## INTASC Standards

### 1. Making Content Meaningful
| | |
|---|---|
| a. understands central content concepts | 5 |
| b. links curriculum to prior learning | 1, 7 |
| c. evaluates and chooses appropriate materials | 10 |
| d. engages students in interpreting ideas | 4 |
| e. uses interdisciplinary approaches | 4, 10 |
| f. uses methods of inquiry central to the discipline | 4 |

### 2. Child Development and Learning Theory
| | |
|---|---|
| a. evaluates student performance to design instruction | 9 |
| b. links teaching to students' prior experiences | 1, 5, 6, 7, 8, 10 |
| c. provides opportunities for active student engagement | 7, 8, 9 |
| d. encourages student reflection | 11 |
| e. accesses student thinking in multiple formats | 10, 12 |

### 3. Learning Styles/Diversity
| | |
|---|---|
| a. designs instruction appropriate to student needs | 3, 6, 7, 10, 12 |
| b. provides student performance opportunities | 6, 9, 11, 12 |
| c. accesses support services when needed | 7, 10 |
| d. adjusts instruction to learning differences | 3, 9, 10, 12 |
| e. uses and connects cultural factors and instruction | 10, 12 |
| f. creates a learning community with respect | 2, 10, 11, 12 |

### 4. Instructional Strategies/Problem Solving
| | |
|---|---|
| a. selects multiple teaching strategies to foster thinking and problem solving | 2, 5, 6, 7, 8, 9 |
| b. encourages student use of learning resources | 5, 8, 9 |
| c. uses multiple strategies and roles to meet learner needs | 2, 3, 7, 9, 10 |

### 5. Motivation and Behavior
| | |
|---|---|
| a. encourages clear procedures and expectations | 1, 2, 5, 6, 9, 10 |
| b. engages students through their interests, choices, and problem solving | 1, 5, 6, 8, 9, 10 |
| c. organizes time, space, and activities to support learning | 2, 7, 9 |
| d. organizes, prepares students for meaningful group work and full participation | 1, 2, 3, 9, 11 |
| e. analyzes and adjusts classroom environment to enhance social relationships, student engagement, and productive work | 9 |

| INTASC Standards | Chapters |
|---|---|
| **6. Communication/Knowledge** | |
|    a. models effective communication skills | 2, 3, 8, 12 |
|    b. provides support for learner expression | 3, 8, 10 |
|    c. demonstrates that communication is sensitive to gender and cultural differences | 2, 9, 10 |
|    d. uses a variety of media communication tools to enrich learning | 3, 10, 12 |
| **7. Planning for Instruction** | |
|    a. plans lessons and activities to address various learning styles, performance modes, problem solving, and exploration | 1, 2, 5, 9 |
|    b. develops plans appropriate for curriculum goals, and based on effective instruction | 4, 5, 6, 9 |
|    c. develops short and long range plans | 4, 10 |
| **8. Assessment** | |
|    a. selects, constructs and uses assessment strategies appropriate to the learning outcomes | 6, 9, 11 |
|    b. uses a variety of formal and informal assessments | 4, 6, 9, 11 |
|    c. uses assessment strategies to involve students in self-assessment activities | 11 |
|    d. evaluates activities, student performance through observation and analysis of student work | 6 |
|    e. maintains and employs useful records of student work | 10, 11 |
|    f. involves parents and other professionals in student evaluation | 11 |
| **9. Professional Growth/Reflection** | |
|    a. evaluates and revises teaching practices | 3, 4, 5, 12 |
|    b. uses professional literature and colleagues, other resources to support self-development | 5, 9, 12 |
|    c. consults with other professionals as support for self-reflection and problem-solving | 1, 4, 6, 12 |
| **10. Interpersonal Relationships** | |
|    a. participates in activities to support a strong learning environment | 5, 10, 11, 12 |
|    b. links with other professionals to support student learning and well being | 1, 4, 5, 10, 12 |
|    c. seeks to establish cooperative partnerships with parents/guardians to support student learning | 2, 10, 11, 12 |
|    d. advocates for students | 4 |

# TEACHING IN K–12 SCHOOLS

## A REFLECTIVE ACTION APPROACH

FOURTH EDITION

**Judy Eby**
*Reflective Action Research Center*
*San Diego, California*

**Adrienne Herrell**
*Educational Partnerships, Panama City, Florida*
*Emeritus, California State University, Fresno*

**Michael Jordan**
*Educational Partnerships, Panama City, Florida*
*California State University, Fresno*

PEARSON
Merrill
Prentice Hall

Upper Saddle River, New Jersey
Columbus, Ohio

**Library of Congress Cataloging-in-Publication Data**

Eby, Judy W.
  Teaching in K–12 schools : a reflective action approach / Judy Eby, Adrienne Herrell, Michael Jordan.—4th ed.
      p. cm.
  Rev. ed. of : Reflective planning, teaching, and evaluation. 3rd ed. 2002.
  Includes index.
  ISBN 0-13-119111-X
  1. Effective teaching. 2. Thought and thinking. 3. Educational tests and measurements. 4. Lesson planning. I. Herrell, Adrienne L. II. Jordan, Michael. III. Eby, Judy W. Reflective planning, teaching, and evaluation. IV. Title.

LB1025.3.E28 2006
371.102—dc22                                                          2005009937

**Vice President and Executive Publisher:** Jeffery W. Johnston
**Executive Editor:** Debra A. Stollenwerk
**Senior Editorial Assistant:** Mary Morrill
**Production Editor:** Kris Roach
**Production Coordination:** Carlisle Publishers Services
**Design Coordinator:** Diane C. Lorenzo

**Cover Designer:** Ali Mohrman
**Cover Image:** Corbis
**Photo Coordinator:** Valerie Schultz
**Production Manager:** Susan Hannahs
**Director of Marketing:** Ann Castel Davis
**Marketing Manager:** Darcy Betts Prybella
**Marketing Coordinator:** Brian Mounts

This book was set in Electra LH by Carlisle Communications, Ltd.

Any mention of the NBPTS Standards or Core Propositions are reprinted with permission from the National Board for Professional Teaching Standards, What Teachers Should Know and Be Able to Do, *www.nbpts.org*. All rights reserved. This book is not endorsed or approved by NBPTS.

**Photo Credits:** Anthony Magnacca/Merrill, pp. 1, 79, 291; Scott Cunningham/Merrill, pp. 21, 55, 109, 215, 261; Anne Vega/Merrill, pp. 169, 195; Judy Eby, p. 135, Patrick White/Merrill, p. 239.

Pearson Education Ltd.
Pearson Education Singapore Pte. Ltd.
Pearson Education Canada, Ltd.
Pearson Education—Japan

Pearson Education Australia Pty. Limited
Pearson Education North Asia Ltd.
Pearson Educación de Mexico, S.A. de C.V.
Pearson Education Malaysia Pte. Ltd.

**PEARSON**
Merrill
Prentice Hall

10 9 8 7 6 5 4
ISBN: 0-13-119111-X

To our friend and colleague, Diane Leonard, who teaches an extraordinary standards-based first grade and makes it look easy.

AH & MJ

# PREFACE

What is *reflective action?* What can a reflective action approach offer you or your students in an educational environment that seems more rigid than reflective? Reflective action is a way of learning from experience, learning from experimenting, and learning by listening to our hearts and to our students. Reflective action grows out of *with-itness,* the capacity to be aware of and responsive to the needs of our students and to make decisions and take actions that will encourage and inspire our students to want to learn and to enjoy coming to school.

We believe that even a standards-based educational program can be presented with enthusiasm, imagination and, yes, even independence. Our goal has always been to inspire and encourage teachers to become as reflective, creative, and independent as possible throughout their teaching careers. We have tried to achieve this goal by searching out the most creative and adventurous teachers we could find and weaving their real-life stories into the text.

At this time in history, we recognize that creativity and independence do not appear to be as highly valued as being able to follow guidelines and meet standards. We struggled with how to balance the reality of today's rather uniform educational expectations with our message that true satisfaction in teaching comes from being a caring and creative artist in the classroom.

At first, this edition seemed like it was going to be difficult to write. But, as we began to collect the stories of teachers who are not only coping in a standards-based environment, but excelling at it, we became much more positive. So, in this edition we are happy to offer what we believe is a balanced description of the realities of a standards-based curriculum with the truly exhilarating stories of teachers who see these standards not as a goal but as a baseline.

Our new aspiration is to inspire teachers to view federal, state, and local standards as meaningful and important, but not the end goal of teaching. We provide the stories of real teachers who begin with standards and then exceed them by creating highly original and creative curricula that take into account and meet the diverse needs of their students. This edition provides you with the knowledge base you need to become highly professional and creative teachers who meet and exceed standards with confidence.

## NEW FEATURES OF THIS EDITION

To accomplish our new aspiration, we have revised this edition to emphasize these new features:

- **A new, updated model of reflective action in teaching** is introduced in Chapter 1 that takes into account the need to plan with standards in mind.

- **Many new teachers' stories** that model how they use reflective action to create school curricula and programs, select teaching strategies, and plan appropriate assessments for their students that achieve the standards of their school districts. These real-life examples, Reflective Action Stories, can serve as models for beginning teachers to think and act with creativity and originality. They can be found in Chapters 2, 4, 5, 6, 9, 10, and 11.

- **NBPTS:** We have anticipated that many teachers may want to begin preparing for the National Board for Professional Teaching Standards (NBPTS) credential. Each chapter of this book ends with a section entitled "Reflective Action Experiences for Your Professional Portfolio." These sections provide beginning teachers with simulated experiences and reflective essays that are drawn from the NBPTS requirements. After completing these simulated activities, many teachers will have the confidence and experience they need to attain this important credential.

- **Praxis:** For those professors who are searching for materials to meet the Praxis II "Principles of Learning and Teaching" exam, you will find that we have highlighted the materials related to Praxis topics. Look for the Praxis margin notes throughout the book.

- **Web site:** The authors have developed a Web site, *www.reflectiveaction.com*, to supplement this text and allow readers to interact with the authors. At this Web site, K–12 teachers and school administrators can learn more about reflective action, take a self-assessment of their capacity for withitness and reflective action, and plan professional book clubs for themselves and their colleagues in a school setting.

## ACKNOWLEDGMENTS

We would like to thank the reviewers for their helpful comments and ideas. They are Sue R. Abegglen, Culver-Stockton College; Suellen Alfred, Tennessee Technological University; Ronald J. Anderson, Texas A&M International University; Kay Brocato, Mississippi State University; and Debra J. Chandler, University of South Florida.

Finally, the authors would also like to acknowledge the contributions of Debra Martin in an earlier edition of this book.

# ABOUT THE AUTHORS

**Judy Eby,** Ph.D., began her teaching career at a Head Start program in Coronado, California. She has been a classroom teacher, a gifted program coordinator, a teacher educator (at DePaul University, University of San Diego, and San Diego State University), and a mentor teacher in the Beginning Teacher Support Academy with the San Diego Unified School District. In 1983, she wrote a master's thesis on gifted behavior and published two articles on that subject in *Educational Leadership* in 1983 and 1984. One of those articles caught the attention of Benjamin S. Bloom, who corresponded with Judy and wrote, "I think you are on the right track."

This led to the opportunity to do her Ph.D. at Northwestern University with Professor Bloom as her dissertation chairman and advisor. In 1986, she wrote her Ph.D. dissertation on gifted behavior as a developmental process rather than an innate and unchanging trait. Essentially, she asked the question, "What are the behaviors that people use to originate and create high-quality original products in the talent area of their choice?" The 10 behaviors that she found to be correlated with this type of success are: perceptiveness, active interaction with the environment, reflectiveness, persistence, independence, goal orientation, originality, productivity, self-evaluation, and communication of findings. She published the *Gifted Behavior Index* and her first book, *A Thoughtful Overview of Gifted Education*, in 1990.

Turning her attention to teacher education as a professor of education at DePaul University in Chicago, Judy reinterpreted her construct of gifted behavior in terms of teacher education, and called this related construct *reflective action in teaching*. This time she asked the question, "What are the behaviors or actions that teachers use to create high-quality original school curricula and programs to meet the needs of their students?" The answers to this question form the basis of this textbook.

You can learn more about Judy at her Web site: *www.reflectiveaction.com*. There, you can learn about her new Reflective Action Book Clubs for Teachers that might benefit you and your faculty in your search for ways to improve your teaching effectiveness, especially in terms of becoming more perceptive, reflective, and proactive in meeting the needs of your students. This process doesn't end when you are awarded your first teaching credential—it continues throughout your career.

One of the central concepts of reflective action is to seek feedback from treasured colleagues. Judy has been very fortunate to have the advice and counsel of her co-authors, Adrienne Herrell and Michael Jordan. Her best critic, however, is her son Alex Eby, who completed his student teaching in Bozeman, Montana, in 2004 and is now in his first year of teaching. His feedback and encouragement keep Judy both honest and realistic about what it is like to be a beginning teacher in the 21st century.

**Adrienne Herrell**, Ph.D., has recently retired from California State University, Fresno, where she was a professor of reading and language arts and taught classes in early literacy, assessment, and strategies for teaching English language learners. *Teaching in K–12 Schools: A Reflective Action Approach* is Adrienne's eighth book for Merrill/Prentice Hall. Her previous books include *Camcorder in the Classroom* with Joel Fowler and *Fifty Strategies for Teaching English Language Learners* with Michael Jordan. Adrienne's writing and research are built on her experiences teaching in Florida's public schools for 23 years. She and Michael Jordan are currently engaged in research in public schools in California and in Florida where they now reside.

**Michael Jordan**, Ed.D., has recently retired as associate professor at California State University, Fresno. He has taught primary grades through high school in Georgia, Alabama, Florida, and California. Michael is also an actor, education director, and board member of Theatre Three Repertory Company in Fresno, California, and is dedicated to providing access to live theatre to children and youth. He and Adrienne incorporate many dramatic reenactment strategies in their joint research, working with vocabulary and comprehension development in children learning English in the public schools of Alaska, California, Florida, Pennsylvania, Ohio, and Oregon. This is Michael's fourth book for Merrill/Prentice Hall.

# Educator Learning Center: An Invaluable Online Resource

Merrill Education and the Association for Supervision and Curriculum Development (ASCD) invite you to take advantage of a new online resource, one that provides access to the top research and proven strategies associated with ASCD and Merrill—the Educator Learning Center. At *www.educatorlearningcenter.com*, you will find resources that will enhance your students' understanding of course topics and of current educational issues, in addition to being invaluable for further research.

## How the Educator Learning Center Will Help Your Students Become Better Teachers

With the combined resources of Merrill Education and ASCD, you and your students will find a wealth of tools and materials to better prepare them for the classroom.

### Research

- More than 600 articles from the ASCD journal *Educational Leadership* discuss everyday issues faced by practicing teachers.
- A direct link on the site to Research Navigator™ gives students access to many of the leading education journals, as well as extensive content detailing the research process.
- Excerpts from Merrill Education texts give your students insights on important topics of instructional methods, diverse populations, assessment, classroom management, technology, and refining classroom practice.

### Classroom practice

- Hundreds of lesson plans and teaching strategies are categorized by content area and age range.
- Case studies and classroom video footage provide virtual field experience for student reflection.
- Computer simulations and other electronic tools keep your students abreast of today's classrooms and current technologies.

## Look into the Value of Educator Learning Center Yourself

A 4-month subscription to Educator Learning Center is $25 but is **FREE** when packaged with any Merrill Education text. In order for your students to have access to this site, you must use this special value-pack ISBN number when placing your textbook order with the bookstore: 0-13-155922-2. Your students will then receive a copy of the text packaged with a free ASCD pincode. To preview the value of this Web site to you and your students, please go to *www.educatorlearningcenter.com* and click on "Demo."

# BRIEF CONTENTS

# CONTENTS

## Chapter 3

## Assessing and Meeting Students' Diverse Needs    55

## Chapter 4

## Using Standards to Guide Your Curriculum Planning    79

## Chapter 5
# Planning Curriculum Units That Give Students a Sense of Purpose    109

## Chapter 6
# Lesson Planning and Sequencing    135

## Chapter 7
## Your Students Want Active, Authentic Learning　　169

## Chapter 8
## Engaging Students in Classroom Discussions    195

## Chapter 9
## Building a Repertoire of Teaching Strategies    215

## Chapter 10

# Integrating Technology into the Curriculum     239

## Chapter 11

# Assessing and Reporting Student Accomplishments     261

## Chapter 12
## Reflective Teachers in the School Community 291

*Note:* Every effort has been made to provide accurate and current internet information in this book. However, the Internet and information posted on it are constantly changing, and it is inevitable that some of the Internet addresses listed in this textbook will change.

## CHAPTER 1

# Reflective Action
# in Teaching

**PRAXIS**

This chapter prepares you to succeed on the PRAXIS™ Exam Section 4a: The Reflective Practitioner.

You can make a decision to be a teacher who reflects deeply and caringly on the actions you take in your classroom. We want to help you reach that goal by sharing some real-life classroom stories told by the teachers who lived them. We've chosen stories that illustrate the reflective-action process. We begin with Jane Speidel, who teaches junior-year–level courses in English at Astronaut High School in Titusville, Florida. Academically, Jane's students are at a midlevel; many of them have not yet passed the FCAT (Florida Comprehensive Assessment Test), which is required to receive a high school diploma.

Jane's students are reading novels and responding to those literary pieces in writing in many forms. They are writing letters to Mrs. Speidel, responding to specific prompts such as "If you were going to take this author to dinner, where would you take him, and why?" These prompts require the student to research the background of the book, think about the setting and plot of the story, and also research local restaurants to find a match for the backgrounds and interests of the author and the literature they are reading. In answering the question of why a particular restaurant was chosen, the student must justify the choice with information gained through research and cite the source of the information.

One year, a few semesters ago, the principal of Jane's school decided to ban parties held to celebrate the end of the school year. Jane and her students responded by doing a research and writing project to provide the principal with justification for a celebration. Their research and writing project had a positive outcome. The principal reinstated the celebrations. Jane has made this project a tradition in her classes. Each year, her students write persuasive essays that the principal uses to justify end-of-year parties. The process is eagerly anticipated by Jane's students and the administration.

Jane and her students produce a cookbook each spring centered on a new theme. The students interview local residents, collect recipes, and research the history of their topic and the recipes. In the past few years they have chosen themes such as the historical recipes of their community, traditional family recipes, and favorite desserts. The first year of this project the classes were made up of about 50% African-American students. They decided to research the African-American culture and traditional foods. Each student found a favorite recipe and researched its origin, preparation, and use. Students also researched traditional celebrations and interesting facts about the African-American culture that were related to food. Each page in the cookbook typically displays a recipe and a sidebar with information about the origins, traditional use of the food, and other interesting information. The students make oral presentations to explain their research and demonstrate some of the discoveries they have made. For example, one student demonstrated the games played by slave children as they shucked the corn used in the traditional sweet cornbread served at African-American meals. The culminating activity is a cookbook reception to which the school administrators are invited and where the recipes included in the cookbook are served.

In this 3-week project many of the Sunshine State Standards for 9–12th-grade English/Language Arts are addressed. For example, one reading standard is the writing of a formal report using information gleaned from reading, interviewing, and relating the information to personal experiences. Another reading standard involves selecting and using appropriate research skills and tools according to the type of information being gathered and organized. Almost all of the writing standards are addressed as the students select and use appropriate prewriting strategies, draft and revise their writing, and produce a final document that has been edited for mechanics and supported by appropriate graphics. The students address the viewing, speaking, and listening standards as they create an oral presentation supported by visuals, and ask and answer questions about their research and the research of their peers. This project encourages students to read widely, respond in written and oral formats, and, perhaps most importantly, provides an authentic reason for celebration that is enthusiastically supported by the school administration.

# STANDARDS THAT APPLY TO REFLECTIVE ACTION IN TEACHING

As Jane Speidel's story demonstrates, teachers are called upon to make many difficult decisions, meet state content standards, and find ways to make curriculum engaging every day. In fact, it is quite possible that teachers make literally thousands of decisions every day. While it is not possible to reflect deeply on every decision, there are many occasions in which caring, reflective teachers search their hearts and minds to find good solutions to problems that confront them and their students every day.

There are guidelines that assist teachers in making good decisions about their curricula and other classroom management issues. Each state has a board of education that publishes a set of standards for teachers to use when planning school programs. A standard is a goal or expectation intended to ensure high quality educational experiences for all students. In the past, school districts made most curriculum decisions independently, but now each state has adopted standards that apply to all schools, so it is important for you to become familiar with those published by your state. Content standards describe what the state wants students to learn for each subject in the K–12 curriculum: reading and language arts, mathematics, science, history and social science, physical education, and visual and performing arts. These content standards identify or define the curriculum and grade level goals that you, the teacher, will be responsible for teaching. It is the standards, not the textbooks, that constitute "the curriculum." The textbooks adopted by your state are simply classroom resources you can use to help your students gain the knowledge and skills defined in the content standards.

As a teacher, you will be planning a sequence of lessons designed to help your students learn and grow toward the grade-level expectations defined in each of the content standards. You will be responsible for monitoring their performance and progress throughout the year and must be ready to plan and adapt your lessons to support students' achievement of the state standards. State assessments will be used to determine whether students in your school are mastering the content standards.

## National Standards

State boards of education also have responsibility for awarding teachers with teaching credentials or licenses. When you complete your teacher education program, you will be awarded a license or credential to teach in your state. However, if you move to another state, you must satisfy the requirements for that state's teaching credential as well. A new, national organization has been formed that awards nationally recognized teaching credentials. The National Board for Professional Teaching Standards (NBPTS) has a mission to advance the quality of teaching and learning by providing rigorous standards for teachers. While state boards of education provide certificates for beginning teachers who demonstrate competence in teaching, the NBPTS provides experienced teachers the voluntary opportunity to attain an additional certificate that demonstrates high levels of proficiency in their chosen profession. This organization synthesized research on teaching excellence and has produced a document describing five core propositions that define standards of excellence that teachers may attain during their careers. The NBPTS seeks to identify and recognize teachers who effectively enhance student learning and demonstrate a high level of knowledge, skills, abilities, and commitment to the teaching profession.

In each chapter, we will feature the NBPTS standards that apply to the chapter topic. We will then discuss how beginning teachers may begin to attain mastery of these standards.

This chapter describes a method teachers can use to reflect deeply and caringly on the many thorny issues that arise in their classrooms each day. We call our concept *reflective action in teaching*. There are several NBPTS (2003) propositions that are related to our model of reflective action. Proposition 1 states that *teachers are committed to students and their learning*. "Proficient teachers learn from their experiences. They learn from listening to their students, from watching them interact with peers, and from reading what they write" (NBPTS, 2003, p. vi). This statement is synonymous with the concept we call "withitness," which you will see is an integral part of our reflective action model.

Proposition 3 states that *teachers are responsible for managing and monitoring student learning*. A subsection of Proposition 3 describes the ways in which teachers can demonstrate that they place a premium on student engagement. "The National Board Certified teacher understands the ways in which students can be motivated and has strategies to monitor student engagement. The teacher's role in building upon student interests and in sparking new passions is central to building bridges between what students know and can do and what they are capable of learning" (NBPTS, 2003, p. vi).

Our reflective action model shows a teacher pondering over the problem of what to do with a class that does not pay attention and does not seem to want to learn the lesson being taught. After considering the problem and talking to colleagues, the teacher determines that the students were not engaged in learning because the original lesson plan did not provide any opportunities for students to be active learners. As the teacher reflects on the failed lesson, an "aha" moment occurs. "They didn't have anything in their hands!" In the next frame, the students are actively engaged in learning by doing. The teacher has demonstrated both the willingness and the ability to reflect on what can be done to build bridges between what her students know and can do and what they are capable of learning, given appropriate teaching methods.

Proposition 4 of the NBPTS document states that *teachers think systematically about their practice and learn from experience*. Our reflective action model is a way of clarifying how teachers think systematically about their practice and learn from their experiences. We are in wholehearted agreement with Proposition 4, which states, "Accomplished teachers are inventive in their teaching and, recognizing the need to admit new findings and continue learning, stand ready to incorporate ideas and methods developed by others that fit their aims and their students" (NBPTS, 2003, p. vii). Proposition 4 also describes the need for teachers to "seek the advice of others and draw on education research and scholarship to improve their practice" (NBPTS, 2003, p. vii). We illustrate this concept by showing a teacher reading up on new methods that may help students learn better and by discussing the problem with trusted colleagues. Our teacher uses reflective action to take new actions that will better fit students' needs.

As we have done in this chapter, we will state the applicable NBPTS standards and connect them to the topic of each chapter. We will discuss and illustrate the ways that you, as beginning teachers, may soon attain the knowledge, skills, and commitment to apply for and receive the NBPTS's nationally recognized certificate of excellence in teaching.

## Preparing Students to Thrive in Our High-Tech World

How do you prepare your students to thrive in the high-tech world of the 21st century? Most of us learned how to do research in encyclopedias and libraries. Now we must teach our students how to do research on the Internet. We learned to make political and economic decisions by reading the newspaper and watching television newscasts to inform our voting decisions. Although our students will continue to gather information from these same sources, much of their information is now gained online, and they may have to sort out opinion from fact when offered hundreds of different points of view from around the world.

We learned how to read, write, and do arithmetic from books and workbooks, but now we will use the latest CDs and computer programs to assist our students in learning the basics. Then we will enrich their curriculum with an amazing array of high-tech ideas such as those found on *www.schoolnotes.com*, a site that allows teachers to share curriculum ideas and teaching strategies with one another. Of one thing we can be certain—nothing is going to stay the same very long in our future. So, how do we prepare our students to cope with change so that they can be flexible and yet have an underlying set of values to guide their decision making? How do we prepare them to respond creatively to the opportunities that come with our world's changing priorities without losing their sense of self?

In January 2000, a recent college graduate named Ravi Chatpar, interviewed for a job with an Internet firm in Boston. He was taken aback when instead of talking about his education and experience, he was asked to "build something with Legos©." He was given 5 minutes to build whatever he wanted, and then he and the interviewers would talk about it. Other job seekers are being asked to solve mathematical brainteasers and riddles to demonstrate their capacity to think under pressure. Another strategy is to ask a candidate to participate in a group game that tests the ability of the candidate to collaborate with others.

If our K–12 curriculum is going to keep pace with and prepare our students to thrive on the changes in our social and economic environment, it must go beyond the teaching of facts and concepts to involve students in problem solving and the use of multiple sources of information. The responsibility for making that a reality depends largely on your problem-solving skills, your ability to collaborate with others, and your capacity to think outside the box and design new learning experiences that will generate enthusiastic responses from your students.

One thing has not changed. Despite the rapid growth and dependence upon technology, we all still need to feel that someone cares for us. Every year, students who enter classrooms yearn for teachers who will like them, inspire them to do their very best, and listen to them, and respond to their needs and longings. There is no high-tech shortcut for this fundamental truth.

Nel Noddings (1992) recognized that "the desire to be cared for is almost certainly a universal human characteristic. Not everyone wants to be cuddled or fussed over, but everyone wants to be received, to elicit a response that is congruent with an underlying need or desire" (p. 17). Caring is a way of relating to one another's needs and points of view, not a set of specific behaviors.

The best, most creative, caring, and reflective teachers realize that, like parenting, good teaching takes time and understanding. Good teaching resembles good parenting in that both require long periods of time and continuity to develop. Good parents and teachers start by creating an environment that encourages trusting relationships and work continually to strengthen that foundation of trust (Noddings, 1992).

This book describes classroom strategies and methods that you can use to become a caring and reflective teacher so that you will thrive in the classroom, not just "get by." We believe that there are two major traits that help teachers achieve the kind of caring relationships that encourage students to relate to ideas, to their peers, and to others in their worlds. The first trait is *withitness*, which refers to a combination of caring and perceptiveness that allows teachers to focus on the needs of their students. The second trait, *reflective action*, is rooted in withitness. It is the ability to monitor your own behaviors, feelings, and needs and to learn from your mistakes. One of the most important things you can do to develop both withitness and reflective action is to get to know yourself and understand your own needs and desires for approval and acceptance from your prospective students. We will return to this theme repeatedly, because your need to receive respect and affection from your students is something you must come to recognize and deal with effectively before you can care for others. We will begin by examining the concept of withitness and then describe reflective action.

## Withitness

When you go into classrooms and observe teachers at work, you probably are curious to discover the differences between classrooms that are well managed and those that are disorderly and chaotic. Kounin (1977) hypothesized that smoothly functioning classrooms were governed by a clear set of rules and that chaotic classrooms had vague rules and discipline strategies. But, when he took his video cameras into classrooms, he found that his hypothesis was wrong. What he observed, instead, was that the most smoothly functioning classrooms were those that were led by a teacher whose management style was characterized by a high degree of alertness and the ability to pay attention to more than one thing at the same time.

Kounin described the teacher characteristic that distinguished good classroom managers from poor ones as *withitness*. The good classroom managers he observed knew what was going on in their classrooms at all times. They were aware of who was working and who was not. They were also able to carry out their instruction while at the same time monitoring student behavior. In the midst of a sentence, they were willing and able to alter their lessons at the first sign of student restlessness or boredom.

If a minor disruption occurred between students, the teacher perceived it immediately and was likely to walk toward a student, using eye contact that said, "I am watching you. You can't get away with that behavior in here."

Withitness is expressed more through teacher perceptiveness and behavior than through rules or harsh words. Eye contact, facial expressions, proximity, gestures, and actions such as stopping an activity demonstrate teacher withitness to students. These teachers are able to continue teaching a lesson while gesturing to a group or standing next to an overactive student who needs to refocus on the lesson. These are examples of the concept of overlapping, in which the teacher is able to deal both with student behavior and the lesson at the same time.

Kounin also studied what he called the *ripple effect*, a preventive discipline strategy that he found to be particularly useful in K–12 classrooms. Kounin observed a student in his own college class reading a newspaper during the lecture. When Kounin reprimanded the student, he observed that his remarks caused changes in behavior among the other members of the class as well. Side glances to others ceased, whispers stopped, and eyes went from windows or the instructor to notebooks on the desk. In subsequent observations in kindergarten classrooms, Kounin found that when teachers spoke firmly but kindly to a student, asking that student to desist from misbehavior, the other students in the class were also likely to desist from that behavior as well. When teachers spoke with roughness, however, the ripple effect was not as strong. Students who witnessed a teacher reprimand another child with anger or punitiveness did not conform more nor misbehave less than those witnessing a teacher correct another without anger or punitiveness.

Ron Clark, Disney's Teacher of the Year in 2001 and author of *The Essential 55* (2003), teaches in Harlem in New York City. He believes that setting up expectations for acceptable behavior at the beginning of the year is vital. He also stresses the importance of maintaining the standards consistently. Withitness in the classroom is an important part of consistency since incidences of rule breaking must be noticed before they can be addressed.

## Reflective Action Builds on Withitness

We all hear that it is good to be reflective and that teachers who are reflective are likely to grow and mature into excellent teachers. But, what does it mean to be reflective and how do you get that way? As educators and authors, we want to create a word picture in your mind that describes positive, caring, reflective teachers in action. We believe that reflectiveness starts with withitness, because it is first and foremost a type of perceptiveness. Perceptive, withit teachers constantly observe conditions and gather information to make good judgments about what is happening in a classroom and what can or should be done to address it. Withitness continually raises the quality and level of reflective thinking because it helps teachers observe more accurately and collect more complete information about classroom conditions. Reflective teachers plan for variations in student response, constantly monitor students' reactions to classroom events, and are ready to respond when students show confusion or boredom. Reflective teachers actively monitor students during group activities and independent seat work, looking for signs that students need clarification of the task or the teacher's expectations. They also consider the quality of developing student relationships and note how students interact with ideas, peers, and others in various settings.

Can withitness and reflective action be learned? We believe so. If you are willing to examine the cause-and-effect relationships in your classroom honestly and search for reasons for students' behaviors, you are likely to develop withitness in the process. If you are willing to ask other adults to observe your interactions with students and give you feedback on how you respond to various situations, you will be able to make changes and improve the quality of your withitness radar and responses. If you are willing to discuss classroom problems openly and honestly with your students, in a problem-solving manner, you are likely to learn from them what their signals mean.

For example, Judy once visited a second-grade classroom where a teacher planned the morning activities to go from reading to math to science without a break. By the time the teacher asked the students to put away their math books and take out their science books, the grumbling and murmuring and shuffling feet had grown to intolerable proportions. With no trace of withitness, this teacher's voice went higher and higher as she scolded the students and told them to be quiet and listen, keep their hands and feet still, sit up, and pay attention. This happened over and over until lunchtime. A reflective, caring teacher using withitness as a tool would have perceived that student grumbling signaled a planning problem—one that could be easily solved by allowing the students to move and stretch for a few minutes before starting another lesson.

Ron Clark (2003) discusses the importance of monitoring students' nonverbal reactions and helping them to recognize that eye-rolling and other negative body language are disrespectful behaviors in the classroom. In order to address these types of behavior the teacher must be extremely observant.

Principals and supervising teachers often note that withitness and reflective thinking grow with experience. They grow in a symbiotic way. The more withitness teachers develop, the more reflective they are likely to become. Similarly, the more teachers reflect on how their own needs may conflict with the needs of their students, the more withitness they display. Few first-year teachers exhibit consistent and accurate withitness. It is gradually developed by teachers as they actively reflect on the effects of their actions and decisions on their students' behavior.

For example, a beginning teacher may gradually become aware that her lessons are too long for the students' attention spans. From that time on, she will be sensitive to whether a particular lesson is moving too slowly or lasting too long. On another day, the teacher may notice that whenever a certain student is made to establish eye contact, the student ceases to misbehave; the teacher reflects on this and actively begins to use eye contact as a way to connect not only with this student but also with others. Then, after further observation and discussion with a colleague, the teacher may also become aware that in some cultures students fail to make eye contact with adults as a sign of respect. In response to a serious disruption, the teacher may notice that using a strong, confident voice causes the students to pay attention, whereas using a tentative, meek voice causes their attention to wander. Through reflecting on these experiences, the teacher develops two effective strategies for redirecting student behavior, and begins to learn which is more effective in a given situation. Her active self-reflection is the first step toward developing greater withitness, and her increasing withitness contributes to greater self-reflection.

## Reflecting on Your Ethics and Principles

Reflective action is a time-consuming practice that requires you to make a personal examination of why you do something, how you can do something better, and how your actions affect others. This intense self-examination leads to increased self-knowledge, but it can also result in feelings of discomfort. When you engage in reflective thinking about actions you have just taken or are about to take, you may become critical of or disappointed in your own behavior or your motives.

When teachers are engaged in reflection about their decisions, actions, and behaviors, they are likely to begin asking themselves questions such as: "Why do I have this rule?" "Why do I care so much about what happens in my classroom?" "How did I come to believe so strongly about this element of my teaching?"

As teachers ask themselves searching questions, they are likely to reexamine their core beliefs and values. For example, if a teacher has grown up and gone to school in traditional settings where students were "seen but not heard" unless they were responding to a direct question by an adult, then the teacher may expect the same type of behavior from his or her students. But, imagine that the teacher observes a classroom where students are allowed to interact, discuss their ideas with other students, and take part in very spirited discussions with the teacher. Based on past assumptions, the beginning teacher may feel uncomfortable in a classroom with this noise level and consider the behavior of the students to be rude. A reflective teacher, however, is willing and able to ask the following questions: "'Why am I uncomfortable with this noise level? Is it because I was never allowed to speak up when I was a child? How did I feel about the rules when I was a child? How do I feel about them now? What are the differences in the way these students are learning and the way I learned? What do I want my future students to learn: how to be quiet and orderly or how to be curious and assertive?"

When teachers confront confusing and ambiguous questions like these with honesty, they are becoming "real." Honest self-reflection can lead to new understandings of how your beliefs influence your present choices and actions. Continued reflective thinking can lead you to begin to clarify your philosophy of life and teaching, your ethical standards, and your moral code.

Do you think it is necessary for you as a teacher to know what you stand for, what you believe and value? Is it important that you be able to state clearly the ethical and moral basis for your decisions? Strike (1993) notes two important reasons for teachers to have a well-articulated philosophy of teaching and code of ethics: (1) They work with a particularly vulnerable clientele; and (2) the teaching profession has no clear set of ethical principles or standards. Strike believes that, in the matter of discipline and grading, the most important ethical concepts are honesty, respect for diversity, fairness, and due process. He also believes that teachers must be willing to consider the ethical implications of equity in the way teachers distribute their time and attention to students, avoiding playing favorites. Are these part of your personal code of ethics?

It is likely that you believe your students ought to have the attributes of honesty, respect for diversity, and fairness. If so, it is important that you demonstrate these behaviors for them, for it is well known that teachers are important models of moral and ethical behavior for the students they teach. When you begin teaching, we want you to

**PRAXIS**
Knowledge of the code of ethics, professional organizations, and literature is tested in PRAXIS™ Exam 4a.

accept the responsibility for setting a good example because your students are vulnerable and likely to be influenced by your beliefs and ethics. Teachers are important role models for behavior and character. In classrooms that we observe, the teacher's character and moral code set the standards and the tone or climate for the classroom. If the teacher is fair, students are influenced to treat others fairly. If the teacher is impulsive and selfish, students are likely to behave in the same way. When teachers demonstrate a willingness to listen openly and honestly to others' points of view, students begin to respect the opinions of others as well. When teachers are closed and rigid in their approach to teaching and learning, students mold their behavior into a search for right answers and rote learning.

Noddings (1992) expresses the need for ethical caring in schools because schools are places where human beings learn how to interact. She proposes that caring is the basis of the Golden Rule. Caring as a moral attribute is probably high on the list of most aspiring teachers. Many choose the career of teaching because they care deeply about the needs of students in our society. Teachers are also likely to feel responsible for meeting the needs of their students. Occasionally, you may observe teachers who seem to have lost the ability to care for others because they are overwhelmed with meeting their own needs. They tend to put the blame on others for why their students fail to behave or achieve. But, reflective, caring teachers willingly accept that it is their responsibility to design a program that allows their students to succeed. They take responsibility for problems that occur during the school day, rather than blaming others. They work every day to balance their own needs with the needs of their students. They are committed to growing as professional educators. To achieve these goals, they are willing to learn systematic ways of reflecting on their own practices so that they can enhance their students' likelihood to succeed. Other moral attributes that teachers cite as important in their personal lives and in their work with children are honesty, courage, and friendliness.

## Definitions of Reflective Thinking and Action

In *How We Think: A Restatement of the Relation of Reflective Thinking to the Educative Process*, John Dewey (1933) defined reflective thinking as the "active, persistent and careful consideration of any belief or supposed form of knowledge in light of the grounds that support it" (p. 9). An analysis of this carefully worded statement creates a powerful verbal image of the reflective thinker and correlates with the concept presented here of a person consciously choosing to use reflective action in teaching.

The first descriptive adjective, *active*, indicates one who voluntarily and willingly takes responsibility for considering personal actions. Reflective action includes an energetic search for information and solutions to problems that arise in the classroom. In teaching, this involves identifying the strengths and needs of individual students and being responsible for finding teaching approaches that work for a diverse group of students. Dewey's use of the word *persistent* implies a commitment to thinking through difficult issues in depth, continuing to consider matters even though it may be uncomfortable or tiring to do so. Although some teachers may begin to seek knowledge and information, they may be satisfied with easy answers and simple solutions. In contrast, reflective teachers are rarely satisfied with quick answers. Instead, they

**PRAXIS**
Knowledge of best teaching practices supported by research is tested in PRAXIS™ Exam Section 4a.

continually and persistently seek to fine-tune and improve ways to teach students and manage classroom events.

The careful thinker is one who has concern for both self and others. Teachers who use reflective action care deeply about ways to improve their own classroom performance and how to bring the greatest possible benefit to the lives of their students. They believe that teaching is relational—meaning that the quality of interactions in the classroom sets the tone for learning. Using reflective action, such teachers set out to create positive, nurturing classroom environments that promote high self-esteem and concern not only between the teacher and her students, but also among students and their peers. Less caring teachers are likely to consider their own needs and feelings to be of greater importance than those of their students. Because they do not reason with care, they may make unreasonable demands on their students or fail to sense and address important student needs. In today's schools there is a focus on meeting standards. One of these standards involves the establishment of an effective learning environment. Teacher caring and reflection are important elements of the leadership that creates a safe and effective learning environment.

Dewey's phrase "belief or supposed form of knowledge" implies that little is known for sure in the teaching profession. The teacher who uses reflective action recognizes the value of informed practice but maintains a healthy skepticism about various educational procedures and theories. While a less reflective teacher might be persuaded that there is only one right way to teach, the reflective teacher observes that individual students may need different conditions for learning and a variety of incentives in order to be successful. A less reflective teacher might adopt each new educational fad without questioning its value; the reflective teacher greets each of these new ideas with an open but questioning mind, considering whether it is valuable and how it can be adapted to fit the needs of individuals within the class.

The final phrase in Dewey's definition, "in light of the grounds that support it," directly relates to the reflective thinker's practice of using evidence and criteria in making judgments. While less reflective teachers may jump to quick conclusions based on initial observations or prior cases, the reflective teacher gathers as much information as possible about any given problem, weighs the value of the evidence against suitable criteria, and then draws a tentative conclusion. After reaching a conclusion, less reflective teachers may stick to them rigidly, but reflective teachers will reconsider their judgments whenever new evidence or information becomes available. Reflective teachers are also willing to adapt their teaching strategies when it becomes evident that their students' needs are not being met.

Although persistent and careful thinking is important to the reflective teacher, such thinking does not automatically lead to change and improvement. Dewey also acknowledged the importance of translating thought into action, and specified that attitudes of open-mindedness, responsibility, and wholeheartedness are needed for teachers to translate their thoughts into reflective actions.

Schon (1990) concurs with Dewey's emphasis on action as an essential aspect of the reflective process. He defines the reflective practitioner as one who engages in "reflection-in-action." This kind of thinking includes observing and critiquing our own actions and then changing our behaviors based on what we see. Reflection-in-action gives rise to on-the-spot experiments. We define a problem, consider how we have addressed it in the past, and think up and try out new actions to test our tentative understandings of them. This process helps us determine whether our moves change things for the better. An on-the-spot experiment may work, or it may produce surprises that call for further reflection and experiment.

Schon also notes that reflectivity in teaching leads to "professional artistry," a special type of competence displayed by some teachers when they find themselves in situations full of surprise, ambiguity, or conflict. Just as physicians respond to each patient's unique array of symptoms by questioning, inventing, testing, and creating a new diagnosis, Schon believes that reflective teachers also respond to the unexpected by asking questions such as: "What are my students experiencing?" "What can I do to improve this situation?" "How does my students' performance relate to the way I am teaching this material?"

Often, during the process of reflection, teachers find that a new, surprising event contradicts something they thought they already "knew." When this happens, reflective individuals are able to cope with paradoxes and dilemmas by reexamining what they already know, restructuring their strategies, or reframing the problem. They often invent on-the-spot experiments to put their new understandings to the test or to answer the puzzling questions that have arisen from the event.

Reflective action is made up of many elements and is related to an individual's willingness to be curious and assertive in order to increase self-awareness, self-knowledge, and new understandings of the world in which we live and work. It is not something that occurs easily for most of us, and it takes time to develop. Writing of this idea, Brubacher, Case, and Reagan (1994) cite the children's story *The Velveteen Rabbit* to suggest that becoming a reflective practitioner has much in common with the process of becoming "real." As the Skin Horse explained to the Rabbit, becoming "real" takes time, and happens after a toy has been loved so much that it loses its hair and becomes shabby. In the same way, becoming a truly reflective teacher involves time, experience, and inevitably a bit of wear around the edges!

## A GRAPHIC MODEL OF REFLECTIVE ACTION IN TEACHING

Consider that, as writers, it is our responsibility to connect with you in the same way teachers must connect with their students. We reflect on memories of ourselves as beginning teachers and think about what we wanted to learn and needed to know in order to be successful. In this fourth edition, we use feedback from readers of previous editions, as well as our own continuing research, to fine-tune the material we want to present.

We know that sometimes students learn better by seeing a picture or a graphic model of a complicated idea. The model of reflective action we present in this edition has changed from earlier editions because we are continually reflecting on how to make it more understandable and usable. Still, we recognize that any model is oversimplified and relies on the readers to fill in details and examples with their own imagination. With feedback from you, we will continue to refine our thinking in future editions. This is exactly how your own teaching can improve over the years if you are willing to seek critical feedback, reflect, and grow as a result of your experiences. In addition, changes in education policies and current research often influence what is expected of teachers. Standards-based teaching requires a focused view to teach the curriculum according to predetermined goals and expectations of state boards of education. This may cause stress for teachers who want to design programs to meet the diverse needs of their students. When all students must meet the same standards, teachers have an enormous task to create lessons that allow all students to be successful.

When you think of your school years, no doubt several of your own past teachers come to mind. Perhaps you recall a teacher who adapted lessons to ensure that all students could succeed. Maybe you had a favorite teacher who reached out to you in a way that made you feel valued and important. Perhaps one of the reasons you are reading this book is because your interactions with a caring teacher helped instill in you the desire to influence others in the same way you were influenced. On the other hand, you may also have had a negative experience with a teacher and determined that you would enter the teaching profession to help ensure that more caring individuals become the teachers of the future. You have probably heard the phrase, "the art of teaching." One aspect of the art of teaching is that each of us enters the teaching profession with a unique set of experiences with people and with institutions. From these individual experiences, each teacher develops a unique perspective, or set of expectations, through which we view the world and from which we determine what we think life in a classroom should be like.

In the field of education, our perspectives or expectations work a little bit like the visual artist's perspective. For example, imagine that three different artists have been asked to paint the same landscape. Figure 1.1 shows the artist in the middle painting the scene as she views it. Notice how she has chosen to depict the scene.

In contrast, note how the first artist's view differs. She focuses on a close-up of the pine tree. If you compared the two paintings, you might not realize from the artist's canvas on the left that there was a sunset in the original scene. Finally, look at the third artist's canvas. How does his view compare to the first two? It is as if the three artists are all painting a different scene entirely.

**Figure 1.1** Different perspectives create a point of view.

Over time, artists develop particular perspectives that become associated with their style of art. In the same way, your unique teaching and learning perspective will lead you to notice some things and overlook others—during your teacher preparation courses and throughout your teaching career. There is nothing wrong with having a perspective or set of expectations about teaching—in fact, you cannot help having one. However, it is important to remember that your personal perspective is not the only view or interpretation of events. In fact, there are at least as many different perspectives for an event as there are participants in it!

The process of planning any type of classroom event is also unique for each teacher. The particular steps you take in planning a lesson or other types of classroom activities will be unique, and may vary from day to day or lesson to lesson. However, we are proposing a general set of steps or guidelines here that we call a *model of reflective action in teaching*.

Reflective action, as the term implies, is a series of steps or processes in which you reflect on what you want to occur in your classroom and then take some type of action. While you are taking the action, you are also likely to be evaluating it, which leads to more reflection, and that points you in a new direction and a new action. A sunflower responds to the sun, rain, wind, and soil and sends out its petals in response. Teachers establish learning goals in response to state standards, district requirements, students' needs, availability of resources, time commitments, and personal limits of energy and creativity. The process teachers use is not linear, but is somewhat circular or cyclical. For that reason, we choose to present it as petals of a sunflower that are interconnected (see Figure 1.2). We use a clockwise direction for a typical or general series of reflection and action steps.

Look at the top petal. The teacher begins to plan a lesson based on state content standards for the grade level and subject matter and to meet school district requirements and goals. This is how most lesson planning begins.

Now look at the next petal, moving in a clockwise direction. The teacher considers what students already know and what they need to learn next. Reflective teachers think about the general needs or readiness of their class as a whole, and they also consider the individual needs of students. Some students will need more scaffolding to be successful, while others may have already mastered the material and need a more challenging assignment.

The next petal reminds us that teachers have expectations of how a lesson or any other classroom activity will be received by the students. Each teacher has a personal concept of what makes a good lesson, how students should act, and what effective teachers do. Just preceding the lesson, many teachers form a mental picture of what is about to occur. This mental image may even be in the form of a moving picture, with a script that the teacher intends to follow. The teacher expects that by following the script, the goal for this lesson will be achieved.

Notice that the next petal is depicted as torn and damaged. This symbolizes the times when unforeseen problems occur and students' responses do not match what was expected. When these problems occur, teachers are forced to rethink their lesson plans. This can occur for a number of reasons. Perhaps the students' experiences with school differ greatly from those of the teacher, or perhaps a physical need (e.g., hunger, fatigue) prevents a student from paying full attention to the teacher's input. For any number of reasons, an unforeseen problem or challenge can (and often does!) arise during even the best prepared lessons.

**Figure 1.2** Graphic model of reflective action in teaching.

The next petal has fallen away from the flower. We use this to symbolize what happens when nonreflective teachers, with dangerously low levels of withitness, ignore warning signals from their students. They continue to teach their lessons just as planned, without adapting them to fit the needs of their students. When the inevitable confusion and inattention occur, they tend to focus only on students who fulfill their expectations and try to ignore the students who do not understand or are not paying attention. Their best-made plans are doomed to fail. Over time, their lack of withitness can result in such frustration with their career that they leave teaching forever.

Back on the flower, the next petal stands for reflective teachers who do use withitness. They notice the behavior of all students and respond quickly to unexpected events. Caring, reflective teachers monitor the ever-changing climate of the classroom by paying close attention to students' nonverbal and verbal responses. When events deviate from expectations, a teacher who uses reflective action responds by changing pace in a lesson, moving about the room, and interacting with students in an effort to redirect and refocus attention and learning.

Withitness is a form of reflection **in** action (Schon, 1990). This means that the teacher is perceiving cues from students, pondering what they mean, and talking out loud or continuing with a demonstration—all at the same time! This is an amazingly difficult feat to accomplish, and most beginning teachers do not achieve this easily. It takes practice and more practice. It also takes commitment and more commitment to teach and reflect at the same time. You will find that your ability to use withitness and reflection-in-action grows just like a sunflower—from a seed nurtured by lots of sun, water, and care.

Afterward, as the next petal demonstrates, the teacher reflects on the event and tries to understand the reasons for the problems that occurred. This is known as reflection **on** action (Schon, 1990). Reflective teachers do not stop thinking about a problem when the bell rings. They try to understand what happened and why. They want to know how the problem might have been prevented. While nonreflective teachers may blame it all on the students, reflective teachers will not be satisfied with such a hasty conclusion. We cannot emphasize enough the importance of this step. Without reflection on action, there is unlikely to be any growth of withitness. Without reflection, there is little or no opportunity to be creative, identify and solve problems, or devise and take a new approach.

The next two petals represent the teacher who responds to difficult situations by doing research to learn more about the teaching dilemma and purposefully talks with trusted colleagues and invites their feedback. A teacher's honest self-reflection leads to the first important action step, inviting the feedback of respected colleagues or looking for other resources to help explain the unexpected classroom event. A concerned teacher might share a discouraging classroom experience with a colleague, who is likely to have a different perspective to offer. Perhaps the colleague will recommend a book or article about the subject or suggest a workshop the teacher could attend. By taking the proactive step of seeking new information, the reflective teacher grows stronger and more capable with each such learning experience.

Next, the teacher reflects again, using the feedback, research, and creativity. Rather than simply adopting a colleague's perspective or ideas, the reflective teacher formulates a unique and creative idea of how to reteach the lesson. We believe that reflectiveness is an integral part of creativity. In addition, the self-awareness that grows from reflection on action enhances teachers' self-confidence and makes them bloom and thrive in their chosen career.

Finally, the teacher creates a new action plan. The teacher imagines the scene in the classroom again and writes a new script. This plan will benefit from the teacher's more accurate awareness of the students' existing knowledge, skills, and interests. There are likely to be additional action steps needed, such as locating appropriate materials and getting them set up in the classroom in time for the next lesson. The entire reflective action process begins again with this newly adapted lesson. Perhaps all will go smoothly, but if a new problem occurs, the reflective teacher uses withitness to perceive the problem and begins the whole reflective action process again.

We hope you can adapt this reflective action model to situations that arise in your classrooms. We hope you will recognize the importance of reflecting before, during, and after a lesson is taught. By reflecting before the lesson, you may be able to imagine or picture what is likely to occur. Then, you can take preventive action by changing your lesson plan to better fit the needs of your students.

In the midst of the lesson, we hope you will use your withitness and reflect on the actions you are taking in real time. What is happening? How are the students responding? Who is paying attention and who isn't? Why do some students seem overwhelmed or bored by this lesson? What can I do to improve the learning experience for them right now? These are questions that reflective teachers ask themselves while in front of the class.

After the lesson, it is time to reflect on what went well and what did not. Beginning teachers may tend to get discouraged when lessons don't go as planned, but experienced teachers know that unforeseen circumstances are not only possible, they are likely. They reflect on what happened without assigning blame to themselves or to their students. They recognize that by reflecting and adapting this lesson, they are learning from their own experiences.

## PROFESSIONAL STANDARDS AND ACCOUNTABILITY FOR TEACHERS

The reflective action model we have presented here is our way of articulating a set of thought processes and action steps that encourage self-understanding and professional growth. As a beginning teacher, you may want to be able to demonstrate your professional growth and your unique teaching style, talents, and abilities to others. You may need to do this in order to earn your teaching credential or, later, to compete successfully for a teaching position. The National Board for Professional Teaching Standards (NBPTS) (2003–2004) names five propositions of accomplished teaching as fundamental requirements for teachers to be able to demonstrate. The NBPTS believes that excellence in teaching is composed of human qualities such as judgment and improvisation, expert knowledge and skill, and unflagging professional commitment. The five propositions include:

**PRAXIS**
The use of professional development to support ongoing personal reflection is tested in Praxis™ Exam Section 4a.

1. Teachers are committed to students and their learning.
2. Teachers know the subjects they teach and how to teach those subjects to students.
3. Teachers are responsible for managing and monitoring student learning.
4. Teachers think systematically about their practice and learn from experience.
5. Teachers are members of learning communities.

We hope you see the links between these five core propositions of excellence in teaching and the processes we have described as reflective action steps. To clarify these links, we believe that teachers who are committed to their students are those who use withitness to perceive their students' needs and are further willing to reflect alone and collegially to meet those needs. Teachers who want to grow in their management capabilities are willing to ask colleagues for feedback on management problems and issues, and consider contingencies before they arise to prevent management problems from occurring.

The fourth core proposition is that teachers think systematically about their practice and learn from experience. What does it mean to "think systematically"? We have tried to offer one version of systematic thinking in this chapter. Our reflective action model is just that—a system of thinking and acting in order to improve your practice and learn from your experience. Our model is purposefully collegial, as we concur with the fifth core proposition that teachers are members of learning communities.

## A Reflective Action Professional Portfolio Based on NBPTS Standards

At the end of each chapter, we provide you with our model of a professional portfolio and describe what it can demonstrate about your own unique style of teaching and knowledge of student needs.

Martin-Kniep (1999) describes portfolios as collections of purposeful and specialized work, capturing a process that can never be fully appreciated unless one can be inside and outside someone else's mind. Portfolios are history in the making. They are fluid, even though they can freeze a moment and make the moment look as if it has a clear beginning and end. They are museums of our work and thinking—displaying our successes, experiments, and dreams (p. 1).

The NBPTS awards its nationally recognized credentials on the basis of a comprehensive portfolio that teachers create through the course of a year. The learning experiences that you include in your portfolio can provide evidence of your ability to plan, teach, and evaluate effectively. We want to provide you with a place to begin thinking about your portfolio. At the end of each chapter in this book, we have suggested activities that are compatible with NBPTS portfolio requirements for the Middle Childhood/Generalist credential and the Early Adolescence/Generalist credential or Adolescence through Young Adult content-specific credentials in English/Language Arts, Mathematics, Science, or Art. You may get a head start on creating your own professional portfolio by following some of these suggestions.

# REFLECTIVE ACTION EXPERIENCES FOR YOUR PROFESSIONAL PORTFOLIO

## Respond to Core Proposition 4 of the NBPTS

Our first activity is a readiness activity designed to get you thinking about creating a professional portfolio. As you recall from this chapter, the NBPTS credentials are awarded on the basis of how well a teacher demonstrates knowledge and ability in the five core propositions:

1. Teachers are committed to students and their learning.
2. Teachers know the subjects they teach and how to teach those subjects to students.
3. Teachers are responsible for managing and monitoring student learning.
4. Teachers think systematically about their practice and learn from experience.
5. Teachers are members of learning communities.

The NBPTS provides documents entitled Early Childhood/Generalist Portfolio, Middle Childhood/Generalist, and Childhood, Adolescence through Young Adult content-specific (English/Language Arts, Mathematics, Science, and Art) Credential Portfolios on its Web page: *http://www.nbpts.org/candidates/portfolios.cfm*. This document includes a section entitled, "Tips for Studying the Standards" (2003–2004, p. 2). We have summarized the tips in these end-of-chapter activities.

Our first portfolio readiness activities respond to core Proposition 4 because it is congruent with the content of this chapter.

1. Write a paragraph about how you have begun to think systematically about your practice as a teacher and what you have done to learn from experience. Tell about one specific activity that you have developed in your work related to students and learning that illustrates your growing ability to think systematically and learn from experience.

2. Think about other teachers you have observed. Describe an event that you witnessed that caused you to see or understand how a highly accomplished teacher reflected systematically about a classroom issue. What was the problem or issue? What was the teacher's first reaction? How did the teacher think or talk through this problem? Who did the teacher consult to get more information? What did the teacher do as a result of this reflection? How did the teacher talk about the experience afterward? Was there a sense that the teacher had learned something from the experience? What convincing evidence could this teacher provide to demonstrate the use of systematic reflective thinking and learning from experience?

3. Think about another teacher who, in your view, appeared to be unwilling or unable to think systematically about classroom events and problems. Describe a situation you observed where the teacher refused to think about a problem or did so very superficially and unsystematically. What convincing evidence could be gathered to demonstrate that this teacher was not using reflective thinking?

4. Write a short commentary on the thought processes you used in preparing the other three sections of this portfolio readiness activity. How did your concept of systematic reflective thinking develop as you completed the assignment? How will you observe other teachers differently as a result of this analysis? How will you monitor your own teaching and learning activities in the future to determine if you are demonstrating a willingness to think systematically and learn from experience?

# References

Brubacher, J., Case, C., & Reagan, T. (1994). *Becoming a reflective educator: How to build a culture of inquiry in the schools.* Thousand Oaks, CA: Corwin.

Clark, R. (2003). *The essential 55.* New York: Hyperion.

Dewey, J. (1933). *How we think* (rev. ed.). Lexington, MA: D.C. Heath.

Kounin, J. (1977). *Discipline and group management in classrooms.* New York: Holt, Rinehart and Winston.

Martin-Kniep, G. (1999). *Capturing the wisdom of practice: Professional portfolios for educators.* Alexandria, VA: Association of Supervision and Curriculum Development.

National Board for Professional Teaching Standards. (2003–2004 cycle). *Middle childhood/generalist portfolio.* Retrieved (May 30, 2003) from *http://www.nbpts.org/candidates/portfolios.cfm.*

National Board for Professional Teaching Standards. (2003–2004 cycle). *What teachers should know and be able to do.* Retrieved (May 30, 2003) from *http://www.nbpts.org/standards/intro.html.*

Noddings, N. (1992). *The challenge to care in schools.* New York: Teachers College Press.

Peters, J. (1991). Strategies for reflective practice. *Professional and Continuing Education, 51,* 83–102.

Schon, D. (1990). *Educating the reflective practitioner.* San Francisco: Jossey-Bass.

Strike, K. (1993). The legal and moral responsibility of teachers. In J. Goodlad, R. Soder, & K. Sirotnik (Eds.), *The moral dimensions of teaching* (pp. 188–223). San Francisco: Jossey-Bass.

## CHAPTER 2

# Creating a Safe, Healthy, and Happy Classroom

Diana Bateman is a third-grade teacher at Lewis Carroll School in Cape Canaveral, Florida. Here is her story of how she and other teachers at her school work together to establish an environment for learning that supports students and helps them to feel they are all part of the school community.

Our whole school operates as if we are part of the same family of learners. We all want to know how the brain works and how students learn best. We have all taken part in the same in-service training and have selected three philosophical bases for our learning programs and for our discipline and classroom management procedures. The three philosophies that we have adopted and adapted are William Glasser's (2001) quality school model, Susan Kavalik's (1994) integrated thematic instruction (ITI) model, and Jeanne Gibbs's (2001) tribes model.

Basically, I manage my classroom by teaching my students how to use the life skills that are the basis of Kavalik's ITI:

**Integrity**—Act on what's right.

**Initiative**—Do what needs to be done.

**Flexibility**—Be willing to alter plans when necessary.

**Perseverance**—Keep at it.

**Organization**—Plan, arrange, and implement in an orderly way.

**Sense of humor**—Laugh and be playful without harming others.

**Effort**—Do your best.

**Common sense**—Use good judgment.

**Problem solving**—Create solutions to problems that arise.

**Responsibility**—Be accountable for your actions.

**Patience**—Wait calmly.

**Friendship**—Make and keep friends through mutual trust.

**Curiosity**—Show a desire to investigate and find out things.

**Cooperation**—Work together toward common goals.

**Caring**—Feel and show concern for others. (Kavalik, 1994, pp. 29–30)

I never assume that my students come to school knowing these life skills. I believe it is my responsibility to teach them each and every skill. I also give them examples of how to use them and plenty of opportunities to put them to use.

## THE FIRST WEEK OF SCHOOL

For the last 4 years I taught a third- and fourth-grade combination class. I loved it because, at the beginning of the school year, the fourth graders already knew what was expected and they could model the life skill behaviors for the third graders. Unfortunately, the combination classes have been eliminated due to the emphasis on meeting state standards for each grade level. This year I am teaching third grade, and at the beginning of the year, they all seemed very young and immature to me. I introduced the life skills and class procedures and told the students what I expected in terms of behavior, but they didn't all get it the first time they heard it. Some students were talkative and inattentive. Every night during that first week of school, I would think about the next day and try to decide what to do next. I had to decide whether to spend my energy on creating great math and reading lessons or thinking of new ways to help my students understand the importance of our class rules and procedures. I decided that, for the first week, the most important thing for me to do was teach my students how to live and work together as a family and to practice and rehearse our class procedures.

On the first day of school, I form tribes, but I prefer to call them learning clubs. Each learning club consists of four students, two boys who are paired and two girls who are paired. The way I assign pairs of students is to think of one as a rookie and one as a veteran. That was a natural effect of having a third- and fourth-grade combination class, but this year, all my students are rookies. I try to pair up one more mature and one less mature student.

Every morning in my class, after we have completed some basic housekeeping procedures, we come together in a community circle. This is our relationship-building time. The first day of school I use activities that will help us all get to know one another. I teach the life skill of problem solving right away on the first day of school by calling one learning club to come and sit near me in a circle. Then, when I call the second learning club to come to the circle, I ask the first group to use their problem-solving skills to make room for the second group. As each group of four students comes to the circle, I say, "How can you use problem solving to figure out how to incorporate the new students into the circle?"

Our school administrators use these same processes with the faculty to build a sense of community among the teachers and the rest of the staff. Before a staff meeting, we might do a tribe activity, which is basically a relationship-building activity. This relationship encourages us all to be more reflective about the thousands of decisions we make each day, and we know we can go to our colleagues to discuss problems we are having and get feedback and new ideas.

I have two basic rules that I use for myself in my classroom. I have promised myself that I will never yell at students and I will never tell a child to shut up. During the first week of school I tell my students that I respect them too much to say shut up or to yell at them. I feel that the minute I yell, I lose their respect, and respect is what I am trying to earn from the first minute I greet them at the door of my classroom.

To avoid yelling, or saying shut up, I use other methods to get their attention, such as chimes or clapping signals. I teach my students the expected procedures so they know exactly what is expected. For example, when I clap three times, the procedure I teach my students is that they will respond to my claps by clapping three times also. I then teach them to put their hands up in the air and then all together we lower our hands as if we are pushing the noise down, down, down. At the same time, we all say a long drawn out "whoooooooooooosh," which sounds like letting all the air out of a balloon. When the whooooooosh ends, it is quiet. We use this noise control method schoolwide. That is one reason it is so effective. When it is completely quiet, the students know that the next step in our class procedure is for them to give me their attentive listening.

This strategy comes from Gibbs's (2001) *Tribes*. In the first week of school, I teach the class what attentive listening is and how to do it. I tell them that when they are listening attentively, their eyes need to be on the speaker and their hands have to be still. They learn to nod their head to show that they are listening. I help them to visualize and practice this procedure with the use of a T chart. On one side of the T chart, I write, "What attentive listening looks like"; on the other side, I write, "What does it sound like?" Together we fill in the chart with their ideas, such as, "All eyes are on the speaker" or "It sounds like a train stopping at a station."

This year, I found it more difficult than usual to teach the procedures. The morning procedures were the hardest thing to teach. The students have four things to do in the morning:

1. Come in and greet the teacher by giving her a hug, a handshake, or a high five. I stand at the door to greet them. I think this lets them know that I value them and that I'm glad to see them.

2. Sign up for lunch. From this procedure, I also take the attendance. They learn that when they come in the room, they are expected to put their nametag either in the lunch or no lunch folder. Two helpers count the number of lunches and take the number to the office.

3. Unpack their belongings and make sure they have a pencil sharpened.

4. Take their seat and do a short learning activity we call our "morning work." I prepare this morning work ahead of time and have it on their desks when they come in the room. This can be a half piece of paper that reviews a math concept or a grammar skill from the day before.

## DIANA'S REFLECTIVE PROCESS

If I didn't have these four procedures and provide them with their morning work, they wouldn't know what to do. They might wander around or make noise or play. I want them to know that school is a place to learn, and these four procedures make that very clear to everyone in the room. I have these four procedures written on a chart stand near the front door. But, this year, with my classroom full of rookies, some students would see the procedures on the chart but not pay attention to them. They didn't seem to understand that it was their responsibility to sign up for lunch. After class, I would reflect on this problem and try to decide how to teach it again more effectively. The next day I pulled the chart stand up and we read the four steps again. I then asked if there was one learning club that was brave enough to use their life skill of courage to model all four steps for the rest of the class. They all wanted to do it. I chose one group and asked them to go outside again and come in the door acting out all the procedures. As they came in, I pointed to procedure #1 and they greeted me. Then, they acted out putting their nametags in the lunch folder, unpacking their belongings, sharpening their pencils, and getting started on their morning work.

If I could tell beginning teachers one important thing, it is that these types of reteaching, practicing, and rehearsing procedures are absolutely necessary. Students need much more modeling and practice than we believe is necessary.

Even when most of the class comes to know and accept the procedures, it is likely that one or two students will need even more reinforcement. For example, this year I had one child who seemed particularly immature and impulsive to me. He needed several rehearsals to learn the morning procedures, and when I asked the students to line up for lunch, he got down on his hands and knees and crawled on the floor.

I didn't say anything at the time. But, when the other students left the classroom, I tapped on his shoulder and asked him to stay and talk with me. I described his own behavior to him and asked him how he thought his actions affected other students. We looked at the chart to read the class procedure for lining up. It read, "When I call your learning club, push your chairs in and line up at the door."

I asked him if he understood that sentence. He said he did. I asked him, "Is this something you can do?" and he answered yes. Then I asked him, "Is it something you are willing to do?" When he agreed that he would follow the procedure, I asked him to show me how to line up and walk to the lunchroom.

I believe in these procedures because I think they free up the class and me to spend our energy on learning. When students know what is expected of them, then they know how to succeed. They feel safer in a classroom where the rules are consistent and well-understood by everyone. These procedures take a lot of time at the beginning of the school year, but after that, I believe I spend less time on discipline the rest of the year. The end result is that we can all focus on learning together as members of a happy, purposeful learning community. I always type these procedures up and have students put them in their notebooks. When we have guest teachers, the students are expected to refer to their procedures. Also, their parents can look at their notebooks and see exactly what my expectations are.

## STANDARDS THAT APPLY TO CLASSROOM MANAGEMENT

As Diana Bateman demonstrates in her story about setting up her classroom for the first day of school, caring, reflective teachers have an intense commitment to meet the needs of their students. This attitude matches the first of the five core propositions of the National Board for Professional Teaching Standards (NBPTS). It states that, "Teachers are committed to students and their learning. Accomplished teachers . . . adjust their practice based on observation and knowledge of their students' interests, abilities, skills, knowledge, family circumstances and peer relationships."

In this text, we use the term *withitness* to refer to this attitude teachers have that compels them to listen, watch, and learn from their students. In their daily practice, reflective, withit teachers adjust their expectations, plans, and schedules to attain and keep students interested and motivated to do well on their studies. If a reflective teacher becomes aware of a family circumstance that may prevent a student from paying full attention to school tasks, the teacher will talk with the student to learn more about the situation and then modify the classroom expectations accordingly.

Another section of the first proposition of the NBPTS is also related to classroom management decisions. It states that, "Teachers' mission extends beyond developing the cognitive capacity of their students. Teachers are concerned with their students' self-concept, with their motivation, with the effects of learning on peer relationships, and with the development of character, aspiration and civic virtues."

We heartily concur with this statement. In this chapter, we will provide descriptions and examples of classroom management strategies and discipline techniques that respect the rights of each individual in the classroom and promote growth of self-esteem and self-responsibility. While there are many discipline methods that seem to "work" in the sense that they cause students to listen quietly and perform adequately, they are not included here if they rely on bribery, threats, sarcasm, or harsh punishments. We believe that you can establish classroom rules and expectations with your students, respecting their rights as well as your own. We believe that you can create a classroom community where the character of each student is encouraged to grow and expand during the school year. We hope you want to be the type of teacher who is recalled by students later in life as the one who helped them understand the need for self-responsibility and respect for others. We also hope you want to establish a classroom environment that is a happy and satisfying place to work and learn.

## PRACTICAL CLASSROOM MANAGEMENT STRATEGIES

### Connectedness

**PRAXIS**
Principles of classroom management are tested in PRAXIS™ Exam Section 1c.

Joy! Does this word remind you of classroom environments you have participated in as a student or an observer? Glasser has been researching classroom management methods that have this goal since the early 1960s. His original work, *Schools without Failure* (1969), persuaded teachers to see the necessity for creating a therapeutic environment that would allow all students to succeed. Today, Glasser (2001) continues to create models of school environments that are characterized by joy, cooperation, and a feeling of connectedness.

In classrooms where students and teachers alike appear to be doomed to fail, there is a noticeable lack of teacher reflectiveness. Instead, Glasser (2001) observes nonreflective teachers who seem trapped into seven deadly habits: criticizing, blaming, complaining, nagging, threatening, punishing, and rewarding to control the behaviors of their students. The mistaken goal of the teacher who uses these negative habits is to control the behavior of students. Teachers use these habits on students; students respond by using them on teachers, creating a dismal, joyless environment that causes a downward spiral of failure.

Glasser suggests that we replace these deadly habits with seven connecting habits: caring, listening, supporting, contributing, encouraging, trusting, and befriending. The teacher's goal should be to connect with students rather than attempt to control them.

But, teachers may say, "What am I supposed to do when a kid in my class is disruptive and obviously testing my authority?" Glasser (2001, p. 25) responds, "Students who give you a hard time have already chosen to separate from you. That's why they're disrupting. If you can't connect with them, they'll give you a hard time all year, resisting your direction, which is their way of trying to control you." Such a student may keep disrupting the classroom until you start to threaten and punish. It's like a game of "Gotcha!" When students see that you have lost control, they may surmise that they are now in control. As the situation escalates, the students are very likely blaming the entire situation on the teacher, who has "lost it."

How do you avoid this nightmare? Glasser describes a couple of familiar situations and suggests a way to use connecting behaviors rather than resorting to blaming behaviors. A third-grade boy starts to hum and keeps humming more loudly, while watching carefully to see what the teacher will do about it. Other students are also aware of the situation and are watching to see what will happen. This is a situation that demands withitness, followed by an appropriate and constructive response. Glasser suggests that the teacher stop teaching, look at the boy, and say, "Tom, I'm having trouble teaching with what you're doing. I'd like to talk with you for a few minutes."

Tell the other students to go back to their work, but do not be concerned if they watch and listen as you talk with Tom, as they can learn from this lesson on human interaction.

When you and Tom are sitting eye to eye, begin by saying, "Tom, I'm concerned about you. I don't think you are happy in this classroom. I'd like you to be happier. I think if you were happier, you wouldn't have been humming this morning. What do you think?"

Tom may be surprised and disarmed by this approach. He expects anger, threats, and punishment. His surprise will likely mean that he is paying attention to you, but he may not know how to answer your question. Instead, he may try to ignore or pretend that he does not need you to care about him. He may answer, "I'm okay, don't worry about it." This is a weak effort to suggest that he does not need a connection with you. But, he does. All students need to feel connected to the important adults in their lives, and, as their teacher, you are one of the most important adults in your students' lives.

Continue to talk quietly with Tom. You might say, "I'm worried about you. If I weren't worried about you, I wouldn't take this time to talk with you about it. You are a smart kid. I'd like to help you get some good work done in this class. I think you'd feel a lot better if you did some work that you are proud of."

Tom may respond with something like, "I hate history. It's boring. Who cares about that old stuff anyway?"

To continue your connective interaction, you might respond, "That's a good question. Why should anyone care about history? We can talk about that with the whole class later this morning. But, for now, I need to get back to teaching. I hope you will get back to your report and finish it in a way that will make you proud of your work. I am not going to try to make you work, but please sit quietly and think about all of this until the period is over."

Tom and the whole class have heard this important exchange. If Tom cooperates at this point, an important victory has been achieved for all members of the class. If Tom begins to hum again with a defiant look in his eye, it may be necessary to send Tom to the principal's office or another quiet place. You can say quite honestly, "Tom, I can't devote any more time to this problem right now. Go to the principal's office and wait for me there. I will come and talk to you during recess." After Tom leaves, you may want to talk to the class about what just happened. Ask the students to give their opinion of what just happened. Allow them to give suggestions for what you might say to Tom when you meet with him during recess. Explain to your students that you want to create a classroom where everybody can work and where everyone feels connected and supported.

## Strategies Designed to Meet Students' Needs

In *Motivation and Personality*, Abraham Maslow (1954) first described a hierarchy of human needs. He recognized that people have basic physical and emotional needs that must be satisfied before the individual can attend to the higher need for achievement and recognition. If the lower needs are not satisfied, the individual is preoccupied by trying to meet them, and other, higher-level, needs are pushed into the background. This explains why hungry or tired students cannot learn efficiently. All their capacities are focused on satisfying the need for food or sleep. To satisfy the real hunger needs experienced by many students, some schools provide breakfast or snacks so students can pay attention to school tasks.

What happens when the student has plenty of food and adequate shelter and is well rested? Then "at once other (and 'higher') needs emerge" (Maslow, 1954, p. 375) and these become dominant. Once basic physiological needs are met, humans need safety and security. Next come the needs for love and belonging. Imagine two classrooms, one led by either an autocratic or a permissive teacher, in which students feel threatened, insecure, and isolated, and the other led by a democratic teacher, in which students feel safe, secure, cared for, and connected with other members of the class community. In the latter setting students are more likely to have their needs met and therefore be ready and able to achieve greater success in academic work.

Glasser (2001) suggests that you may want to begin the school year in a way that creates a sense of connectedness among you and your students. One way to accomplish that is to involve your students in decisions about how to arrange the desks and tables in order to promote good two-way communication and make the students feel connected to you and to one another.

Ron Clark (2003), Disney's Teacher of the year for 2001, stressed the importance of modeling behavior for students. In his book Clark tells of trying to learn to jump rope "double dutch" and failing time after time. His students began to give him the same advice they had gotten: "Keep trying, Mr. Clark. You can do it. Don't give up," until one day he was able to succeed. The whole playground cheered and the students expressed their pride that he "hadn't given up when it got hard." This experience not only reinforced the work ethic he had been trying to instill, it also provided a way in which the students became more connected to him as a person.

## Organization Strategies

When your students walk into your classroom for the first time, they can sense a particular climate or environment within a few moments. A multitude of sensory images enters their consciousness—sights, sounds, and smells, for the most part. The way the room is arranged, its messiness or neatness, wall decorations, open or shut windows, and the smell of chalk dust or an animal cage all combine to create a unique flavor or climate in a classroom.

What do you want your students to see, hear, smell, and feel when they enter your classroom? The appearance of your classroom makes a statement about the extent to which you care for the environment in which you and your students will spend several hours each day. It may be untidy, neat, colorful, drab; filled with objects, plants, animals, and students' art, or left undecorated and unkempt. No two classrooms are alike; each has its unique environment. However, some classrooms (and their occupants) bloom with health, vitality, and strength, whereas others appear sickly, listless, and debilitated.

Reflective teachers want to come to school several days before their contract calls for them to be there. They hang posters, decorate bulletin boards, and carefully consider ways to arrange the students' desks, tables, bookcases, and other furniture to fit their curriculum plans and the needs of their students. You know from the many years you have spent in classrooms as students that a bright, colorful, cheerful, and stimulating classroom leads you to expect that school will be interesting and that the teacher celebrates life and learning. You also know that drab, undecorated spaces lead to expectations of dullness and boredom.

How to arrange the desks is a complex issue. Even though you may decide to involve your students in helping to rearrange the furniture as a way of connecting with them during the first week of class, you must still select an arrangement for the first day of school. Often the room contains many more desks than it was designed to hold comfortably. The number of students in a classroom may vary from 15 to 35, and the precise number of students is not known until the last minute, making preplanning difficult. Generally, though, teachers know approximately how many students they will have in their classrooms, and they set about arranging the desks in a way that uses space economically and strategically. Their plans are governed by an image of themselves and their students in teaching and learning experiences.

While arranging the classroom, reflective teachers envision its "activity flow"— what it will be like when the classroom is filled with students. This imaging process helps reflective teachers decide how to arrange the furniture in the room. As with other important decisions, each option has both advantages and disadvantages. Desks can be arranged in rows, circles, semicircles, and small groups. Each arrangement influences how students work and how they perceive their environment. Rows of desks provide an advantage in keeping order but leave little space for activities (Figure 2.1). A large circle of desks can be used if the teacher envisions that teaching and learning experiences will take place in the center of the circle, but it will be difficult for all students to see the chalkboard (Figure 2.2).

Arranging desks into small groups results in students' spending more time working together, initiating their own tasks, and working without teacher attention when compared with students in traditional rooms. Teachers who value cooperative group learning experiences over teacher-centered learning experiences often use clusters of four to six desks (Figure 2.3).

Activity and workspaces can be arranged by using bookcases and room dividers or simply by arranging tables and chairs in the corners of the room. Some teachers bring in comfortable furniture and rugs to design a space just for quiet reading. Computer or listening stations must also be designated. Room arrangement and the use of space are highly individualized decisions. Teachers make these decisions to fit their personal image of what a classroom should be, by considering what they value most highly and how the room arrangement fits their values as well as the curriculum and grade level of the class.

Reflective teachers also consider the effects of the physical arrangement of the room on developing a healthy classroom environment. Rows of desks imply order and efficiency but do little to build a sense of community. Clusters of desks promote cooperation and communication among groups of students. Large circle or concentric circle arrangements (Figure 2.4) encourage communication and sharing among the entire class. Many reflective teachers change their room arrangements from time to time depending on the goals of a particular learning experience and thus create a variety of classroom environments to fit a variety of purposes.

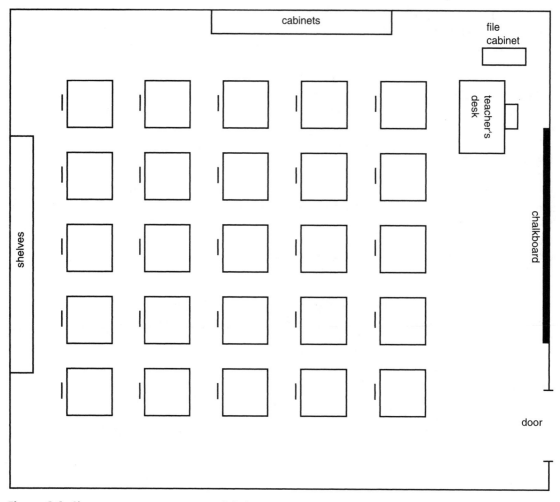

**Figure 2.1** Classroom arrangement: rows of desks.

## Planning for the First Day of School

The physical environment and schedule of the classroom may lead students to expect certain things about the way teaching and learning will occur during the school year. These expectations are reinforced even more strongly during the first few minutes of the first day of school. For example, consider the students' experience on their first day of school in the following elementary and high school classroom scenarios.

You can probably recognize the teachers in these opening-day scenarios and can give them names and faces from your own experiences in school. You have been exposed to a variety of teaching styles, methods, attitudes, and philosophies as consumers of education. You will soon become a teacher yourself. What style will you have? How will your students perceive you? What values and principles will you model? How will your students feel when they walk into your classroom on the first day of school? Consider the scenarios described in Figure 2.5 and Figure 2.6.

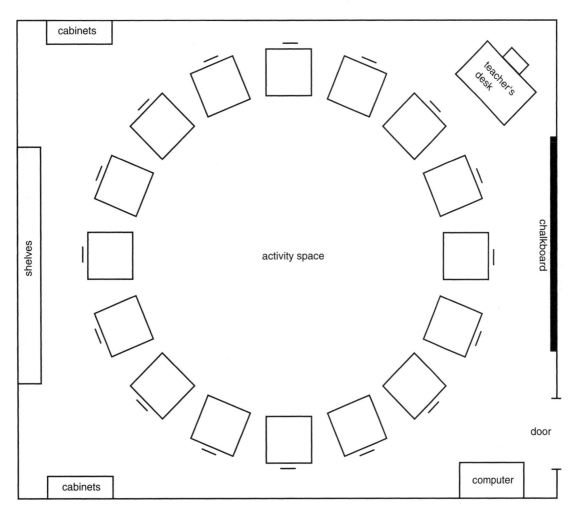

**Figure 2.2** Classroom arrangement: circle of desks.

## Teaching Styles

Each teacher in these scenarios has a unique *teaching style*, a result of personality, philosophy, values, physical and emotional health, past experiences, and current knowledge about the effects of a teacher's behavior on the classroom environment. There are three broad descriptors of teaching styles termed *authoritarian, permissive,* and *democratic.*

Authoritarian teachers tend to plan furniture arrangements to maintain order in the classroom and to plan schedules that seldom vary. Authoritarian teachers believe it is their sole responsibility to make all class rules and establish consequences for misbehavior. Such teachers tend to rely on teacher-centered lectures, discussions, and assignments. It is the student's role to obey the rules and do all assigned work satisfactorily.

In the opening-day scenarios, Miss Adams represented a moderately authoritarian teacher, while Mrs. Destry and Mr. Green are so authoritarian, they could almost be called

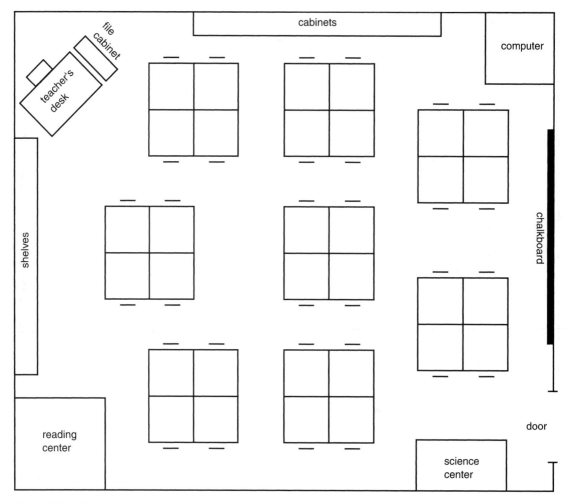

**Figure 2.3** Classroom arrangement: clusters of desks.

autocratic. Teachers exhibiting these leadership styles seem to have as their primary goal the creation of a quiet, orderly classroom climate. There is little positive social interaction in the class. Individuals compete for grades and the teacher's attention. Some students attempt to please the teacher by any means possible, while others revolt and undermine the teacher's efforts to control students' behavior. A positive sense of community is rare in a classroom led by an autocratic teacher; the only sense of community that may develop among the students is a shared sense of resentment or even rebellion in extreme cases.

At the other extreme, there are teaching styles that have been called permissive or laissez-faire. Teachers, such as Mr. Baron, who employ a permissive style appear tentative and powerless. They make few rules and are inconsistent in establishing or delivering the consequences for misbehavior. They accept excuses and seem unable to assert authority over academic work or student behavior. Confusion is the chief characteristic of the classroom climate created by such a permissive teacher. Students don't know what is expected

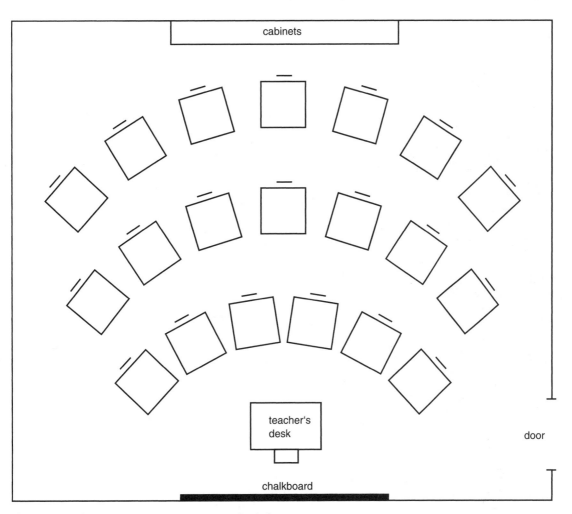

**Figure 2.4** Classroom arrangement: concentric circles.

or how they can succeed. Limits are fuzzy, leading to a constant testing of how much the students can get away with. Little sense of community can develop within a permissive classroom because students often learn to play one against the other to get their way.

A third type of leadership is the democratic style. Democratic teachers, represented here by Mr. Catlin and Mr. Evans, are neither permissive nor autocratic. They are firm and reasonably consistent about their expectations for academic achievement and student behavior. They discuss the need for rules with their students and involve them in establishing the specific rules and consequences for the class. From time to time, they may initiate a reevaluation of certain rules to update them and make them more usable and meaningful. Democratic teachers assert their power to make decisions but are willing to listen to their students' reactions, needs, and desires. The result is that the sense of power and ownership is distributed among students and the teacher in the same way that it is distributed in a healthy community.

*The scene is an elementary school. It is the first day of the new school year. In one corridor, several classroom doors are open. We see and hear four teachers greet the students in their classes.*

## Room 101

Miss Adams is standing at the doorway. As children walk in, she says, in a calm, even-toned voice, to each of them, "You'll find your name on a desk," as she gestures toward six clusters of desks. "Sit in that desk and wait quietly." The children obey and the room is quiet within. When all the children have entered, Miss Adams goes into her classroom and quietly shuts the door behind her. The beginning bell rings at precisely that moment.

## Room 102

Mr. Baron is nowhere to be seen. Children enter the classroom looking for him, but when they don't see him, they begin to talk and walk around the room. The desks are arranged haphazardly in ragged rows. Two boys try to sit in the same desk, and a scuffle breaks out. The beginning bell rings. Suddenly Mr. Baron comes running down the hall, enters the room, and yells, "All right, you guys, sit down and be quiet. What do you think this place is? A zoo?"

## Room 103

Mr. Catlin is standing at the door wearing a big smile. As each child enters, he gives the child a sticker with his or her name on it. "Put this sticker on a desk that you like and sit in it," he says. The children enter and quickly claim desks, which are arranged in four concentric arcs facing the front of the room. They talk with each other in the classroom. When the bell rings, Mr. Catlin enters, leaving the door ajar for latecomers.

## Room 104

Mrs. Destry is sitting at her desk when the children enter. Without standing up, she tells the children to line up along the side of the room. They comply. When the bell rings, she tells a student to shut the door.

*If we were able to enter the classrooms with the students, this is what we might see, hear, and experience.*

## Room 101

Miss Adams stands in front of the class. She has excellent posture and a level gaze. As she waits quietly for the children to find their seats, she looks each child in the eye. They settle down quickly. When the classroom is perfectly quiet, she begins to talk.

"I see that you have all found your desks. Good. Now we can begin. I like the way you have quieted down. That tells me that you know how to behave in school. Let's review some of the important rules of our classroom."

Pointing to a chart entitled "Class Rules," she reads each aloud and tells the children its significance. "Rule 1: Students will pay attention when the teacher is speaking. This is important because we are here to learn and there can be no learning if you do not hear what the teacher is saying. Rule 2: Students will use quiet voices when talking in the classroom. This rule is important because a quiet, orderly classroom is conducive to learning. Rule 3: No fighting, arguing, or name calling is allowed."

The children listen attentively to all items. They do not ask questions or comment on the rules. After the rules are read, Miss Adams assigns helpers for class jobs. The newly appointed monitors pass out the reading books, and the children begin to read the first story in their books. Miss Adams walks quietly from desk to desk to see that each child is reading.

**Figure 2.5** Scenarios of the first day of school.

## Room 102

Mr. Baron rushes in and slams some books and papers on the desk. Some of them land on the floor nearby. Stooping to pick them up, he says, "Sit down, sit down or I'll find cages for you instead of desks." The children sit down, but the noise level remains high.

"Enough! Do you want to begin the school year by going to the principal's office? Don't you care about school? Don't you want to learn something?" Gradually, the noise diminishes, but children's voices continue to interrupt from time to time with remarks to their teacher or to fellow classmates.

Mr. Baron calls roll from an attendance book. He does not even look up when a child says "Here" but stares intently at the book. He has several children pass out books at one time, resulting in more confusion about whether each child received all the necessary books. Finally he tells them to begin reading the first story in their reading books. Some do so, others do not. Mr. Baron begins looking through his file cabinet, ignoring the noise.

## Room 103

Mr. Catlin walks through the room as he talks to the class. From time to time, he stops near a child and puts his hand on the child's shoulder, especially a child who appears restless or insecure. This action seems to help the child settle down and pay attention.

"Welcome back to school! This year should be a good one for all of us. I've got some great new ideas for our math and social studies programs, and we'll be using paperback novels to supplement our reading series. But first, let's establish the rules for our classroom. Why are we here?"

A student raises her hand. Mr. Catlin reads the name tag sticker on her desk and calls on her by name. "To learn," she says timidly.

"Exactly!" Mr. Catlin agrees. "And, what rules can help us to learn the most we've ever learned in a single year?"

Several children begin to call out responses at the same time.

"Wait a moment, class. Can we learn anything like this?"

A chorus of "No's" is heard.

"Then what rule do we need to solve this problem?"

A child raises his hand, is called on, and says, "We need to raise our hands before we talk."

"What a fine rule," Mr. Catlin says with a broad smile. "How many agree?" The hands of most children go up. Mr. Catlin spots one child whose hand is not raised. He walks over to that child, kneels next to the child's desk and says, "Do you agree that this rule will help you learn this year?" "Yes," says the child and his hand goes up.

After the class has established and agreed on several other class rules, Mr. Catlin talks about the reading program. He offers the children their choice of five paperback novels, distributes them, and tells the children to begin reading. As they read, he circulates around the room, stopping from time to time to ask questions or make comments about the stories to individual children.

## Room 104

Mrs. Destry regards the children in their line with an unfriendly gaze. When a child moves or talks, she gives that child a withering stare. From a class list, she begins to read the students' names in alphabetical order, indicating which seat they are to take. The students sit down meekly. No one says a word or makes a sound.

"Now, class, you will find your books in your desks. Take out your reading books and turn to the first page." Going down the rows, each child reads a paragraph aloud while the other children sit silently and listlessly, following along in their books.

*The scene is a high school. It is the first day of the new school year. In one corridor, several classroom doors are open. We see and hear two teachers greet their classes.*

## Room 205

Mr. Evans is waiting at the front door, welcoming his students. The students enter the classroom and can be heard saying, "Hello, Mr. E." Mr. Evans says hello and that he's glad to have each student in class. He tells them to locate their seats by looking at the overhead in the front of the room. He has a seating chart shown on the overhead. Students begin to sit down and talk about their summer experiences.

After the bell rings, Mr. Evans walks to the center of the room and waits for quiet. The students look up and begin to prepare themselves for Mr. Evans's beginning remarks. One bulletin board in the front of the room is completed in the school colors and includes a picture of the school mascot, a pennant, and words from the fight song. The other bulletin board is filled with mathematical symbols and sayings by famous mathematicians. Along the top of the chalkboard is a set of very colorful geometric designs.

A set of rules is posted conspicuously on one of the walls of the room:

Rule 1: Respect each other.
Rule 2: Participate in class.
Rule 3: Help one another.
Rule 4: Everyone tries 100%.

Mr. Evans begins by saying, "Welcome to the best high school in the city. I hope each student has found his or her seat using the chart on the overhead. I believe that it is important that you know how to use such items as charts and graphs. I like to take every opportunity to use mathematics in my classroom. In addition, I would like to review the rules of this classroom. If you have any questions related to the rules, we should discuss them immediately. If you have suggestions for any additional rules, we may want to include them in the initial set of rules I've listed."

## Room 206

Mr. Green leaves the teacher's lounge about 30 seconds before class starts. When he arrives at his classroom, the bell rings. Some students are still outside talking with friends. Mr. Green yells at the students to "get inside or I'll begin writing detention slips on the first day." The students begin to take seats or lean against the side shelves.

As you look around the classroom, there is nothing on any of the bulletin boards. Student books are stacked on the side shelves. They are obviously ready to be distributed to the class.

Mr. Green tells the students to "shut up" so that he can call the roll and tell students where their seats are going to be. He stands behind a podium and begins to call names and assign seats. As students go to their seats, they continue talking among themselves. Frequently, Mr. Green calls for silence, but the noise level does not diminish very much.

After the students are seated, Mr. Green complains that this is a bad beginning to the school year and warns the students again that he is not afraid to send them to detention if they don't know how to behave. He has used this tactic in the past, and he will use it with this class if necessary.

With no discussion of goals, rules, or expectations, Mr. Green appoints some of the boys to pass out the textbooks and writes "Read Chapter 1" on the chalkboard. Some students begin to read, while others continue to talk with each other. Mr. Green gets out his detention slips and begins to write names on them.

**Figure 2.6** First day of high school scenario.

Perhaps you may be considering the important question, "Is it possible to control and decide on my teaching style, or is it simply a function of my personality?" The more information you can gather about how teachers create healthy climates for learning, the more power you have to gain self-understanding and control over this and other important matters pertaining to teaching and learning. To identify the most effective classroom management strategies, Evertson and Harris (2002) conducted a study about how teachers begin the school year and establish their expectations with students. They were especially interested to learn how teachers who are effective classroom managers begin the school year. They hoped to discover some basic principles of effective classroom management that could be taught to beginning teachers. They selected 27 third-grade classrooms in eight elementary schools for their study. Observers were present in each of these classrooms during the first few weeks of school. Using criteria for effective management developed by the team of observers, the 27 teachers were classified into two categories: more effective and less effective classroom managers.

Both groups of teachers had rules and procedures planned for their classes. What distinguished the more effective managers from the others was that they spent a major part of the first day and much time during the next 3 weeks helping their students adjust to their classroom expectations and learn to understand the rules and procedures established for the class. Like Miss Adams and Mr. Catlin, the teachers began describing their carefully planned rules and procedures as soon as most students had arrived at the classroom. In some cases, but not always, students were asked to suggest rules for the class. The rules and procedures were explained clearly, with examples and reasons.

More effective managers did not rely simply on a discussion of the rules. They spent a considerable amount of time during the first week of school explaining and reminding students of the rules. One of the most effective way to communicate your expectations to your class is to lead them through a rehearsal on how to follow the procedures. Teachers take time to rehearse procedures such as how to line up for lunch or what to take out of their desks for math class. Many teachers teach students to respond to specific signals, such as a bell or a hand signal to call for attention. Evertson and Harris (2002) observed that the more effective managers clearly establish themselves as the classroom leaders. They prepare and plan classroom procedures in advance, communicate their expectations clearly, and demonstrate their withitness by signaling their awareness of disruptive student behavior when it occurs. They work on rules and procedures until the students learn them. Teaching content is important for these teachers, but they stress that, initially, socialization into the classroom system is the primary learning goal. By the end of the first 3 weeks, teachers who used these methods have fewer major discipline problems for the rest of the year.

The reflective teacher, guided by moral principles, also recognizes that it is not simply a matter of establishing leadership that is important; the style of leadership counts as well. Miss Adams, Mr. Catlin, and Mr. Evans quickly established that they were the classroom leaders, but Mr. Catlin's style of leadership best exhibited the underlying moral principles of caring, consideration, and honesty as he interacted with his students. The result is that students in such an environment return the caring, consideration, and honesty to the teacher and exhibit it in their interactions with one another.

In contrast, less effective managers (exemplified by Mr. Baron and Mr. Green) did not have well-thought-out procedures. Although teachers like Mr. Baron always have rules, the rules are often vague, and the teachers tend to tell the class the rules and procedures quickly without spending time discussing and rehearsing what they really mean. Others, like Mrs. Destry, try to move quickly to academic matters. They seem to expect the students to be able to comprehend and retain the rules from a single, brief statement. They do not teach the class routines and procedures. As a result, they are often found to waste many, many hours of class time during the year as they remind the students again and again to behave.

The way the two groups of teachers monitor the behavior of their students is also a critical factor in establishing a clear set of expectations for students. The Evertson and Harris (2002) study disclosed that less effective teacher-managers did not actively monitor students' behavior. Instead, they busied themselves with clerical tasks or worked with a single student on a task while ignoring the rest of the class. The consequence of vague and untaught rules and poor monitoring was that the children were frequently left without enough information or a good enough example to guide their behavior.

From this study, you can conclude that if you expect your students to obey the rules of your classroom, you must give them clear directions, allow them to rehearse the procedures until they get it right, and actively observe while your students work, showing them that you expect them to pay attention to the task and do their work.

## Teachers' Body Language

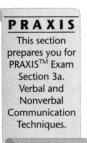

**PRAXIS**
This section prepares you for PRAXIS™ Exam Section 3a. Verbal and Nonverbal Communication Techniques.

Jones (2000) found that effective classroom management and control of student behavior depends a great deal on the teacher's body language. Strong, effective teachers are able to communicate many important things with eye contact, physical proximity, bodily carriage, gestures, and facial expressions. These teachers do not have to be 6 feet 5 inches tall and weigh 230 pounds. Indeed, it is fascinating to observe teachers who are small in stature manage classrooms with a glance by standing next to a student who is disturbing the classroom.

Consider the eye contact of the teachers in the first day of school scenario. Miss Adams had a level gaze and met the students' eyes as she looked at each of them at their first meeting. She communicated that she was aware and in control in a positive, non-threatening manner. Mr. Evans made immediate eye contact with each student in a positive way and demonstrated enthusiasm for the school where he teaches and the students themselves. Mrs. Destry gave the students withering stares that probably caused them to feel anxious and fearful about the year ahead. Mr. Baron and Mr. Green never met the eyes of their students at all, communicating their lack of preparation and confidence to manage the classroom. Mr. Catlin used physical proximity as well as eye contact to put his students at ease and to communicate that he was in charge.

Jones (2000) recommends the concentric circle desk arrangement that Mr. Catlin used because it causes students to focus their attention on the teacher and enables the teacher to provide help efficiently by moving quickly to the side of any student who is having difficulty. A teacher can help students allay their fears and turn the focus to the classroom activity by moving close to the restless student and placing a hand on the student's shoulder. However, to use physical proximity effectively, the teacher must be able to step quickly to the side of the misbehaving student, as Mr. Catlin did. Thus, room arrangement can help or hinder a teacher's ability to control students' behavior.

A teacher's personal bearing also sends messages to students. The strong, straight posture of Miss Adams reinforced the students' perception that she was an authority worthy of their respect. Good posture and confident bodily carriage convey strong leadership, whereas a drooping posture and lethargic movements convey weakness, resignation, or fearfulness (Jones, 2000).

Gestures are also a form of body language that can communicate positive expectations and prevent problems. Teachers can use gestures to mean "stop," "continue," or "quite, please" without interrupting their verbal instruction. When used with positive eye contact, physical proximity, bodily carriage, or facial expression, gestures can prevent small disruptions from growing into major behavior problems.

Facial expressions also vary greatly among teachers. They can show enthusiasm, seriousness, enjoyment, and appreciation, all of which encourage good behavior; or they can reveal boredom, annoyance, and resignation, which may tend to encourage misbehavior (Jones, 2000). Facial expressions that display warmth, joy, and a sense of humor are those that students themselves report to be the most meaningful. You may even want to look in the mirror to see how students will see you when you are happy, angry, feeling good about yourself, or upset.

## Establishing Rules and Consequences

In a healthy democratic community, the citizens understand and accept the laws that govern their behavior. They also understand and accept that if they break the laws, certain consequences will follow. Healthy democratic classrooms also have laws that govern behavior, although they are usually called rules. In the most smoothly managed classrooms, students also learn to understand and accept the consequences for breaking a rule from the very first day.

In the opening-day scenarios, each teacher established rules and consequences for the classroom differently. Miss Adams had established a set of rules beforehand. She read them to the class and explained why each was important. Mr. Baron, Mr. Green, and Mrs. Destry did not present a clear set of rules. Their actions indicated that they expected the students to discover the rules of the classroom. These are likely to be quite consistent in Mrs. Destry's classroom; but in the cases of Mr. Baron and Mr. Green, we suspect that the rules may change from day to day. Mr. Catlin had planned an entire process for establishing rules. His process involved the students in helping to establish the class rules based on shared expectations and consequences.

Two types of consequences are used to guide or shape student behavior. Natural consequences are those that follow directly from a student's behavior or action. For example, if a student gets so frustrated while working on an assignment that he rips the paper in half, the natural consequence is that the work will have to be redone from the beginning. If another student wakes up late, the natural consequence is that she misses the bus and has to walk to school, arrives late, and suffers the embarrassment of coming to class tardy. In these cases, there was no adult intervention; the consequence grew directly from the student's behavior.

Logical consequences are those the teacher selects to fit students' actions; they are intended to cause students to change their behavior. For example, a teacher may decide that the logical consequence of not turning in a paper on time is that the student must stay in for recess or miss another activity period to finish the paper. When the paper is turned in, the logical consequence is that the student may go out to recess or take part in the activity period.

The difference between a punishment and a consequence is that a consequence is not arbitrary and it is not dispensed with anger or any other strong emotion. In his book *What Works in Schools*, Marzano (2003) recommends seven action steps in establishing rules and procedures that will have the effect of managing your classroom with a sense of success for you and a sense of belonging and acceptance for your students.

**Action Step 1:** Articulate and enforce a set of classroom rules and procedures.

**Action Step 2:** Use strategies that reinforce appropriate behavior and recognize and provide consequences for inappropriate behavior.

**Action Step 3:** Institute a schoolwide approach to discipline.

**Action Step 4:** Develop a balance of dominance and cooperation with students.

**Action Step 5:** Develop your awareness of the needs of different types of students and learn ways to alleviate those needs.

**Action Step 6:** Use withitness to heighten your awareness of the actions of your students in your classes.

**Action Step 7:** Maintain healthy emotional objectivity with your students. (pp. 95–102)

By establishing a clear set of rules with objective consequences and clearly communicating these rules and their consequences to your students, you can fulfill many of these seven action steps. In many classrooms, teachers write a set of rules on a large piece of poster board that is prominently displayed. Many teachers try to word the rules in positive ways, describing what they expect rather than what they forbid. They write very specific consequences for each rule on the same poster for all students to see. For example:

| Our Class Rules | Consequences If Not Followed |
| --- | --- |
| We wait in line courteously. | You will go to the end of the line. |
| We listen to the teacher. | You will lose 5 minutes of free time. |
| We turn in work on time. | You will do your work at free time. |
| We work and talk quietly. | You will take a time-out. |
| We treat others with respect. | You will write a letter of apology. |

At the middle or high school level, the posted rules and consequences may resemble these:

| Class Rules | Consequences If Not Followed |
| --- | --- |
| Complete and submit homework. | Attend after-school study hall to complete the missing homework. |
| Show respect for others. | Write an essay explaining your disrespectful behavior and how it affects others. |
| Maintain school property. | Clean and/or repaint property. |

# Using Positive Consequences and Rewards

Many beginning teachers believe that they can reward students with tokens or awards to earn their cooperation and respect. But, Jones (2000) examined the familiar incentive systems of grades, gold stars, and being dismissed first and discovered that these systems appear to benefit only the top achievers; they are not genuine incentives for students who cannot realistically meet the established criteria.

Jones also notes that if teachers offer incentives that are not particularly attractive to many students, the incentives will not positively affect student behavior or achievement. He uses the term *genuine incentives* to distinguish those that students perceive as both valuable and realistic for them to earn from those that students perceive to be of little benefit or impossible to achieve. His system of "responsibility training" focuses on preventing discipline problems by helping students to develop self-control and insight into what is meaningful and important in life.

One important way to develop self-responsibility is a form of time-management training that provides genuine incentives for students to waste less time during the day. If they work efficiently and cooperatively, they can earn their own time to do what they want with it. Jones has observed enough classrooms to conclude that without genuine incentives to save time, many students will simply fritter it away. They move slowly getting to their seats in the morning. They waste time coming to attention, getting out their materials, or lining up. Jones suggests that teachers think about time in the same way we think about money.

To train children to become more responsible with money, it is essential that they earn some money in the first place. Once they have money of their own, it is the adult's responsibility to help them learn how to manage their money effectively. They have to learn that they cannot use credit or borrow more money. They need to learn that if they want more money, they have to earn it. Responsibility training with time is analogous to learning to manage money. Teachers can establish a classroom system that allows students to earn preferred activity time (PAT) to make their own choices. If they fritter away their class work time, then they earn less PAT. If they work effectively and cooperatively during work periods, they become rich (!) in time for their own preferred activities. In this type of system, you can maintain an objective demeanor that is nicely balanced between dominance and cooperation because you are not rewarding or punishing student behavior as much as you are simply keeping an accurate record of the students' decisions, and giving them their payoff in time.

If students are to continue to perceive these favored activities as genuine incentives, they must be delivered as promised. Some teachers promise the incentive but run out of time and do not deliver on their promises. Another counterproductive practice is to continually threaten to reduce or eliminate the incentive if students do not cooperate. Still others deliver the reward even when the work is not done acceptably. When this occurs, the students learn that they can have dessert even if they do not eat their dinner—that is, they can get the reward without doing their work. This practice can destroy the balance of trust between student and teacher so that when the teacher establishes incentives, the students are skeptical that they will be delivered as promised.

Havana Middle School in Havana, Florida, had a history of low test scores, poor attendance, and discipline problems. The principal believed that the students needed some incentives to improve their attendance, behavior, and scholastic efforts. Because his school is in a rural area of the Florida Panhandle, his students all came to school on buses, and after-school incentives were not possible. The administrator and his faculty instituted Friday afternoon clubs. They surveyed the student body to determine what club activities would be interesting and engaging for the students. Every other Friday afternoon the last hour and a half of the school day became devoted to club activities such as model rocketry, softball, computer games, makeup and modeling, and a variety of other things suggested by the students. In order to attend the clubs students must have no discipline or academic reports during the 2-week period. College softball players, local engineers, hairdressers, and cosmetologists (mainly parents) had been recruited from the community to serve as club advisors. The number of discipline and academic reports given out has dwindled to less than 10% of the number prior to the club initiative.

When delivered as promised and as earned, genuine incentives can promote increased achievement among individuals and groups and can cause peer pressure to encourage good behavior. Caring, reflective teachers attempt to understand the real needs and desires of their students and to provide incentives that meet these needs.

## Classroom Meetings

One method democratic teachers often use to build mutual caring, consideration, and honest expression of opinions and perceptions is to hold classroom meetings to discuss problems confronting the class. Some teachers hold regularly scheduled classroom meetings each week; others schedule them only when necessary. When Judy taught fifth grade, she scheduled her meetings just before lunch on Wednesdays so they were in the middle of the week. She found that one of the most important effects of a classroom meeting is the sense of community created when the students and teacher sit down to solve problems together.

The seating arrangement for a class meeting is a single circle of chairs, so each member of the class can see both the teacher and all other members of the class. The teacher has the responsibility of establishing rules and consequences for the meeting. These usually consist of a rule about one person speaking at a time and accepting the ideas and opinions of others without criticism or laughter. It is important that, as the leader of the meeting, the teacher be nonjudgmental. When expressing anger or other feelings, class members are encouraged to use "I"-statements.

The meeting may be divided into several parts. For example, the teacher may choose to open with an unfinished statement such as, "I sometimes wonder why" or "I am proud of" or "I am concerned about." Going once around the circle, every member of the class is encouraged to respond to this opening statement, while the teacher encourages communication from every member of the group. While all class members are encouraged to respond, the teacher makes it clear that any individual may simply say, "Pass." Opening the class meeting in this way has the advantage of allowing everyone to speak at least once during the meeting and may bring out important issues that need discussion.

The second part of the meeting can be devoted to students' concerns. The teacher opens this discussion by asking who has a concern. When a problem is expressed, the teacher moderates discussion on that issue alone until it is resolved. Issues are seldom resolved easily in one meeting, but class members can raise a problem, express different ideas and opinions, then offer possible solutions. When a reasonable solution is worked out, the teacher's role is to restate the solution and suggest that the class try it for a time and discuss how it worked at the next classroom meeting. Other student concerns can then be expressed.

The third part of the class meeting can address the teacher's concerns. The teacher can bring up a problem by expressing personal feelings or stating expectations for future work. Students' responses can be brought out and discussed and solutions proposed. The sense of community that develops from expressing needs and opinions, hearing other perspectives, and solving problems together is translated into all aspects of life in the classroom. When an argument occurs during recess or when students perceive something as unfair, they know they can discuss it openly and freely in a class meeting. When the teacher needs more cooperation or wants higher-quality work, this issue can be brought up in a class meeting, which is designed to develop mutual understanding, tolerance for opposing views, and a way to resolve conflicts. Class meetings can and often do result in a strong sense of ownership and commitment to the academic, social, and emotional goals of the class as a whole.

## Two-Way Communication with Parents

Discipline problems are less likely when teachers communicate their expectations to students and parents so that everyone is working with the same set of expectations. Communication with parents needs to occur early in the school year and continue on a regular basis. Teachers should clearly explain the policies, procedures, and rules that govern the classroom and should establish procedures for parents to ask questions and voice their concerns.

> **PRAXIS**
> Active partnerships and respectful, reciprocal, communication are tested in PRAXIS™ Exam Section 4b.

Susan McCloskey, a first-grade teacher at Greenberg Elementary School in Fresno, California, invites her parents to a parent meeting at the beginning of the year. She reviews the class rules and expectations for behavior and academics with the parents with the help of bilingual assistants in Spanish and Hmong. She also invites the parents to come into the classroom as volunteers or do at-home support in areas such as collecting materials (egg cartons, milk jug caps, etc.) She sends home periodic newsletters (in three languages) with suggestions for ways to help at home. Susan makes frequent phone calls to parents to inform them of outstanding behavior or work being done by the students as well as expressing concerns when needed. Although Susan teachers in a very low-income neighborhood, she makes the parents feel as if they are a part of a learning team.

Jody Salazar teaches seventh- and eighth-grade remedial reading at Martin Luther King Middle School in Madera, California. Jody also invites parents to school for a meeting at the beginning of the year. She explains her program and her expectations and invites the parents to volunteer by sharing their vocations, hobbies, or interests with her classes. When a parent volunteers to talk to a class, Jody has the class read books about the topic to be presented and prepare questions for the speaker (or demonstrator). She also has the class practice the proper way to listen politely, introduce speakers, and thank them for their time. After the visits, the students write letters describing the parts of the presentation they found interesting.

Ron Clark (2003) teaches in Harlem, New York City, and in his initial communication with parents he stresses the importance of parents becoming a part of the educational team. He asks for their cooperation in five important ways:

1. If there's a problem, call *me*, not the principal. Call me first and give me a chance to discuss the problem with you.
2. If you need to talk with me, send a note with your child. I will write back and we can set up a time to meet.
3. Don't allow your children to be late or absent for insignificant reasons. Let them know that school is important.
4. Realize that your child is one of many that I teach every day. I need your help to meet their needs. It's a team effort.
5. Trust that I know what I'm doing. If you don't understand, ask me, not someone else.

## Confronting School Bullies

You may get a call from a parent reporting to you that their child has been coming home from school full of fear and anxiety because another student has been acting like a bully. How will you respond to this parent? How can you find out the truth, and what can you do about it to prevent it from recurring?

"Most students know when there's bullying," say Pepler and Craig (1997) of the LaMarsh Centre for Research on Violence and Conflict Resolution, "but they don't report it." They have found that bullying problems tend to fester under the surface.

A study of Toronto schools found that a bullying act occurred every 7 seconds but teachers were aware of only 4% of the incidents. Teachers may believe that they are withit enough to be aware of bullying behavior in their classroom, but Pepler and Craig found that while 7 out of 10 teachers reported that they always intervene, their students disagree. Only one in four students says that teachers almost always intervene. Three quarters of the students believe that teachers are either unaware or unwilling to get involved in the situation. Parents are not always seen as mediators either. Close to 40% of victims say they have not talked to their parents about the problem. They suffer in silence on the playground or in the classroom, observed only by their peers, who are also reluctant to report the behavior.

Lack of intervention implies that bullying is acceptable and can be done without fear of consequences. Bullies and their accomplices need to understand the harm they cause and that their behavior will not be tolerated at school. They can change.

Ask any child what a bully looks like, and he or she is likely to describe someone who is bigger and stronger. Yet, while bullies certainly are known for their ability to overpower others physically, mental bullying can be just as damaging to students. When bullies are allowed to torment other students, physically or mentally, many feel the need to suffer in silence for fear that speaking up will provoke further torture. But bullying is not a problem that usually just takes care of itself. Action needs to be taken.

As a reflective teacher, using withitness to prevent bullying, you can:

*Use withitness to respond to bullying.* Tell your students that you want to know when they feel bullied. When a bullying act is reported, have a frank discussion with the bully. Try to connect with him or her and find out what he or she wants or needs to feel happier and more successful without the need to bully other students.

*Teach communication skills.* If young, primary-age students are reluctant to discuss the subject, allow them to role-play bullying behavior with puppets or dolls. For intermediate and middle school students, hold a classroom meeting on the subject of bullying. Ask the class to suggest ways for students to express their feelings in a positive way. Practice methods students can use to resolve problems firmly and fairly. It is important for you to identify ways to distinguish between teasing and bullying. Teach students how to ignore routine teasing. Not all provocative behavior must be acknowledged. Help students identify acts of aggression, bossiness, or discrimination. Encourage students not to give up objects or territory to bullies. This discourages bullying behavior.

Students who are victims or witnesses to acts of bullying often suffer from serious emotional problems including depression and anxiety. The "Caring for Every Child's Mental Health Campaign" is part of the Comprehensive Community Mental Health Services for Children and Their Families Program of the federal Center for Mental Health Services. Visit the Web site at *http://www.mentalhealth.org/child.* The federal Center for Mental Health Services is an agency of the Substance Abuse and Mental Health Services Administration, U.S. Department of Health and Human Services.

## Preventing Violence in Our Schools

School violence, bullying, and suicide make the headlines all too frequently these days. As a teacher, it must be daunting to realize that your classroom is not insulated from threats of violence and localized forms of terrorism.

Many people think inner-city schools serving less-affluent students are more susceptible to violent behavior by students or unauthorized outsiders, whereas suburban schools serving middle-class students are viewed as safe and secure. In reality, though, there are angry, depressed individuals in or near all our schools. Teachers are quite literally on the front line, and must develop their withitness to include the ability to discern which students need special support or counseling to prevent them from turning their anger into mayhem.

The National Council on Prevention of Crime (NCPC) discusses this issue on its Web site *(http://www.ncpc.org/ncpc/ncpc/)* and in its report "A Dozen Things Teachers Can Do to Stop School Violence" lists 12 things you can do to ensure that your classroom does not become a headline in tomorrow's news reports.

1. Report to the principal as quickly as possible any threats, signs of or discussions of weapons, signs of gang activity, or other conditions that might invite or encourage violence.

2. [With help from students,] set norms for behavior in your classroom. Refuse to permit violence. Ask students to help set penalties and enforce the rules.

3. Invite parents to talk with you about their children's progress and any concerns they have. Send home notes celebrating children's achievements.

4. Learn how to recognize the warning signs that a child might be headed for violence and know how to tap school resources to get appropriate help.

**PRAXIS**
Strategies for conflict resolution are tested in PRAXIS™ Exam Section 1c: Students as Learners.

5. Encourage and sponsor student-led antiviolence activities and programs ranging from peer education to teen courts to mediation to mentoring to training.

6. Offer to serve on a team or committee to develop and implement a Safe School Plan, including how teachers should respond in emergencies.

7. Enforce school policies that seek to reduce the risk of violence. Take responsibility for areas outside as well as inside your classroom.

8. Insist that students not resort to name-calling or teasing. Encourage them to demonstrate the respect they expect. Involve them in developing standards of acceptable behavior.

9. Teach with enthusiasm. Students engaged in work that is challenging, informative, and rewarding are less likely to get into trouble.

10. Learn and teach conflict resolution and anger management skills. Help your students practice applying them in everyday life. Discuss them in the context of what you teach.

11. Incorporate discussions on violence and its prevention into the subject matter you teach whenever possible.

12. Encourage students to report crimes or activities that make them suspicious.

## Cheating by Students and Teachers

One important element of character development is demonstrating an awareness of right and wrong concerning cheating on schoolwork. Cheating is easier than ever before because of material available to students on the Internet. In earlier eras, students might copy word for word from an encyclopedia. Today, they can go online and buy a term paper or essay to turn in as their own. Confounding this trend is the fact that teachers and school administrators have shown an increasing tendency to cheat. Principals feel driven to show high test scores on standardized tests. Teachers may want their students to look good so they look good as well.

In Walker County, Georgia, the Naomi Elementary School participated in a National Study of School Evaluation (NSSE) parent and student opinion survey on honesty and cheating. The survey indicated that cheating was a possible problem area for Naomi. An alarming 33.9% of students and 29.4% of parents felt that cheating occurred frequently at Naomi, while 61% of students admitted that they were only somewhat honest, fair, and responsible.

To tackle this issue, the school community established a goal (with performance indicators) that students would make a commitment to creating quality work and striving for excellence, while demonstrating that they are self-motivated to act with honesty and put forth their best effort in the pursuit of learning goals and tasks.

The Naomi School community then created a series of action steps to reach their goal. They established a project action team (PAT) consisting of school staff, parents, community members, and students to establish an academic integrity policy that includes a clearly defined honor code for students and a verifiable contract to be utilized during the 2003–2004 school year.

They implemented a curriculum that focused on the ethical traits of honesty, responsibility, self-discipline, citizenship, fairness, integrity, honor, and determination. They commissioned students to create and present drama skits for Parent Teacher

Organization programs to be presented throughout the year on themes of fairness, integrity, responsibility, and work ethics. They conducted seminars for parents and community members to introduce the goal and to open dialogue concerning cheating. They developed a program to assist students, parents, and staff in the recognition and demonstration of character and ethical traits with emphasis on honesty, fairness, and integrity.

Naomi School set up an assessment plan that included the use of surveys that will be distributed yearly to teachers, students, and parents, to determine the perception of progress toward improvement in student demonstration of honesty, integrity, and fairness. Grade-level and schoolwide reviews and evaluations of student progress in relation to work study habits were recorded on student progress reports and permanent records. Administration reviewed discipline referrals to determine any existing or developing trends in relation to honesty, integrity, and fairness. Naomi School published their project with its goals, action plan, and assessment plan on the Web site at *http://www.myschoolonline.com*. Go online and look at May 2001 school archives to see what progress the school has made since this book was published.

## Teaching Students How to Resolve Conflicts

In many schools, conflicts have escalated to violent confrontations. Students bicker, threaten, and harass one another. Conflicts among racial and ethnic groups are on the rise. Truancy is epidemic in some areas. Traditional discipline programs, involving scolding and suspensions, do not appear to improve such situations. What can we do? What will you do when you are confronted with these situations? In some learning communities, teachers are instructing students how to be peacemakers and to resolve conflicts for themselves and their peers. Johnson and Johnson (1995) provide a curriculum for such programs in their book, *Teaching Students to Be Peacemakers*. Through the use of role plays and other learning opportunities to practice conflict resolution skills, students learn how to negotiate and mediate when conflicts arise.

Laurie Mednick, a fifth-grade teacher at Kellogg School in Chula Vista, California, teaches fourth-, fifth-, and sixth-grade students the communication skills they need to resolve conflicts peacefully. Based on the belief that conflict is inevitable and can even be healthy if dealt with in an honest and caring manner, Laurie sponsors the Peace Patrol program at her school.

In the following Reflective Action Story, Laurie describes the process of setting up her Peace Patrol.

## ✳ REFLECTIVE ACTION STORIES ✳

## Teaching Students How to Resolve Conflicts

*Laurie Mednick, Fifth-Grade Teacher, Kellogg Elementary School, Chula Vista, California*

### Teacher Begins to Plan

I was very troubled by the apparent lack of concern my students felt for other people. Instead of treating one another with respect, many of my students were involved in behaviors such as fighting, tattling, putting each other down, and interrupting when others were talking.

## Teacher Considers What Students Already Know

My original belief was that the students were mirroring the prejudices of the society in which we live.

## Reflective Teacher Uses Withitness and Teacher Reflects on the Event

Not willing to accept or perpetuate these behaviors, I asked myself: "How can I help these children to understand that people are different and have different ideas and perceptions, but that they are still very important? How can I help them learn to resolve their own conflicts? How can I teach them to make better choices for themselves?"

## Teacher Does Research and Invites Feedback

I went to see mentor teachers in my district who were investigating a new peace education curriculum and asked them what programs or methods were helpful in building self-esteem. I gained an enormous amount of insight and information from these people as well as an enthusiasm to continue my search.

I did a literature search at a university library on the topic of peace education and found from the articles that I read that this topic is a major concern to teachers across the country and that a number of programs are designed to address this issue. This search took about 2 months. I became so interested in the topic that I wrote my master's thesis on the subject as well.

## Teacher Reflects Again, Using Feedback, Research, and Creativity

I decided that this problem was larger than my own classroom. My students would benefit most if the whole school became involved. This decision was a direct reflection of my values because I believe that all individuals are important and must be shown respect and value, even if you don't agree with them. I also believe that there are alternatives to violence and that we need to teach these alternatives to our students.

## Teacher Creates a New Action Plan

I began my new effort by teaching my students to be more attentive listeners and how to solve problems among themselves without telling the teacher. We also began to practice sharing our feelings using "I" messages (e.g., "It hurts my feelings when you call me that name. I don't like it.")

Then I began to use role playing three to four times a week to involve my students in sharing feelings and practicing conflict resolution by listening to each other with respect. The students were very receptive to the curriculum. They loved being treated with respect by their peers. The class as a whole became cohesive and helpful toward one another.

After implementing these strategies in my classroom. I selected 30 other fourth, fifth, and sixth graders from other classes to become part of a Peace Patrol program for the entire school. I taught them the same communication and conflict management skills that I had used in my classroom. I meet with the Peace Patrol twice a month for continued training. Each day they wear their blue jackets out on the playground and assist other students to resolve their conflicts peacefully.

Now, in our school, when a conflict occurs between students, a conflict manager takes the students involved in the conflict to a quiet corner or passageway to discuss the event. The patroller listens to students involved in a conflict and then asks them to suggest solutions. If a solution can be found by the children themselves, the conflict manager writes a brief report about the conflict and the solution. Copies of the report are given to the students, their teachers, and the principal.

I was concerned that not all teachers would take seriously the reports written by student peace patrollers, so I brought up this problem at a staff meeting. As a faculty, we have agreed that when we receive a Peace Patrol report, we show our respect for these successful conflict management encounters by congratulating the students for re- solving their conflicts peacefully. I feel very proud of the role I took in developing this program for my school community.

---

Effective communication between teacher and student is based on mutual trust that grows from the basic moral principles of caring, consideration, and honesty. Reflective teachers who are guided by these moral principles express them in the classroom by lis- tening empathetically, or as in the case of the Peace Patrol in Laurie's class, by teach- ing students to listen empathetically. Listening is one of the most important ways of gathering information about students' needs in order to make informed judgments about why students behave the way they do.

Discussions between teacher and student must be guided by consideration for the child's feelings and fragile, developing self-concept. There is also a great need for hon- est, open exchanges of feelings and information among all members of a classroom. A sense of community and shared purpose grows from a realistic understanding of each other's perceptions and needs.

## The Self-Fulfilling Prophecy

Students are extremely perceptive. They understand and react to subtle differences in adult expectations. This effect has come to be known as the self-fulfilling prophecy. The process appears to work like this: (1) the teacher makes a decision about the be- havior and achievement to be expected from a certain student; (2) the teacher treats students differently depending on the expectations for each one; (3) this treatment communicates to the student what the teacher expects and affects the student's self- concept, achievement motivation, and aspirations either positively or negatively; (4) if the treatment is consistent over time, it may permanently shape the child's achievement and behavior. High-expectation students tend to achieve at higher and higher levels, whereas the achievement of low-expectation students tends to decline.

What is it that teachers do to communicate their high or low expectations for various students? This is the question that interested Good and Brophy (2002), who found that some teachers treat low achievers this way:

1. Seat them far away from the teacher
2. Call on them less often
3. Wait less time for them to answer questions
4. Criticize them more frequently
5. Praise them less frequently
6. Provide them with less detailed feedback
7. Demand less work and effort from them (Brophy, p. 55)

## Humor in the Classroom

Loomans and Kolberg's (2002) book, *The Laughing Classroom*, is filled with motivating strategies for teachers to use in all areas of the curriculum. They identify four different styles of humor-oriented teaching. The Joy Master is a teacher who inspires students to become warmhearted and humane toward one another. She might use a strategy such as creative debate in which students are assigned a role and debate an issue. Abe Lincoln may be debating on one side and Charlie Chaplin on the other.

The Fun-Meister uses slapstick and clowning as a motivational technique. When teaching a mathematical operation, the teacher may pretend to make mistakes so that students catch them, thereby giving the students a reason to monitor the teacher's demonstration more carefully. Peals of laughter may fill the room as the students point out the teacher's error. This style of teaching, however, can have its dark side, as fun-meisters sometimes mock others, including their students, causing students to laugh at one another's mistakes.

A third type of humorous teacher is the Life Mocker, and this type is almost entirely negative from the students' viewpoints. Teachers who are cynical and sarcastic may cause a few laughs, but the students may experience this style as coldhearted and dehumanizing.

A fourth style is the Joke Maker. Teachers who have a way with telling stories and jokes are always entertaining for their students. These stories can be very instructive and provide insight as examples of an abstract concept. Occasionally, teachers can use jokes or stories that are experienced as insults or stereotypes, which have a negative impact on students.

*The Laughing Classroom* is an excellent resource for teachers at all grade levels and can assist you in planning humorous activities that are supportive, positive, and healing. A Web site devoted to connection between humor and emotional intelligence can be found at *http://www.humormatters.com/*. This Web site provides resources that teachers can use to encourage students to see the humorous aspects of situations.

Goodman (1995) researches ways to use humor to improve working environments. On his Web page *http://www.newhorizons.org*, you can find ways to put humor into the physical environment using a humor bulletin board with lighthearted sayings, such as: "The brain is a wonderful organ. It starts the moment you get up in the morning and does not stop until you get to school" (reworded poem by Robert Frost). He suggests ways that you can defuse potential conflict situations with humor. In fact, he suggests that using humor to prevent trouble from escalating is an important component of leadership. Ron Clark (2003) tells of a situation he encountered when teaching in Harlem. The students would often respond to his requests but exhibit negative body language such as eye-rolling, sighing, and slumping in the process. Ron watched carefully and then when he was asked by one of the students to do something, he responded to the request but gave very exaggerated body language in imitation of their body language until the class was in stitches. They then discussed negative body language and how it demonstrated disrespect. The class added a rule regarding negative body language to the class rule chart as a result of this interaction, tempered with humor.

Goodman warns that we need to use humor as a tool rather than as a weapon. "Laughing with others builds confidence, brings people together, and pokes fun at our common dilemmas. Laughing at others destroys confidence and demolishes teamwork. He suggests that there are many appropriate times for teachers to laugh at themselves. When you do, you model your ability to take your job seriously and yourself lightly. One of the simplest and most powerful ways of doing this is to "tell stories on yourself" whenever possible and appropriate.

Goodman is sad to see that many schools only pay lip service to the idea that humor is important in education. As he travels the country doing presentations for school districts, he frequently hears about mission statements that speak about helping students experience the joy of learning. But, often, he observes that the opposite is true. Phrases like "Don't smile until Christmas" (told to new teachers) reinforce the myth that education and enjoyment are mutually exclusive.

As educators who face a great deal of on-the-job stress, Goodman (1995) encourages you to give yourselves the gift of humor to help you "tickle job-related stress before it tackles you." At the same time, we need to truly invite students to experience the joy of learning and encourage them to nurture humor as a vital life skill. This is more possible if you, as the teacher, can maintain a sense of humor so you can help students to see the joy of life, living, and learning in our classrooms as well as in everyday situations. The power of using humor in our classrooms to create risk-free situations will enable our students to approach learning more eagerly.

# REFLECTIVE ACTION EXPERIENCES FOR YOUR PROFESSIONAL PORTFOLIO

## Reflect on Core Proposition 1 of NBPTS: Teachers Are Committed to Students and Their Learning

In Chapter 1, we provided you with readiness exercises to begin to prepare a professional portfolio for a national credential through the National Board for Professional Teaching Standards (NBPTS). In this chapter, we focus on the first core proposition of NBPTS: Teachers are committed to students and their learning. Specifically, we suggest that you reflect on the actions you can take to demonstrate that you are a person who is committed to your students and their learning. What can teachers do to demonstrate their concern with their students' self-concept? What actions can teachers take to demonstrate their willingness to help students develop good character and civic virtues?

Next, consider how teachers can document the reflective actions they take to meet students' needs. The NBPTS requires that teachers document their attitudes and actions using three methods: description, analysis, and reflection.

Hopefully you are visiting classrooms to observe experienced teachers in action. By observing other teachers, you can plan and document a practice portfolio entry. Later, when you are the teacher in your own classroom, you can revise this entry to make it a genuine document of your own actions and reflections for your real professional portfolio.

1. Select a classroom visit to focus on the classroom management strategies of the teacher you observe. Ask the classroom teacher if you can lead a 30-minute discussion with the students on the classroom rules and consequences for breaking or following the rules. Using *description* (one of the NBPTS requirements), retell what happened during your discussion. To meet NBPTS criteria, your description needs to be logically ordered and detailed enough to allow assessors to have a basic sense of the classroom situation you are describing. For example, describe the rules of the classroom and tell how they are documented. Are they clearly written for all students to see or are they simply "understood" to be the rules? Do the rules seem to be constant or change from situation to situation? What are the consequences of breaking rules? Are the consequences clearly documented or merely "understood"? You must be able to describe all important elements and features of how the rules were created, how the teacher presents the rules to the students, and how the students respond. Include enough detail in your description that would allow an outsider to see what you saw as you observed the situation.

2. The next step is to write your *analysis* of this classroom teacher's rules and consequences. Analysis deals with reasons, motives, and interpretation and is grounded in concrete evidence. What are the reasons the teacher gives for choosing these rules? What are the reasons for the teacher's selection of consequences? What do you think motivated the teacher to choose how to present and document these rules to

the students? How does the student response to these rules and consequences give evidence of their effectiveness?

3. Finally, it is time for *reflection* on the entire process you observed. How would you approach the rule making and presentation process if this were your classroom? What would you do the same way as you observed this classroom teacher do, and why? What would you do differently, and why? Provide enough detail in your reflection to show assessors what you have learned from this experience, and how it will inform and improve your own teaching and classroom management practices in the future.

---

# References

Clark, R. (2003). *The essential 55.* New York: Hyperion.

Dixon-Krauss, L. A. (1996). *Vygotsky in the classroom: Mediated literacy instruction and assessment.* White Plains, NY: Longman.

Evertson, C., & Harris, A. (2002). *Classroom management for elementary teachers* (6th ed.). New York: Allyn & Bacon.

Gibbs, J. (2001). *Tribes.* Windsor, CA: CenterSource Systems.

Glasser, W. (1969). *Schools without failure.* New York: Harper & Row.

Glasser, W. (2001). *Every student can succeed.* Los Angeles, CA: William Glasser Institute.

Good & Brody (2002). *Looking in classrooms* (9th ed.). Boston: Allyn & Bacon.

Goodman, J. (1995). *Laffirmations: 1001 ways to add humor to your life and work.* Sarasota Springs, NY: The Humor Project.

Johnson, D., & Johnson, R. (1995). *Teaching students to be peacemakers.* Minneapolis, MN: Burgess.

Jones, F. (2000). *Tools for teaching.* Santa Cruz, CA: Frederic H. Jones and Associates.

Kavalik, S. (1994). *Integrating thematic instruction: The model* (3rd ed.). Kent, WA: Books for Educators.

Kounin, J. (1977). *Discipline and group management in classrooms.* New York: Holt, Rinehart and Winston.

Lickona, T. (1992). *Educating for character.* New York: Bantam Books.

Loomans, D., & Kolberg, K. (2002). *The laughing classroom.* Tiburon, CA: H J Kramer.

Marzano, R. (2003). *What works in schools.* Alexandria, VA: Association for Supervision and Curriculum Development.

Maslow, A. (1954). *Motivation and personality.* New York: Harper & Row.

Pepler, D., & Craig, W. (1997). *Bullying: Research and interventions.* Toronto, Canada: Institute for the Study of Antisocial Youth.

## CHAPTER 3

# Assessing and Meeting Students' Diverse Needs

As soon as they succeed in getting a teaching position, most teachers are eager to get into their classrooms to arrange furniture, establish schedules, put up bulletin boards, consider rules and consequences, and plan major units of study. But surprises are inevitable when school starts and the classroom is filled with students from many different backgrounds who have a variety of abilities, talents, and needs. Teachers whose classrooms include students who are learning English as a second language (English language learners—ELL) are responsible for meeting an additional set of standards. The national organization Teachers of English for Speakers of Other Languages (TESOL) has established a set of standards that includes three major goals with supporting objectives:

**Goal I:** To use English to communicate in social settings.

*Standard 1:* Students will use English to participate in social interactions.

*Standard 2:* Students will interact in, through, and with spoken and written English for personal expression and enjoyment.

*Standard 3:* Students will use learning strategies to extend their communicative competence.

**Goal II:** To use English to achieve academically in all content areas.

*Standard 1:* Students will use English to interact in the classroom.

*Standard 2:* Students will use English to obtain, process, and provide subject matter information in spoken and written form.

*Standard 3:* Students will use appropriate learning strategies to construct and apply academic knowledge.

**Goal III:** To use English in socially and culturally appropriate ways.

*Standard 1:* Students will use the appropriate language variety, register, and genre according to audience, purpose, and setting.

*Standard 2:* Students will use nonverbal communication appropriate to audience, purpose, and setting.

*Standard 3:* Students will use appropriate learning strategies to extend their sociolinguistic and cultural competence.*

The complete document describing the standards and suggested activities for English learners at different grade levels can be viewed online at *http://www.tesol.org/*. (To read, click on "standards and initiatives" under "advancing the profession of TESOL." To order a copy, click on "publications and products.")

The first day of school can be a daunting experience for a teacher who has spent a lot of time and energy planning the perfect beginning for the school year. Some students may appear to be totally disinterested while others appear to be intent on disrupting the teacher's plans. In most classrooms today, there are likely to be some students who are struggling to understand and speak English. Many new teachers find themselves sitting at their desks thinking, "Whatever made me think I could do this?" Even experienced teachers often find themselves comparing their new class to last

---

*(Copyright © 1997 Teachers of English to Speakers of Other Languages (TESOL). Reprinted with Permission.)

year's class, thinking, "These students have so many more needs than last year's group!" They may be forgetting that last year's class had made a whole school year's worth of progress by the time they parted at the end of the school year.

Teaching today's diverse student population is most definitely a challenge. Students bring a wealth of different perspectives to the classroom, whether they are from mainstream American homes or homes where multiple languages are spoken. We believe all students are teachable, and we hope you agree. Teachers who have faith in their students' abilities to learn are the ones who are able to make the most significant and positive differences in their students' lives.

Stephanie Collom, a resource teacher in Fresno, California, at Hidalgo Elementary School, where native English speakers are rare, observed, "All the students come to school with faith in me, as their teacher. I have to find ways to support their learning so that that faith is justified. I also have to have faith in their abilities as learners and find a way to make sure that they succeed."

Many teachers begin their teaching careers expecting the students in their classes and the curriculum they teach to resemble the students and curriculum they experienced when they were in school. It is sometimes a big shock to realize how much has changed in education in a very short time. The students in today's classrooms come to school from many diverse backgrounds, not only in experiences, but also in language exposure and perceptions of what school is all about. To add complexity to the issue, it seems that at the same time as our student body becomes more diverse, the state-mandated curricula are becoming more focused on meeting a single set of standards for all.

Teachers in today's schools are expected to be able to teach the traditional skills to a very nontraditional group of students. In addition, teachers are also expected to diversify their instructional methods in ways that support students' self-esteem, knowledge of technology, and ethnic and language backgrounds. An added challenge in working with diverse populations is the different expectations that parents from different cultures bring to the school.

## PROFESSIONAL TEACHING STANDARDS RELATED TO DIVERSITY

Celebrating diversity is vastly different than tolerating diversity. At the end of the 20th century, the goal seemed to be for teachers in multicultural settings to show acceptance of students' differences. In the present and hopefully more enlightened century, teachers have the goal of finding ways to encourage all students to value their own cultural heritage and appreciate the contributions of their classmates from other diverse backgrounds. The National Board for Professional Teaching Standards (NBPTS) includes a category entitled "Respect for Diversity," which reads, "Accomplished generalists model and promote behavior appropriate in a diverse society by showing respect for and valuing all members of their learning communities and by expecting students to treat one another fairly and with dignity" (NBPTS Early Adolescent/Generalist Credential Standards, vvi).

One major difference that affects learning is the student's language. In order to teach effectively, teachers must understand how language is acquired and know how to adjust their assessment, curriculum, and planning to take advantage of the multiple language-centered perspectives contained within almost every classroom.

# LANGUAGE ACQUISITION AND THE CLASSROOM TEACHER

**PRAXIS**
This section prepares you for PRAXIS™ Exam Section 1a: Student Development and the Learning Process.

The research into language acquisition issues has become rich and productive. Linguists and educators working together have discovered effective ways to support students in their acquisition of new languages and content knowledge. It is vital that classroom teachers understand the implication of the language acquisition theory so they can provide the scaffolding necessary for their students to be successful in the classroom (Krashen, 1996).

In his study of language acquisition, Krashen makes a distinction between language acquisition and language learning that is vital to the support of students in the classroom in their gradual acquisition of fluency in a new language. Krashen's research demonstrated that language acquisition is a natural process. He observes how easily and readily young students acquire their home language without formal teaching, and no drill and practice! Natural language acquisition is a gradual interactive process based on receiving and understanding messages, building a listening (receptive) vocabulary, and slowly attempting verbal production of the language in a highly supportive, nonstressful environment.

Krashen recommends to teachers that it is necessary to duplicate these conditions as much as is possible in a classroom in order to foster the acquisition of a second language. According to this theory, teachers will be most successful in teaching English if they plan interactive learning activities and speak or write in words selected carefully to match their students' level of understanding. This concept is termed *understandable language* or *comprehensible input*, and it is to be used with props, gestures, pictures, and other strategies that all contribute to the child's acquisition and eventually to the production of the language.

## Language Scaffolding

Scaffolding is a term used in teaching that involves modeling and demonstrating a new skill. It requires a highly interactive relationship between the teacher and the student while the new learning occurs. Bruner's (1997) work with mothers and students led him to recommend that as a mother reads aloud to a toddler, she may simplify the book to meet the attention span and interests of her child, calling the child's attention to material that is appropriate and eliminating material that is beyond the child's present capacity. She is also likely to allow the child to interact with her as they read and discuss the words and pictures on each page. Bruner called this flexible and simplified interaction between child and parent *scaffolding* because it allows the child to connect new ideas to existing schemata at his or her own level.

Teachers can apply scaffolding in the classroom by reducing complex tasks to manageable steps; helping students concentrate on one task at a time; being explicit about what is expected and interpreting the task for the student; and coaching the student using familiar, supportive words and actions. When a teacher coaches the student through a difficult task, he or she must provide sufficient scaffolding through the use of hints and cues so that the student can succeed. As students become more skillful, the scaffolding can be reduced and finally eliminated.

Scaffolding is an especially valuable technique for the primary teacher because most young students require supportive interaction and accommodation to their existing vocabularies to learn new skills. Scaffolding is also appropriate for upper-level students when the tasks are complex or the students have difficulty with the language.

For some beginning teachers, scaffolding may not come naturally because they may not have experienced scaffolded learning in their own school experiences. This technique can be learned only by reflecting on the needs of students, gathering the latest information on such techniques from reading and talking to experienced teachers who have used the techniques successfully, and gradually adding such strategies to personal repertoires.

Scaffolding academic language supports students' successful participation in content area instruction. Academic language is associated with school subjects such as mathematics, science, and social studies. It places a higher cognitive demand on the listener or speaker.

Cummins (1986) identified two types of language that students acquire. The first, Basic Interpersonal Communication Skills (BICS), or social language, is learned more quickly and easily than the second, Cognitive Academic Language Proficiency (CALP), or academic language. Academic language scaffolding supports the student in CALP, the language necessary for the student to participate successfully in classroom learning opportunities.

In order for students to participate successfully in academic lessons in the classroom, teachers use a series of scaffolding strategies that include modeling academic language; contextualizing academic language using visuals, gestures, and demonstrations; and supporting the students in the use of academic language through active learning activities.

Susan McCloskey, a kindergarten–first-grade teacher at Greenberg Elementary School in Fresno, California, provides a perfect example of language scaffolding as she teaches her students the concepts of same and different. She begins her lesson by modeling. She takes two large teddy bears and holds them up for the students to see: "These are the same," she says. She puts one bear down and picks up a stuffed bunny: "These are different," she repeats. She asks students to come up to the front of the class and hold two stuffed animals. The other students repeat the words "same" and "different," depending on the animals the child is holding. Susan then has the students draw pictures of their favorite foods. They show their pictures and talk about the fact that some students like the same foods and others like different foods. During recess she photocopies some of their pictures onto a large sheet of copy paper and when they return to the classroom she arranges the students into pairs, carefully placing them together so that each pair has a relatively strong English speaker. All of her students are English language learners, so she does not have the advantage of strong English models other than herself and classroom volunteers and aides.

As she gives the instructions for the activity, Susan demonstrates. She tells them to cut out the pictures as she models cutting out the pictures. She tells them to paste the pictures together that are the same. As she says this, she models choosing two pictures of hamburgers and placing them together on a large sheet of construction paper. She repeats, "These are the same," as she points to the two hamburgers she has pasted onto the construction paper. The students work together, some talking in English, some in

Hmong, their native language. Susan moves around the room supporting the students, asking questions about the concepts of "same" and "different." To anyone observing, the lesson is obviously a success.

However, it is at the end of the lesson that Susan adds the piece that scaffolds the students into new levels of language. As each pair completes the task, they bring the paper to Susan. She points to one group of pictures on the construction paper and asks, "Why did you put these together?"

The first child says, "Same." "Yes," confirms Susan. "They are all the same. This is a hamburger. This is a hamburger. This is a hamburger. This is a hamburger. They are all the same," she says as she points to each hamburger on the page. She then continues to ask the same child, "Why did you put these together?" as she points to the hot dogs. The child responds, "This is hot dog. This is hot dog. This is hot dog. This is hot dog," as he points to each one. "They all same." Susan then asks the other child in the pair the same questions. Because this child has been watching and listening, she responds in phrases just as Susan has modeled. In just a few minutes these two students have moved from one-word responses to simple sentence responses with the teacher's language scaffolding. Many teachers would have been pleased that the students had completed the task correctly and would have put a smiley face or star at the top of the page without utilizing the "teachable moment" and providing the vital language scaffolding part of the lesson. Knowing how students acquire language is a very necessary part of effective teaching with English language learners.

## The Stages in Language Acquisition

When students are acquiring a new language they go through predictable stages. The stages begin with students listening to language. They are taking in, or receiving, language at this stage, often called the silent period. Teachers should be aware that students are processing the language they are hearing, and it is important that the language be contextualized so it is understandable. After this silent or preproduction period, students move into the early production stage where they can give one- or two-word responses. They then move into speech emergence where they are attempting to speak phrases and short sentences but still making grammatical errors. They then move gradually into intermediate fluency where their sentences lengthen and their errors are fewer. Finally, over time, they become fluent in English.

Teachers need to be aware of these stages so that they can adapt their questioning strategies and expectations to support students' progress into higher language stages. It is especially important that teachers actively seek ways to keep English language learners involved in the classroom community. Allowing students to sit idly, not engaged or processing the instruction that is going on in a classroom, is never acceptable, but teachers must be armed with strategies to use in engaging students.

Leveled questions are used when teachers adapt the way they ask questions so students can answer or respond to them according to their language acquisition stage. The use of leveled questions enables a teacher to include English language learners in the classroom activities and support their active engagement, which, in turn, supports their language acquisition. In order to level the questions the teacher must observe the students and not the way in which they interact in English. Once the teacher knows the level at which a student interacts in English, the questions the teacher poses to the student can be adjusted to assure his or her success in answering. This may involve the teacher using gestures, visuals, or slowing the speech slightly while asking the questions. The teacher asks the question in a way that encourages the student to answer by pointing to a visual, giving a one-word response or a complete sentence or explanation depending on the student's level of language acquisition. The teacher's role in using this strategy involves knowing the student's level of English acquisition and providing enough context in the question so that the student can respond, either verbally or nonverbally, with understanding and confidence.

No matter what grade level they teach, teachers must consider the language development levels of the students in their classrooms when planning for instruction. Teachers at Hoover High School in San Diego, California, have adopted schoolwide teaching strategies that are being used across all curricular areas. They focus on language and literacy in all classes and use read-aloud, graphic organizers, vocabulary instruction, structured note taking, and reciprocal teaching to support understanding in their classes. The Hoover teachers are involved in ongoing staff development to help them develop effective teaching strategies and learn to structure their questions to match the English development level of their students. They are improving test scores yearly (Fisher, Frey & Williams, 2002).

## Optimal Levels of Instruction

Reflective teachers who want to encourage each student to function at the highest level of achievement monitor each student's level of understanding closely to see what interventions are needed. Lev Vygotsky, a Russian cognitive psychologist, identified the optimal level of instruction for each student as the *zone of proximal development* or *zpd*. The zpd for each student is based on the level at which the student can no longer solve problems on his or her own but must be supported by a teacher or more knowledgeable peer (Dixon-Kraus, 1996). In order for the teacher to be able to provide instruction for each student at the optimal learning level, or zpd, the teacher must use reflective actions to gain an understanding of the student's needs. This is especially vital for students who have special needs or who are learning English as their second language.

# FIVE FACTORS IN MEETING THE NEEDS OF DIVERSE STUDENTS

Whether a student is learning English as a second (or third) language or just having difficulty absorbing academic content, there are five factors that reflective teachers consider when planning and implementing instruction.

The first factor is *comprehensible input.* The teacher looks at the lesson and asks, "Is the instruction I am giving understandable to my students?" If the students are experiencing confusion or simply "not getting it" the teacher must consider ways in which the instruction can be made more understandable. It is important to consider how to give explanations while demonstrating something. The teacher may want to ask, "Am I just talking or am I modeling, using pictures, gestures, real objects to demonstrate the concepts I am trying to get across? Am I using words that I have defined and demonstrated? Am I relating new concepts to past experiences, giving examples, showing instead of telling?"

**PRAXIS**
This section prepares you for PRAXIS™ Exam Section 1b: Students as Diverse Learners and Section 3b: Cultural and Gender Differences.

Good explanations require a lot of thought. Giving multiple examples supports understanding. Giving nonexamples is also very helpful. For example, when teaching about the characteristics of mammals, a teacher might say, "A zebra and an elephant are both examples of mammals; fish and birds are not examples of mammals."

The second factor is *quality of the verbal interactions* with and among your students. Ask yourself, "Am I providing opportunities for the students to interact with one another? Do the students have an opportunity to use hands-on materials? Are they given a chance to see the practical importance of what they are being asked to learn?"

The third factor is the *contextualization* of the language experiences you provide for your students. In other words, are new words and ideas presented within a context so the students have an opportunity to link the vocabulary and concepts to a bigger picture? One of the biggest factors in a student's ability to comprehend language is how well that language is supported by context. The direction, "Take out your science book," when spoken while holding up the science book is easily understood even by a student who knows no English, or a student who can't hear well. Just getting in the habit of supporting instruction with the use of gestures, visuals, and showing while telling is highly supportive of language acquisition and student understanding.

The fourth factor is *selecting teaching and grouping strategies that serve to reduce student anxiety* rather than aggravate it. Students who are anxious about being called on or being asked to speak aloud in front of their peers often have difficulty processing information or even listening attentively. Krashen (1996) calls this the affective filter, an emotional process that prevents the learner from hearing or processing new information. Teachers who want to be able to diminish or eliminate the likelihood of triggering a student's affective filter must find ways to create a classroom climate that encourages and motivates students while at the same time reducing their anxiety. One important consideration for you to reflect on is the way you ask questions and respond to errors. If students know that making an error is not going to cause them to be ridiculed in front of the class, they are much freer to answer questions and take risks. It's not enough to refrain from embarrassing students, however. There should be a consistent monitoring of the verbal interactions among students as well. A "no tolerance rule" related to student ridicule is proof of a healthy classroom climate, conducive to learning. This happens only when the teacher models it, discusses it openly, and tolerates no negative verbal interactions among the students.

The fifth factor to be considered is how to *increase the level of active involvement* of students within the classroom. Opportunities to actively engage in classroom activities designed to practice and gradually master the skills being taught is as vital to language acquisition as it is to other aspects of student learning. Activities that provide the students with opportunities to work in small groups on a project that requires the use of new skills and problem-solving strategies also require the students to engage in verbal interactions, contextualize the language they are using, and generally serve to reduce anxiety.

**PRAXIS**
This section prepares you for PRAXIS™ Exam Section 1c: Student Motivation and the Learning Environment.

## BUILDING SELF-ESTEEM AND INTRINSIC MOTIVATION

Students' ability to learn is greatly enhanced when their self-esteem and self-perception is strong and they have a high degree of motivation. Krashen (1996) suggests that students who feel valued, who feel like the tasks they are being asked to accomplish are "doable," and who feel they can make mistakes without recrimination are more open to instructional processes. When students think the work is too difficult or they are afraid to ask questions and to seek help, their "affective filter" is raised, impeding their educational processes. This means that students' emotional needs are screening out any information being presented by the task or the text being read so that they are unable to absorb or thoroughly understand educational input.

Raths (1998) also identified eight emotional needs that people strive to satisfy. These are the need for love, achievement, belonging, self-respect, freedom from guilt, freedom from fear, economic security, and self-understanding. Raths believes that students whose needs are not satisfied exhibit negative, self-defeating behaviors such as aggressiveness, withdrawal, submissiveness, regressiveness, or psychosomatic illness.

Raths recognizes that teachers cannot expect to satisfy the many unmet needs experienced by all the students in their classrooms. However, he does believe that "children cannot check their emotions at the door and we should not expect them to. If unmet needs are getting in the way of a child's growth and development, his learning and his maturing, I insist that it is your obligation *to try* to meet his needs" (p. 141). Raths's book *Meeting the Needs of Children* contains many pages of specific suggestions about what teachers can do to help meet students' emotional needs so they are free to learn.

## The Enhancing Effects of Success

All individuals want to win or succeed. Virtually all students who walk into a classroom on the first day of school hope this year will be *the* year, that this grade will be *the* grade, and that this teacher will be *the* teacher who will make it possible for them to succeed. Some enter secure in the knowledge that they have succeeded before, but they are still anxious to determine whether they can duplicate that success in this new situation. Others enter with a history of failure and harbor no more than a dim, hidden hope that maybe they can succeed if only they can overcome their bad habits and learn how to succeed.

Winning and success are two powerful motivators for future effort and achievement. Glasser (1969) noted:

> As a psychiatrist, I have worked many years with people who are failing. I have struggled with them as they try to find a way to a more successful life. From these struggles I have discovered an important fact: regardless of his background, his culture, his color, or his economic level, *he will not succeed in general until he can in some way first experience success in one important part of his life.* Given the first success to build upon, the negative factors . . . mean little. (p. 5)

It is possible to restate Glasser's message as a significant principle of teaching and learning: when an individual experiences success in one important part of life, that person can succeed in life regardless of background, culture, color, or economic level. Glasser's *Choice Theory in the Classroom*, (1998) is a practical guide to assist teachers as they reflect on the fundamental goals of education and to establish an environment where students can learn to make positive, productive choices that lead to success.

It is especially important for students who may have been raised in culturally different settings to experience success in their new school environments. Caring, reflective teachers are quick to perceive that students new to the school or the community need to experience success very quickly in order to adjust well to their new surroundings. Assign new students a task that you are sure is well within their capability and then show your acceptance and satisfaction with the work they accomplish.

The same is true for students who may appear indifferent or even resentful of school and teachers. Try to understand that they may have a history of being unfairly treated by other, less caring teachers. Students who have faced failure over and over again often develop very negative attitudes toward schoolwork and frequently mask their need for approval with defensive and disruptive behaviors in an effort to hide their hurt and shame. You can be the teacher who helps them change their behavior by perceiving their need for success and structuring some tasks to fit their unique talents and abilities so that they can experience the true and lasting joy of succeeding and being productive.

## Teaching Tolerance

Can students be taught to be more tolerant of others who are different from themselves? An organization called Tolerance.org publishes a magazine entitled *Teaching Tolerance* that provides teachers with classroom activities and resources to guide students in growing toward tolerance. The Web site, *http://www.tolerance.org/teach/index.jsp*, is full of stories shared by teachers who are trying to deal effectively with diversity issues, including homophobia, racial and ethnic bias, and other forms of bias. They have activities designed to help students see the effects of hate, and they offer step-by-step strategies for handling challenging situations in your classroom.

Two of these important goals can be achieved by using cooperative group activities as a strategy for teaching in your classroom. Language acquisition for English language learners is enhanced by taking part in a cooperative group effort where communication skills are required to complete an assigned task, and increased understanding and appreciation of diversity occurs as well.

Slavin (1995) reports that cooperative groups may actually improve race relations within a classroom. When students participate in multiracial teams, studies show that they choose one another for friends more often than do students in control groups. Researchers attribute this effect to the fact that working together in a group as a part of a team causes students to promote more differentiated, dynamic, and realistic views (and therefore less stereotyped and static views) of other students (including peers with special needs or from different ethnic groups) than do competitive and individualistic learning experiences (Johnson & Johnson, 1993).

## Interactive Goal Setting

Teachers can support the growth of their students' levels of performance by using interactive goal setting as a natural forum for celebrating growth and setting goals for the future.

Vince Workman, a fifth-grade teacher in Fresno, California, sets aside time to discuss his students' accomplishments with them during each of the six grading periods in the school year. He schedules these student conferences throughout the year, recycling back through his class in approximately the same order so that students can expect to meet with him for goal setting every 6 weeks. Since Vince and his students work together to select work samples for the student portfolios, he begins the conferences by asking the students to talk about the work they have accomplished since their last student/teacher conference. Students talk about the work they have chosen to share and then, together, the teacher and student look at the grade-level standards and decide which of the standards have been met or are in the process of being met. They decide together on an appropriate challenge for the next grading period.

For example, Alberto, a student who is reading at approximately the third-grade level, has set a goal of reading two library books a week. He is keeping a reading journal and a vocabulary notebook so he is monitoring his own understanding of the books he is reading and focusing on building his English vocabulary. Vince encourages Alberto to use the new words he is learning every day and often calls on Alberto in class to share some of the new words he is practicing. Because vocabulary study is one of Alberto's self-selected goals, he is much more motivated to keep working on his vocabulary journal. Vince talks to him briefly almost every day about new words he is exploring and celebrates Alberto's growing word knowledge with him frequently by simple responses such as, "That's a great word for that, Alberto. Explain where you first found that word and some of the ways you have found to use it." Alberto's first vocabulary goal was to learn two new words a day. He has increased his goal each 6 weeks so that he is now focusing on six new words each day. His vocabulary journal helps both Alberto and Vince to keep track of the progress he is making. A sample page from Alberto's vocabulary journal might look like this:

---

### ALBERTO'S VOCABULARY JOURNAL

**WEEK 1 — GOAL:** Learn two new words each day.

**Day 1: Words from *Stellaluna***

*clutched*     I told my mom that I clutched my bookbag so I would not lose it.

*clambered*     I clambered onto the school bus after school.

**Day 2: Words from science class**

*explored*     We explored drops of water. We looked at them very closely.

*process*     When water changes from water to steam, that is called a process of evaporation.

---

## Classrooms as Communities

How does a class of strangers or competitive individuals develop into a community? As with all the other important classroom effects discussed in this chapter, the teacher has the power to create a positive, healthy, mutually supportive, and productive classroom environment from the first day of school. Through furniture arrangement, schedules, the teacher's body language, words of welcome, rules, consequences, and interaction with the class, the teacher demonstrates a unique leadership or teaching style to the students. A sense of community is also achieved through honest, open communication of needs and feelings among students and their teachers.

It takes more than talk to create a classroom community though. Students need to be taught to work together in obtaining mutually agreed upon goals. These goals can be related to content standards such as supporting one another in learning multiplication tables, working together to complete a community-based project, or writing a collaborative readers theater script to present at back-to-school night.

Communities of learners grow throughout the school year. They grow from roots established at the very beginning by a classroom teacher who accepts students' suggestions and builds on these ideas, integrating content into related studies based on students' unique interests. Communities recognize that diversity among its members is a positive factor. Cultural diversity tends to enrich the classroom communities when reflective teachers choose to celebrate differences among students rather than seek to make all students adapt to one standard.

In Jody Salazar's middle school classroom in Madera, California, the feeling of community is evident although her students change classes every 50 minutes. The students enter the classroom and begin writing in their journals immediately. Three students a day sign up to share their journal entries each day. Jody is aware of the importance of building student confidence. None of her students are native English speakers, but they recognize Jody's support as she leans forward and encourages their verbal participation saying, "Go on, I'm getting it," as they communicate in English. Jody often forms cooperative groups in her classroom and encourages English interaction in discussing the reading of text and writing of responses.

A typical lesson in Jody's classroom might involve creating a collaborative list of words that describe students' feelings when they view a photograph of a sinking ship with a lifeboat loaded with passengers nearby. Next, the group can list a description of the possible feelings experienced by the people in the lifeboat. During the writing activity, the musical theme from "The Titantic" is played softly in the background. The students are then given the opportunity to share their writing within the relative safety of the small group seated at the table. At the end of the period, Jody recognizes students who have used many of the feeling words from the chart and asks some to read their writing aloud. An amazing number of the students volunteer to read. They are obviously confident in their ability to succeed in this activity even though they are assigned to this class because of their below-grade-level reading abilities.

Glasser (1998) believes that students need to feel safe, happy, and proud of themselves in a classroom if they are going to become convinced that schoolwork is worth their time and effort. To enlist their support, he recommends that you allow your students to know you as a human being, not just as an authority figure. Isn't it true that the better you know someone and the more you like them, the harder you will work for that person? Glasser suggests that you use this same principle when establishing the expectations and procedures for your classroom. He suggests that during the first few months you are with your students, look for natural occasions to tell them:

1. Who you are
2. What you stand for
3. What you will ask them to do
4. What you will do for them
5. What you will not do for them (1993, p. 32)

Alex Eby, a first-year teacher at Sacajawea Middle School in Bozeman, Montana, plans to introduce himself to his classroom by explaining that the seventh-grade team of teachers has only one rule for their classes: *All behavior must contribute to the progress of the class.*

Alex will tell his students how he plans to behave in ways that will contribute to the class's progress. He will tell them that he will plan interesting lessons that will add to their knowledge about the world. He plans to describe how he will listen and pay attention to what they tell him and look for other signs of what they need from him. He will tell them that he believes his classroom is a microcosm of the real world and not just a place for kids to hang out until they grow up. "This means that in my classroom students matter, actions matter, learning must be attained through conscious effort in order to be utilized. This means that responsibility is everyone's and we each must be held accountable for our actions and choices."

In this way, Alex plans to reveal who he is to his class and give them the message that he cares about who they are, what they think, and what they need to be successful in school and in life itself.

## Reforming Schools to Provide Multicultural Equity

Did the schools you attended favor one group of students over others? Do you see remnants of racial, ethnic, or gender discrimination in the schools you are observing today? Banks and Banks (2002) seek to create a truly color-, gender-, and race-blind environment where students who are members of diverse racial, ethnic, language, and cultural groups will have an equal chance to achieve academically in school. Banks and Banks believe we must be vigilant in our examination of every aspect of school life in order to root out the effects of discrimination. Every variable in a school, such as its culture, its power relationships, the curriculum and materials, and the attitudes and beliefs of the staff must promote educational equality for students from diverse groups.

But, even teachers who carefully structure their classroom lessons to ensure success are frequently baffled by the tendency of some students to fail to succeed even under optimal conditions. Rimm (1995) observes that there is no single cause for underachievement, nor is there a single cure. Also, no consistent characteristics are associated with underachievement. Some underachievers are bossy and aggressive; others are lonely and withdrawn. Some are slow and perfectionistic; others are hurried and disorganized. A few have adopted a behavior pattern of learned helplessness because of previous experiences in school, overly high expectations at home, or even because of their position in the family as the youngest child. These students perceive that they are certain to fail at whatever they try, so they have learned not to try. They may also have learned to manipulate others to do things for them by acting helpless.

Students from culturally diverse backgrounds or those raised in poverty may underachieve because of low self-esteem or a lack of experiences such as family trips or exposure to English reading materials in the home. You, as teachers, will have an opportunity to confront this difficult issue and create new educational opportunities to improve your students' view of themselves and encourage the people of our nation to grow together rather than apart. There is good news on this topic, however. In recent years there are growing resources available to teachers in the form of multicultural literature to read and discuss in the classroom. Many of the new publications focus on the things all cultures share in common and celebrate the differences as variety and uniqueness. Teachers can begin discussions in the classroom by reading one of these books and supporting students in their acceptance of the variety in our American culture but also in understanding the many similarities among the wealth of cultures in the nation. Books like the series by Ann Morris include titles such as *Bread, Bread, Bread* (1989), *Hats, Hats, Hats* (1989), and *Shoes, Shoes, Shoes* (1995). Other titles that focus on similarities among cultures are *Everybody Cooks Rice* (Dooley, 1991), and *Everybody Bakes Bread* (Dooley, 1996). Even though these are primary picture books, teachers in upper elementary grades and even middle school have found them to be very successful as discussion starters. Some teachers have even encouraged students to find other elements of society shared by all cultures and write their own books with titles such as *Money, Money, Money* or *Work, Work, Work*.

Herrell and Jordan (2004), in their studies of effective teachers of English language learners, found common attributes and behaviors in their classrooms.

The most effective teachers

- truly believe in the ability of all their students to be academically successful.
- convey this belief to the students on a regular and ongoing basis.
- find time to celebrate student achievements and successes in the classroom.

These same effective teachers employed active learning strategies in their classrooms on a regular basis. They also provided daily opportunities for oral and written English practice.

Herrell and Jordan's (2004) *50 Strategies for Teaching English Language Learners* (2nd ed.) is a valuable resource for teachers at any grade level who have multilingual students in their class. The strategies include step-by-step instructions and real-life examples from classrooms, which we do not have room to describe in this text. These 50 strategies can be a valuable resource for reflective teachers who want to widen their perspective and create new action plans to meet the needs of their diverse student body.

## USING ASSESSMENT DEVICES TO IDENTIFY STUDENTS' NEEDS

In many ways the teacher's role in diagnosing students' needs is quite similar to the role of the medical doctor in diagnosing disease. Doctors get information from observing and talking with patients about their medical histories. Similarly, teachers observe and talk with their students to assess their learning histories. But some important information needed for an accurate diagnosis cannot be observed or discussed. Just as doctors may find that laboratory tests provide them with valuable information about the patient, so teachers may find that achievement tests and other assessment procedures can provide them with valuable data about their students.

Many school districts use nationally-normed standardized tests to assess the academic achievement their students make from year to year. The typical standardized test consists of reading, spelling, English, mathematics, science, and social studies exams given over a period of several days. The teacher does not write the questions or establish the criteria to fit a particular classroom. Instead, the tests are created by nationally recognized testing companies, and the items are written to approximate what is taught across the nation in each subject area at each grade level.

Statistical calculations of test scores provide information about a student's performance. The score may be translated into a percentile or a grade-equivalent score. These interpretations are done by comparing the student's raw score with the raw scores of the sample population. A *percentile rank* tells you what percentage of the people tested scored below a given score. For example, if Joe receives a percentile rank of 78, this means that 78% of the students at Joe's grade level scored lower than he did.

*Grade equivalent scores* were created by test publishers especially for use in schools. The results are reported as a function of grade level. For example, if Sally receives a grade-equivalent score of 4.2, this means that her performance is similar to students who are in the second month of fourth grade. If Sally is in the fourth grade, her score tells the teacher that Sally is doing about as well as she is supposed to be doing. If Sally is in the second grade, the score tells the teacher that Sally is capable of functioning like students who are 2 years above her present grade level. However, if Sally is in sixth grade, her score alerts the teacher that Sally is functioning like students who are 2 years below her present grade level.

When they are used well to inform teachers about students' academic needs, standardized tests provide numerical scores that can be used to document the growth of students in their abilities to read, work math problems, and answer questions about academic subjects such as science, social studies, English grammar, and spelling.

Because standardized tests are written by English speakers and assume that students are fluent in the English language, there is a potential for misinformation to occur when they are given to students who are learning English as a second language. Standardized tests also require that standardized procedures be used for administering the exams. All students must hear the same instructions, work under the same time limitations, and have access to the same tools and materials during the test (Tanner, 2001).

English language learners often have difficulty in demonstrating their true abilities on standardized tests because of the inability of the teacher to vary the instructions that are a part of the standardization of the test. For a student with a limited English vocabulary, the instructions may not be clear and the students may not be able to understand what is expected of them. They may be able to perform the tasks if they could understand the directions, but are unable to demonstrate their true abilities when the instructions are a mystery to them.

Teachers must create a variety of ways for English learners to demonstrate their understanding. It is important that teachers provide ways to document the learning of English learners so that appropriate lessons can be planned for continued growth. It is also vital that English language learners be able to show what they are learning and for them to be included in the classroom interaction. Because much assessment can be extremely language based, assessment strategies must be adjusted to find out how well the students understand the concept being taught. Less formal assessment also provides an opportunity for teachers to learn more about the English language learners' understanding of English vocabulary and use of sentence structure.

Assessment strategies appropriate for English language learners include the use of *observation and anecdotal records* (Rhodes & Nathenson-Mejia, 1993) by the classroom teacher and paraprofessionals, watching these students' reactions and responses, and documenting their growth. In addition, *performance sampling*, where students are asked to perform certain tasks, and teachers observe and document their responses, is very effective in monitoring and documenting student growth. The third assessment strategy, *portfolio assessment,* is a way of maintaining records of observations, performance sampling, and ongoing growth. These three assessment strategies, when combined, provide a rich store of information about English language learners and give a more complete picture of their individual growth and learning development (Herrell & Jordan, 2004).

The use of standardized tests varies widely from district to district. In some schools, they are used to diagnose learning difficulties of individuals so that corrective measures can be taken. In some school systems, the test results are published in local newspapers to compare how well students from different schools are doing in the basic skills. This practice is a controversial issue among educators. The tests were not designed to be used as a measure of excellence among schools, but the public and the press have come to believe that they can be used that way.

## Interpreting Data from Students' Cumulative Files

Standardized test scores are recorded in a permanent record for each student. This record of information, called the *cumulative file* (often referred to as a *cume file*) is kept on each student in a school. Each year, the classroom teacher records in the students' files such data as information about the student's family, standardized test scores, reading levels, samples of written work, grades, and notes on parent–teacher conferences. At the end of a school year, the cume files are stored in the school or district office until the next year when they are redistributed to the students' new teachers.

Obviously, these files contain much useful information for teachers to use in preliminary planning. By studying them, the teacher can make judgments about placement in reading, math, or other study groups before meeting the students. Alert teachers may discover information about a student's home environment, such as a recent divorce or remarriage, that can help them in communicating with the student. Some files may reveal little about the students; others may be overflowing with records of conferences and staffings that signal that the student has exhibited a special need or difficulty.

Yet, many teachers resist looking at their students' cume files before meeting the class. Tracy Kidder's (1989) *Among Schoolchildren* provides a realistic look at the entire school year of a fifth-grade class in upstate New York. In the opening chapter, which describes the beginning of the school year, the teacher, Chris Zajac, reflects on the value of cume files as she ponders what to do with a student named Clarence, whose negative attitudes toward school have become apparent on the first day of school.

> Chris had received the students' "cumulative" records which were stuffed inside salmon-colored folders known as "cumes." For now she checked only addresses and phone numbers, and resisted looking into histories. It was usually better at first to let her own opinions form. But she couldn't help noticing the thickness of some cumes. "The thicker the cume, the more trouble," she told Miss Hunt. "If it looks like *War and Peace. . .*" Clarence's cume was about as thick as the Boston phone book. And Chris couldn't help having heard what some colleagues had insisted on telling her

about Clarence. One teacher whom Chris trusted had described him as probably the most difficult child in all of last year's fourth-grade class. Chris wished she hadn't heard that. (pp. 8–9)

Although data and observations about students made by former teachers may be a valuable resource for planning, many reflective teachers, like Chris Zajac, are aware of the power of the self-fulfilling prophecy, in which their own expectations may influence the way their students behave or achieve in school. Teacher expectations can lead to self-fulfilling prophecies. In other words, what you expect from a student may interfere with your ability to make objective observations. If you expect Janie to fail, you may only see the mistakes or misbehaviors she displays. You may overlook or discount her attempts to show improvement. In this way, your expectations can discourage Janie from trying very hard because you fail to notice when she does her work well and she may give up her efforts and live "down" to your expectations

When cume files contain data and descriptions of low academic achievement or misbehavior, nonreflective teachers may assume that the students are unteachable or unmanageable. On the first day of school, the teacher may place them at desks set apart from the rest of the class or hand them textbooks from a lower grade. These teacher behaviors tell the students how the teacher expects them to behave and perform in this class. If these expectations are consistent over time, they are likely to affect the students' self-concepts and motivations in such a way that they achieve poorly and behave badly. In contrast, consider the possible effects of warm and encouraging teacher behavior on these students. If the teacher builds rapport with the students, includes them in all classroom activities from the first day, and works with them to establish their achievement levels and needs, it is likely that their behavior and achievement will improve during the year.

Reflective teachers who understand the great influence of their expectations on their students prefer to assess the strengths and needs of each student independently in the first few weeks of class. They may read the cume folders at the end of September to see how their assessments fit with those of the students' previous teachers.

A good case can be made for either point of view: using cume folders for preliminary planning or waiting to read them until the students are well known to you. This is an issue that you will need to consider and decide for yourself. Perhaps if you understand the power of teacher expectations, you can find a way to use the information in the files to establish positive expectations and resist the tendency to establish negative ones.

## Avoid Labeling Students

Tests and other recorded information about a student can sometimes cause teachers and parents to think about students in oversimplified terms, or labels. Whether you gain information about your students through formal assessments or informal interactions, it is important to avoid the temptation to categorize or stereotype particular students. You can probably recall a time in your own life when you were burdened with a label you resented. Perhaps you dealt with a nickname you detested, or with an academic designation that failed to capture your real potential. Being able to learn about your students and act in their best interests without labeling requires a great deal of care and reflection. How often a quick perusal of a cume file, a glance at a standardized test score, or a few days of observation in the classroom have led a teacher to label a student as a *slow learner, behavior-disordered,* or *underachiever.* These labels can stick for life! When communicated to a student and his or her family (whether indirectly or directly), such labels can have disabling effects all by themselves. Many labels imply that a student is deficient in some way and contribute to a self-fulfilling prophecy where further erosion of self-concept and self-confidence causes even more severe learning difficulties.

Students with excellent school performance can also suffer from labeling. Some teachers refer to their most capable and willing students as *overachievers.* This pseudoscientific term is attached to students whose test scores are only moderate, but whose grades and work habits are excellent. The implication is that these students are working beyond their capacity, and this is somehow seen as a negative characteristic by some teachers (and some peers).

Students with high test scores on standardized tests, especially IQ or achievement tests, are frequently labeled as *gifted students.* At first glance, this label may appear very positive: certainly many parents seek it for their children. But careful reflection reveals that this label can be as damaging as any other. Rimm (1986) notes that "any label that unrealistically narrows prospects for performance by a student may be damaging" (p. 84). Being labeled a gifted student tends to narrow the expectations for performance for that student to a constant state of excellence. Any performance less than excellent can be interpreted by the student (and/or the parent) as unacceptable.

The *gifted* label also has other negative implications. Eby and Smutny (1990) ask the question, if 2–5% of the students in a given school are labeled as gifted, then what are the other 95–98% of the students? Not gifted? What is the hidden consequence for a sibling or a very good friend of a so-called gifted student? Or what about the student who scores a few percentage points below the cutoff score for a particular gifted program? What do we call him, *almost gifted?*

Broader labels also carry damaging consequences. The term *minority* carries a connotation of being somehow less than other groups with respect to power, status, and treatment. Terms such as *economically disadvantaged, culturally deprived,* and *underprivileged* may also create stress and anxiety among those to whom they are applied. These may be especially insidious because they fail to acknowledge the value and unique contributions of various individuals or groups.

As you become aware of the various strengths and needs among your students, you can work to address them without relying on labels. Students who are learning English can be joyfully released to work with a special tutor and be warmly welcomed back to the classroom. Students who encounter difficulty working in large group settings can spend part of their day in small groups and build interaction skills in larger groups under carefully designed conditions. Students who learn more quickly can be challenged to extend their thinking through engaging inquiry projects. No matter what their unique need, our students can be welcomed to our classrooms as unique and valued individuals—labeled only as important, cared for, and wanted.

## Authentic Assessments for a Diverse Student Body

In this text, we use the term *authentic assessment* to describe evaluation procedures that take into account each student's unique and various needs for clarity and support to demonstrate what they are truly capable of doing. Most authentic assessments are designed by teachers in their own classrooms to match what has just been taught. Authentic assessment tasks are very similar or identical to actual tasks that students routinely accomplish in the classroom setting, unlike standardized assessment tasks, which tend to be very unlike everyday classroom activities.

It is vital for the teacher to have a good understanding of English language learners' levels of English development. Herrell and Jordan (2004) recommend that this assessment be done through observation in classroom settings where students are free to interact verbally. Beginning English learners may signal their understanding of verbal interactions with nodding, pointing, or physically responding but not be comfortable giving oral English responses. We call these students *preproductive*, because they are not yet producing English responses although they may comprehend a lot of what is being said. *Early production* English speakers will respond verbally but usually with one or two words. They are much more comfortable responding verbally when given a model to follow or a choice to make. *Speech emergence* English learners begin to verbalize in phrases or short sentences but still make a number of pronunciation and grammatical errors in their English production. *Intermediate fluency* English learners produce longer sentences with fewer pronunciation and grammar errors (Herrell & Jordan, 2004).

In order to fully engage English learners in the classroom activities, teachers must recognize the level of verbal production that is comfortable for each student and adjust the questions that are asked to provide opportunities for these students to become full participants (Herrell & Jordan, 2004). Adjusting the types of questions asked to fit the English language development of the student during a lesson is called "leveling questions." A student at the preproduction stage can be asked to show something. A student at the early production stage can be asked to choose between two alternatives. Speech emergence and intermediate fluency students can be expected to respond in phrases or short sentences, but this is a good stage at which to model the use of the question as a "stem" to the response. For example, if you ask the question, "What is the capital of Florida?" the student can use the question to create a complete response, "The capital of Florida is Tallahassee."

It is often helpful to keep anecdotal records of the verbal responses of the English learners in your classroom for the purpose of noting their English language development, any pronunciation, grammar, or sentence structure errors they are making, and their willingness to participate in verbal interactions in English. Examining these types of records is helpful in planning minilessons for groups of students at the same level or groups of students making similar types of errors.

In Chapter 11, we provide a much more expanded discussion of assessment issues and examples of authentic assessment tasks and procedures. We raise the issue in this chapter because assessment procedures have become such a controversial issue as they relate to student diversity.

## Using Pretests to Diagnose Students' Needs

Pretests are assessment devices designed to gather useful information to plan what students need to learn and what teachers need to teach. At the beginning of a term or a unit of study, teachers use pretests to determine what skills and knowledge pertaining to the subject students already have mastered. Pretests can take the form of brief short-answer quizzes or teachers may ask students to write a paragraph or two telling what they already know about a topic to be studied. They may also describe any prior study they have done on the topic, in another year or another class, family trips, or other experiences they have had that relate to the study about to be explored.

The best use of pretests occurs when the teacher and the student discuss the results together and share their insights into what the student needs to do next. For example, a pretest may reveal a pattern of correctable mistakes in a mathematics operation. The teacher may be able to reteach the process quickly, and the student will be able to proceed successfully. In another instance, the pretest may reveal that the student has mastered the material already, and the conference may then focus on an enriched or accelerated learning opportunity for that student while the others are learning the material.

## Placement and Grouping Decisions

Standardized tests are frequently used to qualify students for special education, classes for the gifted, or bilingual education programs. In most cases these types of placements are no longer made solely on the basis of test results but also include opportunities for the parents and teachers involved in the student's education to provide information and share in the decision.

For many years teachers used pretests and standardized test scores to determine students' placement in reading groups for instructional purposes. In recent years, teachers are using more authentic types of reading assessments such as Marie Clay's (2002) observation survey and reading observations called *running records* to document students' reading abilities, use of strategies, and cueing systems. In kindergarten and first-grade classes the students are grouped in very flexible reading groups for guided reading instruction. They read short paperback books for this instruction so the groups can remain flexible. The short books can be read in one reading group period and then students can be regrouped when they show the need. This practice is helping to eliminate the old, traditional "speedboats, sailboats, and rowboats" reading groups that were set in concrete and served to convince students that they were poor readers because they were always placed in the low (rowboats) reading group, and once there stayed there for their entire K–12 school careers. Teachers today are finding that grouping can help students to learn, if the grouping is done with careful reflection. Heterogeneous groups where each student has a special function are being used frequently in classrooms because students get more opportunities to interact, work together to solve problems, and discuss the task to be done.

Teachers may also use data from pretests, observations, and running records to create cooperative groups and partners for peer tutoring. To strengthen student motivation and interaction, many teachers employ the cooperative team concept. Cooperative groups typically consist of three to five students who are assigned a set of tasks to complete by cooperating with and assisting one another. Each student in the group has an assigned function, and the group must work together in order to complete the assignment. Cooperative groups are extremely effective when they are given instruction in working together to achieve their goals. In some classrooms, teachers use pretest data to decide which students to assign to each team. Often teachers use cooperative groups to promote peer coaching and interactive assistance among their students. In this case, a team of four students may consist of one student with very strong performance, two with moderate performance, and one with relatively weak performance in the subject area. Similarly, peer tutoring dyads may consist of one skilled and one less-skilled student, or one student with very little English vocabulary and another student who speaks the same home language but can speak English at a higher level. These are simply examples; other types of cooperative group placement decisions, for different purposes, are also possible.

## Performance Sampling

Performance sampling is a form of authentic assessment where a student is observed in the process of accomplishing academic tasks and is evaluated on the way in which the tasks are done. Performance samples are well named because the teacher observes a sample of the student's performance in a given academic tasks. Following are examples of the types of tasks used in performance sampling:

- working math problems
- responding to a writing prompt by creating a prewriting activity, writing a draft paper, and then revising the paper
- researching a topic in science or social studies and creating a poster or overhead transparency to demonstrate the main concepts that were researched

Performance sampling is particularly appropriate for assessing English language learners, because the degree of achievement they can demonstrate is based on their ability to perform the task rather than on their fluency in English (Hernandez, 1997).

Portfolio assessment is a term that refers to a system for gathering observations, performance samples, and work samples in a folder or portfolio; analyzing the contents of the portfolio on a regular basis; and summarizing the students' progress as documented by the contents of the portfolio (Herrell & Jordan, 2004). Often students are involved in making selections of work to be kept in the portfolio. Students are also involved in reviewing and summarizing the work, setting goals for future work, and sharing the contents of the portfolio with parents (Farr & Tone, 1994).

This approach to assessment is particularly appropriate for English language learners and special education students because it allows assessment based on actual sampling of the students' work and the growth they are making, with less dependence on scores on standardized tests, which are often difficult for these students to understand (Hernandez, 1997). Portfolio assessment allows students to demonstrate their content knowledge without being so dependent on English fluency or reading ability. The focus in this approach to assessment is celebration of progress rather than focus on weaknesses.

## REFLECTIVE ACTION EXPERIENCES FOR YOUR PROFESSIONAL PORTFOLIO

### Show Evidence of Your Ability to Use Analysis in a Student Needs Assessment Plan

The NBPTS credential requires that the candidate show evidence of being able to analyze a teaching/learning situation. Analysis begins with a description of a learning event, but then goes on to answer questions such as: Why? What was the motive? What was the result? How did the teacher's behavior change the result?

Analysis deals with reasons and motives. It requires that you interpret facts and descriptions and that you give concrete evidence for your conclusions.

To practice analysis of a teaching/learning situation, interview a student to determine the student's academic needs. Select a student whose culture is very different from yours. Talk with the student about what is important and valued in his or her family.

Ask questions to learn about how this student prefers to learn. Sample questions are provided here, but you may want to make up your own as well.

> Do you learn easily by reading about something?
>
> Do you learn well by listening to a teacher explain something?
>
> Do you need the teacher to write examples on the board?
>
> Do you learn best by having somebody show you something or by working alone?
>
> Do you need a quiet room or can you work when others are talking or when the TV is on?
>
> Does it bother you when there is movement around you?

After your interview, write an initial description of what conditions this student needs in order to learn and feel safe and comfortable in your classroom.

Ask yourself what else you need to know in order to make a thorough assessment of this student's needs.

What can you find on the Internet that relates to needs assessment? Talk to an experienced teacher or try a chat with other teachers on the Merrill Methods Cluster page *http://cwx.prenhall.com/bookbind/pubbooks/methods-cluster/* or on *http:/www.Schoolnotes.com.*

If possible, try to meet the student's family and learn what the parents' hopes and expectations are for their child.

Now write an analysis of this student's academic and social/emotional needs in the classroom. What do you think motivates this student to learn? Why does the student have certain strengths and weaknesses? Give evidence to support your analysis and conclusions. Then, write a brief action plan describing the classroom conditions you believe to be important for this student to learn effectively. Include in your plan ideas for encouraging this student to feel safe and comfortable in your classroom.

# References

Banks, J., & Banks, C., Eds. (2002) *Multicultural education: Issues and perspectives*. New York: Jossey-Bass.

Bruner, J. (1997). *The culture of education*. Cambridge, MA: Harvard University Press.

Clay, M. (2002). *An observation survey of early literacy abilities* (2nd ed.). Portsmouth, NH: Heinemann.

Cummins, J. (1986) Empowering minority students: A framework for interaction. *Harvard Review, 56,* 18–36.

Dixon-Kraus, L. (1996). *Vygotsky in the classroom: Mediated literacy instruction and assessment*. White Plains, NY: Longman.

Dooley, N. (1991) *Everybody cooks rice*. Minneapolis, MN: Carolrhoda Books.

Dooley, N. (1996) *Everybody bakes bread*. Minneapolis, MN: Carolrhoda Books.

Eby, J., & Smutny, J. (1990). *A thoughtful overview of gifted education*. White Plains, NY: Longman.

Farr, R., & Tone, B. (1994). *Portfolio performance assessments*. Fort Worth, TX: Harcourt Brace.

Fisher, D. (2002). Seven literacy strategies that work. *Educational Leadership, 60,* 70–73

Fisher, D., Frey, N. & Williams, D. (2002). Seven literacy strategies that work. *Educational Leadership,* 70–73.

Glasser, W. (1969). *Schools without failure*. New York: Harper & Row.

Glasser, W. (1998). *Choice theory in the classroom*. New York: Perennial.

Hernandez, H. (1997). *Teaching in multilingual classrooms*. Upper Saddle River, NJ: Merrill/Prentice Hall.

Herrell, A., & Jordan, M. (2004). *50 strategies for teaching English language learners* (2nd ed.). Upper Saddle River, NJ: Merrill/Prentice Hall.

Johnson, D., & Johnson, R. (1993). *Circles of learning: Cooperation in the classroom*. Alexandria, VA: Association for Supervision and Curriculum Development.

Kidder, T. (1989). *Among schoolchildren*. Boston: Houghton Mifflin.

Krashen, S. (1996). *The natural approach: Language acquisition in the classroom*. Upper Saddle River, NJ: Merrill/Prentice Hall.

Morris, A. (1989). *Bread, bread, bread*. New York: Lothrop, Lee & Shepard.

Morris, A. (1989). *Hats, hats, hats*. New York: Lothrop, Lee & Shepard.

Morris, A. (1995). *Shoes, shoes, shoes*. New York: Lothrop, Lee & Shepard.

Raths, L. (1998). *Meeting the needs of children*. Educator's International Press.

Rhodes, L., & Nathenson-Mejia, S. (1993). Anecdotal records: A powerful tool for ongoing literacy assessment. *The Reading Teacher, 15,* 503–509.

Rimm, S. (1995). *Why bright children get poor grades*. New York: Crown.

Slavin, R. (1995) *Cooperative learning* (2nd ed.). Boston: Allyn & Bacon.

Tanner, D. E. (2001). *Assessing academic achievement*. Needham Heights, MA: Allyn & Bacon.

## CHAPTER 4

# Using Standards to Guide Your Curriculum Planning

PRAXIS

Chapters 4, 5, and 6 prepare you for PRAXIS™ Exam Section 2b: Planning Instruction.

One of classroom teachers' most important responsibilities is to plan the curriculum, the course of events and learning experiences for their students. To illustrate the complexity of the planning process, here is a brief account of some issues that Diane Leonard faced during her first three months at Balderas Elementary School in Fresno, California.

When I first walked into my second-grade classroom in July, I encountered a large empty room with piles of textbooks on every counter. I knew that I had the freedom to create my own curriculum using the texts. But I also knew that I had to address the state-mandated standards in reading, writing, math, science, social studies, visual and performing arts, and physical education. I also knew that most of my second graders were just learning English and I would also have to address the English language development standards with them.

I didn't know my students yet, so I didn't want to presume to plan an entire year's curriculum until I had met them and determined their needs. I knew I wanted to plan integrated units and collaboratively build the group into a learning community. I found my answer in the history/social science standards. Standard 2.1 reads, "Students differentiate between things that happened long ago and things that happened yesterday." The standard suggests activities such as tracing family histories, conducting family interviews, time lines, and mapping family travel and relocations. I thought, "What a perfect way to get to know my students while addressing the social studies standards." I began to think of all the other grade-level standards that could be addressed in the process of the family history study. We would be practicing oral English as we interviewed our parents and grandparents. We would be addressing writing standards as we wrote the stories that we learned from our families.

I began to collect family-related literature to read to the students. I found stories about families doing things together, stories of grandparents and how they had lived long ago, and folk tales from the different ethnic backgrounds represented by my students. I looked through the softback leveled readers I would be using for my guided reading groups to find family stories. I found short poems about families that I printed onto charts for daily choral reading. I also made copies of the poems so the students could illustrate them and practice reading them as their homework.

Because we were housed in a brand-new school, none of the students had attended our school the previous year, so we began the year with a short mapmaking activity where we created a map of our new school. We took walks around the school and practiced our oral English by interviewing the secretary, cafeteria manager, librarian, custodian, and principal. We placed their offices on our school map and used shared writing to create their stories. We learned how to ask questions and how to transfer our newfound knowledge into stories about our school. We talked about the new school becoming a community and wrote a class-book about our school. I used the big book *I Went Walking* (Williams, 1990) as a shared reading where I read aloud and we reread the repetitive text together and related the story to our walk around the school. We recreated the book, writing our own big book using our newfound school friends in place of the animals seen in the original story.

During this same time we were generating questions to ask our parents and grandparents. We were preparing for our family history unit. The students began to interview their parents and grandparents. They focused on questions about what life and school were like a long time ago when the parents and grandparents were 7 years old. The students brought their stories back to the classroom, and we began to write our family history books. Some of the students brought in photographs and crafts to add to the discussion. We used roll-type fax paper and created family time lines, and whenever possible, we invited parents and grandparents in to demonstrate the art, crafts, cooking, dances, or music of their cultures. Whenever we had guests, we asked questions about how things had changed since the guests were students.

Our culminating activity was a family covered-dish dinner where we shared the family books, time lines, and oral reports. Since my students come from many different cultures, we couldn't always communicate in English, but the older siblings served as translators. There were many tears shed as the students shared their family history books that evening. We had electronically scanned some of the photos so we could include them in the family books. The parents were excited about the new family treasures created by the students.

We were able to incorporate math into our study as we created the time lines and determined the number of years between events. We also used math in creating the maps showing the travels of the families and the great numbers of miles they traveled to come to Fresno. We incorporated science as we compared the way things were done in the past, for example, the types of machines used to get work done when our parents and grandparents were young. We even discovered simple levers and pulleys in some of the modern machines we use today. We learned a lot about the visual and performing arts as we examined the art and craft work done by the different cultural groups. We even practiced several types of dances, taught by our fellow students or their parents. One grandfather came to school and taught tai chi as a physical exercise. Some of the boys thought it rather "sissy" until they tried it for 20 minutes. We also learned a number of new playground games from the different cultures.

The morning after the family history dinner the students were very excited about how well the families had received their books. They had discovered a number of new foods they liked and they were ready to plan a new unit of study. Many of them had been very interested in the folk tales we had read and wanted to do more of that. Several of them had been told traditional folk tales by their parents and grandparents in the course of the family history interviews and wanted to write and illustrate the stories to create story books for their younger brothers and sisters. So began our second unit, writing and telling folk tales. I immediately began to find ways to integrate other content areas into the study so I could address multiple content standards.

As Diane's account shows, teachers face a multitude of complex issues and judgments in their own classrooms. As a teacher, Diane has a great deal of freedom (and responsibility!) to decide what to teach and when to teach it; but her decisions are influenced by many forces, both past and present. We all tend to focus on the way federal, state, and local standards are being used as the basis for educational decision making, but we should also be aware of how history and tradition exert powerful influences over what is taught in schools. The three Rs have served as the basis for planning in U.S. schools for more than a century, and there are active and vocal groups of citizens who believe that the primary goal of K–12 schools should be to instill these basic skills in their students.

Some groups believe that schools are the custodians of the culture and that the primary goal of education should be to develop good citizenship and understanding of the great ideas and literature produced by Western civilization. Others believe strongly that the primary goal of a modern education is to teach students how to use reasoning, problem solving, and communication skills as a means of learning how to learn so that they are able to gather the information they will need in their lives.

Still others believe that the new wave of computer technology available to future generations makes older forms of learning obsolete. They call for an emphasis on the use of technology in K–12 schools to prepare students for a future that will be vastly different from the present. There is also a growing trend toward creating school programs that are multidisciplinary and multicultural by design, with a new emphasis on investigation, inquiry, research, experimentation, and conflict resolution.

Diane discovered how difficult it is to plan so many different types of school programs all at once. Like many beginning teachers, she wanted to incorporate the best ideas from all of the influential groups she had read about in her teacher education program. At times the responsibility seemed so overwhelming that she might have wished that there was just one standard curriculum for all teachers to follow. Her task was made easier, however, because she could refer to the content standards for which she was responsible and choose activities that would help move her students toward meeting those standards.

# HOW SCHOOL CURRICULA ARE PLANNED
## National Standards and Federal Mandates

**PRAXIS**

National and state learning standards are addressed in PRAXIS™ Exam Section 2b: Instruction and Assessment.

Many nations have uniform standards for school curricula. When these standards exist, individual teachers plan their daily programs to coincide precisely with national expectations. In some countries, if you were able to visit several schools in various cities at the same time of the school year, you would find the students using the same textbooks and working on the same chapter as students in other cities and rural areas of that country. Periodically, all students attending the schools take national examinations as a means of testing whether they have learned the requisite material and, at the same time, whether schools are accomplishing their mission of teaching the national curriculum.

Other countries, including the United States, have no such tradition of a uniform mandated curriculum. Historically, the regulation and supervision of K–12 curriculum has resided with the states; and although many states have established curriculum guidelines and examinations, there has also been a strong public sense that the best curriculum is the one planned at the local level based upon local interests, values, resources, and the needs of a particular group of students in each school district.

Recently, however, some school districts have been criticized by the media or by citizen watchdog groups because their students have performed badly on a variety of tests and measurements of academic progress. As a result of the public's perception that some school districts prepare students for the world much better than other school districts do, a debate is growing over the value of establishing national standards for student performance. Recently, several movements to establish national standards for the preparation of teachers and for teaching effectiveness have entered the debate. The first step in improving the quality of teaching and learning has been recently implemented with the passage of federally legislated mandates in the No Child Left Behind

Act, which requires that any school receiving federal education funding must employ "highly qualified teachers." The federal definition of highly qualified teachers does not simply mean that teachers hold a teaching credential but that they also have passed a standardized test that documents the mastery of all the subject matter they will teach. For K–12 school teachers this means they must demonstrate mastery of reading, writing, science, social studies, health, and physical education. A variety of nationally standardized assessments are being used across the states to document the subject matter competency of credential candidates.

In addition to the testing of teacher candidates, and in response to the public's desire to be able to measure and compare the progress of students across the nation, Congress mandated the U.S. Department of Education to provide a set of assessment tools to measure K–12 students' subject-matter knowledge in five areas. They produced a document known as the National Assessment of Educational Progress (NAEP), which is commonly referred to as the nation's report card. NAEP provides *benchmarks* for each subject area, describing what students should be able to do or demonstrate at various grade levels.

As is often the case in a vigorous, multicultural democracy such as the United States, there is little agreement about the form educational standards should take or how they should be used. Subject-area specialists, for example, argue that their disciplines are so different from each other that standardizing performance expectations across the disciplines would be impossible.

Many other philosophical debates concern the purpose of national standards in education. Before establishing one set of universally accepted standards, educators will need to agree on issues such as whether the national standards and benchmarks ought to describe basic or minimal competency in each subject area or whether they ought to describe higher level expectations. A national debate remains over the value of emphasizing content or process knowledge in most subject areas, and this causes the authors of standards and benchmarks to disagree about whether to assess content knowledge or performance standards.

## State Standards Are the Basis for Curriculum Planning

In the United States, each state has a department of education that has traditionally taken responsibility for establishing guidelines for curriculum development. Recently, these state departments of education have become much more interested in measuring achievement as well.

Currently, 49 of the 50 states have adopted content standards in K–12 programs. This movement is not without its critics, however. Brooks and Brooks (1999) observe that most standards-based reform efforts are illogical because they ignore the differences in the way students learn and the diversity of experience that students bring from their multicultural backgrounds. Assessing state standards for many states depends on constructing or buying standardized assessments that equate test results with student learning. These types of systems tend to reward schools whose students score well on the assessments and sanction schools whose students do not. Brooks and Brooks (p. 20) decry the "un-deviating, one-size-fits-all approach to teaching and assessment in states that have crowned accountability king. Requiring all students to take the same courses and pass the same tests may hold political capital for legislators and state-level educational policymakers, but it contravenes what years of painstaking research tells us about student learning."

Constructivists such as Brooks and Brooks believe that only by analyzing students' understandings and ways of learning and then customizing our teaching approaches to each student's cognitive processes can we hope to increase student achievement. This constructivist approach to learning and assessment of learning is closely aligned with the concept of reflective action in teaching that we propose in this book. Reflective action in teaching calls for teachers to use their withitness to perceive students' needs, individual student's needs in this case that vary widely depending on background experiences, multiple intelligences, and physical development of the brain and nervous system. Diane Leonard's approach to the planning of units based on content standards, described in the beginning of this chapter, taking into account the needs and functioning levels of her students, is a reasonable way of addressing both sides of the debate, however. Another role of state departments of education is to publish curriculum guidelines for all of the subject areas in public K–12 education. Many states revise their curriculum guidelines by inviting representative teachers and administrators from all areas of the state to form a committee responsible for considering ways to incorporate both state and subject matter standards into meaningful curriculum outlines. The resulting documents are then published and distributed to all of the school districts they serve.

Curriculum frameworks at the state level change frequently based on the latest research in education. They are also heavily influenced by political pressures and interest groups within the state. As a beginning teacher, you will be expected to become familiar with the latest curriculum frameworks for your state and implement them in your classroom.

## Curriculum Mapping Provides a Big Picture

Heidi Hayes-Jacobs (1997) recommends that faculty members in a school work together to map the curriculum so that everyone on the staff knows what is actually going on in classrooms. This strategy requires teachers to meet and create the maps for each subject area or grade level. The maps include a brief description of the content to be covered, a description of the processes and skills that will be emphasized, and the type of assessments that will be used to demonstrate that students have achieved the goals and met the standards that apply.

For example, a K–4 science curriculum content map might look like this:

| Topics | Kindergarten | 1st Grade | 2nd Grade | 3rd Grade | 4th Grade |
|---|---|---|---|---|---|
| Environment | Seasons | Weather | Seashore | Ecology | Water Cycle |
| Physical World | Sink & Float | Magnets | Attributes | States of Matter | Electricity |
| Human Body | Five senses | Safety | Nutrition | Health | Circulatory System |
| Living Things | Animal Families | Seeds & Plants | Habitats | Life Cycles | Adaptation |

# Other Influences That Affect Curriculum Development

Ralph Tyler (1949) observed that in planning educational goals, teachers should first consider the needs of the learners, then the needs of society, or what he termed "contemporary life," and finally the suggestions or recommendations of subject-matter specialists. It is precisely those subject-matter specialists, in the form of professional organizations designed to further the various content disciplines, who took on the daunting task of designing standards for the curriculum areas. Beginning in 1989, with the first publication of national mathematics standards by the National Council of Teachers of Mathematics (NCTM), a series of national standards projects have been implemented to identify the vital curricular areas in each discipline. See Figure 4.1 for a list of those organizations and their Web sites. You might want to look at the national standards for your grade level and compare them with your state standards.

The notion that the learner's needs must be satisfied in order to be a successful teacher is not a new idea. Tyler (1949) observed this in his earliest work. Since 1949, there has been consistent support for Tyler's elegant (simple but not simplistic) curriculum planning method. He proposed four fundamental questions that should be considered in planning any curriculum (1949, p. 1):

1. What educational purposes should the school seek to attain?
2. What educational experiences are likely to attain these purposes?
3. How can these educational experiences be effectively organized?
4. How can we determine whether these purposes are being attained?

Reflective educators are likely to use Tyler's basic principles in planning, organizing, and evaluating their programs because they are remarkably similar to the process of reflective thinking. Essentially, he suggests that teachers begin curriculum planning by perceiving the needs of students, gathering information, making a judgment about an educational purpose, selecting and organizing the strategies to be used, and then evaluating the effectiveness of their curriculum plan by perceiving its effects on their students. These are very similar processes to those outlined in the model of reflective action presented in Chapter 1.

Although reflective teachers are not likely to memorize Tyler's four questions word for word, they are likely to carry with them the fundamental notion of each:

1. What shall we teach?
2. How shall we teach it?
3. How can we organize it?
4. How can we evaluate it?

With the adoption of state-mandated standards, question 1 is answered for us. However, reflective teachers must still address questions 2 through 4 with respect to the needs and functioning levels of their students. Reflective teachers ask themselves these questions each year because they have probably noticed subtle or dramatic changes in their communities, subject-matter materials, students, or themselves from year to year that cause them to reexamine their curricula. On reexamination, they may confirm that they want to continue to teach the same curriculum in the same way or that they want to modify some aspects of the curriculum. As teachers grow in experience

| Discipline/Year of Implementation | Professional Organization/Web Site |
|---|---|
| Mathematics/1989 | National Council of Teachers of Math<br>*www.nctm.org* |
| Social Studies/1994 | National Council for Social Studies<br>*www.ncss.org* |
| Physical Education/1995 | National Association for Sport and PE<br>*www.aahperd.org* |
| Business Education/1995 | National Business Education Association<br>*www.nbea.org* |
| Reading/Language Arts 1996 | National Council of Teachers of English<br>*www.ncte.org*<br><br>International Reading Association<br>*www.reading.org* |
| Economics/1997 | Economics America<br>*www.ncee.net* |
| ESL/1997 | Teachers of English for Speakers of Other Languages (TESOL)<br>*www.tesol.org* |
| Crossdisciplinary/1997 | National Center on Education and the Economy "New Standards"<br>*www.ncee.org* |
| Oral Communication/1998 | National Communication Association<br>*www.natcom.org* |
| Crossdisciplinary/1998 | The Council for Basic Education<br>*www.ecs.org* |
| Technology/2000 | International Technology Association<br>*www.iteawww.org* |
| Mathematics/2000 New Math Standards | National Council of Teachers of Mathematics<br>*www.nctm.org* |

**Figure 4.1** Content standards, professional organizations, and Web sites.

and skills, most greet each new year as an opportunity to improve on what they accomplished the previous year. Rather than continue to teach the same subjects in the same ways year after year, reflective teachers often experiment with new ways of teaching and organizing the curriculum.

An obvious contrast between more reflective and less reflective teachers is that after teaching for 20 years, a reflective teacher has accumulated 20 years of experience, while a less reflective teacher is likely to have repeated one year of experience 20 times. Reflective teachers want to have an active role in the decision-making processes in their schools, and curricular decisions are the ones that count the most. They also display a strong sense of responsibility for making good curriculum choices and decisions, ones that will ultimately result in valuable growth and learning for their students.

## Evaluation and Use of Textbooks

School textbooks have enormous impact on the curriculum. K–12 school textbooks are undergoing major revisions to meet the demand for updated, student-centered, active learning rather than the older emphasis on receptive, rote learning. Many of these changes are controversial, reflecting the often divisive issues that are hot topics among adults in our society.

One of the greatest controversies regarding textbooks today is the rewriting of social studies textbooks to include multiple perspectives on history. Critics of traditional textbooks suggest that they are written solely from the perspective of the white European male. They believe students should learn history from multiple perspectives. Traditionalists believe that eliminating or ignoring content in the traditional textbooks will misrepresent history and that the subject will become diluted in an effort to please every interest group. Reflective teachers attempt to clarify their own values and their own curriculum orientations and beliefs as they make decisions about the curriculum they teach.

When first-year teachers move into their classrooms, the textbooks are already there, in formidable rows or piled in cumbersome stacks. Novice teachers have been told about the importance of individualizing education and meeting the needs of all students in their professional preparation programs. When reality sets in, they realize that many of the materials they need to plan a highly creative program that meets the students' individual needs are not in the classroom. A less reflective teacher will, without thinking, distribute the textbooks and begin teaching on page 1, perhaps emulating former teachers, with the intent of plowing through the entire book by the end of the year.

Reflective teachers, however, are more inquisitive and more independent in their use of textbooks. They ask questions of other teachers: "How long have you been using these textbooks? How were they chosen? Which parts match the school or district curriculum guides? Which parts are most interesting to the students? What other resources are available? Where do you go to get your ideas to supplement the textbook? In your first year of teaching, how did you meet the individual needs of your students when you had only textbooks available to you?"

Less reflective teachers tend to assume without question that the "approved" or "correct" curriculum is the one found in textbooks because it is written by "experts." They attempt to deliver the curriculum as written, without questioning its effects or adapting it to the students' needs and interests.

More reflective teachers consider decisions about curriculum planning to be within their jurisdiction, their domain of decision making. They consult with others, but they take responsibility for deciding which parts of a textbook to use to meet the needs of their own class and to match the goals and learning outcomes their state and local curriculum committees establish.

Reflective teachers are seldom satisfied to use textbooks alone. They know that students must have a motivation to search for meaning and create their own understanding of the world of ideas. "When students want to know more about an idea, a topic, or an entire discipline, they put more cognitive energy into classroom investigations and discussions and study more on their own," state Brooks and Brooks (1999, p. 22). Fortunately, there are many trade books, books not written to be used as textbooks, now available on many topics related to science, social studies, mathematics, and literature that are written at a variety of reading levels. Many of these are beautifully illustrated, sometimes with full-color photographs and add much depth to any study in the classroom. Some schools have a fund that can be used for the purchase of these types of books. Teachers often collect text sets, sets of books on one topic or by one author, that can be used to add multiple perspectives to the unit studies.

## Bloom's Taxonomy of Educational Objectives

**PRAXIS**
Important theorists are tested in PRAXIS™ Exam Section 1a: Students as Learners.

Benjamin Bloom, a student of Ralph Tyler, extended Tyler's basic principles in a most useful way. Bloom and his colleagues Max Engelhart, Edward Furst, Walker Hill, and David Krathwohl (1956) attempted to respond to the first of Tyler's questions as completely as possible. In meetings with other teachers, they brainstormed and listed all the possible purposes of education, and all the possible educational objectives they could think of or had observed during many years of classroom experience. Then they attempted to organize and classify all of these possible objectives into what is now known as the *Taxonomy of Educational Objectives.* Their intent was to provide teachers with a ready source of possible objectives so they could select ones that fit the needs of their own students and circumstances. They also intended to help teachers clarify for themselves how to achieve their educational goals. A third purpose for the taxonomy was to help teachers communicate more precisely with one another.

The taxonomy first subdivides educational purposes into three domains of learning: cognitive, affective, and psychomotor. The *cognitive domain* deals with "the recall or recognition of knowledge and the development of intellectual abilities and skills"; the *affective domain* deals with "interests, attitudes, and values"; and the *psychomotor domain* concerns the development of manipulative and motor skills (Bloom et al., 1956, p. 7).

## Clarifying Educational Goals and Outcomes

All three domains are considered to be important in the curriculum because together they support the growth and development of the whole student. Educators used to begin writing curriculum documents by carefully wording their educational goals. An educational *goal* is a general long-term statement of an important aim or purpose of an educational program. For example, most schools have a goal of teaching students how to read and write, another to ensure that they understand the cultural heritage of the United States, and another to help them develop attitudes and habits of good citizenship.

Although standards-based education is relatively recent, it is based on an approach that has been in place for a number of years. In the past, the translation of goals into operational plans were specified as *outcomes*. Teachers thought about what outcomes were expected as a consequence of being in school and taking part in the planned curriculum. Eisner (1985) alerts educators to be aware that goals express intentions but that other factors may occur that alter the intentions in the educational process. According to Eisner, "outcomes are essentially what one ends up with, intended or not, after some form of engagement" (p. 120).

Standards and outcomes are statements that describe what students will demonstrate as a culmination of their learning. Spady (1994) proposes that outcomes must specify "high quality, culminating demonstrations of significant learning in context" (p. 18). A high-quality demonstration means one that is thorough and complete, showing the important new learning the student has gained or demonstrating the mastery of a new skill or process. Outcomes are designed to be assessed at or near the end of a learning period.

Written outcome statements are used to translate goals into actions. They describe what students will be able do as a result of their educational program. If educators can envision what they want students to be able to do or know after a series of learning experiences, they can plan with that outcome in mind. Learning outcomes generally describe actions, processes, and products that the student will accomplish in a given period.

Cognitive outcomes are expressed in terms of students' mastery of content or subject-matter knowledge. For example, kindergartners are expected to master the alphabet, third graders are expected to master multiplication facts, and sixth graders are expected to show mastery of the history of ancient civilizations.

Educators also write many psychomotor outcomes, including strategies, processes, and skills that involve both the mind and the body in the psychomotor domain. For example, K–12 students are expected to learn how to decode symbols to read, write, calculate, solve problems, observe, experiment, research, interpret, make maps, and create works of art, music, and other crafts.

Most teachers view affective outcome statements as being related to the development of character. Typically, schools highlight the affective outcomes emphasizing good citizenship, self-esteem, respect for individual and racial differences, and an appreciation of art, music, and other aspects of our cultural heritage.

Individual teachers may write outcome statements for their own classes, but when they work collectively to clarify a set of schoolwide outcome statements, the effect on students is likely to be much more powerful and result in greater growth and change. This enhanced growth is a result of the consistency of experiences that students have in every classroom and with every adult in the school. Many school districts have statements of philosophy (often called mission statements) and outcome statements written in policy documents, but they may or may not be articulated and applied in the schools themselves. For effective change to take place, the school faculty must consider its educational purposes each year, articulate them together, and communicate them to the students through words and deeds.

In a classroom, each teacher has the right and the responsibility to articulate a set of educational outcomes for his or her own students. Working alone or with teammates at the same grade level or subject area, the classroom teacher may want to articulate approximately two to four yearly outcome statements in each of the three domains. Tyler encourages teachers to select a small number of highly important goals "since time is required to change the behavior patterns of human beings. An educational program is not effective if so much is attempted that little is accomplished" (1949, p. 33).

## Writing Useful and Appropriate Outcome Statements

The wording of standards or outcome statements must be general but not vague. This is a subtle but important distinction. Some school documents contain goals such as "to develop the full potential of each individual." What does this mean to you? Can you interpret it in a meaningful way in your classroom? Can you translate it into programs? Probably not. This goal statement is so general and vague that it cannot be put into operation, and it would be very difficult to determine whether it is being attained.

An outcome statement should be general, in keeping with its long-term effects. It should also describe, clearly and precisely, how you want your students to change and what you want them to be able to do at the end of the term of study.

Here are some examples of useful *cognitive* outcome statements:

Kindergarten students will be able to recognize and name all the counting numbers from 1 to 20.

Fifth-grade students will demonstrate that they understand how technology has changed the world by creating a time line, graph, chart, or set of models to show the effects of technology on human experience.

Tenth-grade students will demonstrate their understanding of practical uses for plane geometry by interviewing people of various professions to determine the connections between geometry and the world of work.

Here are some examples of *psychomotor* (sometimes referred to as skill or process) outcome statements:

Third-grade students will be able to measure and compare a variety of common objects using metric units of measurement of length, weight, and volume.

Sixth-grade students will be able to compose and edit written works using a word-processing program on a computer.

Ninth-grade students will use the Internet to map and determine mileage and best routes between their residence and locations of national parks and monuments.

Here are some examples of *affective* outcome statements:

Second-grade students will demonstrate that they enjoy reading by selecting books and other reading materials and spending time reading in class and at home.

Students at all grade levels will demonstrate that they tolerate, accept, and prize cultural, ethnic, and other individual differences in human beings by working cooperatively and productively with students of various ethnic groups.

In many school programs, outcome statements are intended to be accomplished over the course of a school year. Yearly outcome statements can be written for one subject or across several disciplines. Outcome statements can also be written for a shorter period such as a term or a month. They are used as guides for planning curriculum and learning experiences for that length of time. At the end of a given time, the teacher assesses whether students have successfully demonstrated the outcome. If not, the teacher may need to repeat or restate the outcome statement to ensure that it can be met.

Some outcome statements may need to be modified because they are too vague. In the following example, compare the first vague statement with the improved second statement:

*Original outcome statement:* Students will be able to demonstrate that they understand the U.S. Constitution.

*Improved outcome statement:* Students will be able to describe the key concepts in the articles of the U.S. Constitution and give examples of how they are applied in American life today.

Other outcome statements may need to be modified because they are too difficult for the students. Compare these:

*Original outcome statement:* Ninth-grade students will demonstrate that they know the key concepts of the Bill of Rights by creating a time line showing how each has evolved over the past 200 years.

*Improved outcome statement:* Ninth-grade students will be able to create an illustrated mural showing pictorial representations of each of the articles in the Bill of Rights.

Some outcome statements may need to be improved by adding learning opportunities that will stimulate student interest and motivation to learn the material. Consider the following:

*Original outcome statement:* Students will be able to recite the Bill of Rights.

*Improved outcome statement:* Students will work in cooperative groups to plan and perform skits comparing how life in the United States would differ with and without the constitutional amendments known as the Bill of Rights.

Standards and outcome statements are useful guides for educational planning but must be adapted to fit the needs of a particular teacher and class. For this reason, curriculum planning is an evolving process. A curriculum is never a finished product; it is constantly being changed and improved from day to day and year to year.

Standards might appear in one of three formats. Some standards are *procedural;* they refer to what procedures the students will be able to perform. Others are *declarative;* they state what broad concepts students will be able to understand. Still others are *contextual;* they refer to the ways and contexts in which the knowledge will be used. For example, a procedural standard might state that "students will be able to locate mountain ranges and rivers on a state map." A declarative standard might state that "students will understand the concept of regional weather conditions." The contextual standard might state that "students will determine when to use a map and when to use a globe to locate needed information" (Kendall & Marzano, 2000).

# EXAMPLES OF LONG-TERM CURRICULUM PLANNING
## Language Arts Planning for the Primary Grades

The language arts curriculum of the 21st century places roughly equal emphasis on cognitive, affective, and psychomotor outcomes. Teachers now tend to believe that the best environment for learning is one that enhances a child's love of reading, writing, speaking, listening, and being creative. But, they also know that students must master the basic skills of phonics, sentence construction, and word usage in order to be proficient readers and writers.

In an integrated language arts curriculum, students listen to or read literary works, write in journals, participate in editing groups, and speak for a variety of purposes. They also have skills lessons to master the proper grammar, punctuation, spelling, and other conventions of the English language.

As a first-grade teacher in Carpentersville, Illinois, Ginny Bailey and her colleagues planned this integrated curriculum together. She explains:

> *We began our plan by deciding that we would use thematic units to address the state standards. We quickly discovered that language arts cannot be separated from science, social studies, and mathematics when you use a unit approach, so we incorporated those areas into our planning. All of us had attended numerous classes and workshops on using thematic units and had read every book we could find on the subject of using an integrated language arts curriculum in the classroom. But now it was time to sit down and make our plan for the coming school year. We began by going through the state standards for science, mathematics, and social studies to familiarize ourselves with what had to be covered in those areas at our grade level. We then studied the language arts standards. We chose to teach one or two thematic units a month depending on the length of the units.*

Figure 4.2 on model curriculum planning presents a brief overview of Ginny's year-long plan for an integrated language arts curriculum. The state curriculum standards that are addressed in just the first two themes include:

English/language arts standards include concepts about print, decoding and word recognition, vocabulary and concept development, reading comprehension, literary response and analysis, and writing in response to reading.

Science standards addressed include studying plants and animals, including their needs for survival, their cycles of growth and development, investigation and experimentation including recording information and data, and reading to gather information and data (English/language arts).

## An Example of a Middle School Plan for Mathematics

We will use the subject of mathematics in order to provide an example of how curriculum plans are designed at the middle school level. The teaching of mathematics has changed over the years at every grade level. No longer a time for drill and practice, mathematics is often one of the most highly interactive parts of the K–12 school curriculum. Manipulatives that primary students use to demonstrate their

These three teachers like to use a multidisciplinary approach for curriculum planning. They use themes that may be related to social studies, literature, or science, but all of them incorporate and emphasize language arts activities. In each unit, students read, write, speak, and otherwise investigate the topic. The themes change from year to year, but this is a typical example.

**Author Study: Norman Bridwell (Clifford Books)**

The purpose of this unit is to make the children feel comfortable in school. Young children relate to these familiar books. For the first week of school, we read the Clifford Books and do many art and music activities related to the stories. The students discover that they can learn to read through singing and express themselves through art.

**Changes**

This unit emphasizes the patterns of cause and effect in life and encourages students to notice that things in the world change and evolve over time. Subtopics include:

1. Butterflies and moths
2. Frogs
3. Colors
4. Apples
5. Seasons
6. Self

**Zoo Animals**

The purpose of this unit is to learn the characteristics of animals and to classify them as mammals, amphibians, reptiles, or birds. It is primarily a mathematics and science theme, but we integrate literature and writing activities in it and culminate the unit with a trip to the zoo. Subtopics include:

1. Mammals
2. Amphibians
3. Reptiles
4. Birds

**Human Bodies**

In this unit, we help students understand their physical and emotional selves. Subtopics include:

1. Inside the human body
2. Nutrition
3. Five senses
4. Feelings

**Families**

In this unit, we emphasize the importance of families and how each family is alike and different. Subtopics include:

1. Family members
2. Different types of families
3. Families from different cultures
4. Family homes

**Astronomy**

The purpose of this unit is to understand that we are part of the universe and how the laws of science govern our lives. Subtopics include:

1. Day and night
2. The sun and the nine planets
3. The force of gravity

*(continued)*

**Figure 4.2** A yearlong plan for primary school language arts.

---

**The Earth**

In this springtime unit, we examine earth science concepts and how they relate to our everyday lives. We emphasize the new beginnings that occur in the spring in each of the following subtopics:

1. Rocks and minerals
2. Farm animals
3. Insects
4. Plants

**Community Helpers**

The purpose of this unit is to acquaint students with the variety of jobs that people in the community do and how interconnected our lives are. Subtopics include:

1. Police
2. Fire protectors
3. Postal workers
4. Nurses and doctors

**Transportation**

The purpose of this unit is to study geography and learn where things are in the world by studying how we travel from place to place. Subtopics include:

1. Trains
2. Airplanes
3. Automobiles
4. Ships and boats

---

**Figure 4.2** *(Continued)*

SOURCE: Ginny Bailey, Judy Yount, and Sandra Krakow, Woodland School, Carpentersville, Illinois, Barrington Community Unified School District.

understanding of number concepts include beans, beads, and number lines. But many teachers also use such motivating materials as pretzels, fish-shaped crackers, jelly beans, or coated chocolate candies. Recently, a little girl was asked how she knew it was math time and she answered, "That's easy! Math is when we have our snacks."

Kendall & Marzano (1995) provide a summary of recommendations made by the National Council of Teachers of Mathematics (NCTM) and the Mathematics Assessment Framework of the NAEP. These groups stress the importance of teaching mathematics in the context of real-life situations, and they recommend that school curricula should be designed so that the student

1. Effectively uses a variety of strategies in the problem-solving process
2. Understands and applies properties of the concept of number
3. Uses a variety of procedures while performing computation
4. Understands and applies the concept of measurement
5. Understands and applies the concept of geometry
6. Understands and applies concepts of data analysis and distributions

7. Understands and applies concepts of probability and statistics
8. Understands and applies properties of functions and algebra
9. Understands the relationship between mathematics and other disciplines, particularly science and computer technology. (Kendall & Marzano, pp. 88–89)

With this emphasis on problem solving and application of mathematical concepts to real-life situations, the curriculum in many K–12 schools has changed dramatically from drill and practice to mathematical explorations and investigations. Teachers who try to incorporate these recommendations into their mathematics curricula find that the best way to do it is through the use of projects and multidisciplinary units. A year-long plan in mathematics will be divided into several strands or concepts with opportunities for reviewing previously learned material from time to time. It may resemble the plan illustrated in Figure 4.3.

## Long-Term Planning in Science

In the high school curriculum, we will use science as an example of how teachers plan long-term goals. Science consists of a survey of the basic ideas in the academic disciplines of earth and space, life sciences, physical sciences, and environmental studies and the relationship between science and technology. When most of you were in elementary school, you may have learned about science as a collection of facts, laws, principles, and theories that have been found to be important in each of the science disciplines. When this content-oriented approach is used as the basis for curriculum planning in science, students are expected to read, comprehend, discuss, and take tests to demonstrate their mastery of the subject matter. This academic orientation toward science assumes that content is what students must learn to be able to understand science in later schooling.

Project 2061 (an educational study group of the American Association for the Advancement of Science) and the National Committee on Science Education Standards and Assessment (NCSESA) are among several national study groups recommending that we change that approach significantly. The new recommendations stress the need for students to have realistic, hands-on opportunities to experience the methods and processes scientists use to imagine possibilities, speculate on causes, hypothesize effects, gather and weigh evidence, and reach conclusions.

Reflective teachers who believe in teaching science processes use fewer textbooks and more laboratory experiences. Rather than teach *about* science, they believe that students must learn how to *do* science in order to understand it. They are likely to create a science curriculum that consists of a series of laboratory and experimental situations in which students observe, hypothesize, experiment, and evaluate their results in each topic of science. They may test rocks or create a model of plate tectonics for earth science. They may observe the moon or simulate an eclipse for astronomy or collect and classify plants and engage in microscopic examinations of pond water for biology. They may build and test simple machines for physics.

Reflective teachers recognize that the process approach provides students with many more opportunities for developing their critical and creative thinking about science than the textbook-centered, content-oriented approach does. Jim Hicks and Chris Chiaverina, two high school science teachers in Illinois, have created a curriculum that

**Outcome Statement**

Students will demonstrate the ability to discern mathematical relationships, reason logically and strategically, apply mathematical operations accurately, and use technology to solve mathematical problems.

**Assessment Plan**

A mathematics portfolio will be initiated and will contain examples of students' work during each month of the school year. Timed tests will be used to demonstrate mastery of math facts in addition, subtraction (primary grades), and multiplication and division (upper elementary grades).

**First Month: Patterns in Mathematics**

Hands-on activities allow students to discover patterns, relationships, and appreciation for the nature of mathematics. Manipulatives such as beads, geoboards, tangrams, Unifix Cubes, Cuisenaire® rods, and attribute blocks are used. When possible, activities will be coordinated with other areas of the curriculum.

**Second Month: Numbers and Place Value**

Students will learn to compute arithmetic operations: addition, subtraction (primary grades); multiplication and division (upper elementary grades); and use algorithms to solve problems. Place value activities will be stressed. Math facts will be learned and students will demonstrate accuracy and speed in using basic math facts. Students will also solve and create word problems related to other themes being studied in literature, social studies, and science during this month.

**Third Month: Measurement**

Students will have many opportunities to measure length, weight, and volume in a variety of hands-on experiences. Many of these experiences will be designed to relate to other curricular themes being taught.

**Fourth Month: Geometry**

Using real objects, students will examine, compare, and analyze one-, two-, and three-dimensional features. They will identify and classify the attributes of various geometric figures. Related activities will be designed to fit the rest of this month's curriculum.

**Fifth Month: Logic and Reasoning Strategies**

By confronting a variety of real-life problems, students will learn to use logic and problem-solving strategies to make comparisons, decisions, and choices. Many of the problems will be taken from other parts of the curriculum for this month.

**Sixth Month: Mathematics and Technology**

Students will use calculators, computers, and other technological aids to explore ways to use mathematics to solve real-life problems, conduct business, and keep records. Whenever possible, these activities will relate to other curricular areas.

**Seventh Month: Statistics and Probability**

Students will work in cooperative groups to do research and use statistics and probability. The results of the research will be displayed for other students to see. These research studies will be coordinated with other curriculum units being taught during this time period.

**Eighth Month: Patterns and Functions**

Patterns and functions will be examined in a search for understanding the rules that govern mathematical relationships. When possible, these patterns will come from other curricular areas.

**Ninth Month: Review of Mathematical Understandings**

All aspects of the mathematical curriculum will be reexamined. Individual needs will be addressed to improve understanding and strengthen skills. Portfolio assessments will be reviewed by students, and summaries of students' understandings and needs will be written by students and teacher.

**Figure 4.3** A yearlong plan for middle school mathematics.

SOURCE: Pam Knight, Twin Peaks Middle School, Poway, California.

involves their students in active explorations designed to stimulate their curiosity, make them aware of the wonders that surround them, and equip them with skills to help them function effectively in the world. As you can see in their yearlong plan for physics (Figure 4.4), they build toward a culminating activity in which students do physics at a Great America theme park.

The yearlong plan in science may be planned in a wide variety of sequences. Teachers may decide to offer an earth and space science unit for the first 6 weeks, followed by units on life science, then science and technology, and end with physical sciences. Since most of the states organize the science standards into these same categories, this makes the planning of activities to address the standards more logical. The order of presentation of the science themes may easily be changed; many elementary teachers choose to coordinate their science units with other academic subjects. For example, at the same time as a unit on measurement is presented in mathematics, the science unit may emphasize measurement tools and strategies. When the social studies curriculum focuses on themes of exploration of new worlds, the science unit may be coordinated to emphasize scientific frontiers in technology.

## Long-Term Planning in Social Studies

As in science, development of the social studies curriculum can follow a content-oriented approach or a process-oriented approach. Educators committed to an academic or content-oriented view of social studies believe that students need to know and understand the important facts, persons, events, and sequences in the history of our country and the world. Also important to the academic orientation toward social studies are the important concepts that distinguish various cultures and the basic facts about world geography. Recent critics of U.S. schools have decried the lack of knowledge of history and geography among young people. Televised tests and magazine quizzes have demonstrated that many young people lack knowledge about geography. Content-oriented curriculum planners seek to improve this condition by providing history and geography courses that emphasize knowledge and comprehension objectives to teach facts and concepts.

Process-oriented curriculum planners believe that instead of memorizing facts, names, places, and dates, learners should experience the processes of acquiring information on their own. The National Center for History in the Schools (NCHS, 1994) provided benchmarks for teaching students how to think historically, by learning to do their own research in social studies and learning how to use tools such as maps, globes, atlases, charts, graphs, and other resources to enable them to find information when the occasion demands it. The credo of this orientation toward curriculum development can be summed up in the adage, "Give a man a fish and he will be hungry the next day; teach him to fish and he'll never go hungry again." Reflecting this philosophy, many states include research skills in the grade-level social studies standards.

Decision making is also a key focus in the process-oriented approach to teaching social studies. Harlan Cleveland defined social studies as "the study of how citizens in a society make personal and public decisions on issues that affect their destiny" (Bragaw

Planning as a team, Jim and Chris have incorporated these basic guidelines into their plan for their physics course.

**Measurement Techniques (Four Weeks)**

Focusing on the question "What is time?" this unit is designed to enrich students' concepts of time. Students learn how to measure short time intervals using stroboscopic photography and a cathode ray oscilloscope (CRO) and how to measure long time intervals using time-lapse photography and motion pictures. Students create motion picture machines called *xeroscopes.* Measurement of length is also covered. To investigate probability, estimation, and errors in measurement, students throw paper snowballs into a hidden trash can to estimate how large the trash can opening is. The probability nature of the second law of thermodynamics is also investigated.

**Wave Phenomena in Light and Sound (10 Weeks)**

In this unit we deal with reflection of light, refraction of light, and properties of waves associated with light and acoustics. The unit culminates in a field trip to the University of Wisconsin at Whitewater, where students learn the theory of holograms and then make and develop their own.

**Forces, Vectors, and Equilibrium (Seven Weeks)**

In this unit, students learn that forces come in pairs: action and reaction. We examine the forces of nature—gravitational, electromagnetic, nuclear, and the weak force.

In our exploration of vectors, students learn how to add forces. We examine the directions of forces and how they relate to each other. We construct graphs to demonstrate the effects of various forces and vectors.

Our study of equilibrium demonstrates how to combine forces to make a net force of zero. We examine Newton's first law of motion (an object at rest tends to remain at rest).

**Acceleration (Two Weeks)**

Using Newton's second law of motion (force equals mass times acceleration), we explore acceleration with ordinary objects. Students design and build a hovercraft and also spend a day measuring the mass of a car by applying a net force and measuring the resulting acceleration.

**Kinematics (Five Weeks)**

Kinematics is the study of motion. Our students investigate the properties of motion and its relationship to time, velocity, and acceleration through racetrack games. We also study projectile motion and circular motion, which extends the study of motion to two dimensions.

**Work and Energy (Three Weeks)**

We discuss all the types of energy that can be observed and learn to classify them into kinetic and potential energy.

**Momentum (Two Weeks)**

We explore practical applications of the concept of momentum by focusing on automobile safety, especially the use of seatbelts and air bags. We explore forces in collisions. This unit culminates in a field trip to an amusement park to explore energy conservation and circular motion. We have created a guidebook for physics experiences in an amusement park.

**Electricity (Two Weeks)**

We explore electrostatic forces between stationary charges and charges in motion or current electricity and emphasize their uses in the home and the workplace.

**Figure 4.4** A yearlong plan for high school in science.

SOURCE: Jim Hicks, Barrington High School, Barrington, Illinois, and Chris Chiaverina, New Trier High School, Winnetka, Illinois.

& Harloonian, 1988, p. 9). To accomplish this, Bragaw and Hartoonian suggest that the curriculum planner must make sure that students do the following:

1. Develop an information base in the social sciences.
2. Think using the logic and patterns of history and the social sciences.
3. Communicate with others about social science data.
4. Make enlightened personal and policy decisions and participate in civic activities.

David Ramert is a social studies teacher at Francis Parker Upper School in San Diego, California. When asked what he would like new teachers to know about long-term planning, he reminisced about his first years of teaching.

*When I began to plan my U.S. history course, I read several textbooks written for my course and I knew that I couldn't teach all of the material in one year, nor did I want to. I reasoned that it can't all be of equal value. Some parts are definitely more equal than others, but how was I to decide which parts to emphasize? I began to look for events and ideas that would be most likely to stimulate high school students' interests and imagination and involve them in discussion. At the time I had a personal interest in political cartoons that have been published in newspapers for several centuries. I believed that these could be used effectively to spark student interest in controversial issues, which, in my view, is what history is all about. U.S. history can be viewed as one controversy after another, from Columbus to Clinton.*

*I also wanted to seek out primary sources rather than rely on textbooks alone. You can yap for hours about Christopher Columbus and students will yawn and doodle. But show them the letter he wrote home to Spain describing the natives of this new land, their facial features, clothes, crops, and what they valued, and students sit up and start asking questions. They are surprised to learn, for example, that Columbus's men learned that the natives would trade gold for bits of pottery or scraps of leather. Because of his own values, Columbus forbid his crew to continue in this exchange because it wasn't fair. He had a moral problem with that. This experience offers students an interesting contrast to the present day image of Columbus as a destroyer of an ancient culture.*

*Basically, what I want to accomplish by teaching U.S. history is for my students to scuttle all the simplistic, black and white notions of history that they read in the newspaper and see on television. When they leave my class I want them to have learned how complex human beings are and how complex every historical event has been and continues to be. Controversy is the middle name of my course. No one is spared, even the teacher.*

*My responsibility as a teacher of U.S. history is to present a survey of the entire span of our nation's history, but my responsibility to myself is to give an emphasis to the stories that best illustrate the controversial nature of historical events. There have always been so many different interest groups seeking attention and power. So, to plan my year, I select the most interesting and controversial topics in the textbook and organize them chronologically. I begin with Colonial America, emphasizing the demographics, people's life spans, diseases, and the rise of public schools. Then I move on to the American Revolution, the Declaration of Independence, the Constitution and the new nation, the Jeffersonian Era, nationalism and Western expansion, Jacksonian America, issues leading to the Civil War beginning with the struggle over slavery. I always spend too much time on the Civil War.*

*From there I go to reconstruction, industrialization, immigration, and urbanization in the late 19th century. I choose to do the Spanish American War and the controversial issue known as "U.S. imperialism." I deal with the rise of the populists and progressives that takes us through World War 1. Then I move on to the 1920s as the era of wonderful nonsense, the Jazz Age. Then, in contrast, we learn about the economic collapse of 1929, the Great Depression, and the New Deal of the Roosevelt era. World War II is a complex subject because I have to deal with both the European and the Pacific War. I don't have time to teach it battle by battle, so I focus on political and economic events leading up to the war and the treaties and commitments made by the United States after the war. Lots of controversy there!*

*That takes us to the cold war. I give this era a lot of time, looking at both foreign and domestic issues. I remember this era. I lived it as a child. Now most of my students don't know what a communist is and why our country was so fearful of them. As we reach the 60s, we discuss the rise of civil rights and civil liberties for all groups—women, Indians, Blacks, Chicanos. I always spend significant time on that era. The college board exams place a lot of emphasis on this era, on questions relating to the social history of our country. That illustrates one of the major changes in the teaching of history. When I went to school, the teachers used to focus on diplomatic and political history and so did the textbooks. Now, the focus has turned to social history, emphasizing changes in the way people live, interact, and view one another. Teaching a year of U.S. history is a constant struggle to get at the truth. Controversy is a tool I use to undo the myths created in students' minds by popular culture's simplistic notions.*

You can read a unit plan from David's U.S. history course in Chapter 5 and a lesson plan in Chapter 6.

## Redesigning the Curriculum to Reflect Multicultural Values

One of the enduring controversies in curriculum planning is how to design a curriculum that accurately reflects and honors the wide variety of cultural values represented by students in our schools. As David Ramert provokes his students to think by posing controversial questions, he is also trying to encourage them to see the world from points of view different from their own.

James Banks, director of the Center for Multicultural Education at the University of Washington, has similar goals when he advises teachers to redesign their curricula to promote "cultural excellence." Banks (1992) believes that the redesigned curriculum should describe the needs and contributions of all Americans, all their struggles, hopes, and dreams. It should not be an add-on to the existing curriculum, but should become an integral part of every subject we teach. Ask students to reflect, discuss, and write about questions such as: "Who am I?" "Where have I been?" "What do I hope for?" Banks believes that when students can answer these questions they will be better equipped to function in their own world, as well as in the larger community that may be populated by people who answer the same questions very differently.

To develop a multicultural curriculum for your classroom, no matter what subject you teach, plan learning experiences that reflect the concerns of the diverse cultural groups that make up the class, the school, and the community. Encourage your students to share their different perspectives and opinions and show that you value the different ways they solve problems and view the world around them.

Reissman (in Sleeter & Grant 1994) recommends that as you assign learning tasks, consider how each assignment can be used to strengthen intergroup understandings, respect for each other's cultures, and the development of skills that will later be needed in community, national, and global citizenship. Her book entitled *The Evolving Multicultural Classroom* may be a very valuable resource for you in your curriculum planning.

> Students "develop knowledge by interacting mentally and to some extent physically with people and objects around them. This interaction requires active involvement. Knowledge that is poured into a passive mind is quickly forgotten." (Sleeter & Grant, 1994, p. 218)

One side benefit of the multidisciplinary curriculum is that it has led teachers to share what they are doing and work together to plan learning experiences. Teachers who come to school, close the doors of their classrooms, and teach in isolation are becoming a thing of the past. For example, in curriculum planning, many districts team beginning teachers with experienced teachers to develop and share curriculum materials.

This new trend has created an environment in which teachers do not structure their curricula into separate blocks of time. As Beane (1991) points out, when confronted with a problem, individuals do not say, "Now which part of this is science and which part of this is language arts?" Instead, people address problems with a multidisciplinary approach and use whatever resources and content they need to resolve them.

In his analysis of subject-matter teaching, Brophy (1992) emphasizes the importance of teaching fewer topics with more depth. This practice allows students to have a greater understanding of the topics and lets teachers emphasize higher-order applications. Brophy indicates that state curriculum guides and textbooks should be modified in order to accomplish this task, and in many cases they are being revised to include a greater emphasis on integrated curricula such as whole language programs.

In middle school, much energy is being focused on restructuring the curriculum. In many cases, middle school faculty are reflecting on whether to continue with the concept of the middle school as a mini high school, where students take subject-specific courses, or whether to consider alternative structures that combine subject matter into integrated curricula. Beane (1991) proposes a vision of the curriculum centered around themes rather than abstract or artificial subject areas. He suggests that middle school curricula could be focused on themes such as "living in the future," "wellness," or "cultural diversity."

When this integrated thematic approach is used in a middle school, the faculty plans together to design curricula that include literature, writing, mathematics, history, science, and health instruction within the selected theme. The result is often a highly motivating set of learning experiences designed specifically for the special needs of young adolescent students. Faculty members also report increased satisfaction with their own careers when they are involved in actively restructuring the curriculum to meet the needs of their students and celebrate their own special interests and talents.

At the middle school and high school levels, where teachers are usually responsible for teaching only one major subject area at a time, it may be more difficult to design a multidisciplinary curriculum than it is in K–6 schools. It requires that several teachers agree to try this approach and collaborate to plan common goals and themes so that students can experience an integrated, multidisciplinary curriculum even though they still go to math, social studies, and English classes during different class periods.

If a team of secondary teachers decides to plan a multidisciplinary curriculum, they might, for example, choose a common theme such as "change." Individual science, mathematics, language arts, and English teachers then design learning experiences that allow students to identify how things change and to relate these changes to their own experiences. The mathematics teacher might choose to do the unit on renaming fractions during this period to illustrate how number concepts need to be changed in order to carry out mathematical operations. The social studies teacher may choose to focus on the changes in a community over a period of time. The English teacher will look for a novel or a series of other readings that fit the theme of change and carry out discussions of how change affects the characters' lives and beliefs.

To extend this example of the multidisciplinary curriculum to include a multicultural approach as well, the same teachers can highlight various cultural aspects within the theme. The mathematics teacher can describe the contributions made by various cultures to change the way in which mathematics is done. The social studies teacher can ask students to explore the way the changes in the community have affected various cultures and encourage students to express how these changes are experienced today by their own families. The English teacher can select a variety of readings on the theme of change, each one expressing the point of view of a different cultural or ethnic group.

We can also find examples of high schools that are using the integrated curriculum. One is the Humanitas program in the Los Angeles Unified School District. This program integrates English, social studies, and art; some teams also include philosophy, mathematics, science, studio art, or dance. The Humanitas programs are built around themes such as: "women, race, and social protest"; "the Protestant ethic"; "the spirit of capitalism." Students take core classes in these thematic programs, which may include literature, writing, artistic expression, and discussion of social issues. They attend regular subject-matter classes for mathematics, science, and physical education. Teachers who work with the Humanitas program are responsible for planning the program together; and as a result, they report that they believe a spirit of renewal and empowerment was missing when they worked alone.

## Planning Curriculum for a Multicultural, Bilingual Classroom

Ruth Reyes teaches sixth grade at Washington School in downtown San Diego, California. This school follows a special policy of developing biliteracy among all its students. All classes are taught in both Spanish and English. In her class, Ruth teaches one day in Spanish and the next day in English. Her curriculum is designed to allow students to move from one language to another very flexibly. When she designs a unit of study, she selects resources in both English and Spanish. The students use both or select the ones that fit their own level of language development.

Ruth has chosen to use a yearlong theme that she calls "environment/survival." This theme grows out of her own special interest in biology. It also ties in with the social studies curriculum and grows out of her belief that sixth-grade students need to be aware of the concept of environment and the relationship between humans and their environment. She wants her students to leave her class with a commitment to saving our natural environment. She also wants them to begin to develop survival skills and strategies to improve their own environment.

Ruth describes how she translates this important goal into daily learning experiences that cover the state- and district-mandated curricula for math, science, social studies, and language arts. Ruth describes the process in this way.

*I looked through the course of study provided by the school district and the content standards from the state and the school district. Then I opened up all the teacher's manuals for the textbooks we use in sixth grade. As I looked for a way to organize all this material into meaningful chunks, it was clear to me that I should use the social studies standards as the basis for planning. At sixth grade, we focus on the study of world history and geography. That's a perfect fit with my interest in the environment and its relationship to mankind. I can teach the historic material and at the same time bring in contemporary issues and show how they relate to each other.*

*But before I plunge into the yearlong thematic curriculum, I spend the first week of school assessing students' interests and needs. My goals are to get to know my students and learn their strengths and interests. For that week, I use a short literature book that really interests me. This year, I used Kurusa's (1981)* The Street Is Free *and the Spanish edition,* Las Calle Es Libre. *This book about the rainforests fits my theme and allows me to introduce the major ideas we'll be studying all year long. The students do a lot of reading, writing, discussion, and group assignments, so I can observe them as they work together. I spend most of my time during that week observing and taking notes on students as they are working in various groupings. I try to identify what each student enjoys, what is easy, and what is a challenge for each of them. As I walk around with my clipboard, I take notes on computer labels (one label per student), which I can then transfer to their portfolios without rewriting. I look for as many positives as possible while also jotting down what appears to be challenging for each student. Everyone in my class is learning a new language so I have to be alert when I hear them speak in the unfamiliar language, so I can encourage them and plan activities that will allow them to be successful.*

*During the second week of school, we begin our study of the first social studies/literature unit for the year. The topics covered in the social studies curriculum include: early man, the beginning of civilization, ancient Hebrews and Greeks, India, China, and Rome. For language arts, I locate several literature books that are related in some way to each of these topics. We spend about 3 weeks on each novel. For example, with the study of early man, I use a book about a girl who lived during the ice age who has to help her family survive by moving to a winter cave. See, it fits my theme in every way. For math and science, we study the time lines and the ages of prehistoric earth. We also write word problems for math involving the characters in the novel.*

*I am not rigid in my organization of the whole year, but we spend about 3 weeks per book. For some historical eras, we read two or three books. I try to get each book in Spanish and in English. When this isn't possible, then I get similar books on the topic so that my students can choose to read in English for one book, Spanish for another.*

*We begin a new unit by brainstorming what we already know about rainforests. We make a chart of what we know and put it up in the classroom. Then, we make another chart of what we want to learn about rainforests. Based on what we want to know, I create five categories and divide the class into five groups. Each group focuses on re-searching one of the categories, such as animals or trees. Each group researches their topic for about 3 days and then they begin to organize their material into a book. They use the computer to write, edit, and illustrate their books. When they are completed, they teach what they have learned to the rest of their classmates. The books they write become part of the school library's collection for the rest of the year.*

*When I think of what my students experience during the entire year, I want them to see that every subject is related to each other. When they see the connections between subject matter, I feel that I have been successful. Some students come to school believ-ing that in order to do math, they have to use a math book. I want them to learn that we do math every day of our lives. I also want them to see the relationships between dif-ferent authors and their style. We concentrate a lot on comparing and analyzing in my room. Whenever we read a new book, we are constantly looking for ways that this book compares to other books we've read or to the social studies book or to some idea in math or science. When I hear my students making these analyses, I feel that my methods of teaching are validated.*

## Time Lines That Fit Your Goals and Outcome Statements

Time is the scarcest resource in school. Reflective teachers who organize time wisely are more successful in delivering the curriculum they have planned than are teachers who fail to consider it. Teachers who simply start each subject on page 1 of every text-book and hope to finish the text by June are frequently surprised by the lack of time. In some cases, they finish a text early in the year, but more often the school year ends and students never get to the subjects at the back of the textbook. In mathematics, some classes never get to geometry year after year. In social studies, history after the Civil War is often crammed into a few short lessons at the end of the year.

Will you be satisfied if this happens in your classroom? If not, you can prevent it by preplanning the time you will give to each element or subtopic of each subject area you are going to teach. This may seem like an overwhelming task at first, but it can be less threatening if you understand that you are not required to plan every outcome and ob-jective for every subject before the year begins. You need to give the entire curriculum an overview and determine the number of days or weeks you will allot to each element.

Begin by examining the standards for your grade level and comparing them to the textbooks in your classroom, looking at the way in which they are organized. Most books are divided into units, each covering a single topic or collection of related top-ics within the academic subject. Mathematics books are likely to contain units such as place value, operations, measuring, and geometry. History books are divided into units on exploration, settling the new frontier, creating government, and others. English books contain units such as listening, writing, and speaking. If you have a range of reading abilities within your classes, it is also important to bring books of varying levels of reading difficulty into the classroom. No matter what the reading abilities of your students, a range of resource books adds interest to your units.

Curriculum units are excellent planning devices because they show students how facts, skills, concepts, and application of ideas are all related. The alternative to plan-ning with units is planning a single, continuous, yearlong sequence of experiences of planning unconnected and unrelated daily experiences. Units will be used as the basis for planning throughout the rest of this book.

Decide if the units in your school's textbooks are valuable and important as well as whether you agree with the way in which they are organized and the quality of learning experiences they contain. Consider whether using the textbook will result in achieving the state-mandated standards. Will it result in achieving the goals and outcomes you have for your class? If the textbook learning experiences match your outcomes and the state standards, you can plan the year to coincide with the sequence of units in the book.

If the textbook does not coincide with your planned outcomes or if you disagree with the quality or the organizational pattern of the book, you have several options. In reviewing the textbooks you must also decide if the textbooks fit your students and if they respond to the learning needs of your students. You can plan to use the book but present the units in a different order. You can delete units, or you can use some units in the book as they are written but supplement with other materials for additional units not covered or inadequately covered in the book. The most adventuresome and creative teachers may even decide to use the textbook only as a resource and plan original teaching units for the subject. They then search bookstores and the Internet for resources.

In any case, you should carefully consider the amount of time you want to allot to each unit you plan to teach. Create a time line, chart, or calendar for each subject and use it as you judge how much time to spend on each subtopic. For time-line planning, you can divide the school year into weeks, months, or quarters. For a subject such as mathematics, you may think about the year as a total of 36 weeks and allot varying numbers of weeks to each math topic you want to cover during the year. For a subject such as language arts, you might think of the school year as eight months long and create eight different units that involve students in listening, speaking, writing, and reading activities. You may divide the year into four quarters for subjects such as science or social studies with four major units planned for the year. These examples are only suggestions. Each subject can be subdivided into any time segment, or you may combine subjects into interdisciplinary units that involve students in mathematics, science, and language arts activities under one combined topic for a time.

Making reasonable and professional judgments about time-line planning depends on having information about your students' prior knowledge and their history of success or failure before the year begins. The pace of your curriculum depends to some degree on the skills and knowledge your students have acquired before you meet them. But your own expectation for their success is also important. You want to avoid the trap many teachers fall into of reviewing basic skills all year because a majority of your students have been unsuccessful in the past. If you expect them to succeed in your curriculum and be ready to move on to new challenges, then you should provide them with new challenges. They are likely to respond to your positive expectations.

The time lines you create at the beginning of the year need not be rigid and unchanging. They are guidelines based on the best knowledge you have at the time. As the year progresses, you will undoubtedly have reasons to change your original time line. Students' needs, interests, and success will cause you to alter the pace of the original plan. Current events in the country, your classroom, or your local community may cause you to add a new unit to your plan. Interaction with other faculty members may bring you fresh insights about how you want to organize the way you allocate time in your classroom.

## Collaborative Long-Term Planning

Long-term planning, either individually or collectively, is an important job for teachers. If you are teaching in a self-contained classroom, you have the freedom to write your own curriculum as long as it relates to the district and state standards and responds to the learning needs of your students. If you are working in a team-teaching school, you will need to articulate your vision of curriculum to your teammates and adjust yours to include their ideas as well as your own. In either case, the curriculum you create will improve with experience. As you see the effects of your original planning and assess your students' mastery of the standards, you will reflect on your planning and find ways to improve it with each succeeding year.

When you begin teaching, you may be assigned to a curriculum task force or planning committee. In discussions with your colleagues, you are likely to gain new insights and information, but you may also experience frustration with points of view that differ from your own or ideas that come from a different perspective. Be prepared to speak assertively about your own ideas and beliefs. You may be the one to suggest innovative ways of dividing the curriculum into units. Although your ideas may meet skepticism or resistance from some teachers, it is quite appropriate for you to articulate them because schools rely on fresh ideas from faculty members with the most recent college or university training to enhance the curriculum and create positive innovations and change.

## REFLECTIVE ACTION EXPERIENCES FOR YOUR PROFESSIONAL PORTFOLIO

### Give Evidence of Your Reflection on Long-Term Curriculum Planning

We provided a model of reflective action in Chapter 1 of this book. The NBPTS describes reflection as a thought process that allows you to make decisions about how you would approach similar situations in the future. They want to see that you can reflect on a teaching/learning situation in a way that shows evidence that you can learn from teaching experiences to inform or improve your practice in the future (NBPTS, p. 15).

1. Choose one state standard that you will be expected to use in your curriculum planning for student teaching. Write the standard and then analyze it to discover the reasons and motives that resulted in this state standard being adopted. What is this standard going to accomplish? Why do you think it was adopted by your state? How will this standard affect the way you create curriculum in this subject area? How will this standard make your planning easier than if you had no standards to follow? How will it make your planning more difficult?

2. Imagine that you are beginning to plan a yearlong curriculum for this subject area. How would you use this state standard to begin planning? Write a brief long-term plan to achieve this standard. Will you teach it continuously for a period of time or come back to this subject matter every week or so during the year? How will you assess your students' accomplishment of this standard? How will you prove to yourself that your students have successfully mastered this standard? How will you prove this to your school administrators?

3. Reflection always requires self-analysis. Reflect on the difficulties you had in planning this sample curriculum. How will you improve this process when you are called upon to plan a real curriculum? What evidence can you provide that you can use what you learned from this sample planning experience to apply to future planning experiences?

## References

Banks, J. (1992). Multicultural education: For freedom's sake. *Educational Leadership, 49*, 4.

Beane, J. (1991). Middle school: The natural home of the integrated curriculum. *Educational Leadership, 49*(2), 9–13.

Bloom, B., Engelhart, M., Furst, E., Hill, W., & Krathwohl, D. (1956). *Taxonomy of educational objectives: Cognitive domain*. New York: Longman.

Bragaw, D., & Harloonian, M. (1988). Social studies: The study of people in society. In R. Brandt (Ed.), *Content of the curriculum* (pp. 9–29). Alexandria, VA: Association for Supervision and Curriculum Development.

Brooks, J., & Brooks, M. G. (1999). In search of understanding: The case for constructivist classrooms. *Educational Leadership, 57, 3*, 18–24.

Brophy, J. (1992). Probing the subtleties of subject-matter teaching. *Educational
Leadership, 49*(7), 4–8.

Eisner, E. (1985). *Educational Imagination*, 2nd ed. Upper Saddle River, NJ:
Merrill/Prentice Hall.

Hayes-Jacobs, H. (1997). *Mapping the big picture*. Alexandria, VA: Association for
Supervision and Curriculum Development.

Kendall, J., & Marzano, R. (1995). *The systematic identification and articulation of content
standards and benchmarks*. Aurora, CO: Mid-Continent Regional Educational
Laboratory.

Kendall, J., & Marzano, R. (2000). *Content knowledge: A compendium of standards and benchmarks for K–12 education*. Aurora, CO: Mid-Continent Regional Educational
Laboratory.

Kurusa, D. (1981). *The streets are free (Las calles son libres)*. Caracas: Ekare-Banco del Libro
(Spanish version); New York: Annick Firefly Books (English version).

National Center for History in the Schools (1996). *National standards for history*. Revised.
UCLA, Los Angeles, CA.

National Committee on Science Education Standards and Assessment (1996). *National
science education standards*. Washington, DC: National Research Council.

National Council for Social Studies (1994). *Expectations of excellence: Curriculum standards
for social studies*. Washington, DC: Author.

National Council of Teachers of Mathematics (2000). *Principles and standards for school
mathematics*. Reston, VA: Author.

Reissman, R. (1994). *The evolving multicultural classroom*. Alexandria, VA: Association for
Supervision and Curriculum Development.

Sleeter, C., & Grant, C. (1994). *Making choices for multicultural education*. Upper Saddle
River, NJ: Merrill/Prentice Hall.

Spady, W. (1994). Choosing outcomes of significance. *Educational Leadership, 51*(6),
18–22.

Tyler, R. (1949). *Basic principles of curriculum and instruction*. Chicago: University of
Chicago Press.

Viadero, D. (1993, June 16). Standards deviation: Benchmark-setting is marked by diversity. *Education Week*, pp. 14–17.

Williams, S. (1990). *I went walking*. Boston: Red Wagon Books.

## CHAPTER 5

# Planning Curriculum Units That Give Students a Sense of Purpose

Do you have a vision of yourself teaching a roomful of students who are excitedly investigating, experimenting, discussing, and reporting on what they are learning? Beginning teachers and student teachers often report that what they want to do most is create a learning environment that motivates their students to want to come to school and learn as much as they can about important matters.

Current national standards and state curriculum guides are also the products of the vision of experienced teachers working in collaboration to provide beginning teachers with guidelines for what to teach and how to teach it. These documents encourage teachers to create programs that develop students' deeper understandings of a few important subjects rather than provide them with superficial surveys of data. At the local school district level, teachers are responsible for translating the curricular visions described in national and state standards into practical classroom learning experiences. The word *vision* is carefully chosen in this discussion, because at the local level teachers and principals are often encouraged to develop a common vision and create a mental image of what they want to accomplish with students.

One of the most natural and authentic ways to translate a vision of core curriculum goals into practical classroom experiences is by planning thematic units of study that engage students in actively seeking information on a topic that has meaning in their lives. Many teachers use a series of thematic units for their long-term planning. There is something refreshing and inherently motivating for both teachers and students using this plan. A unit of study lasts a specified number of days or weeks, during which everyone is motivated to investigate and find out everything they can about the topic. Then, during an exciting culmination, the students proudly display what they have learned. After a brief period devoted to assessment, the unit ends, and a new one begins. When this rhythm is established in a classroom, complaints of boredom or repetition are rare from students or the teacher. The pace is quick, the goals are clear, and the expectations are high when everyone is involved in a thematic unit on an interesting, challenging topic.

**PRAXIS**

Effective unit planning is tested in PRAXIS™ Exam Section 1a, Students as Learners and 2a, Instruction and Assessment.

## PLANNING THEMATIC UNITS TO FIT YOUR CURRICULUM

No other model of curriculum development involves teachers in a more active and professional capacity than in the planning, teaching, and evaluation of thematic curriculum units. They appeal greatly to reflective teachers who want to be part of the decision-making process and use their own creative ideas and methods. However, planning thematic curriculum units also adds greatly to the responsibility of classroom teachers. To create a successful unit, teachers must be willing to explore the state-mandated standards, gather a wide variety of information, and create an excellent knowledge base about the topics they have chosen so that the learning experiences they plan will be based on accurate and interesting information. They must also be willing to work with their colleagues to make sure that their curriculum units do not repeat or skip over important material in the K–12 curriculum. Care must be taken to articulate their units with what was covered in earlier grades and what their students will learn in subsequent years.

Even when teachers decide to create their own thematic curriculum units to translate curricular visions into actual classroom experiences, many are not certain how to do that, or what can or should be covered in each unit. In this chapter, we examine how teachers decide what units to teach and how they organize the learning experiences in a curriculum unit to ensure that students acquire the knowledge, skills, and processes that are intended.

## Deciding on Unit Topics

The first step is to analyze state and local standards to be implemented at that grade level in math, science, social studies, language arts, and fine arts. Most teachers also examine the curriculum materials supplied by the school district, looking for recommended themes or topics. The teacher may choose to look for topics within a subject, such as a math unit on fractions, a science unit on magnets and electricity, or a social studies unit on the electoral process. Other units may be interdisciplinary—that is, designed to include information and material from several subjects at one time. For example, a theme of "change" may include learning experiences in science, math, social studies, and literature.

Although many teachers choose to work alone, some teachers at the same grade level frequently work together to create units of study. When this occurs, their combined knowledge and ideas are likely to result in a much more comprehensive set of units and greater variety of learning experiences. Whether a teacher works alone or with a team, the first step is to decide on a series of curriculum units that correspond to the major educational goals for that grade level.

When a unit topic comes to mind, you need to reflect on whether it is appropriate according to several criteria. Roberts and Kellough (2000) suggest that you consider the following questions. Is this theme one that has a proper length, not too short or too long? Will I be able to find good materials and resources on this subject? Does it have a broad real-life application? Does it have substance? Is it worth spending time on this topic? Will the students be interested in this topic and be motivated to learn about it?

Wiggins and McTighe (1999) recommend using a backward design for unit planning. What are the goals or standards that you want to accomplish and how can your unit plan achieve these goals and meet these standards? This approach also requires you to think about the evidence that will prove that your students have met the standards. Evidence of achievement is usually gathered through some type of assessment of learning or understanding. Therefore, using the backward design approach for your unit plan, you will want to (1) identify the desired results; (2) determine what evidence can measure or assess the accomplishment of these results by your students, and (3) plan the learning experiences and methods of instruction that you will use in your unit plan.

When teachers select unit topics, Wiggins and McTighe (1999) recommend that the focus be on a topic that will result in students gaining "enduring big ideas that have lasting value beyond the classroom" of the subject rather than simply learning facts or skills (p. 78). For example, if you wanted to plan a unit on nutrition, they suggest that you create a unit that will result in students learning that a balanced diet contributes to both physical and mental health throughout one's lifetime. This "enduring understanding" is more important than simply having students learn which foods fit into the various food groups.

## Creating a Curriculum Unit Using Reflective Actions

First, consult your state standards for the subjects you want to include in your unit. When reflective teachers approach the development of a curriculum unit, they consider their long-term goals for that subject or subjects. By consulting the state standards for the subjects to be included in the unit, you can have confidence that your long-term goals and those in the standards are congruent. You may begin with the questions: "What are my major social studies goals this year? What are the state standards in social studies that support and coincide with my goals? What should I include in this unit of study to accomplish these goals?" Or you may begin by considering the core outcomes your students are expected to achieve during the year, and plan curriculum units that will encourage your students to learn the content and enhance the skills that make up those outcomes.

**Consider What Students Already Know.** Consider and reflect on the skills and knowledge the students will need to bring to the unit to be successful in learning new material. Pretest your students to assess prior knowledge and skills they bring to the new unit. Some may have already mastered most of the content you intend to teach. Consider ways to challenge them by compacting the curriculum so they can go on to more challenging material. Other students may have serious gaps in their knowledge or may lack background experiences or language structures necessary to successfully participate in the planned activities. Consider how you will scaffold the new material to make it accessible to them.

Teachers who think and plan using the reflective actions described in Chapter 1 are likely to consider the cues they perceive from their students' interests and talents when planning thematic units. As they plan curriculum, they tend to ask themselves: "What do my students need to learn? How do they enjoy working? What learning experiences will motivate my students to become actively engaged in the learning process? What language skills and vocabulary will need to be taught so that students can express their newly acquired knowledge?"

**Create an Initial Plan for the Unit.** When they have decided on a topic, teachers who use reflective actions then sketch out a preliminary draft of a unit and begin to consider some interesting ways to teach it. The first draft may resemble a concept web or something they've read in a curriculum guide, seen online, or perhaps even the type of unit plan they recall from their own school experiences.

**Reflect on the Initial Plan and Make It Fit the Needs of Your Students.** Reflective teachers are likely to begin to establish some criteria for selecting certain content or methods while omitting others. As reflective teachers consider what to include and what to exclude, they ask themselves: "What knowledge and skills am I responsible for teaching at my grade level, and how can I help my students understand the application of this content to their success in school or in life? How can this curriculum assist them in developing what they need most? What attitudes do I want to instill among my students? How can this unit help them to attain those attitudes? What values do I want to model for my students during this curriculum unit? How can I best model those values for them?"

**Research or Confer with Colleagues.** At many points along the way, reflective teachers are likely to do additional research on the subject or on teaching methods they can include in their new unit. They are also likely to talk with other trusted colleagues about how they have taught the subject. Many teachers share their unit plans with others, but most agree that sharing a unit plan is very much like sharing their recipes for making spaghetti sauce. No two sauces or units are identical. Still, a trusted colleague can point out things for the beginning teacher to consider, share strategies for motivating student interest, and suggest new materials to include in the unit.

**Revise the Unit.** What changes have occurred to you as a result of your interaction with colleagues? Do you have a new and original way to approach the topic? Have your basic goals changed? Teachers who use reflective action tend to enjoy the process of combining all the content materials and methods they have learned during planning into an original set of learning experiences that fit their own teaching style and the needs of their students. No two thematic units are ever alike. Even when teachers plan together up to this point, they are likely to interpret the materials they have gathered differently and add their own unique spin to the way they teach the unit.

Throughout the process of planning and teaching the unit, teachers who use reflective action are likely to be asking themselves: "How can I adapt the materials I have available to meet my goals? What new instructional materials shall I create to teach this material effectively? What risks are possible if I try to teach this unit in my own way? Which risks am I willing to take? What gains are possible if I take these risks? Do the possible gains outweigh the risks?"

During a thematic unit, teachers create original bulletin boards, group activities, work or activity sheets, processes for promoting student interaction, methods to assess student accomplishments, and ways to allow their students to perform or display what they have learned. Teachers also carefully examine standards across disciplines. In planning a social studies unit, for example, many standards in reading and writing, science and mathematics, and visual and performing Arts can be infused in the planned unit activities. If there are English language learners in the class, then language objectives must be included in each of the activities to ensure their full participation and success. For many reflective teachers, these opportunities for creativity are some of the most important sources of pride and are often cited as some of the most significant perks of their careers.

**Consider Alternate Plans.** All teachers encounter challenges in teaching and managing their classrooms. But teachers who use reflective action are able to prevent some of these challenges because they try to imagine the consequences of their plans before putting them into action. For example, if you are planning to introduce innovative learning materials to motivate students, you will want to consider what types of management procedures will be needed for distributing and using these materials. The introduction of new and interesting materials may need to include time for the students to explore the materials before they are asked to implement their use in activities.

Teachers who use reflective actions in their thinking and planning anticipate the students' need to explore. Making your expectations very clear will assist in arriving at a positive outcome in student interaction with materials. If unexpected problems arise, teachers use withitness in the midst of the problem to observe what is happening and respond appropriately. Afterward, they talk with the students themselves and with their colleagues in order to reframe the problem and create a new plan, if necessary.

**Put the Plan into Action and Get Student Feedback.** The day you present your new unit plan to your students is usually an exciting day for you and your class. There is a sense of heightened expectations as you reveal the plan. Students may have a lot of questions. You may be able to answer some but not all of their questions right away. You will use withitness during the initial presentation to get feedback from your most important critics: your students. They will give you cues as they react to the plan with excitement, confusion, fear, or increased motivation to learn. You can also discuss the first day's presentation with your colleagues and get ideas about how to reframe the plan for yourself or for your students. After the first day, you will be even better equipped to rethink and adjust certain parts of the plan. If your students react with fear or confusion, you can make changes now, before it is too late. If they react with excitement, you can consider adding even more challenging material to the plan.

Reflective teachers are also able to laugh at their own mistakes and learn from their errors in judgment without an overwhelming fear of the consequences or feelings of guilt. As they plan their thematic units, they are likely to encounter difficulties in locating suitable materials. When this happens, teachers become very good at scrounging for the materials they need or they substitute and go on anyway.

When they begin to teach their units, some of the lessons they planned are likely to turn out quite differently than they expected, but they simply assess, regroup, and reteach as needed. As the unit nears completion, they may discover that, due to their students' choices and actions, some unplanned effects occur. These are simply accounted for and evaluated along with the outcomes that were planned.

Throughout the process of planning, organizing, teaching, and evaluating a thematic unit, good communication skills are necessary. Reflective teachers must often convince or persuade their colleagues or administrators to allow them to take the time, spend money, take certain risks, and establish certain priorities necessary to teach their thematic units the way they want. Assertiveness is a very important trait in curriculum development, especially considering the different curriculum orientations that various members of the faculty adopt. The ability to clearly connect the unit and its outcomes to established and mandated standards continues to be a powerful influence on these types of decisions.

Conflicts may arise with students as well. When reflective teachers introduce a creative new way to learn a difficult subject, some students may react by stating their own preferences. When this occurs, teachers who use reflective actions simply explore new ideas with the students and attempt to address the needs of the students and the possibility of working those needs into revised approaches and activities within the unit plan.

## SEQUENCING LEARNING EXPERIENCES

Practically speaking, the process of developing a curriculum unit also includes the following:

**PRAXIS**
Scope and sequence in planning is tested in PRAXIS™ Exam Section 2b: Instruction and Assessment.

1. Defining the topics and subject matter to be covered in the unit
2. Defining the cognitive, process, and affective goals or outcomes that tell what students will gain and be able to do as a result
3. Outlining the major concepts that will be covered
4. Gathering resources that can be used in planning and teaching

5. Brainstorming learning activities and experiences that can be used in the unit

6. Organizing the ideas and activities into a meaningful sequence

7. Planning lesson plans that follow the sequence

8. Planning evaluation processes that will be used to measure student achievement and satisfaction

Analysis will reveal that these statements correspond to Tyler's (1949) four questions. Items 1, 2, and 3 pertain to the question "What shall we teach?" Items 4 and 5 relate to the question "How shall we teach it?" Items 6 and 7 respond to the question "How shall we organize it?" Item 8 answers the question "How will we know if we are successful?"

When seen in print, as they are here, these steps appear to depict an orderly process, but curriculum planning is rarely such a linear activity. Instead, teachers find themselves starting at various points in this process. They skip or go back and forth between these steps as ideas occur to them. For example, a team member may begin a discussion by showing a resource book with a particular learning activity that could be taught as part of the new unit. Discussions may skip from activities to goals to concepts to evaluation to organization. Nothing is wrong with this nonlinear process as long as teachers are responsible enough to reflect on the overall plan to determine if all of Tyler's questions have been addressed fully and adequately. When the plan is complete, it is important to review it and ask yourself: "What are the outcomes I expect from this unit? Are the learning experiences directly related to the outcomes? Is my organization of activities going to make it possible for my students to achieve my outcomes? Are the assessment systems I've established going to measure the extent to which the students have accomplished the outcomes?"

Thematic units vary in types of learning experiences and in organization. Some subjects, such as math, are organized very sequentially, and others are not. The type of learning experiences also vary greatly depending on the subject, the resources available, and the creativity or risk taking of the teacher.

Most teachers use the textbook or a district curriculum guide as the basis for planning and as an important resource. *Do not limit yourself, however, to a single textbook as the source of all information in planning your unit or in teaching it.* A good textbook can be a valuable resource for you as you plan and for your students as they learn about the topic, but a rich and motivating unit plan will contain many other elements.

Supplemental reading materials from libraries or bookstores might include biographies, histories, novels, short stories, plays, poems, newspapers, magazines, how-to books, and myriad other printed materials. Other resources to consider are films, videotapes, audiotapes, and computer programs on topics that relate to your unit. Many interesting student-centered computer programs allow your students to have simulated experiences, solve problems, and make decisions as if they were involved in the event themselves. A good example is the computer game called "Oregon Trail," distributed by the Minnesota Educational Computer Consortium (MECC), in which the student travels along the Oregon Trail, making decisions about what supplies to buy, when and where to stop along the way, and how to handle emergencies. This program can enrich a unit on westward expansion by providing more problem-solving and critical-thinking experiences than reading and discussion can ever yield.

Many educational games also provide students with simulated experiences. Some are board games that can be purchased in a good toy store or bookstore. Others are more specialized learning games sold by educational publishers or distributors. Your school district probably receives hundreds of catalogs from educational publishers. Locate them and find out about the many manipulative and simulation games available on your topic.

Consider field trips that will provide your students with experiences beyond the four walls of the classroom. Which museums have exhibits related to your topic? A simple walk through a neighborhood to look for evidence of pollution or to view variations in architecture can add depth to your unit. If you cannot travel, consider inviting a guest to speak to your students about the topic. Sometimes parents are excellent resources and are willing to talk about their careers or other interests.

In thinking about how to organize a unit, many reflective teachers prefer to begin with a highly motivating activity such as a field trip, a guest speaker, a simulation game, a hands-on experiment, or a film. They know that when the students' initial experience with a topic is stimulating and involving, interest and curiosity are aroused. The next several lessons in the unit are frequently planned at the knowledge and comprehension levels of Bloom's Taxonomy to provide students with basic facts and concepts so that they can build a substantial knowledge base and understanding of the topic. After establishing the knowledge base, further learning experiences can be designed at the application, analysis, synthesis, and evaluation levels to ensure that the students are able to think critically and creatively about the subject. This model of unit planning is not universal, nor is it the only logical sequence, but it can be adapted to fit many topics and subjects with excellent results.

## EXAMPLES OF THEMATIC UNITS

The following sections illustrate the processes teachers use as they select, order, and create unit plans in several subjects from the K–12 curriculum. Because each teacher has a personal curriculum orientation and philosophy, the process of decision making is more complex when teachers plan together than when they plan alone. The following examples demonstrate how teachers create their own curriculum units and what they put down on paper to record their plans for teaching. You will notice many variations in the way units are created and what they contain depending on their purposes and the philosophies and values of the teachers who create them.

### A Multidisciplinary Primary Unit

Adams (1999) suggests that multidisciplinary units are the way to develop literacy across the curriculum. Literacy is much more than reading in today's educational environment. We are equally concerned with promoting mathematical, historical, social, and scientific literacy.

To create such units, teachers frequently choose themes or topics and plan learning experiences that involve students in reading, writing, speaking, science investigations, mathematical problem solving, music, and art. A single teacher can certainly plan and teach a multidisciplinary unit, but we have found that the units planned by two to four teachers are often more exciting because they incorporate each teacher's different perspectives and strengths. For example, at Woodland School in Carpentersville, Illinois, three first-grade teachers often plan their whole language thematic units together. Ginny Bailey, Judy Yount, and Sandra Krakow recently planned an interdisciplinary unit on "change," highlighting the changes of caterpillars and butterflies.

They begin with the State of Illinois language arts standards, such as the reading standard for primary grades that reads, "Apply reading strategies to improve under-standing and fluency." Section 1.B.1a requires teachers to "[e]stablish purposes for read-ing, [m]ake predictions, connect important ideas, and link text to previous experiences and knowledge." Section 1.C.2b calls upon teachers to create opportunities for students to "make and support inferences and form interpretations about main themes and topics."

Bailey, Yount, and Krakow also know that teachers often have difficulty fitting in all the subjects of their busy curricula. They find that by using a thematic unit, they can teach several subjects simultaneously. To plan a unit, these teachers use a graphic or-ganizer known as a *planning web*. They sit down with a large piece of paper and write the thematic topic in the middle of the page. They write the various disciplines they want to cover at different positions on the paper and then brainstorm learning experi-ences that fit the topic under the appropriate subject areas. An example of one of their planning webs is shown in Figure 5.1.

Through their observations of the students they teach, the three teachers learned that, in the minds of first-grade students, reading and writing are very closely related. Their interdisciplinary thematic units allow students to read, write, and investigate interesting topics such as caterpillars, cookies, and planets. In each unit they select appropriate topic-specific children's books of fiction, nonfiction, and poetry. They locate songs on the topics when possible. Skill teaching is embedded in the unit, within the context of the literature, poetry, or music. The science and social studies facts and concepts are easily mastered by students when they are presented in the

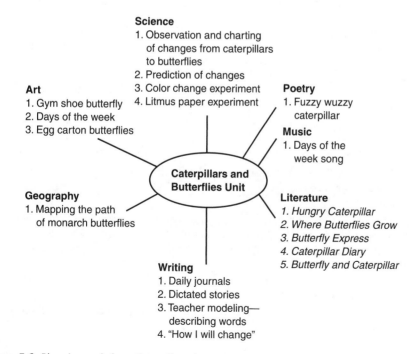

**Figure 5.1** Planning web for a thematic unit.

SOURCE: Virginia Bailey, Judy Yount, and Sandra Krakow, Woodland School, Carpentersville, Illinois.

context of hands-on experiments and are reinforced by illustrated stories, poems, and songs. Math concepts are introduced by counting, measuring, sequencing, and patterning games and activities appropriate to each unit. Figure 5.2 shows a written plan for the unit "Changes," describing some of the specific learning experiences and how the unit is evaluated.

---

### Description

This primary learning unit was planned to provide students with a set of varied learning experiences to understand the concept of change, with an emphasis on changes in the life cycle of living things.

- **Cognitive goal:** Students will understand that all living things change over time.
- **Affective goal:** Students will accept change as a natural part of their own lives and environment.
- **Psychomotor goals:** Students will use observation skills to identify changes. They will use writing and speaking skills to report what they have learned through observation.

### Activities

**Nature Walk:** Before the nature walk, students are asked to imagine what they might find out about caterpillars and butterflies on their walk. During the walk, they look especially for cocoons. When they return to the classroom, they discuss their findings. They predict whether the cocoons they found will become butterflies or moths. Then they write about what they saw on their nature walk.

**Observing Caterpillars:** Caterpillars ordered from a science supply dealer arrive in plastic jars. Students observe them climb to the top of the jar preparing to form a chrysalis. In just a few days, they begin to spin their chrysalis. They remain in this form for three or four days and then emerge as butterflies or moths.

As a follow-up activity, students are asked to illustrate the various changes they observe. A strip of 18-inch by 6-inch paper is prepared for each child. Children fold the paper into fourths and draw each stage of a butterfly's development: (1) egg on a leaf, (2) caterpillar, (3) chrysalis or cocoon, and (4) butterfly or moth.

In groups of four, children evaluate their products and check the proper sequence. Each child can then tell the other children a story about his or her butterfly.

**Color Changes:** In a learning center, students experiment to discover how colors change. Working with diluted red, blue, and yellow food color, the children use an empty cup and an eye dropper to mix colors and experiment on their own to create new colors from the original primary colors.

**Children's Literature:** The teacher collects a variety of picture books for use in this unit. Some books will be read aloud by the teacher and used as a focus for discussion. Others will be selected by the children to read on their own.

**Caterpillar/Butterfly Art Activity:** Students create a wiggly caterpillar by cutting 12 cups from an egg carton and turning them upside down. They make a small hole in the bottom of each cup, tie a knot at one end of a piece of yarn, and string the 12 cups together. Then they add paper eyes and decorate the caterpillars with crayons or paint.

They create a butterfly by cutting out 3 of the 12 cups from an egg carton for the body. Then they add wings and pipe-cleaner antennae.

**Gym Shoe Butterfly:** Each child places his or her gym shoes on a large piece of pastel paper (arches facing out) and traces the shoes into a butterfly shape. The child then cuts out the shape and adds antennae. The child can write a poem inside the butterfly shape.

**Figure 5.2** A multidisciplinary primary unit on "Changes: Butterflies and Moths."

**Days of the Week:** Students create a caterpillar with seven circles cut from construction paper. They then copy the name of a different day of the week on each circle and glue them onto a background paper in the correct order. Afterward, they add a face, legs, and antennae. Students learn a song about the days of the week.

**How People Change:** Students bring in pictures of themselves as babies and put them on a bulletin board. Current school pictures are also arranged on the bulletin board. Students have to try to match the baby pictures with the current pictures of their classmates. Discussions focus on how people change (observing differences in size, hair, and other physical features) and what people are able to do at different ages. As a follow-up, students write in their journals about how they have changed.

**Growth Charts:** Charts on the students' current heights and weights are initiated during this unit. Each student measures and weighs a partner. The data are recorded on a wall graph. The charts are updated three times during the year.

**Poetry about Change:** Poems about caterpillars and butterflies, seasons, and other changes are distributed frequently during the unit. Students read them, memorize and recite them, discuss them, and illustrate them. The poems are also used to teach language structure and vocabulary skills. A poem is projected onto a screen using an overhead projector. Students also have copies of the poem on their desks. We teach skills such as these:

1. Reading from left to right
2. Finding and reading individual words
3. Using the context of the poem to decode words
4. Learning specific phonics skills (such as beginning sounds, endings, rhyming words)

**Art/Nutrition:** Create a caterpillar out of fruit, vegetables, and peanut butter. Eat it for a snack and discuss its nutritional value.

**Unit Evaluation Activity**

Provide students with a paper that has the beginning of three paragraphs (shown below). Use a copy on the overhead projector and clarify for students how to begin and what is expected.

Because primary students are unable to write all that they know and have observed, this evaluation can be extended by asking children from an upper elementary grade to interview the primary children and write the younger students' responses for them.

This week, I learned about butterflies and moths. First, I learned _____
_____
_____

Next, I learned _____
_____
_____

Finally, I learned _____
_____
_____

SOURCE: Virginia Bailey, Judy Yount, and Sandra Krakow, Woodland School, Carpentersville, Illinois. Barrington Community Unified School District.

## Fourth-Grade Social Studies/Literature Unit

Janet Gengosian, a fourth-grade teacher at Greenberg Elementary school in Fresno, California, begins her exploration of the westward movement with a series of books related to the gold rush era in California. The first of the books, *Nine for California*, (Levitin, 1996) describes a family's trip across the broad expanse of middle and western America on a stagecoach to join their father, who was already working in the goldfields of California. The second in the series, *Boom Town* (Levitin, 1998), gives us a look at the growth of a small town around the mining activities, taking into account the ideas of supply and demand and a variety of economic interests. The third book in the series, *Taking Charge* (Levitin, 1999), gives us an account of the responsibilities of maintaining a family in the early days of a boom town. It gives us an opportunity to contrast children's lives of the past with those of today. Janet chose this series of books because she can use them to explore a great variety of the content contained in the history/social studies standards in the context of high interest stories. They will also provide opportunities for active learning strategies for the students through simulations, active vocabulary role play, reader's theatre, and so forth.

Janet's planning begins with reviewing both the history/social science standards and the reading/language arts standards for the fourth grade. She then begins to gather support materials for her California history unit, which will begin with a simulation based on *Nine for California*. She plans to come dressed as the character of the mother in the book. The students will begin a "simulation journal" by writing a daily entry as the story unfolds day by day. Janet plans this 3-week unit to coincide with the book's description of the family's 21-day stagecoach trip to California. She also includes activities such as mapping the family's route across the country. These maps will include topographic features encountered in their journey. Janet plans to integrate a number of the history/social science standards related to the westward movement, the gold rush, and basic economics into this study.

Under the reading/language arts standards, she will be addressing a number of standards related to comparing and contrasting information from several sources and writing narratives based on experiences and simulations, with a focus on descriptive writing. Because her students are second language learners, she plans to focus on vocabulary development and comprehension through the writing and multiple readings of reader's theatre scripts.

Janet begins the unit with the reading and simulation activities. She quickly grabs the students' interest and creates a heightened level of excitement by using *Nine for California*, a book that tells the story through the eyes of children who are relatively the same age as her students. In talking about the gold rush, it becomes evident to Janet that there are some gaping misconceptions about certain terms related to the study, for example, "gold fever." The students relate this to an "illness" that the miners had, based on the students' understanding of what having a "fever" means to them. Janet sees the need for an activity to help clarify this term. She paints some rocks with gold paint and plans a simulated "gold fever" activity. While the students are out of the room, Janet hides the gold rocks throughout the room. She greets her students at the door and explains that the room has been turned into a goldfield. Before she allows them to enter the room, she gives them each a length of yarn with which to mark their "claim" area. Janet has set up a video camera to capture the actions of the students as they search for gold and "stake their claims" around the room. Once started, the activity is quite frenzied as the students rush from place to place within the room, discovering gold and staking their claims. The video camera captures all the action and when Janet reviews the tape with the students at the end of the activity, they are quite surprised at how frantic their actions appeared. The discussion following the viewing of the videotape allows Janet to clarify the term "gold fever." She follows this activity with a writing prompt, leading the students to write descriptive entries in their simulation journals telling how they felt when they suffered from "gold fever."

In the exploration of *Boom Town*, they will set up a mock frontier town, including needed businesses to stimulate discussion of economy and concepts of supply and demand. As students begin to choose businesses to open, they will deliver an oral presentation to the "town council" with supporting reasons as to why they should be allowed to bring their business to the town. They will continue adding to their simulation journals, describing how the town is growing and developing.

*Taking Charge*, the third book in the series, leads the class into a study of the way of life in the boom town, and the responsibilities of adults and students. It gives Janet an opportunity to engage her students in a comparative analysis of life in the gold rush days versus life today. She also takes this opportunity to challenge the students to investigate the differences in the types of information that might be gained from different types of texts, e.g., narrative text versus informational or expository text.

Janet's culminating activity for the unit is the writing of a class poem using a format called "I used to think, but now I know." She starts the poem off for the students with the line "I used to think gold fever was a disease, but now I know it describes the way the miners rushed to search for gold and stake their claims." The students then continue adding their own verses to the poem, stating new things they had learned or correcting misconceptions they had prior to the unit study.

Janet also includes a variety of activities in the unit that address a number of other content standards. Math is included by mapping, documenting distances traveled, economic transactions in the mock village, measurements in creating products to be sold, and so forth. Visual and performing arts standards are addressed in the simulations and dramatic representations, illustrations, and songs produced by the students during their "travels" across the country. Science standards are included in investigations of machines, geology, and navigation. Physical education standards are incorporated in a variety of games and dances the students recreate from the period.

Janet used the California history/social science and language arts standards in preparing her unit plan. Then, she used her imagination and creativity to make sure her unit engaged her students in active learning. Her unit action plan is shown in Figure 5.3.

## A Middle School Mathematics Unit

Mathematics is generally thought of as a subject that does not lend itself to multidisciplinary planning, but recently, many teachers have been experimenting with ways to connect mathematics to other subject areas and life experiences. As Piaget

To plan her California History Unit, Janet identified the following standards and then put them into a sequence of learning experiences as described in the text:

**California Fourth Grade History/Social Science Standards**

Identify physical geographic features.

Use maps, charts, and pictures to describe how communities vary.

Compare how and why people traveled to California and the routes they traveled.

Analyze the effects of the gold rush on settlements, daily life, politics, and the physical environment.

Study the lives of women who helped build California.

Explain how the gold rush transformed the economy of California.

Discuss immigration and migration to California and its effects on diversity.

Describe the daily lives of the people.

**California Reading/Language Arts Content Standards**

Read and understand grade-level-appropriate material using predictions and comparing information from several sources.

Identify sequential and chronological order to strengthen comprehension.

Compare and contrast information on the same topic from several sources.

Create multiple paragraph compositions.

Write compositions that describe and explain events and experiences using concrete sensory details.

Ask thoughtful questions and respond to relevant questions with appropriate elaboration in oral settings.

Summarize major ideas and supporting evidence in effective oral presentations.

**Figure 5.3** Integrating standards into a history/social studies unit plan.

SOURCE: Janet Gengosian, teacher, Greenberg Elementary School, Fresno, California.

demonstrated, mathematics is a subject that requires early experiences with concrete examples and hands-on experiences allowing students to manipulate materials to understand mathematical relationships. Later, upper intermediate grade students can be expected to understand these same relationships at a more abstract level without the need to "see" them in a concrete way. Many teachers like to plan their mathematics curriculum using thematic units so students have many opportunities to experience and investigate the mathematical relationships they are learning.

Mathematics is also a subject that requires lateral thinking, reasoning, and problem-solving strategies that cannot be taught in a sequential series of lessons. Current mathematics units encourage students to explore mathematical relationships and select from a variety of strategies to set up and solve problems. Skillful computation is no longer sufficient as an outcome or performance expectation; it is also important that students be able to apply mathematical operations to real-life problems and tasks.

Based on these organizational principles, an effective curriculum unit in math is likely to (1) present new skills and concepts in order of difficulty; (2) initiate new learning with concrete, manipulative experiences so that students can understand the concepts involved; (3) teach students a variety of problem-solving strategies; and (4) provide examples, tasks, and problems that call on students to apply their newly learned skills and strategies in lifelike situations to problems they can relate to and want to solve.

Mathematics is an example of a *spiral curriculum*. This means that certain concepts and skills are taught every year but in an upward spiral of difficulty. Each year begins with a review of skills from previous years, then an introduction of new skills and concepts. For this reason, the topics of mathematics units are likely to be similar from year to year, but the way these topics are addressed and the complexity of the concepts vary greatly. Mathematics education now emphasizes problem solving and investigation as a means of developing mathematical power.

California state mathematics standards for the upper elementary grades ask teachers to provide learning experiences that will challenge students to "use data samples of a population and describe the characteristics and limitations of the samples." A good example of a mathematics unit that involves students in realistic data collection and interpretation is presented in Figure 5.4. Pam Knight created this unit, entitled "Television Viewing Habits," for her sixth-grade students. She uses it during the first week of school to engage her students' interest in mathematics, help to develop a sense of confidence in their mathematical power, and show them how useful and important mathematics can be in their everyday lives.

## A Science Unit at Yellowstone National Park

John Graves is a middle school teacher at Montforton School, in Bozeman, Montana. Living near Yellowstone National Park gives him the opportunity to make geology and earth science come alive for his students. Each year, John plans a 3-day outdoor education experience as the culmination of his unit on geologic history. Before going to Yellowstone, he provides his students with many hands-on experiences in the classroom that will get them thinking like scientists. They examine rock specimens and test for geologically distinguishing features. They simulate the examination of rock layers using three-dimensional cut-and-fold papers colored differently for different layers.

Then, when they arrive at the national park, they are ready to think and act like scientists. They have a different focus on each of their 3 days in the park. On day 1, they visit Mammoth Hot Springs to learn about geothermal phenomena. On day 2, they take a 4-mile hike to Specimen Ridge, where they discover petrified trees still standing where they grew eons ago. John asks students to observe and take field notes. The students list, describe, and draw what they can see from Specimen Ridge. By the time they leave the ridge, their notebooks contain information about kettle lakes, U-shaped valleys, lateral moraines, glacial erratics, and other geologic features of the region. (For more on the Yellowstone petrified trees, go to: *http://www.grisda.org/origins/24002.htm*).

Day 3 finds John and his students climbing Bunsen Peak, the core of an old volcanic mountain. From the top of this mountain, they can see the effects of ancient glaciers and modern erosion on the land below them.

John developed this unit of study several years ago, but now, in the era of state and national standards, he is happy to find that his goals are very much in synch with these guidelines. The National Science Education Content Standard D states that as a result of their activities in grades five through eight, all students should develop an understanding of the structure of the Earth system and the history of the Earth.

## Description

This unit functions both as a personal exploration of how students use their free time and as a mathematics investigation. Students keep a log of all the time they spend watching TV every day for a week. With parental permission, students may also log the TV viewing habits of their parents. After a week of data gathering, students carry out a variety of mathematical calculations and interpret the data they collected.

## Cognitive and Skill Outcome Statements

- Students will be able to collect and record data accurately and efficiently.
- Students will be able to calculate percentages of time spent watching television and compare those with percentages of time spent doing other activities.
- Students will be able to create bar and circle graphs based on the data they collected and the percentages they calculated.
- Individually, students will interpret the data they collected about their own television-viewing habits.
- As a class, students will combine their data with that collected by other members of the class to make interpretations and generalizations regarding TV-viewing habits of their age group.
- Individually, students will write articles describing the conclusions and generalizations they reached from this study.
- In small groups, students will make oral presentations on the findings of their group.

## Affective Outcome Statement

Students will become aware of the amount of time they and their classmates spend watching television and will make value judgments about whether they want to continue spending their time in this way.

## Calendar of Events

I plan this investigation for the first week of school. It gives me insight into the students' incoming work habits and mathematical power.

## First Week of School

*Friday:* Introduce unit and distribute data collection materials. Assign students the task of collecting data, beginning Sunday, on the amount of time they watch television. Because video games are played on a TV screen, my students also decided to count the time spent playing video games. I ask students to be as honest as possible and to keep track to the nearest quarter of an hour.

## Second Week of School

*Monday–Friday:* Data collection continues. Discussions in class focus on data collection problems and techniques.

## Third Week of School

*Monday:* Bar Graphs. Individually, students create bar graphs demonstrating the amount of time they watched TV each day of the preceding week.

**Figure 5.4** A middle school mathematics unit on "Television Viewing Habits."

*Tuesday:* Calculating Percentages and Circle Graphs. Individually, students calculate the amount and percentage of time they spent sleeping, in school, in after-school or weekend activities, and watching television, as well as extra time not spent watching television. They create circle graphs showing these percentages.

*Wednesday–Friday:* Group Data Interpretation. Cooperative groups combine class data in order to answer these questions:

1. Which grade level watches more television? Explain how you came to this conclusion.
2. Which day of the week do people watch the most television? Explain how you came to this conclusion.
3. Who watches more television in general—boys or girls? Does any particular age group watch more television? How did you come to your conclusions?
4. By using data about parent viewing habits, have you discovered any relationship between the television-viewing habits of a parent and the habits of a child?

**Fourth Week of School**

*Monday:* Writing Articles. Individuals are assigned to write an article about their conclusions about the television-viewing habits of fifth and sixth graders. They must answer the questions "Who? What? When? Where? and Why?" in the articles.

*Tuesday–Wednesday:* Oral Presentation Planning. Cooperative groups plan presentations on the findings of their groups. They create visual displays to show the data they collected.

*Thursday:* Oral Presentations. Cooperative groups present their findings to the rest of the class.

*Friday:* Unit Evaluation. Students evaluate their accomplishments in this unit. Individuals participate in a teacher–student conference to discuss the points each student earned in the unit. Cooperative groups discuss the processes they used in their group planning sessions, the visual displays they made, and the effectiveness of their oral presentations.

SOURCE: Pam Knight, Poway School District, Poway, California.

A major goal of science in the middle grades is for students to develop an understanding of Earth and the solar system as a set of closely coupled systems. The idea of systems provides a framework in which students can investigate the four major interacting components of the Earth system—geosphere (crust, mantle, and core), hydrosphere (water), atmosphere (air), and the biosphere (the realm of all living things). In this holistic approach, students investigate the physical, chemical, and biological processes of the planet. Students can investigate the water and rock cycles as introductory examples of geophysical and geochemical cycles. Their study of Earth's history provides some evidence about co-evolution of the planet's main features—the distribution of land and sea, features of the crust, the composition of the atmosphere, global climate, and populations of living organisms in the biosphere.

By plotting the locations of volcanoes and earthquakes, students can see a pattern of geological activity. Earth has an outermost rigid shell called the lithosphere. It is made up of the crust and part of the upper mantle. It is broken into about a dozen rigid plates that move without deforming, except at boundaries where they collide. Those plates range in thickness from a few kilometers to more than 100 kilometers. Ocean floors are the tops of thin oceanic plates that spread outward from midocean rift zones; land surfaces are the tops of thicker, less-dense continental plates.

Closer to home, there are the Montana Standards for Science to consider. John finds his unit to be in close congruence with Montana's educational requirements. Montana Science Content Standard 4 states that students demonstrate knowledge of the composition, structures, processes, and interactions of Earth's systems and other objects in space. John's science program also coincides with the state benchmarks for students to achieve by the end of eighth grade. They should be able to: (1) model and explain the internal structure of the Earth and describe the formation and composition of Earth's external features in terms of the rock cycle and plate tectonics, (2) differentiate between rocks and classify rocks by how they are formed, and (3) explain scientific theories about the origin and evolution of the Earth and solar system by describing how fossils are used as evidence of climatic change over time.

John takes his students to the top of the world to learn about the Earth and its history. He believes that by providing his students with these real-life hands-on experiences, they will learn to care deeply about the Earth and will also learn to think and act like scientists in the classroom. It is after these experiences that the classroom discussions get interesting, and students show much greater interest in reading textbooks, doing research on Earth history online, or even listening to the occasional lecture on the topic. By providing these science explorations, John believes that he gives his students a reason to learn. They want to know more and are motivated to find out as much as they can about the world we live on as a result of their science investigations in class and their class field trip to the national park.

## A Social Studies Unit in U.S. History

Social studies combines several academic disciplines, including geography, history, economics, political science, anthropology, sociology, and psychology. By adding learning experiences in literature and the arts, a teacher can fairly easily create a high-quality multidisciplinary thematic unit. If your goal is also to infuse the unit with multicultural learning experiences, then social studies is a very appropriate subject. Typically, the social studies curriculum is designed as an ever-widening circle of ideas, in keeping with the developmental stages of students. In the early grades, the curriculum centers on the home and the community; the middle grades focus on the states and the United States; concepts related to nations and the world are dealt with in the later grades. At each level, teachers can find many interesting ways to address the issues and contributions of various cultures.

Primary teachers often create units on the community, including maps of the school neighborhood, history of the community, roles of community helpers, economic activities related to stores in the community, and other similar experiences. To make this unit a valid multicultural experience, primary teachers invite family members of the students to participate by sharing their cultural heritage with the rest of the class.

Upper elementary teachers frequently create units on the life experiences and cultural beliefs of the first citizens of North America, the Native Americans. They also bring in the wide variety of contributions made by the people who immigrated from Asia, Europe, Africa, and Central and South America. Upper-grade teachers may offer units comparing nations of the world in terms of culture, geography, politics, economics, and history.

U.S. history is a topic that is taught in elementary, middle, and high schools. It is an example of the spiral curriculum, where students are introduced to a topic in elementary school, revisit it at middle school, and then learn about it again, in greater depth, in high school. As a teacher planning curriculum for a subject such as U.S. history, the trick is finding a way to engage the learners' interest in a subject they think they already know. David Ramert uses controversy to generate interest.

In Chapter 4, David described an overview of how he plans for a year of U.S. history. One of his favorite units of study is the Jacksonian Era, spanning the time from 1828 through 1840. This period of history includes many of the controversies having to do with the changing status of the American Indian in the United States. Because he relishes teaching the controversial issues that he finds throughout history, he enjoys challenging students to examine how President Jackson created policies that dealt with who gets to create Indian policy, and the changing status of the Indian in the burgeoning U.S. growth. Ramert challenges his students to think about the questions that Jackson and other American politicians at the time posed, such as: "Is an Indian a citizen? Is he a person? Does he get to vote? Does he have any of the rights provided by the Constitution?" Some of these questions got decided during Jackson's presidency for better or worse.

David allocates only 5 to 7 days of class time to this important era in our history. His unit plan in Figure 5.5 illustrates one of the most perplexing dilemmas faced by high school history teachers. One academic year is approximately 180 days, and each of the exciting and valuable eras of our history must be brutally condensed to fit within this time limit. In this unit of study, there is no time for a hands-on project, but David does view it as a separate and unique unit of study because it deals with so many overriding issues that are still meaningful to our culture today.

Using a form of authentic performance-based assessment, David informs his students of the essay questions on the first day of the unit. On the final day, they write their essay responses to these questions. There are no surprises. At the beginning of the year, students tend to ask, "Are these really going to be the questions on the test?" He does this in order to relieve anxiety and worry about what they are expected to learn. He tells them what he expects them to learn on the first day and gives them an opportunity to demonstrate it on the final day. He may vary the essay questions to fit the academic levels of different classes. Advanced placement classes will be offered more complex questions.

To determine grades in his course, David assigns a point value to each unit of study and combines these points to assign a letter grade at the end of each reporting period. Every assignment has a point value based on its importance as an assignment. A quiz might be worth 10 points, while a test might be worth 50 points. David enters each student's numerical score in his gradebook as a ratio made up of the student's score above the possible score, for example, 9/10 or 45/50. These ratios can then be converted to percentages—for example, 90%—which are then translated into letter grades. Examples of this type of grading system are found in Chapter 11 in the section called "Computation of Grades."

### Description

We deal with the questions, "Was Jackson a curse or a blessing?" "Was he good for this country or bad?" The Jacksonians viewed themselves as guardians of the constitution, of individual rights and promoters of equality. Is that view of themselves accurate? It illustrates some of the enduring contradictions of our country since its inception. It was the era of the common man, and the rise of the common man, but that term applied only to white male property owners. It was known as an era of Jacksonian Democracy, even though it didn't apply to women, Blacks, or Indians.

### Outcomes

I start with questions such as those in the description above. My outcomes grow from these questions. Students will write answers to these questions at the end of the unit to show what they have learned and to demonstrate that they are able to view the Jacksonian era and others in U.S. history in all its controveries.

> *Question 1:* Was Jackson a curse or a blessing in our country?
>
> *Question 2:* Was he defender of the Constitution in the area of individual liberty and human rights and equality? Was that view of themselves valid?

### Time Line

### Day One

I pose my two basic questions (see above) as dramatically as I can and back them up by writing them on the blackboard. As I write, I tell the students that these are the essay questions that they will have to deal with at the end of the unit. The questions remain there in writing for all of us to see so that we all stay focused. I also provide a handout that lists the questions, the subject matter outline, and the list of readings.

For the remainder of the class period, I introduce Andrew Jackson. Who was he? Where did he come from? Why did he cough and spit pus and blood every day?

### Day Two

What was the vocabulary of the Jackson era? What was Jacksonian democracy? Who was the common man at that time? What was the frontier aristrocracy? How was it similar to the Marxian struggle between the classes?

### Day Three

What was Andrew Jackson's Indian policy? What were the contradictions of that policy? What was the role of the Supreme Court in deciding the status of Indians? What was the "trail of tears"? What did it mean for the future of the Indian? How did this era determine the present-day status of the Indian in the United States? Why can Indians now have gambling casinos on their reservations? Isn't it interesting that the Indians have turned the tables on the white man? Now, they get the White man drunk and take their money at their gambling casinos.

**Figure 5.5** A high school history unit on "Jacksonian Democracy."

### Day Four

What were the major political issues of the Jackson Era? Why did he kill the bank of the United States? How much of his presidency was vindictive because of his electoral loss in 1824? What was universal manhood suffrage? Who was actually eligible to vote at the end of his term? How did his economic policies help to create the panic of 1837? What were the petticoat wars? How much of his presidency was purely personal? Why did his view of women and the rights of women cause his vice president to resign?

### Day Five

What was the issue known as states rights? What was the struggle that divided the federal government and the states? What court cases illustrated these state rights? Is nullification of federal law a valid concept? Is it possible or legal for a state to secede?

### Day Six

What is the legacy of Andrew Jackson? We review our questions for essays by brainstorming answers to the controversial questions. (See David's Lesson Plan in Chapter 6.)

### Day Seven (Evaluation) Students Write Essays.

I pose the basic questions and students choose one to write. Essays are worth 50 points toward a final grade in the course and are evaluated on the following criteria:

There must be a thesis statement that takes a stand on the controversial question posed. (10 pts)

It had better be interesting and keep me awake. (10 pts)

Quote from primary sources or the text to support your statements. (10 pts)

Use the vocabulary of the era of study correctly and appropriately. (10 pts)

You must argue your controversial issue using evidence and examples from the era and the people and events we studied. (10 pts)

SOURCE: David Ramert, U.S. history teacher, Francis Parker Upper School, San Diego, California.

## Two Science Teachers Collaborate to Create a High School Science Unit

Chris Chiaverina and Jim Hicks are high school science teachers who believe that the world is a richer and more interesting place when people are aware of the principles of physics that operate around us. They plan their physics units to replace students' misconceptions about science as a dull and abstruse body of knowledge, with a new view that science consists of exciting opportunities to satisfy their curiosity about how things work.

Working as colleagues, Jim and Chris have created a number of science units that begin with concrete explorations that encourage students to explore and investigate science phenomena. When they begin to create a new unit, they think about spectacular opening demonstrations to pique the students' interest in the topic. Jim and Chris report that they work very hard to plan and teach science units that are full of active exploration, real-life applications, and opportunities for students to experience the wonders of science. The say the payoffs for them and their students are worth the effort. When a student looks at Jim with a light in her eyes and says, "Hey, that's neat!" he knows that all the work that went into the lesson was well spent. Their unit on wave phenomena is shown in Figure 5.6.

The curriculum of any subject or of a combination of subjects may be subdivided into thematic units of study that are often highly motivating to students and a source of pride for the teachers who create them. Teacher-crafted curriculum units are often very creative and original products. For teachers who choose to create them rather than rely on textbook lessons and content, units are a way of individualizing the curriculum to capitalize on the interests and talents of the teacher and the students.

We hope these unit plans will inspire you to think outside the box when you have your own classroom and are able to plan curriculum. The state standards you must meet are easily incorporated into highly creative and motivating thematic units. Your students will experience the thrill of researching and investigating topics of high interest, and you will experience the pride and success that comes when the whole class is engaged in active learning for a real-life purpose.

---

### Description

In this unit about wave phenomena, we study both sound and light waves. As with all our units, we begin with dramatic and puzzling demonstrations by the teacher to generate students' interest in the topic. Students then explore waves in a qualitative laboratory experience in order to observe them in action. This enables students to construct their own meaning and understanding of the properties of waves. During class discussions, we probe students' preconceived ideas about the phenomena and help them unlearn their preconceptions in order to construct more accurate understandings. Only after students have experienced the phenomena in action do we introduce mathematical relationships. At this point, students do a quantitative laboratory experiment in which they learn to express their new understandings in a formula or mathematical expression.

### Outcome Statements

### Cognitive Outcomes

- Students will investigate wave phenomena and identify key features of light and sound waves.

- Students will distinguish between energy transfer by waves and particles.

### Skill and Process Outcomes

- Through kinesthetic learning experiences, students will derive the relationship among wave speed, wave length, and frequency.

- Students will investigate constructive and destructive interference of waves and apply the principle of superposition.

- Students will demonstrate how sound is produced and transmitted.

**Figure 5.6** A high school physics unit on "Wave Phenomena."

## Affective Outcome

Students unlearn their preconceived notions of physical phenomena and replace them with scientifically accurate observations and understandings.

## Time Line and Calendar of Events

### Slinkies® and Human Slinkies

Students create and observe waves in the hallways using Slinkies. They explore their views, preconceptions, and observations of wave phenomena and examine different types of waves. Mathematical relationships are derived from students' observations. Students learn to communicate what they have observed about the speed of waves, what happens when waves meet and interfere with each other, and other basic properties of waves using mathematical expressions.

### Sound Waves

We explore what happens when sound waves meet and interfere with each other. We discuss acoustics and how sound is produced and perceived. We look at the sources of sound, including musical instruments, and how sound is recorded and reproduced. We make Edison record players so that students can experience the reproduction of sound.

### Light and Its Properties

Using mirrors and lenses, students look at how light interacts with matter. As a culminating activity, we go to the University of Wisconsin, where the students attend college classes and create their own holograms. They keep a journal of their observations on this trip.

### Sound and Light Show

In the school auditorium, we use loudspeakers connected to a signal generator. Students line up in the regions in the auditorium that have no sound because of wave interference. We also explore how the walls act as acoustical mirrors. Using primary colors, we produce all the other colors of the spectrum by mixing light.

### Evaluation Plan

Students complete both quantitative and qualitative laboratory explorations, worksheets, and paper and pencil tests. They take notes and write reports on holograms and the sound and light show. They create acoustical and optical devices.

*Tests and quizzes:*    50 percent

*Laboratory experiments:*    25 percent

*Homework:*    20 percent

*Special projects:*    5 percent

SOURCE: Chris Chiaverina, New Trier High School, Winnetka, Illinois, and Jim Hicks, Barrington High School, Barrington, Illinois.

## REFLECTIVE ACTION EXPERIENCES FOR YOUR PROFESSIONAL PORTFOLIO

## Write a Unit Plan Entitled "Writing: Thinking Through the Process"

The NBPTS Middle Grades/Generalist credential requires each candidate to demonstrate their mastery of teaching in three subject areas: writing, social studies, and the integration of mathematics and science. For this portfolio experience, we suggest you write a unit plan on writing for the grade level or subject matter of your choice. The title we have suggested, "Writing: Thinking Through the Process," is the same one that candidates for the NBPTS Middle Grades/Generalist credential must submit. If you are working on an Early Adolescence/Generalist credential or an Adolescence through Young Adult Subject-Specific credential (art, English/language arts, science, mathematics, or social studies), write a unit plan that incorporates the writing process in subject-related study.

Think about this unit plan as a 3-to-4 week learning experience. Begin by examining the reading/language arts standards for your state that apply to the writing process.

Next, visit a class and talk with the teacher about unit plans for teaching writing. Ask to see samples of unit plans used in the class. If possible, ask to observe the students at work on writing assignments. Then, ask to examine the student responses or writing projects.

Sketch out an initial plan for the 3-to 4-week unit. What will you do the first week? What will be the focus of weeks 2, 3, and 4? How will you conclude the unit? How will you assess the students' mastery of the writing process?

Show your initial plan to the classroom teacher or to other trusted colleagues. Brainstorm and share ideas for the unit topic. Ask your colleague to predict possible roadblocks or other sources of difficulty standing in the way of implementing your unit plan successfully. Ask for advice about the types of materials you need to gather or create. Ask for suggestions about teaching strategies and assessment strategies that are appropriate for your unit.

Begin to rewrite your unit plan. This time, ask yourself, "What are the *cognitive, affective*, and *psychomotor* outcomes that are possible for my students in this unit?" Sketch out a planning web as you brainstorm learning experiences that will allow your students to achieve these outcomes. What are the likely consequences of each step of your plan? Which outcomes will be easy to achieve and which will be difficult? Use a calendar to plan the sequence of learning events for your unit. Create a time line of events for your students and a complementary one for yourself so that your teaching plans coincide with the events in the unit.

Now begin to plan a way to assess the outcomes for your unit. What types of products or tests will you use to evaluate the degree to which your students achieve success on each of the outcomes you have for the unit? Show your assessment plan to a colleague, and get feedback on making this important part of your unit a meaningful and accurate representation of what students have learned.

Write the final version of your unit to include in your professional portfolio. Give your writing unit an interesting, motivating title. Make a folder for the paper copy of your unit plan so that you can file it for safekeeping. Keep another copy on your computer.

Reflect on the curriculum planning process you used in this assignment to consider how you would improve on the process in the future. Can you envision your students accomplishing these outcomes, learning the skills, and mastering the process of thinking through the writing process?

# References

Adams, D. (1999) *Literacy today: New standards across the curriculum*. New York: Garland.

California Department of Education (2001). *History-social science framework*. Sacramento, CA: California Department of Education.

Illinois Learning Standards (2004). Retrieved Dec, 2004 from *http://www.isbe.state.il.us/ils/english/eng1.html*

Levitin, S. (1996). *Nine for California*. New York: Orchard Books.

Levitin, S. (1998). *Boom town*. New York: Orchard Books.

Levitin, S. (1999). *Taking charge*. New York: Orchard Books.

Roberts, P., & Kellough, R. (2000). *A guide for developing interdisciplinary thematic units* (2nd ed.). Columbus, OH: Merrill.

Tyler, R. (1949). *Basic principles of curriculum and instruction*. Chicago: University of Chicago Press.

Wiggins, J., & McTighe, G. (1999). *Understanding by design handbook*. Alexandria, VA: Association of Supervision and Curriculum Development.

# Lesson Planning and Sequencing

**PRAXIS**

Chapter 6 prepares you for PRAXIS™ Exam Section 2b: Instruction and Assessment.

When you think of *lesson plans*, what comes to mind? Perhaps you think of a piece of paper containing very detailed directions that describe how to teach something to a class of students. Or perhaps you envision a weekly plan book with very brief notations that serve to remind experienced teachers what they have planned to accomplish each period in the school day.

Beginning teachers often want to find examples of excellent lesson plans so they can see how other, more experienced, teachers have organized their teaching. How do they write meaningful learning objectives? How do they ever think of every detailed instruction? How do they write out a way to assess what students have gained from the lesson? It can seem like a mystery to many new teachers.

This chapter is designed to further demystify the process of writing your first lesson plans. We will describe ways to use the reflective action processes to envision and then describe on paper the goals and objectives you want to achieve, the materials you will need to gather, the step-by-step procedures you will use to teach your lesson, and the assessment devices you will employ to measure what your students have achieved.

## WRITING OBJECTIVES TO FIT GOALS AND OUTCOME STATEMENTS

As you recall from Chapter 5, *goals* are the broad, long-term descriptions of how you want your students to grow and develop; *outcome statements* refer to what you want students to know, understand, and be able to do during a given time. As you try to visualize your students accomplishing these goals and outcomes, it is useful to envision a sequence of events that will lead to successful accomplishment of the goal. Teachers often find it useful to write down these sequential steps as a series of objectives that work together to accomplish the goal or outcome. Reflective teachers rarely plan a lesson in isolation. Rather, they consider each lesson in relation to what students already know as well as what they hope students will be able to do at a later time. This big-picture thinking characterizes reflective teachers, who realize that larger goals guide the selection of small daily tasks.

### Educational Objectives

Educational objectives are short-term, specific descriptions of what teachers are expected to teach and/or what students are expected to learn. As described by Bloom and colleagues in the *Taxonomy of Educational Objectives* (1956), they are intended to be used as an organizational framework for selecting and sequencing learning experiences. Embedded in any large goal (such as teaching students to read) are hundreds of possible specific objectives. One teacher may have an objective of teaching students how to decode an unfamiliar word using phonics and another objective of teaching students how to decode an unfamiliar word using context clues. Another teacher may select and emphasize the objectives of decoding unfamiliar words by using syllabification or linguistic patterns in order to meet the same overall goal.

Objectives are also used to describe the *sequence of learning events* a teacher feels will help students achieve a given outcome. They also allow teachers to assess and chart group or individual progress. Teachers can ascertain students' needs more accurately if they have established a guideline of normal progress with which to compare each student's achievement.

Teachers who prefer to be very specific about their lesson planning choose to write *behavioral objectives.* These include: (1) the conditions under which the learning will take place; (2) the action or behavior that will provide evidence of the learning; and (3) the criteria for success (how well a task must be completed or how often the behavior will occur). For example, a behavioral objective could be written as follows:

> After building words using initial consonants added to the word "at," students will insert the correct "at" words in 8 out of 10 cloze sentences.

This statement includes a description of the *conditions for learning (After building words using initial consonants added to the word 'at'),* the *behavior (students will insert the correct 'at' words),* and the *criterion for success (in 8 out of 10 cloze sentences).*

Behavioral objectives can have a very positive effect on teaching effectiveness; teachers who use them become better organized and more efficient in teaching and in measuring the growth of students' basic skills. When following a planned sequence of behavioral objectives, the teacher knows what to do and how to judge students' success. This system of planning also allows the teacher to better explain to students exactly what is expected of them and how to succeed.

As with any educational practice, however, there are positive and negative aspects to planning this way. Critics of behavioral objectives believe that when curriculum planning is reduced to rigid behavioral prescriptions, much of what is important to teaching and learning can be overlooked or lost. Thus, reflective teachers use behavioral objectives in their lesson planning for those learning events and activities that warrant them and rely on other less rigid objectives when appropriate.

As an alternative form for learning that cannot be predicted and calibrated, Eisner (1985) suggests the *problem-solving objective:*

> In a problem-solving objective, students are given a problem to solve—say, to find out how deterrents to smoking might be made more effective, how to design a paper structure that will hold two bricks 16 inches above a table, or how the variety and quality of the food served in the cafeteria could be increased within the existing budget. In each of these examples, the problem is posed and the criteria necessary to resolve the problem are clear. But the forms of its solution are virtually infinite. (pp. 117–118)

Eisner points out that behavioral objectives have "both the form and the content defined in advance. There is, after all, only one way to spell aardvark." The teacher using behavioral objectives is successful if all the students display the identical behavior at the end of the instructional period. "This is not the case with problem-solving objectives. The solutions individual students or groups of students reach may be just as much a surprise for the teacher as they are for the students who created them" (p. 119).

As an example, a problem-solving objective might be written:

> Following a brief introduction on electric circuitry, students are given a battery, a light bulb, and a piece of copper wire. The student will work alone or with a partner to figure out how to make the bulb light.

This objective describes the conditions and the problem that is to be solved, but does not specify the actual behaviors the student is to use. The criterion for success is straightforward but is not quantifiable, and in fact, some of the most important results of this experience are only implied. The teacher's primary aim is to cause the student to experiment, hypothesize, and test methods of solving the problem. This cannot be quantified and reported as a percentage. Problem-solving objectives, then, are appropriate when teachers are planning learning events that allow and encourage students to think, make decisions, and create solutions. For that reason they are frequently employed when teachers plan lessons that are designed to develop critical, creative thinking. They are especially valuable when teachers are planning learning events at the higher levels of Bloom's taxonomy (1956).

## Bloom's Taxonomy

**PRAXIS**

Important theorists in education are tested in PRAXIS™ Exam Section 1a: Students as Learners.

Many teachers use Bloom's *Taxonomy of Educational Objectives* (1956) as the basis for organizing instructional objectives into coherent, connected learning experiences. The term *Bloom's taxonomy* (as commonly used by teachers) refers to the six levels of the cognitive domain described here. Any curriculum project, such as a yearlong plan, a unit, or a lesson plan can be enriched by the conscious planning of learning events at all six levels of the taxonomy:

Higher level objectives:      Level 6: Evaluation
                              Level 5: Synthesis
                              Level 4: Analysis
                              Level 3: Application

Lower level objectives:       Level 2: Comprehension
                              Level 1: Knowledge

*Knowledge-level* objectives can be planned to ensure that students have a knowledge base of facts, concepts, and other important data on any topic or subject. *Comprehension-level* objectives cause students to clarify and articulate the main idea of what they are learning. Behavioral objectives are very useful and appropriate at the knowledge and comprehension levels.

At the *application level*, problem-solving objectives or expressive outcomes can be written that ask students to apply what they have learned to other cases or to their own lives, thereby causing them to transfer what they have learned in the classroom to other arenas. *Analysis-level* objectives and outcomes call on students to look for motives, assumptions, and relationships such as cause and effect, differences and similarities, hypotheses, and conclusions. When analysis outcomes are planned, the students are likely to be engaged in critical thinking about the subject matter. Because the *synthesis level* implies an original response, expressive outcomes are very appropriate. They offer students opportunities to use creative thinking as they combine elements in new ways, plan original experiments, and create original solutions to problems. At the *evaluation level*, students engage again in critical thinking as they make judgments using internal or external criteria and evidence. For these levels, problem-solving objectives or expressive outcomes are likely to be the most appropriate planning devices.

For example, in planning a series of learning events on metric measurement, the teacher may formulate the following objectives and outcome statements:

**Knowledge-level behavioral objective:** When given a meter stick, students will point to the length of a meter, a decimeter, and a centimeter with no errors.

**Comprehension-level behavioral objective:** When asked to state a purpose or use for each of the following units of measure, the student will write a short response for meter, centimeter, liter, milliliter, gram, and kilogram, with no more than one error.

**Application-level problem-solving objective:** Using a unit of measure of their choice, students will measure the length and width of the classroom and compute the area.

**Analysis-level problem-solving objective:** Students will create a chart showing five logical uses or purposes for each measuring unit in the metric family.

**Synthesis-level expressive outcome:** A group of four students will hide a "treasure" on the playground and create a set of instructions using metric measures that will enable another group to locate the treasure.

**Evaluation-level expressive outcome:** Students will debate their preference for metric or nonmetric measurement as a standard form of measurement.

When we review the six objectives and outcomes for metric measurement, we see clearly that the first two differ from the others in that they specify exactly what students will do or write to get a correct answer. In addition, the criteria for success are not ambiguous. These two qualities are useful to ensure successful teaching and learning at the knowledge and comprehension levels. After successfully completing these first two objectives, students will have developed a knowledge base for metric measurement that they will need to do the higher-level activities. In the problem-solving objectives, students are given greater discretion in determining the methods they use and the form of their final product. In the expressive outcome statements, discretionary power is necessary if students are to be empowered to think critically and creatively to solve problems for themselves.

Although the taxonomy was originally envisioned as a hierarchy, and although it was believed that students should be introduced to a topic beginning with level 1 and working upward through level 6, most educators have found that the objectives and learning experiences can be successfully taught in any order. For example, a teacher may introduce the topic of nutrition and health by asking students to discuss their opinions or attitudes about smoking (an evaluation-level objective). The teacher may then provide the students with knowledge-level data about the contents of tobacco smoke and work back up to the evaluation level. When students are asked their opinions again, at the end of the lesson, their judgments are likely to be stronger and better informed.

As in the example about smoking and health, it is often desirable to begin with objectives that call on students to do, think, find, question, or create something and thereby instill in them a desire to know more about the topic. Knowledge- and comprehension-level objectives can then be designed to provide the students with the facts, data, and main concepts they need to know to further apply, analyze, synthesize, and evaluate the ideas that interest them. Figure 6.1 shows a planning device offering teachers ideas for learning events that correspond to each level of the taxonomy.

Learning objectives can be planned at all levels of Bloom's taxonomy. Behavioral objectives are best suited for knowledge and comprehension levels; problem-solving and expressive objectives are best suited for application, analysis, synthesis, and evaluation levels.

| **Examples of Objectives** | **Appropriate Action Verbs** |
|---|---|
| **Knowledge Level** | **Knowledge Level** |
| Can recognize and recall specific terms, facts, and symbols. | Find, locate, identify, list, recite, memorize, recognize, name, repeat, point to, match, pick, choose, state, select, record, spell, say, show, circle, underline. |
| **Comprehension Level** | **Comprehension Level** |
| Can understand the main idea of material heard, viewed, or read. Is able to interpret or summarize the ideas in his or her own words. | Explain, define, translate, relate, demonstrate, calculate, discuss, express in own words, write, review, report, paraphrase, summarize. |
| **Application Level** | **Application Level** |
| Is able to apply an abstract idea in a concrete situation, to solve a problem or relate it to prior experiences. | Change, adapt, employ, use, make, construct, demonstrate, compute, calculate, illustrate, modify, prepare, put into action, solve, do. |
| **Analysis Level** | **Analysis Level** |
| Can break down a concept or idea into its constituent parts. Is able to identify relationships among elements, cause and effect, similarities and differences. | Classify, distinguish, categorize, deduce, dissect, examine, compare, contrast, divide, catalog, inventory, question, outline, chart, survey. |
| **Synthesis Level** | **Synthesis Level** |
| Is able to put together elements in new and original ways. Creates patterns or structures that were not there before. | Combine, create, develop, design, construct, build, arrange, assemble, collect, concoct, connect, devise, hypothesize, invent, imagine, plan, generate, revise, organize, produce. |
| **Evaluation Level** | **Evaluation Level** |
| Makes informed judgments about the value of ideas or materials. Uses standards and criteria to support opinions and views. | Appraise, critique, consider, decide, judge, editorialize, give opinion, grade, rank, prioritize, value. |

**Figure 6.1** Curriculum planning using Bloom's taxonomy.

SOURCE: From Benjamin S. Bloom, et al., *Taxonomy of Educational Objectives.* Published by Allyn and Bacon, Boston, MA. Copyright © 1984 by Pearson Education. Reprinted by permission of the publisher.

# PLANNING LESSONS FOR ACTIVE LEARNING

Teachers can use their reflective actions to ensure a high quality learning experience for their students. They begin by using withitness when they write the first draft of their lesson plan. Reflective teachers try to mentally picture what a lesson will look like in real life. They try to anticipate what their students need, what they can do easily, and where they will need the most guidance and positive feedback.

Reflective teachers recognize that students are more motivated to learn when they understand why this learning experience is important. For this reason, they often explain the purpose of each lesson and tell students what they will be able to do after they master the skill or concept in the lesson. On other occasions, teachers who enjoy using an inquiry or discovery approach to learning may present students with challenging or puzzling conundrums that may cause students to experience a state of "disequilibrium," and cause them to work feverishly to discover the answer to the puzzle or solve the dilemma. A talented teacher may be able to do both by describing the objectives, and causing students to wonder how something works and how they can solve the problem. It is important, in either case, for you to use words and examples that are easily understood by the students at your grade level. For example, during a science lesson, a reflective teacher might say:

> We are doing this experiment today to help you see for yourselves how solids can literally disappear in a liquid. The procedures we are going to use are the same type of procedures that real scientists use when they want to discover something new about the laws of science and the physical nature of a substance.

> I want you to carefully observe what happens when I pour this white powder into a glass of water. Where has the powder gone? Why does the water turn blue? What could possibly be making this substance change so dramatically and so quickly?

After this introduction, students are likely to be eager to begin. They want to get on with the experiment and see for themselves what happens. They enjoy acting as scientists do during the process.

To make learning tasks even more inviting, reflective teachers know that it is very important to model the physical behaviors or mental processes needed to do the work. Kindergarten teachers model how to write a capital letter *A*. Elementary teachers demonstrate how to divide a pizza into equal fractions. Middle school teachers show students how to place their hands on the keyboard of the computer. High school teachers do a sample algebra problem on the chalkboard. After modeling, reflective teachers take just as active a role on the sidelines, encouraging and guiding students as they begin the active process of finding out how things work.

Another role that the most effective teachers take while teaching a new skill is to model internal behaviors (such as problem solving) by thinking aloud while they model the first example for their students. By telling the students orally what they are thinking when they work on a problem, teachers provide real-life examples of how learning occurs. Thinking aloud is particularly helpful when asking students to comprehend an unfamiliar skill or a difficult concept. At all stages of lesson planning and presentation, reflective teachers carefully observe and interact with their students—learning what students already know and where they need extra help. This observation and assessment is critical to the success of any given lesson, as well as to the planning and sequencing of future lessons. It also helps to think again about this three-step process when things happen during a lesson that surprise you or upset your plans.

## Planning Assessments That Fit Your Lesson's Objectives

**PRAXIS**

Assessment strategies are tested in PRAXIS™ Exam Section 2c: Instruction and Assessment.

How does a teacher measure success? Chapter 11 covers in detail the topic of assessing students' needs and accomplishments, with a focus on creating authentic assessment systems that describe students' progress over time. In designing lesson plans, however, it is useful to consider some options for assessing students' accomplishments on a single lesson.

Traditionally, the methods used to assess individual achievement are either written or oral quizzes, tests, and essays. When K–12 teachers want to determine whether the class as a whole has understood what was taught in a lesson, they frequently use oral responses to questions that usually begin with "Who can tell me?" These are useful and efficient ways to assess student achievement at the knowledge and comprehension levels of Bloom's taxonomy, but reflective teachers are seldom satisfied with these measures alone. They seek out other methods that are less frequently used but more appropriate in evaluating learning at the higher levels.

*Knowledge-level* objectives are tested by determining if the student can remember or recognize accurate statements or facts. Multiple-choice and matching tests are the most frequently used measuring devices.

*Comprehension-level* objectives are often tested by asking students to define terms in their own words. (Only knowledge would be tested if the students were asked to write a definition from memory.) Another frequently used testing device is a question requiring a short-answer response, either oral or written, showing that the student understands the main idea. Essays that ask students to summarize or interpret are also appropriate. Multiple-choice tests are also used as a test of comprehension, but the questions call on the students to do more than recall a fact from memory; they ask students to read a selection and choose the best response from among several choices.

At the *application level*, students are usually asked to apply what was learned in a classroom to a new situation. For that reason, application-level objectives are usually assessed by presenting an unfamiliar problem that requires the student to transfer what has been learned to the unfamiliar situation. Essays in which the students describe what they would do to solve an unfamiliar problem can be used. In classrooms where students are encouraged to use manipulative materials and experiment with methods to solve problems, teachers assess the processes used by the student and the end product such as a hand-drawn or computer-generated design of a new device, a written plan for solving a problem, or a model of a new product. These products may or may not be graded, depending on the teacher's need to quantify or qualify students' success.

*Analysis-level* objectives may also require that the teacher present unfamiliar material and ask the student to analyze it according to some specified criteria. In these situations, students may be asked to analyze various elements, relationships, or organizational principles, such as the way in which elements are categorized, differences and similarities, cause and effect, logical conclusions, or relevant and irrelevant data.

Again, essays may be used to assess analytical behavior, but the essays must do more than tell the main idea (comprehension) and describe how the student would apply previously learned knowledge. Analytical essays must clarify relationships, compare and contrast, show cause and effect, and provide evidence for conclusions. Other student products that are appropriate for assessing analysis are time lines; charts that compare, contrast, or categorize data; and a variety of graphs that show relationships.

The types of student products that demonstrate *synthesis* are infinitely variable. Written work such as creative essays, stories, poems, plays, books, and articles are certainly appropriate for assessing language-arts objectives. Performances are just as useful, including original speeches, drama, poems, and musical compositions. Student-created products may include original plans, blueprints, artwork, computer programs, and models of proposed inventions. Student work may be collected in portfolios to demonstrate growth and achievement in a subject area.

Evaluating the relative success of synthesis products is very difficult. No objective criteria may exist for judging the value or worth of a student's original product. When student products are entered in a contest or submitted for publication, outside judges with expertise in the subject area provide feedback and may even make judgments that the classroom teacher cannot make. Many K–12 teachers simply record whether a finished product was turned in by the student rather than attempt to evaluate or grade it.

*Evaluation-level* objectives call upon students to make a judgment. To test a student's ability to make a judgment, the teacher must provide all of the needed data, perhaps in the form of charts or graphs, and ask the student to draw certain conclusions from these data.

Another form of evaluation is to ask students to state their opinions on a work of art or to judge the validity of a political theory, offering evidence to support their opinions. The types of products that students create at this level are critical essays, discussions, speeches, letters to the editor, debates, drama, videotapes, and other forms that allow them to express their points of view.

Like synthesis outcomes, evaluation outcomes and objectives are difficult to grade. A teacher who offers students an opportunity to express their own views usually places high value on independent thinking and freedom of expression. Therefore, the teacher cannot grade a student response as right or wrong. The teacher, however, can assess whether the student has used accurate, sufficient, and appropriate criteria in defending a personal opinion. Student work that has cited inaccurate, insufficient, or inappropriate evidence should probably be returned to the student with suggestions for revision.

In summary, evaluation of student accomplishment should be directly linked to the lesson's objectives. To assess basic knowledge and skills, behavioral objectives are useful because they state exactly what the student will be able to do and specify the criteria for success. For higher-level objectives, problem-solving objectives may be less precise but still should describe the type of student behavior or product expected and give some general criteria for success.

When teachers plan by writing clear behavioral, problem-solving, and expressive objectives for their lessons, they are, in effect, clarifying their expectations regarding what students will gain from the lesson and their criteria for success. The evaluation section of a lesson plan is then usually a restatement of the criteria expressed in the objectives. You will see an example of this in the sample lesson plans in this chapter.

## Predicting Possible Outcomes of Your Lesson Plans

Imagine that you have written your first lesson plan and decide to show it to some experienced teachers and ask them what they think about it. Congratulations! You are using this very important reflective action of inviting feedback. Now, you hope the veteran teachers will read your plan and look up with huge smiles to tell you that you have done a great job.

What is more likely is that one of the teachers will begin the discussion with, "What if . . . ?" Another will say, "Have you thought about. . . ?" One might even laugh and tell a story about the "perfect lesson plan" that turned into a disaster in the classroom. When Judy Eby was a student teacher at the University of Illinois in Urbana, Illinois, she planned just such a perfect lesson. Within a unit on animal behavior, she planned a series of lessons in which students were allowed to conduct experiments on live animals. Following her written lesson plan, she asked students to bring in small animal cages from home to house the animals. The students brought in leftover gerbil cages, bird cages, and other small containers. On the first day of the new unit, Judy went to the university and got one white mouse per student and put the mice into the students' cages. The mice were smaller and more agile than expected, however, and they quickly squeezed out of the cages and began running around the classroom. Chaos ensued. She asked the students to help catch the mice and put them all into a glass-walled aquarium. Although planned objectives were not met that day, there were certainly many opportunities for problem solving and unintended outcomes.

Judy and her master teacher spent the afternoon rethinking the entire lesson plan without separate cages. They decided to identify individual mice by using different colors and patterns of ink dots so that students could tell their mice apart. Having done this, they went home for the night. But, when they returned the next morning, the mice had disrupted the plan again. Baby mice had been born during the night and some of the adult mice were dead or wounded by attacks from their own species. The third revision of this lesson plan called for mealworms instead of mice to be used as the experimental animals.

Most veteran teachers have experienced this type of scenario more than once. Even the best plans can go wrong. Indeed, part of the nervousness many teachers feel before teaching a lesson comes from this very realization. It is hard to prepare for the unexpected!

Even when the basic lesson plan runs smoothly, it is almost a given that in any lesson, some students will require different experiences or explanations to understand the new concept or skill being taught. Some teachers can think on their feet and address student confusion on the spot, but this can be a challenge for a new teacher. We suggest that you consistently plan a second way of introducing or extending any given concept just in case you need it. We think you will often be glad you did. Reflective teachers are aware that students learn differently and that some may need a second strategy to achieve the lesson objective.

As we observe new teachers presenting lessons, one thing we have noticed is that discipline and management problems rarely occur when the lesson content is focused slightly above students' current knowledge base. This is probably due to the fact that students feel challenged but not overwhelmed by the experience, so they are engaged in learning and feel happy to cooperate. In contrast, problems seem to arise when a teacher prepares a lesson that covers content the students already know. They act restless and may become disruptive when they feel that the teacher is babying them or talking down to them. What should you do when you arrive in a setting, materials in hand, and find out the students have already mastered the content you have planned to teach?

Should you press bravely on, working your way through the lesson because it is what you worked so hard to prepare? To do so is to ignore the learning needs of your students. We have often seen this, and believe that the biggest reason for this choice is a simple one—the teacher has nothing else prepared, and has not thought through the next steps in the learning sequence.

## Varying Objectives for Students with Special Needs

Often teachers plan their lessons with a set of objectives for the students in their class whose knowledge and skills are at grade level. The term *at grade level* means the average or typical level of understanding or skill that most students are able to achieve at that age and in that grade. As teachers gain experience teaching at a grade level, they are able to describe what the typical learner at that grade level can accomplish. Because most students in the class will have skills and knowledge near the average, it makes sense for teachers to plan lessons with difficulty levels conforming to that average.

**PRAXIS**
Approaches for teaching students with special needs and/or varying learning styles are tested in PRAXIS™ Exam Section 1b: Students as Learners.

Reflective teachers realize that in any classroom, there is likely to be a wide range of student achievement and experience. There are bound to be students who have already learned and mastered the concepts being taught. Many kindergarten students come to school knowing the entire alphabet and how to count to 100. Some sixth-grade students could teach teachers a thing or two about their computer usage. Planning for ways to extend the knowledge of these students is just as important to the success of your lesson as is planning for ways to help students who do not understand the concept right away. When you enter a classroom with a plan for extending a lesson's concepts and content, you will feel more confident and you will enhance the learning experiences of more of your students.

There are also likely to be students who appear to be completely bewildered during a lesson. Others give no readable cues for you to tell whether they understand or do not understand the lesson concepts. Some students may sit quietly but refuse to try the learning task you have assigned to them. Reflective teachers accept that there are many reasons students may fail to respond in the ways we hope and plan for. For example, a student may be hungry, tired, or preoccupied with a concern (outside or inside of school) that is more compelling than this lesson (remember Maslow's hierarchies). Students may doubt their ability to succeed at the task and avoid it in an attempt to save face, or feel that the task is far too easy and therefore not worth the effort to complete. Students may also need more experience with new or unfamiliar vocabulary.

If you consider reasons a student may not respond appropriately to your lesson, you can begin to write variations in your lesson plan to accommodate these students. For example, if you realize that some students may feel threatened by a particular task such as reading aloud to the entire class from their book report, you can plan an alternate task, such as allowing students to work in pairs and discuss their book reports with a peer. By having a back-up plan, you will know what to do when a student stares blankly instead of working. By visualizing and trying to predict the possible outcomes of your lesson plan, you can avoid these uncomfortable situations, maintain the flow of the lesson, and involve all your students more productively.

# WRITING A WELL-ORGANIZED LESSON PLAN

When teachers plan for day-to-day learning experiences, they are creating lesson plans. Usually a lesson plan is created for a single subject or topic for one day, although some experiential, hands-on lessons may be continued for several days in a row. Teachers in self-contained classrooms must devise several different lesson plans each day, one for each subject they teach, unless they choose to use multidisciplinary units. Teachers in the upper grades who work in departmentalized settings where students travel from class to class for various subjects must still create different lesson plans for each grade or group of students they teach.

In the university or college courses designed to prepare teachers, the lesson plan is an important teaching or learning device. The professor and experienced classroom teachers can provide the aspiring teacher with models of good lesson plans. Students can look on the Internet or purchase books that contain well-written lesson plans. But it is only by actively creating their own plans that they are able to demonstrate the extent to which they understand and can apply the theories and principles they have learned about reflective thinking and planning.

For that reason, many university and college programs require students to create a number of precise and detailed lesson plans. Sometimes students observe that the classroom teachers they know do not write such extensive plans for every lesson. Instead, these teachers write their lesson plans in large weekly planning books, and a single lesson plan may consist of cryptic notations such as Math: p. 108; or Social Studies: Review Ch. 7; or Science: Continue Nutrition. Although experienced teachers may record their lesson plans with such brief notes, novice teachers need to write lessons in great detail to know which resources to gather for a lesson. Writing detailed lesson plans also enables novice teachers to communicate their plans to the professor or mentor teacher, who can provide feedback on the plan before the lesson is taught.

Well-written lesson plans have additional value: They can be shared. A teacher's shorthand notes that serve as a personal reminder can rarely be interpreted by an outsider. If a substitute teacher is called to replace a classroom teacher for a day or longer, the substitute needs to see the daily plans in language he or she can understand and use. Teams of teachers often write lesson plans together or for one another. In this case, they need to have a common understanding of the lesson objectives, procedures, evaluation, and resources.

The form may vary, but most lesson plans share a number of common elements. Three essential features of a complete, well-organized lesson plan are the objectives, procedures, and evaluation. These correspond to the four questions of curriculum planning formulated by Tyler (1949). Lesson objectives specify the "educational purposes" of the lesson. The procedures section describes both "what educational experiences can be provided" and the way they can be "effectively organized." The evaluation section describes the way the teacher has planned in advance to determine "whether these purposes are being attained" (Tyler, 1949, p. 1).

The description, another feature in a lesson plan, is used to identify it and give the reader a quick overview of its purpose or description. Also, a lesson plan often contains information about the resources teachers need as background preparation for teaching the lesson as well as any materials necessary for actual execution of the lesson.

A suggestion for teachers in this age of computers is to create a basic outline of a lesson plan on a word processor and save it on a disk. Then, whenever you wish to write a lesson plan, you can put the outline on the screen and fill in the spaces. You may also want to take some time to access the Internet and look at various lesson plans posted there. Many sites are available through commercial publishers, as well as through groups of teachers at local and state levels.

The Internet also provides some new clues and models that can inform and enliven your teaching. Almost any search engine on the World Wide Web has a category called *education*, and a subcategory called *K–12 education*. Type *K–12 lesson plans* into Google to find web pages filled with real-life examples of teachers' lesson plans in every subject and at every grade level.

For example, "Ask Eric Virtual Library" can be accessed at *http://ericir.syr.edu/ Virtual/*. This web page contains a library of lesson plans created by teachers and submitted to ERIC, the Educational Resources International Clearinghouse. The "Gateway to Educational Materials" is another source of ready-to-use lesson plans at *http://www.thegateway.org/*. Once you have located these web pages, you can bookmark them and refer to them frequently. When you have mastered the art of writing your own lesson plans, you can submit one of your best to these types of organizations for others to see.

## A Lesson Plan Model

Including all of the ideas discussed in this chapter in one lesson plan can sound pretty daunting, but it is something that will become second nature to you with experience. To help you remember the important aspects of a lesson, we offer you a model of a lesson plan format in Figure 6.2. Take some time to review it now, and see if you can describe the reason each part has been included. This outline can be copied on your computer disk for use in college and the rest of your teaching career.

After you have put in the title, subject, grade level, and lesson duration, you can describe what you want students to gain from this lesson. We suggest using from one to three objectives for each lesson to help you maintain focus and avoid overwhelming students with too many ideas at once. Once you have established your basic objectives for the lesson, think about some of the students in your class who have special needs. Write notes to yourself to describe how you will scaffold the lesson for students who do not understand or who are learning to speak English. Write notes about enriching the lesson for students who have mastered the concept you are teaching and need a more challenging curriculum.

By listing the materials you need ahead of time, you avoid getting part way through the lesson and missing something you need. Each step of the procedures in our model may help you to think through what you will do to prepare for and teach the lesson. The preassessment step refers to the process of finding out what your students already know prior to teaching a new lesson. Reflective teachers use this strategy to avoid behavior problems from bored students as well as from those who do not have a clue what you are talking about. This strategy also helps you to build the background for the day's lesson. For example, to preassess students' knowledge of metric measurement, you might want to show a meter stick to your students and ask if they know what it is and what it is used for.

**Title of Lesson:**

**Subject Area:**

**Grade Level:**                    **Lesson Duration:**

**Description:** (What will students experience during this lesson?)

**Materials and Resources:** (What do you need to teach this lesson? What do students need in order to participate?)

**Objectives:** (What will students be able to do at the conclusion of this lesson?)

1.

2.

3.

**Varying Objectives for Students Who**

(a) Do not understand:

(b) Have already mastered the concept:

(c) Are learning English:

**Figure 6.2** Reflective action lesson plan model.

**Reflective Action Procedures**

1. *Preassessment:* (How will I find out what students already know about this topic?)


2. *Motivation:* (What will I do to make a connection between students and this topic?)


3. *Statement of Purpose:* (What will I say to explain the importance of learning this lesson?)


4. *Teacher Modeling or Demonstration:* (What will I do to show students what is expected?)


5. *Guided Practice:* (What will we do together as they learn how to succeed at the new task?)


6. *Check for Understanding:* (What will I ask, to see if students understand so far?)


7. *Independent Practice or Activity:* (What will you do on your own to internalize the knowledge?)


8. *Assessment:* (What will students do to demonstrate what they have learned?)


9. *Closure:* (What will students be able to say or do to show what they learned?)

After you have written a draft of your lesson plan, imagine yourself teaching it and consider the possible outcomes that may result. Think through what you will do if students do not understand or appear to be bored because they have already mastered the concept. What can you predict about the reaction of students in your classroom who are learning English? What will they need from you and their classmates in order to be successful in this lesson? You can see that the outcome prediction is a vital aspect of withitness and reflective action in teaching.

In the active learning experience example, the teacher can aid the students in comprehending what they have learned by having them share what they did that worked and did not work. Concepts can be developed by articulating and generalizing what they learned about electricity. Such a teacher-led discussion is an essential part of active, hands-on learning. It provides a sense of closure.

Every lesson or presentation can benefit from some thoughtful consideration to its ending. It is important to allow time for closure. You may use this time to ask questions that check for understanding so that you will know what to plan for the lesson that follows. You may allow the students to close the lesson with their own conclusions and new insights. A few moments spent summarizing what was learned is valuable in any form. If insight is to occur, it will probably occur in this period. At the close of one lesson, you can also indicate what will follow in the next lesson so that your students know what to expect and how to prepare for it.

# SEQUENCING OBJECTIVES IN SCHOOL SUBJECTS

## Sequencing Objectives in Mathematics

Some subjects are necessarily sequential in nature. Mathematics is the best example in the K–12 curriculum because its concepts and operations can be readily ordered from simple to complex. Teachers can organize effectively the teaching of computational skills in the basic operations of addition, subtraction, multiplication, and division very easily. For example, outcome statement 1 describes a possible sequence for teaching an essential understanding about the concept of numbers:

> *Mathematics outcome statement 1:* Primary students will be able to show how addition and subtraction are related to one another.

To accomplish this outcome, primary teachers will introduce the students to the concept of numbers and give them concrete, manipulative experiences in adding and subtracting one-digit numbers. Students may act out stories in which students are added and subtracted from a group. They may make up stories about animals or objects that are taken away and then brought back to demonstrate subtraction and addition.

Math textbooks offer a sequence of learning activities and practice of math facts, but reflective teachers find that the math textbook must be used flexibly and supplemented with other learning experiences. Before planning math lessons for a particular group of students, the teacher must pretest their entry-level knowledge and skills. Pretests will reveal that some students have already mastered some of the skills in the sequence and do not need to spend valuable time redoing what they already know. They need enriched math activities to allow them to progress. Other students may not have the conceptual understanding of number relationships to succeed on the first step. For them, preliminary concrete experiences with manipulative materials are essential for success.

Sample math objectives to fit outcome statement 1:

**Students will be able to:**

1. Use blocks to show addition of two single-digit integers.
2. Use blocks to show subtraction of two single-digit integers.
3. Use pennies and dimes to show place value of 1s and 10s.
4. Subtract pennies without regrouping.
5. Add pennies and exchange 10 pennies for a dime.
6. Subtract pennies by making change for a dime to show regrouping.
7. Tell how subtraction is related to addition using coins as an example.

These sample objectives are representative of the basic knowledge- and comprehension-level skills needed to accomplish the outcome statement. They can be written in the behavioral objective form, specifying what percentage of correct answers must be attained to demonstrate mastery.

These objectives emphasize basic computational skills that all students need to learn. However, in keeping with the National Council of Teachers of Mathematics' recommendations to emphasize problem solving over computation, reflective teachers are likely to plan lessons that allow students to explore the relationships between addition and subtraction. They are also likely to include many additional math outcomes and objectives at the higher levels of Bloom's taxonomy (1956) to teach students how to apply the math facts and computation skills they are learning to actual problem-solving situations. However, this example does illustrate the importance of matching objectives to outcome statements in a logical sequence. Each of the objectives builds on the one before it. As students master each objective, they are continually progressing toward mastering the outcome statement.

## Sequencing Objectives in Language Arts

Not all subjects in the K–12 curriculum are as sequential as mathematics. Language arts consists of knowledge, skills, and abilities that develop students' understanding and use of language. Reading, writing, speaking, listening, visually representing, and interpreting visual information are all part of the language-arts curriculum, and each one can and should have its own outcome statement(s). Outcome statement 2 suggests one illustration of how the language arts curriculum is designed:

> *Language arts outcome statement 2:* Students will be able to write standard English with correct spelling, accurate grammar, and well-organized meaning and form.

Again, this outcome statement will take years to accomplish, but teachers at every grade level are responsible for providing learning experiences that build toward the ultimate goal. The objectives to reach this goal may be similar each year for several years but written in increasing levels of difficulty. This is known as a *spiral curriculum*.

Sample language-arts objectives to fit outcome statement 2:

**By the end of grade two, students will be able to:**

1. Write a sentence containing a subject and a verb.
2. Use a capital letter at the beginning of a sentence.
3. Use a period or question mark at the end of a sentence.
4. Review and edit sentences for complete meaning.

**By the end of grade four, students will be able to:**

1. Write a paragraph that focuses on one central idea.
2. Spell common words correctly in writing samples.
3. Use capitalization and sentence-end punctuation correctly.
4. Review and edit a paragraph to improve the organization of ideas.

**By the end of grade six, students will be able to:**

1. Write several paragraphs that explain one concept or theme.
2. Use a dictionary to spell all words in a paper correctly.
3. Use correct punctuation, including end marks, comma, apostrophe, quotation marks, and colon.
4. Review and edit papers to correct spelling, punctuation, grammar, and organization of ideas.

**By the end of grade eight, students will be able to:**

1. Write papers with introductory paragraph, logical reasons, data to support the main idea, and a closing statement.
2. Use a dictionary to spell all words in a paper correctly; use a thesaurus to add to vocabulary of the paper.
3. Eliminate fragments and run-on sentences.
4. Review and edit papers to correct spelling, punctuation, grammar, organization of ideas, and appropriateness for the purpose.

When teachers have curriculum guidelines such as these, they must still translate the outcome statements and objectives into actual learning experiences that are appropriate and motivating for their students. To pretest how well your students can use written language when they enter your classroom, plan a writing experience in the first week. Analyzing these writing samples will allow you to plan suitably challenging activities for your students. In this example, the second-grade teacher must decide what topics to have students write about and when to limit students to copying teacher-made examples or allow them to begin to write their own sentences. The fourth-grade teacher knows that students will not learn all of these skills in just one writing lesson. It is necessary to provide many interesting classroom experiences so that students will have ideas to express in their writing. The sixth-grade teacher has to plan a series of research and writing experiences so that students will have ample opportunities to synthesize all of the skills required at that grade level.

Curriculum planning of subjects such as language arts is a complex undertaking because it contains so many varied outcomes and objectives. The previous example illustrates only a single outcome for teaching students how to write. Teachers must also plan outcome statements and objectives for reading, listening, speaking, visually representing, and interpreting visual methods.

## Sequencing Objectives in Science

As discussed in Chapter 4, the science curriculum should inform students of the basic facts and concepts of science topics, but it should also allow students opportunities to experience how scientists work. These dual goals of the science curriculum are often expressed as *teaching both content and process*. An example of an outcome statement in science that covers both content and process follows:

*Science outcome statement 3:* Students will demonstrate the properties of electricity and magnetism, and show how their energy can be used to benefit mankind.

If Judy was planning a series of lesson plans to accomplish this outcome, she would use a sequence of process-oriented learning experiences that allow students to discover some important properties of electricity and magnetism, followed by a few content-oriented lessons to review and articulate what they discovered. As a culmination, she would allow students to apply what they have learned and synthesize their own inventions using the energy from batteries and magnets. The order of these learning experiences would be as follows:

Sample science objectives to fit outcome statement 3:

**By the end of the unit on electricity and magnetism, students will be able to:**

1. Demonstrate how electricity travels in a closed circuit.
2. Demonstrate how magnetism attracts and repels certain metals.
3. Investigate the basic properties of electricity and magnetism.
4. Be able to compare and contrast electricity and magnetism and identify key properties of each.
5. Invent some beneficial ways to use electricity and magnetism.

Using this approach, the first lesson plan would involve hands-on experiences using batteries, copper wire, and light bulbs so that students can demonstrate to themselves how electricity travels in a closed circuit. On subsequent days, lessons would be planned to allow students to investigate the properties of magnets and electricity. Then, Judy would plan a lesson in which students created charts comparing the two and there would be a lesson in which students discussed the properties and learned to use terminology correctly. Students might then have a written, individual test on these properties and terms. Finally, there would be several days for students to work on their inventions, and present them to classmates and parents.

## Sequencing Objectives in Social Studies

Reflective K–12 teachers can also see the need for both content and process in their social studies curriculum. They attempt to help their students build a knowledge base in history and geography, but they also give attention and time to teaching students how to acquire information on their own.

An example of an outcome statement in social studies that covers both content and process follows:

*Social studies outcome statement 4:* Students will be able to use a map and a globe to find place names and locations. They will then create a chart listing the countries, major cities, rivers, and mountain ranges in each continent.

Sample social studies objectives to meet outcome statement 4:

**At the end of the map and globe unit, students will be able to:**

1. Identify the seven continents on a world map and a globe.
2. Interpret the country boundaries with a map legend.
3. List the countries in each continent.
4. Interpret the symbol for rivers on the map legend.
5. List the major rivers in each continent.
6. Interpret the symbol for mountain ranges on the map legend.
7. List the mountain ranges in each continent.
8. Create a chart showing the countries, cities, rivers, and mountain ranges in each continent.

In this example, the teacher has planned a set of learning activities that will add to the students' knowledge base about world geography. This set of activities also equips the student to be able to find and interpret information on maps and globes. This social studies curriculum demonstrates that by employing hands-on learning experiences, students are able to learn both content and processes simultaneously and that they are active rather than passive learners throughout the entire set of activities. An oral or written pretest might consist of having students name or point to certain geographical locations and read and interpret a map legend. The information from the pretest is valuable in planning lessons that use students' existing knowledge and add to it.

## Sequencing Objectives in Interdisciplinary Units

Whenever possible, many teachers enjoy enriching the curriculum units they plan by incorporating fine-arts experiences into the academic subjects. Primary students are often asked to illustrate math examples by drawing one pumpkin plus two pumpkins or to create 10 different pictures using a rectangle. Songs and rhymes frequently accompany learning about historical events and people. Many such events are dramatized as well. Stories and films are often used to augment many aspects of the curriculum.

In later years, emphasis on the fine arts may decline except in special art and music classes or on special occasions and holidays. This is due, in part, to the crowded curriculum that teachers are required to deliver. Given the prevailing culture of the early 21st century, the fine arts often take a back seat to academic and social subjects. But each teacher must consider the place of fine arts in the curriculum. Reflective teachers are likely to consider the importance of the arts in enhancing the joy of living and to make them an integral part of every learning experience. This has the effect of increasing students' active involvement, creative thinking, and inventiveness.

Here is an example of an outcome statement that includes fine arts with an academic subject:

*Fine arts/social studies outcome statement 5:* Students will be able to distinguish the important contributions made by various world cultures in sports, art, music, literature, and drama.

Sample objectives to meet outcome statement 5:

**Each learning team of students will be able to:**

1. Select one country of the world to study.
2. Locate at least three sources of information about that country.
3. Draw a map of the country's geographical boundaries and features.
4. Describe the country's contributions to sports.
5. Play or sing an example of the country's music.
6. Draw examples of the country's art and architecture treasures.
7. Read aloud a story or a poem from that country.
8. Work with other learning teams to create a dramatic event featuring the stories, poems, art, and music of all the countries.

This ambitious set of learning experiences demonstrates how well the fine arts can be incorporated into an academic subject. Cognitively, students who take part in this series of experiences will learn a knowledge base of facts, ideas, and concepts about the world. They will also gain understanding and use of such processes as communication and problem-solving skills. Affectively, they will learn to appreciate and understand differences and similarities among people by sharing the cultural arts of each country.

## SAMPLE LESSON PLANS

Lesson plans are written scripts that teachers write so that they can present a well-organized set of learning experiences for their students. The objectives of the lesson specify the teacher's expectations for what the students will learn or be able to do as a result of the lesson. When teachers plan objectives that specify the criteria for success, they are clarifying for themselves what the students must be able to do to demonstrate mastery of the skill or understanding of the lesson's concepts.

To plan the procedures of a lesson in advance, many reflective teachers visualize themselves teaching the lesson. They write what they must do to teach the lesson successfully and what the students must do to learn the material. Teachers who can visualize the entire process of teaching and learning can write richly detailed lesson plans. When they begin to teach the lesson, they have a supportive script to follow.

As teachers become more proficient and experienced at planning and teaching, their written lesson plans are likely to become less detailed. But for beginning teachers, a thorough, richly detailed plan is an essential element for a successful lesson.

## A Student Teacher Plans and Replans a Science Lesson

Alex Eby recently graduated from the teacher education program at Montana State University in Bozeman, Montana. During one of his paraprofessional school observations, he visited John Graves's classroom. Mr. Graves invited him to teach a science lesson on geology. Alex found a lesson plan online entitled "Cupcake Geology." He referred to the Montana State Standards to see whether this lesson plan was compatible and found that it fit Science Content Standards 1 and 4 very well.

The Montana State Science Standard 1 states that students will design, conduct, evaluate, and communicate scientific investigations. His plan was designed with student investigation as a major goal and with communication of findings as an important element. He also found that Montana State Science Standard 4 expects that students will demonstrate knowledge of the composition, processes, and interactions of Earth's systems and other objects in space. His lesson plan would give students an opportunity to see for themselves how the composition of the earth varies.

To prepare for his lesson, Alex baked 30 cupcakes. He divided the cupcake batter into three portions and used food color to distinguish them. He swirled together the chocolate, yellow, and green batters before baking them. After they were baked, he covered them with chocolate frosting.

The next morning he arrived at Mr. Graves's class and passed out paper towels to each student as he introduced himself and described his goals for the lesson. He tried to create a bond by saying, "Just like you, I am a student of Mr. Graves's in a science methods course at the university." He told the class that in the next hour, they would talk for a minute, do an activity, have a discussion, and write up their observations. To describe the content goals for the lesson, he told the class that scientists often cannot see things they want to study, so they create models and study those instead. He asked students to give examples of other scientific models and pointed out that the fish tank in the back of their room was a model of the unseen depths of a lake or ocean. He told the students that simulation is a powerful way to learn new and unfamiliar material.

One student raised her hand and told Alex that another student teacher had taught them a lesson the year before using cupcakes. Alex was shocked. The students had already experienced the lesson he had planned for them. "Now what should I do?" he tried to think quickly. But, he had no other lesson planned so he knew that he had to proceed. He hoped that it would not just be a waste of the students' time to do the same experiment over again.

After the experiment was over, Alex discussed with the class whether repeating the simulated experience was useful or not. The students reassured him that they had gained new information and ideas from the lesson. Figure 6.3 shows a copy of Alex's lesson plan.

Soon you will be the student teacher who is responsible for planning lessons for a classroom. Take your sense of humor with you, and especially your ability to laugh at your own mistakes. Like Alex, you may find that your carefully planned lesson has already been taught or that your students do not respond the way you expected them to. Your written lesson plans are great guides or scripts, but a reflective teacher is always willing to ad-lib if necessary. The art of teaching is a balance between careful planning and improvisation.

---

**Title of Lesson:** Cupcake Geology

**Subject Area:** Science

**Grade Level:** Sixth grade        **Lesson Duration:** 1 hour

**Description:** Students will simulate geological exploration by taking core samples from a cupcake to discover what is underneath the frosting layer.

**Materials and Resources:** Frosted cupcakes made with several different colors of cake batter, straws, paper towels, science notebooks, or journals

**Objectives:**

1.  Students will discover that taking core samples is a useful method for learning about the earth below its surface. (Application)

2.  Students will be able to make inferences from sample data. (Analysis)

3.  Students will be able to think and behave like scientists in a simulation, as well as write their conclusions in a scientific notebook. (Synthesis)

**Varying Objectives for Students Who:**

(a) Do not understand:

Students will write their observations in their own words. Results will vary. If students have difficulty writing about what they learned, I will discuss it with them and assist them in the writing process.

(b) Have already mastered the concept:

Some students may work quickly, and accurately write up their observations. I will encourage them to read more about how scientists use core samples in real life.

(c) Are learning English:

English learners may draw what they see and may not be required to write their observations in their notebooks. Some new vocabulary will be learned during this lesson, such as *core sample, simulation, geology,* and different colors.

---

*(continued)*

**Figure 6.3** Science lesson plan.

**Reflective Action Procedures**

1. *Preassessment:* During my opening discussion, I will ask how scientists find out about the earth below its surface. I will ask students to name other models they have studied.

2. *Motivation:* I will discuss how simulations, such as the fish tank in their classroom, help us to imagine or picture those parts of the world that we cannot easily see.

3. *Statement of Purpose:* Simulation helps us understand what we couldn't otherwise experience. Scientists use simulation to create models of natural phenomena. Today, we can take the role of scientists who are examining the geology of the earth.

4. *Teacher Modeling:* When I distribute the cupcakes and straws, I will use a straw to drill for a core sample of my cupcake.

5. *Guided Practice:* I will ask students to practice taking a core sample of their cupcakes while I watch and ask questions in response to their questions.

6. *Check for Understanding:* I will walk around the room and observe students as they work. I will ask questions such as, "How many core samples do you need before you can make an inference about what is below the surface? Why? When you encounter a layer near the surface, does it always continue deep down?"

7. *Independent Practice or Activity:* Students will decide how many core samples to take. They will write up their observations, using the questions, "In this lab, I did. . . ." and "In this lab, I learned. . . ."

8. *Assessment:* I will collect and read the students' lab write-ups. If a student has not answered the questions accurately, I will confer with that student to assess what he has learned.

9. *Closure:* We will discuss worldwide uses of core sampling, and especially focus on the use of this technique in Montana in the mining industry and in paleontology research. I will also encourage students to come up with other uses of core sampling both real and imagined.

**Figure 6.3** *(Continued)*

SOURCE: Alex Eby created this lesson while a student in the teacher education program at Montana State University, Bozeman, Montana, in 2004.

## Sample Bilingual Kindergarten Lesson Plan

Conchita Encinas teaches in a bilingual first-grade classroom in Chula Vista, California. To encourage her students to interact and use oral language in small groups, she likes to plan many of her lessons using learning centers. For each topic she wants to teach, she designs four different activities that students can do independently or in a small group. For example, her spring curriculum includes a unit on plants and growing things. For the lesson on plants and seeds she designs four different learning center activities.

She begins the lesson with the students sitting in a circle, where she provides students with some general information in both Spanish and English about plants and seeds. She encourages her Spanish-speaking students to learn and use new English words related to the topic being studied. She also teaches English-speaking students to learn Spanish words related to the subject in the lesson. Then she introduces the four different activities they will be able to explore in the centers. She divides the class into four groups, and each group travels from one center to another for 20-minute intervals. At the end of the morning, the students gather in a circle again to share what they have done and learned about seeds and plants. Conchita reads aloud the stories the students have written at the first center. Figure 6.4 shows Conchita's lesson plan for the exploration of seeds and plants.

---

**Title of Lesson:** Seeds and Plants

**Subject Area:** Science and Language Development

**Grade Level:** First grade    **Lesson Duration:** Time for a four-center rotation

**Description:** Students will explore how seeds grow into plants.

**Materials and Resources:** Fruits, vegetables, knife, paper, pencils, posterboard, crayons, rye seeds, paper cups, soil, water

**Objectives:**

1. Students will observe that seeds are different sizes, shapes, and colors.

2. Students will be able to identify various fruits and vegetables and describe how seeds grow into plants. By doing so, they will increase their English vocabulary, oral speaking, and listening skills.

3. Students will compare and make graphs to show the variation in number and type of seeds among several different types of plants.

**Varying Objectives for Students Who:**

(a) Do not understand:

I will pair them with other students who are likely to understand. The teacher's aide and I will talk with them during the activities.

(b) Have already mastered the concept:

They can read or look at books about seeds and plants. They can make graphs on the number of seeds in a plant.

(c) Are learning English:

I will pair them with other students who are likely to understand. The teacher's aide and I will talk with them during the activities, focusing on vocabulary and oral expression.

---

*(continued)*

**Figure 6.4** Primary bilingual lesson plan on seeds and plants.

**Reflective Action Procedures**

1. *Preassessment:* Begin in a circle. Review concepts students have already learned about plants. Have students give a thumbs-up signal if they agree, a thumbs-down signal if they disagree with statements such as, "Flowers are plants. Plants need water to grow. Plants need milk to grow."

2. *Motivation:* Open up a papaya or cantaloupe and show students the seeds. Tell students that with the seeds from one piece of fruit, it is possible to grow a new piece of fruit for everyone in the room. Discuss how this helps people grow food for everyone in the world.

3. *Statement of Purpose:* Tell students that today they will get to be scientists and investigate how many seeds are in different fruits and vegetables.

4. *Modeling or Demonstration:* Teach children the English words *plants*, *seeds*, *garden*, *grow*, and *food*.

5. *Guided Practice:* Have children repeat these words in the circle and use them while working in the centers.

6. *Check for Understanding:* Ask students to define the vocabulary words again. Then, review with the whole group directions for the activities at the four centers. Divide the class into four groups. Assign a rotation schedule so that each group goes to all four centers.

7. *Independent Center Activities*
   *Center 1:* Students cut out parts of a plant, glue them on a piece of paper, and write a story about it.
   *Center 2:* Students examine and count a variety of vegetable and fruit seeds, including an apple, cantaloupe, pea pod, and green pepper. They graph the number of seeds from each vegetable.
   *Center 3:* Students plant rye seeds in a paper cup and discuss what happens to seeds under the ground.
   *Center 4:* Students identify various vegetables, cut them up, and taste them. They list words about the way each vegetable tastes.

8. *Assessment:* Story boards and stories from center 1 are read aloud at the closing circle. Graphs from center 2 are displayed on the bulletin board. Seeds in cups from center 3 are placed near a window to grow.

9. *Closure:* Students discuss the tastes of different vegetables during the closing circle.

**Figure 6.4** *(Continued)*

SOURCE: Hands-on science lesson designed for learning centers by Conchita Encinas, first-grade bilingual class, Chula Vista School District, California.

## Sample Middle School Lesson Plan in Mathematics

Students like to explore their own world. A large portion of time in the middle school student's world is devoted to watching television. Figure 6.5 shows a lesson plan from Pam Knight's unit on television-viewing habits (see Chapter 5). On the surface, this appears to be a mathematics lesson. However, after analyzing the objectives and activities in it, you will see that it involves the social sciences and language arts as well.

This lesson plan requires more than one class period. One day is needed to prepare for data collection; a week is needed to collect and record the data; and a day or two are required for constructing the bar graphs and describing the findings.

Pam's lesson demonstrates how students can use mathematics in their lives. They become researchers who collect and organize data. For the data to be relevant, they must be able to analyze them and explain what they found. Finally, the students are expected to make inferences and evaluate an important factor in their lives.

## Sample High School Lesson Plan in Social Studies

David Ramert discussed the way he uses controversy in planning his U.S. history course in Chapter 4. In Figure 6.6, we can see an example of a lesson that engages students in active discussions on an important but controversial topic from the history of the United States. This lesson plan also illustrates the way a reflective teacher designs curriculum so that students know how to succeed, then scaffolds the lessons so that students have many opportunities to get the information they need from readings as well as class discussion. Note David's willingness to adapt the lesson plan to meet the needs of learners who are not fluent in English.

---

**Title of Lesson:** Television-Viewing Habits of Students

**Subject Area:** Mathematics/social sciences

**Grade Level:** Middle school

**Description:** Students will keep records of the amount of television they watch and present this information using graphs.

**Materials:** Graph paper, rulers, and pencils

**Objectives:**

1. *Application level:* Students will construct bar graphs using data collected on television-viewing habits.

2. *Analysis level:* Students will interpret and make inferences based on the analysis of the data gathered by writing a statement that describes the data on the graph.

3. *Evaluation level:* Students will evaluate their television-viewing habits and the television-viewing habits of the class as a whole.

---

*(continued)*

**Figure 6.5** Mathematics lesson plan.

**Varying Objectives for Students Who:**

(a) Do not understand:

Provide samples of graphs for students to use as models

(b) Have already mastered the concept:

Students may design additional research questions about television viewing habits

(c) Are learning English:

Allow them to work with an English-speaking partner on this project. Take time to talk one to one with them about their projects at all stages.

**Reflective Action Procedures**

1. *Motivation:* The lesson begins with a discussion of the observations students have made about their own television-viewing habits. This is an open-ended discussion, and students may talk about types of shows seen (MTV, movies, sports contests, etc.). Ask students: "Do students watch too much television and play too many video games? How much TV do students really watch? Are there methods by which students can gather data on their television-viewing habits?"

2. *Statement of Purpose:* We will learn how to gather information and data to make informed decisions about important matters in our lives.

3. *Teacher Modeling and Demonstration:* Teacher models data collection by surveying students on their favorite TV show. Teacher tallies these data and, with class participation, creates a bar graph of the data at the chalkboard.

4. *Guided Practice:* Students duplicate the teacher's tally and bar graph at their desks.

5. *Check for Understanding:* Ask questions to determine whether the students know the processes of recording data and constructing a bar graph.

6. *Independent Practice or Activity:* Students gather data on their television-viewing habits for one week.

7. *Check for Understanding:* At the end of the week, students choose ways to display their data using bar graphs. Examples of displaying the data could be the amount of television boys watched compared with the amount girls watched, the amount of television watched on different days of the week, or the types of programs watched. In groups of three, students construct the graph and identify an inference they could make based on their graph. They share their graph and inference and display them on a bulletin board.

8. *Assessment:* Students write in their journals about the activity completed. Students graphs are examined to see if the data have been correctly graphed. The inferences made by students are checked against the constructed bar graphs. The graphs become part of the students' mathematics and social studies portfolios.

9. *Closure:* Students discuss what they have learned about their television-viewing habits. They discuss what the results mean to them. For example, do they think they watch too much television? Do they watch more or less television than they expected? Is the bar graph an effective way to display the data they gathered?

**Figure 6.5** *(Continued)*

SOURCE: Pam Knight, Twin Peaks Middle School, Poway, California.

**Title of Lesson:** The Legacy of Andrew Jackson (A review of the unit)

**Subject Area:** U.S. History

**Grade Level:** Junior in high school          **Lesson Duration:** 45 minutes

**Description:** (What will students experience during this lesson?)
Students will be bombarded by comments and statements contributed by everybody in the room about the Jacksonian era. Students will take notes for their essays, hoping they will be able to collect their ideas for the essays they will write the next day.

**Materials and Resources:** (What do you need to teach this lesson? What do students need in order to participate?) Chalkboard, chalk, ideas, brains engaged, notepaper and pens.

**Objectives:**

(What will students be able to do at the conclusion of this lesson?)

1. Students will use correct vocabulary from the era.

2. Students will contribute ideas (hopefully original) in answer to controversial questions.

3. Students will be able to articulate that Jackson initiated a change in the movement from a republic to a democracy.

**Varying Objectives for Students Who:**

(a) Do not understand:

   I walk around during the period to observe students as they write. Those who don't seem to be contributing or writing during class will be invited to an extra tutoring session. As independent school teachers, we are willing to meet with students even on weekends if it is necessary to make certain a student succeeds.

(b) Have already mastered the concept:

   Occassionally, I have them teach part of a lesson. They prepare a presentation for the class on an area of strength or interest.

(c) Are learning English:

   I tutor them and make arrangements for them to write the essays at home so that they can use their notes, dictionaries, and textbook in their own time. I also allow them to revise and rewrite their essays before they are evaluated.

**Reflective Action Procedures**

1. *Presassessment:* (How will I find out what students already know about this topic?) This lesson serves as a preassesment for the essay evaluation for the course.

2. *Motivation:* (What will I do to make a connection between students and this topic?) I ask, "How can this man be the champion of the common man and destroy the lives of thousands of Indians at the same time? Is it possible to be both these things? Do we find these same types of controversy present in every major figure in the history books?"

*(continued)*

**Figure 6.6** History lesson plan.

3. *Statement of Purpose:* (What will I say to explain the importance of learning this lesson?) Today we're going to work together to gather all of the information we need to write our essays separately tomorrow.

4. *Teacher Modeling or Demonstration:* (What will I do to show students what is expected?)

   I write two columns on the chalkboard: **Curse or Blessing.** (20 minutes)

   I write: (20 minutes)

   **In what ways did Jacksonians view themselves as Guardians of:**

   **The Constitution, Individual Liberty, Human Rights, Equality?**

   We discuss: **How valid was their view?**

5. *Guided Practice:* (What will we do together as they learn how to succeed at the new task?) I ask the class to brainstorm examples of how Jackson was bad for the country and how he was good for the country. I write their responses in no order of importance.

6. *Check for Understanding:* (What will I ask to see if students understand so far?) If a student offers an incorrect response or uses incorrect vocabulary, I probe and question. I may write it so that everyone can see it, but I ask, "Are you sure about this?"

7. *Independent Practice or Activity:* (What will you do on your own to internalize the knowledge?) On the following class day, the students write their own essays on one of the two controversial questions posed in this unit. They must write in ink on lined paper in class for a class period. (See option above for English Language Learners).

8. *Assessment:* (What will students do to demonstrate what they have learned?) Essays will be written the next class day. See Unit Plan in Chapter 5 for essay criteria and grading system.

9. *Closure:* (What will I say to sum up the unit?) Despite all of his enigmas and contradictions, Jackson moved the country one step closer to democracy at a time when democracy was not really popular or "cool," in the rest of the world. Remember, you're going to have to argue both sides of this issue.

**Figure 6.6** *(Continued)*

SOURCE: David Ramert, U.S. history teacher, Francis Parker Upper School, San Diego, California.

## Sample High School Lesson Plan in Science

The lesson plan for science in Figure 6.7 is taken from the unit developed by Chris Chiaverina and Jim Hicks described in Chapter 5. Their plan is exciting because they are constantly trying to find ways to make science interesting, practical, and fun. In their words, "If there isn't a common understanding of the application of a concept in science, then it isn't worth teaching." As you read their lesson plan, remember that the philosophy of their approach to science is to use a smorgasbord of examples and demonstrations as well as a hands-on approach by their students. Their lessons clearly meet the expectations of the new science frameworks that require teachers to take an active and exploratory approach to the learning of science.

**Title of Lesson:** Sound Production

**Subject Area:** Science

**Grade Level:** High school physics          **Lesson Duration:** 1–2 class periods

**Description:** Using a variety of items that vibrate and produce sounds, students investigate sound production.

**Materials:** Tuning fork, guitar, carpet tubing, music box, 78 RPM record, needle, pencil, "talking strip," Fisher burner, aluminum rod, resin, "sound wagon" toy, rubber bands, file cards, tongue depressors, string

**Objectives:**

1. *Comprehension:* Students will become aware of their naïve ideas about sound and be able to describe how sound is produced.

2. *Application:* Students will make their own source of sound through a device called the hummer.

3. *Knowledge:* Students will develop their science vocabulary by being able to define and use acoustical terminology appropriately.

**Varying Objectives for Student Who:**

(a) Do not understand:

   Have students review previous laboratory work and movie on waves. Students can explore waves with a pool of water to observe how agitation of a medium generates disturbances.

(b) Have already mastered the concept:

   After building their hummer, students can design a guitar-like apparatus and explain the purpose of changing the tension of a vibrating wire or rubber band.

(c) Are learning English:

   Allow for group work or peer tutoring. Students can explore the wave pool. Students can explore a working model of a hummer.

**Reflective Action Procedures**

1. *Preassessment:* Students have done laboratory work, seen demonstrations, and watched a movie on waves. They have also done labs using Slinkies and a ripple tank. After students have observed the demonstration of sounds in the motivation activity, they are asked to relate their observations to the concepts learned in the previous lessons on sound production, including reflection and transmission. They are also asked to relate this to the terminology of wave speed and amplitude.

2. *Motivation:* The teacher demonstrates a variety of common vibrating systems that produce audible sounds. For example, strike a tuning fork and have the students observe if there is a noticeable visible vibration on the fork. Strike the tuning fork and place it in a glass of water and observe what happens. The water will be stirred. The teacher plucks a guitar string and the students listen to the sound.

3. *Statement of Purpose:* Students will learn how sound is produced by vibrations.

*(continued)*

**Figure 6.7** High school science lesson plan.

4. *Modeling/Demonstration:* The teacher then demonstrates some unusual sources of sound. An old record is played with a straight pin. A carpet tube is placed over a Fisher burner, which makes a sound like a fog horn. A talking plastic strip is pulled across a fingernail and delivers a message. An aluminum rod is stroked with resin and produces a high-pitched tone.

5. *Guided Practice:* Students are assigned problems on the sources and transmission of sound. These problems relate to the earlier examples as well as the hummer.

6. *Check for Understanding:* Teacher interacts with students while they work on assigned problems.

7. *Independent Activity:* Students produce their own hummer. (a) A rubber band is stretched around a tongue depressor and acts as a vibrating object. (b) A file card is stapled to the tongue depressor and used to amplify the vibrations. (c) A string is attached to an end of the device. (d) The hummer is spun around in a circle by the string, and a sound is produced.

8. *Assessment Plan:* Students create hummers and describe in their own words how the hummer produces sound, using correct acoustical terminology.

9. *Closure:* Students decipher this phrase: "Sound equals vibrations." They demonstrate their hummers.

**Figure 6.7** *(Continued)*

SOURCE: Chris Chiaverina, New Trier High School, Winnetka, Illinois, and Jim Hicks, Barrington High School, Barrington, Illinois.

## Conclusions about Lesson Planning

Lesson plans are scripts that teachers write so they can present a well-organized set of learning experiences for their students. The objectives of the lesson specify the teacher's expectations for what the students will learn or be able to do as a result of the lesson. When teachers plan objectives that specify the criteria for success, they are clarifying for themselves what the students must be able to do to demonstrate mastery of the skill or understanding of the lesson's concepts.

To plan the procedures of a lesson in advance, many reflective teachers visualize themselves teaching the lesson. They write what they must do to teach the lesson successfully and what the students must do to learn the material. Teachers who can visualize the entire process of teaching and learning can write richly detailed lesson plans. When they begin to teach the lesson, they have a supportive script to follow.

As teachers become more proficient and experienced at planning and teaching, their written lesson plans are likely to become less detailed. But for beginning teachers, a thorough, richly detailed plan is an essential element for a successful lesson.

# REFLECTIVE ACTION EXPERIENCES FOR YOUR PROFESSIONAL PORTFOLIO

## Write a Lesson Plan Entitled "Writing: Thinking Through the Process"

As part of the NBPTS requirement to demonstrate mastery of teaching the writing process, we suggest that you write a lesson plan on writing for the grade level of your choice. This lesson can become part of the unit plan you wrote in Chapter 5, "Writing: Thinking through the Process."

Think about this lesson plan as a 30- to 60-minute learning experience, depending on the grade level you choose. Begin by examining the reading/language arts standards for your state that apply to the writing process.

Next, visit a class and talk with the teacher about lesson plans for teaching writing. Ask to see samples of lesson plans used in the class. If possible, ask to observe the students at work on writing assignments. Then, ask to examine the student responses or writing projects.

Sketch out an initial plan for the lesson. How will you introduce the lesson? Describe what students will experience during the lesson. What materials and resources will you need? How will you conclude the lesson? How will you assess the students' mastery of the writing process?

Show your initial plan to a classroom teacher or to other trusted colleagues. Brainstorm and share ideas for the lesson together. Ask your colleague to predict possible roadblocks or other sources of difficulty standing in the way of implementing your lesson plan successfully. Ask for advice about the types of materials you need to gather or create. Ask for suggestions about teaching strategies and assessment strategies that are appropriate for your lesson.

Begin to rewrite your lesson plan. This time, ask yourself: "What are the *learning objectives* that are most important for your students to achieve in this lesson? How will you vary these objectives to meet the needs of individual students in your classroom who have special needs? How will you vary the lesson for students whose primary language is not English? How will you vary the lesson for students who write fluently and easily? How will you vary it for students whose writing skills are below grade level? What are the step-by-step procedures you will use to teach this lesson? How will you motivate students to want to learn to write more effectively? How will you model or demonstrate what you want them to be able to achieve? What will you give them to do as a guided practice of the concept you are teaching? How will you check to see who understands and who needs more instruction? What will you give them for an independent activity to show what they have learned? How will you assess the writing products they turn in to you? How will you help your students put into words what they have learned in this lesson?"

Write the final version of your lesson to include in your professional portfolio. Give your writing lesson an interesting, motivating title. Put a paper copy of this lesson in a writing folder and keep another copy on your computer.

Reflect on the lesson-planning process you used in this assignment to consider how you would improve on the process in the future. Can you envision your students accomplishing these objectives, learning the skills, and mastering the process of thinking through the writing process?

---

# References

Bloom, B., Engelhart, M., Furst, E., Hill, W., & Krathwohl, D. (1956). *Taxonomy of educational objectives: Cognitive domain.* New York: Longman.

Eisner, E. (1985). *Educational imagination* (2nd ed.). Upper Saddle River, NJ: Merrill/Prentice Hall.

Tyler, R. (1949). *Basic principles of curriculum and instruction.* Chicago: University of Chicago Press.

## CHAPTER 7

# Your Students Want Active, Authentic Learning

Remember the times in your own school experience when you could hardly wait to get to school each morning? Remember the teachers who encouraged you to put imagination and creativity into your work? Remember the times you and your classmates became obsessed with finding out how something works or what happened next? Chances are that these learning experiences all had two things in common: (1) they were designed to allow you and your classmates to be active rather than passive learners and (2) what you were learning seemed important, useful, and authentic. We use the term *authentic* to mean learning that students recognize to be something they need to know in order to develop into capable, knowledgeable adults.

## NBPTS STANDARDS THAT APPLY TO ACTIVE, AUTHENTIC LEARNING

The NBPTS views the mission of teachers to be knowledgeable about the subjects they teach, but also about how to teach those subjects to students. Proposition 2 describes the need for teachers to demonstrate that they have attained specialized knowledge of how to convey a subject to students. The NBPTS recognizes that knowledge of subject matter, while essential, is not enough to become a master teacher. Certified teachers must also be able to demonstrate knowledge and skills needed to present the subject matter to students effectively. Proposition 2 suggests that teachers employ a variety of teaching methods, including analogies, metaphors, experiments, demonstrations, and illustrations. In this chapter, we describe these methods and many more that you can learn how to use in your classroom.

**PRAXIS**

Chapters 7, 9, and 10 prepare you for PRAXIS™ Exam Section 2a: Instructional Strategies.

Proposition 3 is concerned with the way teachers take responsibility for managing and monitoring student learning. One subheading of NBPTS Proposition 3 states that "Teachers place a premium on student engagement." Our model of reflective action in teaching also makes active student engagement a priority. Proposition 3 goes on to state that facilitating student learning is not simply a matter of placing young people in educative environments; teachers must also motivate them, capturing their minds and hearts and engaging them actively in learning.

Another subset of Proposition 3 states that teachers need to use multiple methods to meet their goals. Accomplished teachers should know how to employ a variety of instructional skills—how to conduct Socratic dialogues, how to lecture, how to oversee small cooperative learning groups. The following sections of this chapter will provide you with the basic ideas of these and many other teaching strategies. As a reflective teacher, you know that the information in this textbook is just a starting place. You will need to do more research on each strategy to become proficient in it.

The term *authentic learning* is used to distinguish between the achievement of significant, meaningful, and useful knowledge and skills from that which is trivial and unrelated to students' lives. The Wisconsin Center on Organizing and Restructuring of Schools has concentrated on defining standards of authentic instruction. Its studies have led to the conclusion that many conventional instructional methods do not allow students to use their minds well and result in learning that has little or no intrinsic meaning or value to them beyond achieving success in school.

These studies recommend establishing standards for teachers to use as guidelines in selecting and learning to use teaching strategies that promote authentic learning.

According to their research, the standards for authentic instructional methods should emphasize higher-order thinking, depth of knowledge, connectedness to the world, and substantive conversation and should provide social support for student achievement (Newman & Wehlage, 1993).

As a learner, you may have had teachers who used teaching strategies that stimulated you to use your higher-level thinking and problem-solving skills. You may recall learning experiences that encouraged you to delve deeply into a subject that had real meaning to your life. You may recall class discussions that sparkled with enthusiastic exchanges of ideas and opinions within a social system that encouraged you to challenge yourself to make more and more meaningful accomplishments. If you recall school experiences such as these, you have experienced authentic learning.

You may have had other teachers who relied on conventional methods that required rote memorization of facts and dates or other content. You may recall learning a lot about a little or participating in boring recitations in which students were expected to parrot what they had memorized. You may recall competitive social systems that rewarded those students who were able to memorize and recite quickly and those who were able to figure out what the teacher wanted to hear. If you recall school experiences such as these, you will need to overcome the natural tendency to repeat learned patterns and challenge yourself to learn to use many new and exciting instructional strategies.

Your personal conception of the teaching-learning process is drawn from your own experiences as a learner, but for reflective teachers it is also drawn from the values and beliefs they hold about what students need to know and how students ought to behave and from perceptions and reflections about the theories and practices of other classroom teachers they observe. To become a reflective teacher, you must make yourself aware of the emerging research and knowledge base about teaching and learning. Gathering information from research is an important attribute of a reflective thinker and teacher.

# RETRIEVAL PROCESS

## Schema Theory

The retrieval process is obviously a critical factor in being able to use stored information. Knowledge, concepts, and skills that are learned must be stored in the brain until they are needed. According to Piaget's *schema theory* (1970), each subset of knowledge is stored in a *schema*, an outline or organized network of knowledge about a single concept or subject. It is believed that young children develop *schemata* (the plural form of schema) made up of visual or other sensory images and, as language increases, verbal imagery replaces the sensory images.

For example, an infant stores sensual images in the schemata for mother, bottle, bed, and bath. Later the verbal labels are added. A schema grows, expands, or otherwise changes due to new experiences. If the infant sees and touches a large, round, blue ball, he or she can store sensory images of its size, color, rubbery feel, and softness. At a later encounter, the infant may experience it bounce, and he or she can store these images in the same schema. A year later, when the child learns to say the word *ball*, the label is acted on in working memory and stored in long-term memory within the schema for ball.

**PRAXIS**
Important educational theorists are tested in PRAXIS™ Exam Section 1a: Students as Learners.

Students come to school with varied schema. Some students who have had many experiences at home, in parks, at zoos, in museums, and in other circumstances may enter kindergarten with complex schemata for hundreds of topics and experiences. Other students, whose experiences have been severely limited by poverty or other circumstances, are likely to have very different schemata, and some of these may not match the prevailing culture's values or verbal labels. Similarly, if students come from highly verbal homes where parents talk with them frequently, their schemata are likely to contain accurate verbal labels for stored sensory experiences and phenomena. Students who are raised in less verbal homes, however, will have fewer verbal components to their schemata. This theory complements Piaget's observations of stages of development and helps us to understand how a child's vocabulary develops.

Schemata also vary according to their organizational patterns. As students mature, each schema expands to include many more facts, ideas, and examples. In cases of healthy development, the schemata are frequently clarified and reorganized. Learning new information or observing unfamiliar examples often causes a schema to be renamed or otherwise altered. For example, very young children have a schema labeled *doggy* that includes all four-legged, furry creatures. As they see new examples of animals and hear the appropriate labels for each type, the original schema of doggy is reorganized to become simply a subset of the schema *animal*. New patterns and relationships among schemata are forming every day of a child's life when the environment is full of unfamiliar concepts and experiences.

Schema theory helps to explain why some students are able to retrieve knowledge better than others. Students who have many accurately labeled schemata are more likely to have the background knowledge needed to learn an unfamiliar concept. Students whose schemata are richly detailed and well organized into patterns and hierarchies are much more likely to be able to retrieve useful information on request than are students whose schemata are vague and sparse.

Reflective teachers who believe it is in their power to help their students improve their cognitive processing recognize that one of the best ways to do this is to stimulate students to actively create more well-developed, accurately labeled, and better-organized schemata.

At the elementary grade levels, teachers recognize that one of their most important responsibilities is to aid students in schema development with accurate verbal labels. At the earliest grades (especially kindergarten), teachers emphasize spoken labels, teaching students to recognize and be able to name objects and concepts such as numbers, letters of the alphabet, and colors. At the primary grades, teachers emphasize the recognition and decoding of written labels as an integral part of the reading program. When students exhibit difficulties in learning to read, the reflective teacher is likely to plan learning experiences that assist the student in developing schemata that are prerequisites for reading.

Students who have been raised in environments characterized by few experiences with books are likely to have an underdeveloped schema for reading and books. This may also prove true for English language learners, who may not have access to text material in the home, or whose parents are reluctant to read books to them, even in the first language. Reflective teachers who consider the needs of the whole individual are likely to provide their students with many opportunities to hear stories read aloud, to choose from a tempting array of books, and to write their own stories as a means of developing a rich and positive schema for the concept of reading.

# Advance Organizers

When teachers want to assist students in retrieving information from their schemata, they provide verbal cues that help the students access the appropriate information efficiently. In the case of English language learners, this may require multisensory cues, gestures, and visual cues as well. Teachers can also provide cues to assist students in accurately and efficiently processing and storing what they read, see, or hear. Ausubel (1960) proposed that learners can comprehend new material better when, in advance of the lesson, the teacher provides a clear statement about the purpose of the lesson and the type of information that learners should look or listen for. This introductory statement is known as an *advance organizer.* English language learners benefit from a similar teaching strategy called "preview/review" in which the students are given an advance organizer prior to the lesson and a review following the lesson, both in the native language. This allows them to be prepared for the information they are about to receive and to clear up any questions or misunderstandings following the lesson.

When we relate this theory to information processing theory, it is apparent that the advance organizer provides the learner with an important cue as to which schema will incorporate this new knowledge. The learner can be more efficient in processing the information in working memory and transferring it to the appropriate schema in long-term memory than if no advance information was presented. For example, consider what is likely to happen when a third-grade teacher introduces a lesson on long division with no advance organizer. Some students will simply reject the new knowledge as incomprehensible. Using an advance organizer, the teacher might begin by writing an example on the board of a large number such as 100, and then ask students to subtract 10 from that number. Students will compute the subtraction problem $100-10$ and get 90. Then, they will compute $90-10$, $80-10$, and so on until they reach zero. In this way, students can use a previously learned skill of subtraction to organize their thoughts and make division more comprehensible. When the teacher asks how many 10s are in 100, the students can look at their subtraction problems and count the number of 10s they subtracted from 100. When the teacher then tells the students that division is a short way to solve this problem, it provides students with the cues they need to retrieve their subtraction schema in advance of the new learning.

In Chapter 6, we read about Alex's geology lesson plan on the methods and uses of core sampling to determine what is hidden beneath the surface of the earth. If Alex had just begun lecturing on this topic, many students might have been bewildered by the concept. Instead, Alex used cupcakes—something every child can understand—as an advance organizer for his lesson. Students were motivated by their desire to learn what was hidden beneath the surface of the cupcake, and as they performed their experiments, they were able to organize their thoughts about how scientists discover hidden geological phenomena as well.

In follow-up studies of Ausubel's hypothesis, many educational researchers designed experiments that showed the same effects. Therefore, this knowledge has been added to our growing common knowledge base about teaching and learning. In fact, this particular study demonstrates the way in which the knowledge base grows. The original hypothesis and study conducted by Ausubel (1960) led others to apply the principle to different types of students and environments. As the hypothesis was confirmed in subsequent studies, the knowledge was gradually accepted as a reliable principle of effective teaching. You probably experience the beneficial effects of advance organizers when your teachers tell you in advance what to listen for in a lecture or what to study for an exam. Now you can learn how to use this principle in your teaching career for the benefit of your students.

## Differentiated Instructional Strategies

One size does not fit all. This commonsense idea is used as a metaphor for learning by Gregory and Chapman (2002) as they describe methods teachers can use to respond to students' individual differences. It is possible to differentiate your school program in four important ways: content, assessment tools, performance tasks, and instructional strategies.

The first requirement for a differentiated curriculum is the creation of a safe and nurturing classroom environment much as we described in Chapter 2. For students to be able to express their needs and acknowledge their differences, there needs to be a climate of warmth, safety, and nurturance. Students need to be encouraged to take risks and to recognize that what is a safe and easy task for one student may pose a risk for others. The classroom environment must be collaborative and inclusive of all ranges of ability, talents, interests, and special needs without making a big point about it, without calling attention to it. This can frequently be accomplished by the creation of cooperative groups or tribes as described in Gibbs (2001). Tribes are communities, and communities tend to be inclusive and collaborative. In addition, there needs to be a sense of heightened interest, challenge, and stimulation in the classroom so that all students feel suitably challenged.

In every class and for almost every assignment, there are likely to be students who have great difficulty achieving the objective of the lesson. They are not likely to succeed unless the teacher modifies the initial lesson plan to provide them with individual or small-group lessons to reteach the skills they lack. For some students to achieve successful growth of skills and understanding, the teacher must be willing to alter the pace of the lessons, the difficulty of the material, and the criteria for success.

For students who learn more slowly, one modification that is needed is to reduce the volume of material in a lesson. If the grade-level lesson calls for the students to complete 20 problems in one class period, the teacher may reduce this requirement to 10 or 15 problems for a student who works slowly. If 20 were expected of this child, there would be little chance for success, resulting in frustration for both teacher and student. When the pace is lowered, the student has an opportunity to succeed and is likely to show the increase in motivation that accompanies success.

A child may have missed or not learned some important basic skills in previous grades for a variety of reasons. Illness, family problems, emotional difficulties, inferior teaching, or frequent moves may have prevented a child from learning the skills that most students his or her age have attained. For students who have not attained the basic skills necessary for a grade-level task, the modification needed is to teach the prerequisite skills before introducing the new material. When these prerequisite skills have been successfully mastered, the student may proceed at the pace of the rest of the class.

Some students in your classroom may have been identified as having *learning disabilities*. This label may mean that a child has one or more of a variety of learning disorders, some physical and others social or emotional in origin. When a student has been labeled learning disabled, a teacher who specializes in working with such students will be called on to create an individualized educational plan (known as an IEP) for that student. The classroom teacher will receive some guidance from the IEP on how to modify lessons for that student.

In some schools, many students come from backgrounds where the primary language of the home is not English. This has implications for instruction and lesson planning. Although these students may be able to understand the content of the lessons, the teacher may need to vary the delivery of the content in order to make it comprehensible to them. English as a second language (ESL) or sheltered English programs may be available for students learning this new language. When this is the case, the ESL teacher can assist teachers in assigning appropriate materials, adjusting teaching styles, and helping students acquire language skills that will help them to succeed. For students learning the language, it is necessary to offer contextualized learning experiences, lessons that provide context clues using props, visuals, graphs, and real objects. Teachers may need to speak more slowly and enunciate more clearly while encouraging their classmates to do so as well.

Students with hearing impairments need lessons that are modified to provide directions and instruction using visual aids. Similarly, students who have sight impairments may require extra auditory learning aids. Less obviously, some students in your classroom may have strong auditory, visual, or kinesthetic learning style preferences. To meet the needs of these students, teachers must modify their lessons to accommodate all three types of learning styles. This is usually accomplished by providing instructions and examples using visual aids to learn, such as the chalkboard, books, and written handouts. For auditory learners, the teacher may allow students to use tape recorders to record the instructions and examples given in class. Kinesthetic learners require manipulative materials and hands-on experience to make sense of unfamiliar material. When a teacher provides visual, auditory, and kinesthetic learning aids and experiences, students may modify their own lessons by taking in the needed information in the form that fits their own learning style preferences.

For students who work unusually rapidly and accurately on grade-level material, the task is to provide appropriately challenging learning experiences so that these students are able to continue to make gains even though they have mastered the grade-level requirements. Two standard methods serve the needs of highly able learners: *acceleration* and *enrichment*. Although both strategies are valuable modifications, acceleration is appropriate for sequential subjects such as math, and enrichment is appropriate for other subject areas. An inappropriate modification is to give the child more work at the same level. For example, if 20 math problems are required of the students working at grade level, an inappropriate modification is to require the highly able learner to do 40 problems. This practice is common but does not serve the student's real need to be challenged to gain new skills and understanding.

Some acceleration strategies that teachers can choose from include ability grouping, curriculum compacting, and mastery learning. *Ability grouping* requires the teacher to modify the curriculum to correspond to three different groups in the classroom. High, middle, and low groups are created, with variations in material and expectations for success. Reflective teachers must consider the possible negative consequences of lowered self-esteem and the possible positive benefits of academic fit and organizational efficiency when deciding whether or how to use ability grouping in the classroom.

In some schools, ability grouping may be organized across several grade levels. Subjects such as math and language arts may be scheduled at the same time of day, allowing students who work above or below grade level to leave their own classrooms and travel to other classrooms where the instruction is geared to their learning level.

*Curriculum compacting* can occur in a single classroom. This strategy requires the teacher to pretest students in various subject areas. Those students who demonstrate mastery at the time of the pretest are allowed to skip the subsequent lessons altogether. This strategy compacts the grade-level curriculum for them. Teachers then provide materials at a higher level of difficulty for these students, who typically work on their own through the more difficult material with little assistance from the teacher, who is busy instructing the students at grade level.

*Mastery learning* is a highly individualized teaching strategy designed to allow students to work at their own pace on material at their own difficulty level. Pretests are used to place students at the appropriate difficulty level. As each new skill is learned, a posttest demonstrates mastery. This technique is described in more detail in Chapter 10.

Enrichment strategies vary according to the imagination of the teacher who creates them. The teacher provides students who demonstrate mastery of a basic skill with a challenging application of that skill. Objectives and learning experiences at the higher levels of Bloom's taxonomy are often used as the basis for enrichment activities. A child who easily masters grade-level material is frequently allowed to investigate or research the topic in greater depth. For outcomes of enriched activities, students typically create an original product, perform an original skit, or teach the class something they have learned from research.

Modification of lessons is a continual challenge to teachers. It is not easy to decide whether a student needs a modified lesson. Reflective teachers struggle with this decision because they know that when they lower their expectations for a student, one of the effects may be lower self-esteem, creating the conditions for a self-fulfilling prophecy that the student cannot achieve at grade level. But they also know that when adult expectations are too high, students experience little or no success, leading to a similar downward spiral. For beginning teachers, it is wise to consult with other teachers in the school, especially teachers who specialize in working with students who have special needs. Talk over your concerns with these specialists and make informed decisions about lesson modifications.

# PRESENTATION SKILLS THAT INCREASE CLARITY AND MOTIVATION

Teaching is more than telling. You have been on the receiving end of teachers' lectures, discussions, and other forms of lessons for many years. You know from your own experience that the way teachers teach or present material has an effect on student interest and motivation, which are both integral aspects of the classroom climate. You may have been unable to understand the beginning of a lesson taught by a teacher who failed to get the full attention of a class before speaking. You have probably experienced sinking feelings when a teacher droned on in a monotonous voice during a lecture. You may have experienced frustration when a teacher explained a concept once and hurried on, ignoring questions or comments from the class. Reflective teachers are not likely to be satisfied with a dull, repetitive, or unresponsive presentation style. Most of them are eager to improve their presentation skills to stimulate interest and motivate student achievement.

## Getting Students' Attention

To consider systematically the way in which you present a lesson, think about the beginning. The introduction to a lesson is very important, whether it is the first lesson of the day or a transition from one lesson to another. As Kounin (1977) found in his study of well-functioning classrooms, transitions and lesson beginnings start with a clear, straightforward message or cue signaling that the teacher is ready to begin teaching and stating exactly what students should do to prepare themselves for the lesson. To accomplish this when you teach, you need to tell your students to get ready for a certain lesson and to give you their full attention. Some teachers use a visual cue for this purpose, such as a finger on the lips or a raised arm. Others may strike a chime or turn off the lights to cue the students that it is time to listen.

**PRAXIS**
Strategies for increasing student motivation to learn are tested in PRAXIS™ Exam Section 1c: Students as Learners.

It is unlikely that students will become quiet instantly. It will probably take a few moments to get the attention of every student in the class. While you are waiting, stand up straight and establish direct eye contact with those who are slow to respond. Watch quietly as the students get their desks, pencils, books, and other needed materials ready for the lesson. The waiting may seem uncomfortable at first. You will be tempted to begin before they are ready because you will think time is being wasted. Do not give in to this feeling. Wait until every voice is quiet, every chair stops scraping, every desk top stops banging, and every pencil stops tapping. Wait for a moment of pure, undisturbed silence. Then quietly begin your lesson. You will have the attention of every student.

Some teachers use a bit of drama to begin a lesson. They may pose a question or describe a condition that will interest their students. Richard Klein, a teacher at the Ericson School on Chicago's West Side, begins teaching a unit on aviation by asking students what they know about the Wright brothers. The students' replies are seldom very enthusiastic, so he unexpectedly asks them, "Then what do you know about the Wrong brothers?" They show a bit more interest but are still unable to provide many informed responses. So Mr. Klein turns off the lights and turns on a videotape of the Three Stooges in a skit called "The Wrong Brothers." Afterward, partly in appreciation of Mr. Klein's humor, the students show a greater willingness to learn about the real historical events.

Often teachers begin with a statement of purpose, describing how this particular lesson will help their students to make an important gain in skills or knowledge. Still others begin by doing a demonstration or distributing some interesting manipulative materials. This technique is called providing an *anticipatory set* both to gain attention and to motivate students to be interested in the lesson. Your presentation skills can benefit by using a variety of anticipatory sets appropriate to the lesson content and objective.

In contrast, less reflective teachers begin almost every lesson with: "Open your books to page _____. David, read the first paragraph aloud." This example employs no presentation skills. This nonmethod relies on the material itself to whet the students' interest in the topic. Although some materials may be stimulating and appealing, most are not. The message the teacher gives to the students is "I do not care much about anything; let's just get through this." The students' motivation to learn drops to the same level as this message and can best be expressed as "Why bother?"

Teachers often display a greater degree of excitement and interest for material they themselves enjoyed learning, and they pass that excitement about learning on to the students. A teacher who reads aloud with enthusiasm conveys the message that reading is fun. A teacher who plunges into a science investigation with delight causes students to look forward to science.

After you gain your students' attention and inspire them to want to know more, you move on to the lesson itself. Presentation skills that you can learn to use systematically in your lessons include the following:

Enthusiasm

Clarity

Smooth transitions

Timing

Variation

Interaction

Active, authentic learning experiences

Closure

## Enthusiasm

Animation is the outward sign of a teacher's interest in the students and the subject. Enthusiasm is the inner experience. There are at least two major aspects of enthusiasm. The first is conveying sincere interest in the subject. The other aspect is vigor and dynamics, and both are related to getting and maintaining student attention. Outwardly, the teacher displays enthusiasm by using a bright, lively voice; open, expansive gestures; and facial expressions that show interest and pleasure. Salespeople who use animated, enthusiastic behavior could sell beach umbrellas in the Yukon in January. Why should not teachers employ these techniques as well? You can "sell" long division better with an enthusiastic voice. You can convince your students that recycling is important with a look of commitment on your own face. You can encourage students' participation in a discussion with welcoming gestures and a warm smile.

Is animation something you can control? Absolutely. You can practice presenting information on a topic with your classmates, using an animated voice and gestures. They can give you feedback, which you can use to improve your presentation. Have yourself videotaped as you make a presentation. When you view yourself, you can be your own best teacher. Redo your presentation with new gestures and a different voice. Repeat this procedure several times, if necessary. Gradually, you will notice a change in your presentation style. You will add these techniques to your growing repertoire of effective presentation skills.

## Clarity

The clarity of the teacher's presentation of lesson directions and content is a critical factor in student success. Good and Brophy (2002) listed the importance of teacher clarity as a consistent finding in studies of teacher effectiveness. Their review of research on teacher clarity describes negative teacher behaviors that detract from clarity. These include using vagueness terms, mazes, discontinuity, and saying "uh" repeatedly.

As an example of *vagueness terms*, how would you expect students to respond to a lesson introduced in the following way:

> See if you can find page 76 and look at this division problem. This example might help you to understand a little more about how this all works. Maybe, if you read this, you can even get some idea of how to do these problems.

The vague terms such as *might, maybe, some* and *how this all works* in this example have the effect of making the teacher sound tentative and unsure of the content. As an introduction to a lesson, it is not likely to capture students' attention or interest. Clarity can be improved, in this example, by exchanging the vague terms for specific ones, resulting in a simple, straightforward statement:

> Turn to page 76 and look at the long-division problem at the top of the page. We will work through this example together until you feel confident that you know how to do this type of problem.

Clarity also suffers from what Good and Brophy (2002) call *mazes*: false starts or halts in the teacher's speech, redundancy, and tangled words. For example:

> Okay now, let's turn to page . . . um, just a minute. Okay, I've got it now. This chapter, er, section in the book lesson will *hopefully*, um, *it better or we're both in trouble*, get you to understand multiplication, *uh*, facts . . . I mean the patterns behind, underlying the facts.

Even when students attempt to pay attention, they may be unable to decipher the meaning of the teachers' words if the presentation is characterized by the false starts in this example. It is obvious that the way to improve this statement is to eliminate the redundant words. This example is a very simple one.

Clarity is also reduced when the teacher has begun to present a lesson, is interrupted by a student's misbehavior or a knock at the door, then begins the lesson again. Kounin (1977) observed that the most effective teachers are able to *overlap* teaching with other classroom management actions. That is, they are able to continue with the primary task, presenting the lesson to the class, while at the same time opening the classroom door or stopping misbehavior with a glance or a touch on the shoulder. When teachers can overlap their presentations, the clarity of their lessons is greatly enhanced.

The third teacher behavior that detracts from clarity is *discontinuity*, in which the teacher interrupts the flow of the lesson by interjecting irrelevant content (Good & Brophy, 2002). This is why lesson planning is so important. Without a plan, teachers may simply begin a lesson by reading from a textbook. As they or the students are reading, the teacher (or a student) may be reminded of something they find interesting. They may discuss the related topic for quite some time before returning to the original lesson. This side discussion may or may not be interesting or important, but it is likely to detract from the clarity of the original lesson.

The fourth detractor from teacher clarity is repeatedly saying "uh." It is also likely that other repetitive speech patterns are just as annoying, such as "you know." For the beginning teacher, it is likely that some of these teacher behaviors will occur simply as a result of nervousness or unfamiliarity with the content being taught. It is likely that these four detracting behaviors decrease as a result of teaching experience. In other words, as a teacher gains experience, the four detracting behaviors subside and clarity increases. Two other teacher behaviors found to enhance clarity were an emphasis on key aspects of the content to be learned and clear signaling of transitions between parts of lessons.

## Smooth Transitions

Just as lesson introductions are important to gain students' attention, smooth transitions are essential to maintaining that attention and making the classroom a productive working environment. Transitions occur within a lesson as the teacher guides students from one activity to another. They also occur between lessons as students put away what they were working on in one lesson and get ready for a different subject.

Good and Brophy (2002) note that knowing when to terminate a lesson is an important element of teacher withitness. When the group is having difficulty maintaining attention, it is better to end the lesson early than to doggedly continue. This is especially important for younger students, whose attention span for even the best lesson is limited. When lessons go on after the point where they should have been terminated, more of the teacher's time is spent compelling attention and less of the students' time is spent thinking about the material.

In addition to moving students to another classroom, transitions between activities and lessons may require that students move from place to place in the room, such as having one group come to the reading circle while another group returns to their seats. Usually students are required to exchange one set of books and materials for another. These movements and exchanges have high potential for noise in the form of banging desk tops, scraping chairs, dropped equipment, and students' voices as they move from lesson to lesson.

Jerky, chaotic transitions result when the teacher gives incomplete directions or vague expectations about student behavior. "Take out your math books" is incomplete in that the teacher does not first specify that the students should put away other materials they have been working with. The result may be that the students begin to work on desks cluttered with unnecessary materials.

Often, inexperienced teachers begin to give directions for a transition, and the students start to get up and move around while the teacher is speaking. When this happens, teachers may attempt to talk louder so that they can be heard over the din. A way to prevent this from occurring is to inform students clearly that they are to wait until all directions have been given before they begin to move.

Smooth transitions are characterized by clear directions from the teacher about what is to be put away and what is to be taken out, who is to move and where they are to go. Clear statements of behavioral expectations are also important. The same techniques for getting attention that were described previously apply to the beginning of each new lesson. After a noisy transition between lessons, it is essential for the teacher to have the students' complete attention before beginning the new lesson. The teacher should wait until all students move into their new positions and get all their materials ready before trying to introduce the lesson.

The teacher can use a signal to indicate that the new lesson is about to begin. A raised hand, lights turned off and on, or a simple verbal statement such as "I am ready to begin" will signal to the students that they should be ready for the next lesson. After giving the signal, the teacher should wait until the students have all complied and are silent before beginning the new lesson.

In considering strategies that result in smooth transitions, teachers do well to reflect on the students' needs for physical activity. In a junior high or high school, students can move between periods. At the elementary school or in a block period of time in the middle school, it is unrealistic to expect students to be able to sit still through one lesson after another. Some teachers take 5 to 10 minutes to lead students in singing or movement games between two working periods. Other teachers allow students to have a few moments of free time in which they may talk to friends, go to the washroom, or get a drink of water. Some transitions are good opportunities for teachers to read aloud from a storybook or challenge students to solve a brain teaser or puzzling mathematics problem. Reflective teachers find that when they allow students a respite and a change of pace during a brief transition period, the work periods are more productive and motivation to learn is enhanced.

## Timing

Actors, speakers, and comedians give considerable attention to improving the timing of their presentations. Good use of timing engages the attention of an audience, emphasizes major points, and sometimes creates a laugh. Teachers also work in front of an audience, and class presentations can be improved by considering timing and pacing as a means of getting attention and keeping it. Pausing for a moment of complete silence before you begin teaching is a good example of a way to incorporate timing into your presentation.

In most instances, students respond best to teachers who use a brisk pace of delivering information and instructions. Kounin's (1977) research on the most effective classroom managers demonstrated that students are best able to focus on the subject when the lesson has continuity and momentum. Interruptions result in confusion. When teachers forget to bring a prop, pause to consult a teacher's manual, or backtrack to present material that should have been presented earlier, inattention and disruptive behavior are likely to occur (Kounin). Jones (1987) found that students' attention improved when teachers gave them efficient help, allocating 20 seconds or less to each request for individual help or reteaching. When this time was lengthened, the result was restlessness and dependency on the part of students.

However, there are times when a pause in instruction can improve your presentation. Researchers have found that it is important to present new information in small steps, with a pause after the initial explanation to check for understanding. Students may not respond immediately during this pause because they need a moment to put their thoughts into words. Wait for them to do so. Encourage questions and comments. Ask for examples or illustrations of the fact or concept being discussed. This pause allows your students to reflect on the new material and allows you to test their understanding.

# Variation

Lesson variation is an essential presentation skill for teachers who want to develop a healthy, vital classroom climate. In analyzing classroom videotapes, Kounin (1977) noticed that satiation results in boredom and inattentiveness. If presentations are monotonous, students will find a way to introduce their own variation by daydreaming, sleeping, fiddling with objects, doodling, or poking their neighbors.

Planning for variation is important whenever you plan a lesson of 30 minutes or longer. Divide your lesson into several segments. Use lecture for only part of the time. For example, include segments of discussion, independent practice, small-group interaction, and application activities. If you cannot break a single lesson into segments, plan to use a variety of strategies during the course of a day. Use quiet, independent work for one subject, group interaction for another, lecture for a third, and hands-on activities for a fourth. In this way, your students will always be expectant and eager for each new lesson of the day. They will feel fresh and highly motivated to learn because of the variations in the way you choose to present material. If teachers attempt to address different learning styles in each lesson, they cannot help but provide variation in the classroom. All lessons should be checked for activities that address the different learning modalities. This is discussed in more detail later in this chapter.

# Interaction

Students thrive on interaction with the teacher and with their classmates. Rather than employing a traditional teacher-to-student, student-to-teacher communication pattern, open up your classroom to a variety of interactive experiences. Pushing the desks into a large circle encourages open-ended discussion from all students. Arranging the desks in small groups encourages highly interactive problem solving. Moving the desks aside leaves a lot of space in the middle of the room for activities. Pairing the desks provides opportunities for peer teaching or partnerships of other kinds. Your presentations can include all these types of activities, and you will find that it is motivating not only to your students but to you as well. You will feel a sense of expectant excitement as you say, "All right, students, let's rearrange the desks."

The need for interaction derives from the powerful motivational need for belonging described by Maslow (1954) and Glasser (2001). When these needs are frustrated or denied, disruptive behavior is likely to occur as a means of satisfying them. When teachers consciously plan interactive learning experiences, they allow students to satisfy their important drive for belonging and thereby prevent unnecessary discipline problems.

# Active, Authentic Learning Experiences

Teachers who value authentic learning present material in ways that engage their students in active rather than passive learning by including many verbal, visual, or hands-on activities. Consider a lecture on a topic such as the closed circuit in electricity. Ho hum. Add a visual aid such as a poster or an overhead projection. Students sit up in their seats to see better. Now add a demonstration. Turn off the lights. Hold up a battery, some copper wire, and a light bulb. Your students watch expectantly with a new sense of interest.

Turn on the lights again. All these techniques are adequate to teach the students a concept, but none is as valuable as a hands-on experience for in-depth learning and understanding. Picture this scene instead. After lunch the students come into their classroom to find a battery, a flashlight bulb, and a piece of copper wire on each desk. After getting their attention, the teacher simply says, "Working independently, try to get your bulb to light up." Lights go on all over the room as well as in students' eyes and in their minds as they struggle with this problem. The motivation to succeed is intense and intrinsic, not tied to any exterior reward. Each individual has a sense of power and a need to know.

The key to authentic learning is in allowing your students to encounter and master situations that resemble real life. Simulated experiences are often just as valuable as real life for elementary school students and are much safer and more manageable for the beginning teacher. While your students may never invent a marketable product, you can simulate this type of exploration by inventing products that are needed in your classroom. You can simulate the debate and communication skills necessary to solve international crises by creating a mini United Nations in your room, in which each student studies one country in depth and engages in substantive conversations about the varied needs and strengths of each country.

## Closure

At the end of most learning experiences, the teacher can ensure that students have mastered the objectives of the lesson or have integrated the new concepts into their existing schema by having them share what they did that worked and didn't work or by articulating and generalizing what they have learned about a new concept. For example, after a period of independent investigation about how batteries and light bulbs work, the teacher may ask students what they could do to make a light bulb give off more light. Such a teacher-led discussion is an essential part of active, hands-on learning. It provides a sense of closure.

Every lesson or presentation can benefit from some thoughtful consideration of its ending. It is important to allow time for closure when you plan your lessons. You may use this time to ask questions that check for understanding so that you will know what to plan for the lesson that follows. You may allow the students to close the lesson with their own conclusions and new insights by asking them an open-ended question such as, "What did you discover today?" If insight is to occur, it is likely to occur during this summary experience. At the close of one lesson, you can also indicate what will follow in the next lesson so that your students know what to expect and how elements of the lessons fit together to make a whole concept.

Michael Jordan and Adrienne Herrell were working recently as consultants at Hoover High School in San Diego, California. Hoover is a highly diverse school in an urban section of San Diego, which has been involved in a project in collaboration with San Diego State University to raise teacher effectiveness and student performance. As a part of their work at Hoover they were asked to plan and teach a 10th-grade lesson on *The Odyssey*, a required piece of literature in the 10th-grade English curriculum.

Michael taught the lesson in the classroom employing a sequence of activities that combined a number of the strategies discussed in this chapter. The lesson was planned to include an advance organizer, a video clip from the film version of the book, and an interactive discussion of book nine of *The Odyssey*. The video clip was selected in order to visually introduce new characters encountered in book nine and to set the stage for book 10.

Michael introduced the lesson with an advance organizer in the form of a web drawn on the whiteboard, allowing students to visualize the connections between the characters and the sequence of events so far.

Because of the number of second language learners in the class, Michael spent some time introducing new vocabulary, listing the words and short definitions on the whiteboard, and asking students to use the words in sentences related to the book to be read. Michael also treated them to a fun activity by reciting a rather funky rendition of "The Odyssey Rap" from Hart and Mantell's book, *Ancient Greece!* (1999), with the students taking on the role of the Greek chorus in appropriate places. The students took great delight in his futile but animated attempt at being "Rapper 0."

Michael then introduced the video clip, saying that it would show scenes from book nine and then show the characters they would meet in book 10. The students watched the 6-minute clip with interest. Michael paused the tape at intervals to discuss the individual characters. One student said, "Bernadette Peters looks just like I thought the goddess would look."

Another student added, "The part where the men are turned into pigs was funny. That's a good movie. Can we see the whole thing when we finish reading the book?" Their teacher promised them that this would be done.

A colorful pictographic map handout from Adrian Mitchell's (2000) book *The Odyssey*, showing the routes of the journeys of Odysseus, allowed the students to trace the journey up to book 10. As they explored the maps, they were working in small groups writing summaries of the events encountered so far. The discussion that followed the mapping activity asked student to predict what might happen next in book 10. When Michael told the students that they were to read the first part of book 10 for the next day's assignment, Yolanda said, "You can't leave now. We need to know what's going to happen next." Michael's response was, "Well, when you read the next book you will find out for yourself. Then we'll discuss it." Michael and the students were all smiling as he left the class. They all felt successful.

## SYSTEMATIC CLASSROOM INSTRUCTION

### Direct Instruction of New Knowledge and Skills

**PRAXIS**
Appropriate uses of direct instruction are tested in PRAXIS™ Exam Section 2a: Instruction and Assessment.

The curriculum contains a high proportion of basic knowledge and skills that learners must master thoroughly to succeed in the upper grades. Basic language concepts such as letter recognition, phonics, decoding words, writing letters and words, and the conventions of sentence and paragraph construction must be mastered. Basic mathematical concepts such as number recognition, quantity, order, measurement, and the operations used in computation must be learned.

Many models of direct instruction are appropriate for teaching this type of material. They are known as the five-step or seven-step lesson because they have been described in a chronological sequence of steps that results in getting students' attention; reviewing what has been learned up to the current lesson; systematically teaching, modeling, and practicing the new material; then demonstrating individual and independent mastery of what was taught.

The direct instruction model includes the following steps:

1. Create an anticipatory set to interest your students in the lesson by asking a thought-provoking question, providing an interesting visual aid, or using a puzzling and intriguing opening statement about the topic.

2. Connect this lesson with what has come before by providing a short review of previous, prerequisite learning or otherwise describing relationships between the current lesson and other subjects being studied by the class.

3. A short statement of the purpose of learning this new information is likely to convince your students that this lesson has a meaning to their lives beyond just achieving well in school. Tell them what they are going to learn and why it is important.

4. Present new, unfamiliar, and complex material in small steps, modeling each step by doing an example yourself. Give clear and detailed instructions and explanations as you model each process.

5. Provide a high level of active practice for all students. After you model a step, allow every student to practice the example on his or her own or with a learning partner.

6. Monitor students as they practice each new step. Walk around and look at their work as they do their sample problems. Ask a large number of questions to check for student understanding. Try to obtain responses from many students so that you know the concept is being clearly understood by the class. Provide systematic feedback and corrections as you see the needs arise.

7. At the end of each practice session, provide an opportunity for independent student work that synthesizes the many steps students have practiced during the lesson. This may be assigned as seatwork or homework. It is important to check this work and return it to students quickly, with assistance for those who have not demonstrated independent mastery of the new material.

When these seven strategies are reviewed quickly, many readers may respond with reactions such as, "But is not that what all teachers do? What is new about these methods?" It is true that many teachers have used these strategies throughout the history of education. Unfortunately, many other teachers have not. We have all observed classroom teachers who take a much less active role than these systematic procedures call for. They assign work, collect it, and have students exchange papers and correct it.

On close examination, these seven steps describe methods that would be used by a teacher who takes an active role in helping students process the new information being taught. They are also highly compatible with the concept of authentic learning because students are encouraged to think about what they are learning, construct the new knowledge in a meaningful context, and respond to substantive discussion in a supportive environment for learning. Although direct instruction is frequently associated in peoples' minds with whole-class instruction, you can readily see that these systematic steps can be used during small-group instruction as well.

In selecting appropriate teaching methods and strategies, reflective teachers are likely to look for and discover relationships among various theories of learning and methods of teaching. One such relationship exists between this direct instruction model of systematic teaching and the process of thinking and learning known as *information processing*.

The first step is to begin a lesson with a short review of previous, prerequisite learning. This strategy is a signal to the learner to call up an existing schema that will be expanded and altered in the new lesson. Beginning a lesson with a short statement of goals provides the student with an advance organizer that allows more efficient processing. In practice, these first two steps are often presented together and can be interchangeable with no ill effects.

Current information processing theories suggest that there are limits to the amount of new information that a learner can process effectively at one time (Gagne, 1985). When too much information is presented at one time, the working memory becomes overloaded, causing the learner to become confused, to omit data, or to process new data incorrectly. This overload can be eliminated when teachers present new material in small steps, with student practice after each step. This allows learners to concentrate their somewhat limited attention on processing manageably sized pieces of information or skills.

Teachers who model new skills and give clear and detailed instructions and explanations are likely to provide students with the support they need while they are processing new information in their working memories.

Providing students with a high level of active practice after each step, and again at the conclusion of a series of steps, is important because the practice enhances the likelihood that the new information will be transferred from working memory to long-term memory, where it can be stored for future use. Each time a new skill is practiced, its position in long-term memory is strengthened.

As teachers guide students during initial practice and ask a large number of questions, check for student understanding, and obtain responses from all students, they are also encouraging their students to process the information accurately. Learning occurs when schemata stored in long-term memory are expanded, enriched, and reorganized. Effective teacher questions and checks for understanding cause students to think about new ideas from a variety of perspectives and to update their existing schemata accordingly.

Providing systematic feedback and corrections and monitoring students during seatwork also increases the likelihood that students will process the important points and practice the new skills in the most efficient manner.

## Teacher Modeling and Demonstration

**PRAXIS**
Modeling is addressed in PRAXIS™ Exam Section 2b: Instruction and Assessment.

When teachers present new information to students, they must carefully consider the method they will use to introduce it. For students, it is rarely sufficient for teachers simply to talk about a new idea or skill. A much more powerful method of instruction is to model or demonstrate it first and then give students an opportunity to practice the new learning themselves.

A simple example of this technique occurs at the primary grades when teachers say, "First, I will say the word; then you will say it with me." In the middle grades, the teacher may first demonstrate the procedures used in measuring with a metric ruler and then ask students to repeat them. In the upper grades, teachers may write an outline of a paragraph and then ask students to outline the next one.

Teacher demonstration and modeling is an effective instructional technique for almost every area of the curriculum. It is useful in teaching music: "Clap the same rhythm that I do." It is vital in teaching mathematics: "Watch as I do the first problem on the chalkboard." It can be easily applied to the teaching of creative writing: "I'll read you the poem I wrote about this topic, and then you will write your own."

When teachers circulate throughout the classroom to monitor students as they practice or create their own work, it is efficient to use modeling and demonstration on a one-to-one basis to assist students in getting started or in correcting mistakes.

## Structuring Tasks for Success

Researchers have found that the degree of success that students have on school tasks correlates highly with achievement in the subject area. This supports the widely known maxim that "success breeds success." Both formal research and informal discussions with students reveal that when students experience success on a given task, they are motivated to continue working at it or to tackle another one. The number and type of successful learning experiences that students have affect their self-knowledge, leading them to have expectations regarding probable success or failure in future tasks.

To structure tasks for success, a teacher must create a good fit among his or her expectations, student ability, and the difficulty of the task. Rimm (1995), who has specialized in assisting underachieving students reach their potential believes that

> students must learn early that there is a relationship between their effort and the outcome. If their schoolwork is too hard, their efforts do not lead to successful outcomes but only to failures. If their work is too easy, they learn that it takes very little to succeed. Either is inappropriate and provides a pattern which fosters underachievement. When teachers select and present academic tasks to their students, they need to reflect continually on how well the task fits the students' present needs and capacities. (p. 327)

Glasser (1969) has been committed to improving schools throughout his career. As a psychiatrist, he strongly believes that a person cannot be successful in life "until he can in some way first experience success in one important part of his life" (p. 5). Glasser recognizes that children have only two places in which to experience success: home and school. If they are lucky enough to experience success in both settings, they are likely to be successful in their adult lives. If they achieve success at home, they succeed despite a lackluster school experience. But many students come from homes and neighborhoods where failure is pervasive. For these students especially, it is critical that they experience success in school. Glasser's (1969) book, *Schools Without Failure*, offers many realistic and practical methods for teachers to develop a classroom environment that breeds success. His newer book, *Every Child Can Succeed* (2001), updates this classic and valuable philosophy for your classroom.

## Matching Learning Styles and Teaching Styles

Learning styles are human characteristics that make some teaching methods more effective and appealing than others: Each person has a particular pattern of needs for optimum learning. Some students learn best in quiet rooms; others prefer a certain level of noise in the room. Students have individual preferences for light and dark, temperature, and seating.

Learning styles have been described in enormous variety including preferences for the structure of tasks and the best time of day for learning. Although you cannot accommodate all the needs of all your students, you will want to become aware of some of the many variations in learning styles so that when a student with an unusual sensitivity or a severe impediment to learning appears in your classroom (and this will happen), you will be able to reflect on the student's particular needs and provide a learning environment or restructure your teaching style to better match the student's learning style. A set of learning styles based on sensory preferences is especially useful to reflective teachers. Eight studies in the 1980s examined preferences for visual, auditory, and kinesthetic learning. Most learners were found to prefer receiving information either visually (by viewing or reading), auditorially (by hearing), or kinesthetically (by touching, working with, or otherwise manipulating materials). Teachers have a strong tendency to teach using the modality they prefer as a learning modality. Specifically, visual learners who rely on reading and viewing material to learn tend to rely on reading and other visual aids as teachers. Similarly, if you learn best by hearing, you may assume that others do also, and as a result, you may teach primarily using lecture and discussion. Kinesthetic learners who enjoy hands-on activities as students tend to provide many of these active learning materials in their own classrooms.

Currently, two major approaches exist for matching learning styles with teaching styles. One solution requires schoolwide cooperation. At each grade level, teachers may be identified as having visual, auditory, or kinesthetic preferences. Students are then tested and placed in the classroom with the teacher whose style matches their own. But this approach offers few opportunities for learners to improve their weaker learning modalities. Another approach is for each teacher to conscientiously plan to teach using all three modalities. For example, when presenting a lesson, the teacher will provide visual aids in the form of pictures and reading material; auditory aids in the form of lecture, a discussion, or tape-recorded material; and kinesthetic aids in the form of models or other manipulative materials. Studies show that providing all three types of learning experiences to all students is likely to result in higher achievement than simply by matching one style.

## Learning Experiences Designed for Multiple Intelligences

For students to experience success in school, it is necessary for teachers to understand that each individual perceives the world differently and that there is not just one way to learn or one way to teach. Prior to the emergence of this theory, most people were convinced that there was just one type of intelligence and that all human beings had an intelligence quotient (IQ) that ranged from zero to approximately 200, with the great majority of individuals in the average range near 100, plus or minus 16 points.

Gardner's (1983) theory of multiple intelligences disputes that old belief system. He proposed the alternate theory that humans have more than one type of intelligence. He originally described seven different intelligences: verbal/linguistic (word smart), logical-mathematical (logic and math smart), visual/spatial (art smart), musical (music smart), bodily-kinesthetic (body and movement smart), interpersonal (people smart), and intrapersonal (self-awareness smart). Later, he added another intelligence known as the naturalist, describing people who are very smart about nature and natural phenomena and a ninth intelligence called the existentialist. Other researchers have suggested that there are additional intelligences as well. In her teaching and curriculum planning, Judy Eby proposed that there is an intelligence related to mechanical and technical inventiveness. She created curriculum projects that encouraged students to be inventive and expand their technical and mechanical skills.

Teachers who wish to acknowledge and support the varied intelligences of their students try to provide learning experiences that allow students to use their special strengths in learning a subject or skill. For example, when teachers present new material to a class, they are likely to describe it in words and ask for verbal feedback for linguistically talented students. They attempt to provide problem-solving activities related to the subject for logical-mathematically oriented students. They give spatially talented students visual cues and allow them to react to the new material with drawings or diagrams. They may encourage musically talented students to commit the new material to memory via a song or allow them to create a musical response to what they have learned. They set aside time and space for bodily-kinesthetically gifted students to learn with their bodies by modeling, acting out, or pantomiming the material they are learning. For students with a special facility for interpersonal communication, teachers plan stimulating classroom discussions, and for students who are especially good at intrapersonal examination, they provide opportunities for written or oral responses related to how the new material relates to their own sense of self.

Kagan and Kagan (1998) provide a teacher's guide to using the multiple intelligences (MI) in their classrooms, entitled *Multiple Intelligences: The Complete MI Book*. This resource suggests three MI visions: matching, stretching, and celebrating. The first vision describes methods teachers can use to match instructional strategies with their students' varied intelligences. The second vision encourages teachers to stretch students' capacities in their nondominant as well as their dominant intelligence. The third vision suggests ways of celebrating and respecting one another's differences and unique patterns of learning.

By incorporating the concept of multiple intelligences in your curriculum planning, you are taking a large, positive step toward accomplishing the goal of differentiated instruction. One size does not fit all and neither does one teaching strategy. Lesson plans that take advantage of the various strengths, talents, and intelligences of your students are much richer and more interesting to everyone. Give visual/spatial learners the opportunity to do a visual presentation of what they learn. Ask kinesthetic learners to do an activity to demonstrate the concept. Let musicians create a musical response. Your classroom will hum with activity and enthusiasm.

Armstrong (2000) has explored ways that teachers can apply this concept to K–12 educational experiences. He describes these intelligences as:

Linguistic intelligence ("word smart")

Logical-mathematical intelligence ("number/reasoning smart")

Spatial intelligence ("picture smart")

Bodily-kinesthetic intelligence ("body smart")

Musical intelligence ("music smart")

Interpersonal intelligence ("people smart")

Intrapersonal intelligence ("self smart")

Naturalist intelligence ("nature smart")

Instead of a single IQ number, each individual has a different profile of strengths and talents among these eight domains. One child might have a very high spike in logical-mathematical intelligence and low levels of the seven other intelligences. Another student may have several high peaks on her profile. Some students may have relatively high levels for six or seven or more of the intelligences. In fact, it is our belief that people who choose elementary education as their field of study and career are often people who have relatively high levels of many intelligences. They are good, but not great, at math, language arts, sports, music, and art, for example. This profile may predispose a person to consider being a teacher at the elementary level where they are able to use all their talents and interests in creating curriculum and teaching the many varied subjects in the elementary curriculum. Reflective teachers are those who also embody high levels of interpersonal and intrapersonal intelligence. They know themselves and they want to know and understand others.

These teachers are aware of the relative strengths of their students in their multiple intelligences and plan activities to enable their students to learn best through their strongest ones. They also provide a variety of ways for the students to demonstrate their learning utilizing their differing intelligences.

As reflective teachers present new material to their students, they are aware of the variety of strengths in their students. They present material verbally for the linguistically intelligent, but add visuals to support the spatially intelligent, and problem-solving for the logical-mathematical learners. They encourage role play for the bodily-kinesthetic learners and present concepts in song and rhythm for the musically intelligent. They allow those strong in intrapersonal intelligence to read and study alone while providing discussion groups and cooperative learning for those stronger in interpersonal intelligence. Reflective teachers also recognize that students will need opportunities to demonstrate their mastery of concepts through their strong intelligences, as well. Students will be encouraged to share their learning in varying ways such as power point presentations, songs and jingles, posters and murals, journal writing, word problems in math using information and concepts from the area of study, or skits and games. This is not to imply that the teacher needs to present eight different lessons in order to meet the needs of the various intelligences. Instead, reflective teachers use a wide variety of presentation techniques, learning activities, and assessment strategies that allow all students to utilize their strengths while supporting their ability to learn in a variety of modes.

Reflective teachers also recognize the need for students to practice new skills using their strongest intelligences and provide learning centers for extended practice. These learning centers focus on new skills and concepts while providing experiences related to multiple intelligences such as; reading, writing, or listening centers (linguistic intelligence), puzzles, mathematic and logical problem-solving centers (logical-mathematical intelligence), art, diagramming, or spatial problem-solving centers (spatial intelligence), role playing or physical games (bodily-kinesthetic intelligence), listening to music, singing, rapping (musical intelligence), discussion, conferencing, debating, or group interactions (interpersonal intelligence), quiet reading with personal response, or personal reflection shared through audio-taping (intrapersonal intelligence), use of materials from nature, applying new concepts or skills to examples from nature (naturalistic intelligence). Once designed, these centers can be adapted for many different curricula areas.

Armstrong (2003) describes methods for using multiple intelligences to promote literacy. He retells the story of the blind men who touch various parts of an elephant and then report that an elephant is like a rope or a wall or a tree stump based on their individual experiences. Armstrong suggests that the concept of "literacy" is just as complex as an elephant and hence, is not easily described by any single individual. If a king were to ask several blind educators in his village to examine the concept of literacy, one educator might respond that literacy is made up of words—whole words. The second educator might return to the king saying: "Literacy is not made of whole words! It's made up of sounds! All kinds of sounds! Sounds like 'thhhh' and 'buh' and 'ahhhhh' and 'ayyyyy' and 'juh' and many more. In fact, I counted all the sounds, and there are exactly 44!" A third educator might examine the concept and claim that it is not made up of sounds or whole words at all. It's constructed out of stories, and fables, and songs, and chants, and poems, and books. And, a fourth educator might return saying, "They're all wrong! Literacy is made up of whole cultures. It's about understanding who we are and what we're capable of, and how each of us can speak, and read, and write with our own voices, and in this way contribute to the good of all" (Armstrong, 2003, pp. 5–6).

Reflective, caring teachers are likely to confer with their colleagues and try to understand concepts as complex as literacy with open minds and hearts. They will try to see one perspective and then look for other perspectives or sides to each issue. They search and reflect, search and reflect, actively trying to improve their own understanding of educational dilemmas. They are not threatened by the complexity or ambiguities inherent in their chosen profession. Rather, they become excited by the opportunities to learn more about each student's learning style and preferred intelligence patterns. They can use this information to create original unit plans or lesson plan activities that encourage their students to become active searchers and interpreters of knowledge rather than passive recipients of knowledge. With this philosophy, reflective teachers attempt to plan varied and interesting lessons, which their students view as authentic, meaningful, and purposeful learning experiences.

## REFLECTIVE ACTION EXPERIENCES FOR YOUR PROFESSIONAL PORTFOLIO

### Show Evidence of NBPTS Core Proposition 5: Teachers Command Specialized Knowledge of How to Convey a Subject to Students

**The NBPTS states in its core Proposition 5 that accomplished teachers possess knowledge of the most appropriate ways to present subject matter to students through analogies, metaphors, experiments, demonstrations, and illustrations. Teachers must be able to make well-reasoned and careful decisions about what aspects of the subject matter to emphasize, what type of presentation skill to employ, and how to pace their instruction.**

In this chapter, we have described many presentation skills that increase clarity and student motivation. To perceive your own teaching performance, it is important to see yourself in action. Teach a lesson that is videotaped. As you observe the videotape of your own teaching, observe your presentation skills and rate you enthusiasm, clarity, smooth transitions, timing, variation, interaction, active learning, and closure. If possible, teach the lesson again, making improvements according to your perceptions.

As you observe your videotape, allow yourself to see your own strengths and weaknesses. What does your body language say? How does your voice sound? Do you make false starts in your phrasing, such as "Here is an example . . . I mean . . . Look at this . . . "? Do you have eye contact with your students? What facial expressions and gestures do you want to work on? Choose one of the presentation skills described in this chapter that you want to improve in your own teaching. For example, you may choose *enthusiasm* if you feel that your presentation style is low key. For the next four occasions that you have to work with students, focus on the skill and attempt to improve it. Ask the classroom teacher for feedback and work to refine and master this skill to your own satisfaction.

Videotape the lesson again to see if the presentation skill you worked on has improved. Decide which are your strongest presentation skills. Write a one- to two-page description, analysis, and reflection of the videotape to include in your portfolio to give evidence of your ability to learn from experience.

## References

Armstrong, T. (2000) *Multiple intelligences in the classroom* (2nd ed.). Alexandria, VA: Association of Supervision and Curriculum Development.

Armstrong, T. (2003) *The multiple intelligences of reading and writing: Making the words come alive.* Alexandria, VA: Association of Supervision and Curriculum Development.

Ausubel, D. P. (1960). The use of advance organizers in the learning and retention of meaningful verbal material. *Journal of Educational Psychology, 51,* 267–272.

Gagne, E. (1985). *The cognitive psychology of school learning.* Boston: Little, Brown.

Gardner, H. (1983). *Frames of mind.* New York: Basic Books.

Gardner, H. (2000). *Intelligences reframed.* New York: Basic Books.

Gibbs, J. (2001). *Tribes.* Windsor, CA: CenterSource Systems.

Glasser, W. (1969). *Schools without failure.* New York: Harper & Row.

Glasser, W. (2001). *Every child can succeed.* Los Angeles: William Glasser Institute.

Good, T., & Brophy, J. (2002). *Looking in classrooms* (9th ed.). Pearson Boston: Allyn & Bacon.

Gregory, G., & Chapman, C. (2002). *Differentiated instructional strategies: One size doesn't fit all.* Thousand Oaks, CA: Corwin Press.

Hart, A., & Mantell, P. (1999). *Ancient Greece!* Charlotte, VT: Williamson.

Jones, F. (1987). *Positive classroom discipline.* New York: McGraw-Hill.

Kagan, S., & Kagan, M. (1998). *Multiple intelligences: The complete MI book.* San Clemente, CA: Kagan Cooperative Learning.

Kounin, J. (1977). *Discipline and group management in classrooms.* New York: Kreiger.

Maslow, A. (1954). *Motivation and personality.* New York: Harper & Row.

Mitchell, A. (2000). *The odyssey.* New York: Dorling Kindersley.

Newman, F., & Wehlage, G. (1993). Five standards of authentic instruction. *Educational Leadership, 50*(7), 8–12.

Piaget, J. (1970). *Science of education and the psychology of the child.* New York: Viking Compass Book.

Rimm, S. (1995). *Why bright children get poor grades.* New York: Crown.

CHAPTER 8

# Engaging Students
# in Classroom Discussions

In Chapter 7, we described a lesson on *The Odyssey* that Michael Jordan taught to a class of 10th graders. In this chapter, we want to focus on the way he conducted a highly interactive discussion about the book.

| | |
|---|---|
| **MJ:** | *We've been reading The Odyssey. Recently this book was listed as number one on a list of the 100 best books of all times. Why do you think it was ranked this high?* |
| **Amanda:** | *Well, it's really an old book and it's been read for many years.* |
| **Jose:** | *It's an action story with lots of strange twists.* |
| **MJ:** | *Those are two good reasons. What are some other things you think would need to be a part of a book in order for it to make the list?* |
| **Jose:** | *Must have to be pretty interesting.* |
| **Carlos:** | *It would have to have "stood the test of time."* |
| **MJ:** | *What does that mean?* |
| **Amanda:** | *Like I said before, it's been around for a long time and people still want to read it.* |
| **Maria:** | *It also has to have something different about it. It can't be like a lot of other books.* |
| **Jose:** | *This book reminds me of some of the great action movies too, like Matrix or Spiderman.* |
| **Carlos:** | *I agree with Jose. It just has a lot of action and a lot of surprises like men being turned into pigs and big monsters with one huge eye in the middle of their foreheads.* |
| **MJ:** | *Well, those things certainly make it kind of weird and interesting to read, but what was special about having those kinds of characters in the story?* |
| **Claudia:** | *It was more about what Odysseus did with those characters, how he reacted to them.* |
| **MJ:** | *You're right, Claudia, we read a lot about how he interacted with the characters and situations he encountered. So, thinking about that, Jose, how did it remind you of Spiderman and the Matrix?* |
| **Jose:** | *Well, like, they had to deal with some bad dudes and situations, like this guy did.* |
| **MJ:** | *And did they have to be creative in solving problems like Odysseus did?* |
| **Jose:** | *Yeah, they had to come up with special ways of taking care of every problem they came up on.* |
| **Maria:** | *And they were heroes, like he was, like always good defeating evil.* |
| **Claudia:** | *Yeah, that's kind of what makes this a great book. It's about a hero struggling against evil and winning. And that kind of story is still being used today, like in the movies Jose is talking about. It's still heroes taking on the bad guys and winning.* |
| **Jose:** | *Is that what you mean when you say it "stood the test of time?" It's like a story that's been around for a long time and it's still being talked about and copied.* |

This introductory discussion then led into further discussions and writing activities based on the idea of "heroes"—examples from fiction and real life—and what makes them a hero. Michael encouraged the students to identify the present-day heroes they admired, and they compared their examples to Odysseus. Bringing these "old ideas" into the present, and relating it to students' experience, made the classic story and theme more relevant and comprehensible to the students without distorting the ideas of the original story.

When students become actively and enthusiastically interested in thinking about and discussing an idea, they are experiencing *cognitive engagement*, a powerful new concept for teachers to aim for when they select teaching strategies for their classrooms.

Cognitive engagement results in the opposite of the sterile, passive classroom environment in which students attend listlessly to the lessons and carry out their seatwork and homework with little real effort or interest. When students are fully engaged in reading, listening, discussion, or creation, the classroom climate is likely to be as lively and stimulating as a thundershower. When teachers structure classroom discussions to engage their students fully in substantive, meaningful, and highly interactive exchanges of information and ideas, authentic learning is likely to occur, even without the use of hands-on manipulatives.

Can you recall a classroom learning experience so powerful that you have almost total recall of it many years later? When you recall the event, do you feel as if you are reliving it because the memory is still so vividly etched in your mind? Do you think of this event as life changing? Perhaps it altered the way you think about an issue or caused you to change your career goal or provoked you into making a lifestyle change. Bloom (1981) calls these relatively rare classroom events *peak experiences.*

For many students, peak learning experiences occur during especially stimulating classroom discussions in which all members of the classroom community are expressing ideas, opinions, and points of view. Students experience these discussions as authentic, substantive, and valuable. Teachers also have a sense of exhilaration and pride when they are able to create the environment and structure needed for such powerful exchanges. In this chapter, we will examine some of the strategies you can use to stimulate and guide substantive and satisfying classroom discussions.

## ASKING QUESTIONS THAT STIMULATE HIGHER-LEVEL THINKING

Imagine you are observing a classroom discussion after the students have read a biography of Dr. Martin Luther King, Jr. The teacher asks the following questions:

When and where was Dr. King born?

Who were the other members of his family?

How did King's father and mother earn a living?

What career did Dr. King choose?

What does the term *ghetto* mean?

What does *prejudice* mean?

What did Dr. King accomplish that earned him the Nobel Peace Prize?

**PRAXIS**
This chapter prepares you for PRAXIS™ Exam Section 3c: Communication Techniques That Stimulate Discussion.

As you watch and listen to this discussion, you might reflect on the way you would lead it and the questions you would like to ask the students. Perhaps you believe that there are other, very different types of questions that the teacher could use to stimulate higher-level thinking and engage the students in a discussion that connects what they have read to their own lives.

Many reflective teachers use Bloom's taxonomy (Bloom, Engelhart, Furst, Hill, & Krathwohl, 1956) to think of discussion questions that promote the use of higher-level thinking processes. Discussion questions can be readily planned at every level of the taxonomy, just as other learning experiences are planned. The term *higher-level* refers to the top four levels of the hierarchy:

Higher Level Thinking Processes

> Evaluation
>
> Synthesis
>
> Analysis
>
> Application

Lower Level Thinking Processes

> Comprehension
>
> Knowledge

In the previous example, the teacher has asked only lower level (knowledge and comprehension) questions. But you can plan your discussions to highlight the thinking processes of application, analysis, synthesis, and evaluation. Although this system can be used at any grade level and with any topic, the following examples are taken from the discussion of Dr. King's biography.

**Knowledge Level.** At this level, the learners are asked to recall specific bits of information, such as terminology, facts, and details.

> When and where was King born?
>
> Who were the other members of his family?
>
> What were the jobs King's father did to earn a living?
>
> What jobs did his mother do?
>
> What career did Dr. King choose?

**Comprehension Level.** At this level, the learners are asked to summarize and describe the main ideas of the subject matter in their own words.

> What does the term *ghetto* mean?
>
> What does *prejudice* mean?
>
> How did the church affect King's life?
>
> What did Dr. King accomplish that earned him the Nobel Peace Prize?

While the teacher in the previous example stopped here, a reflective teacher is likely to use those questions only as a beginning to establish the basic facts and ideas so that the class can then begin to engage in a spirited discussion of how Dr. King's life and accomplishments have affected their own lives.

**Application Level.** At this level, the learners are asked to apply what they have learned to their own lives or to other situations. Are there ghettos in this community? What are they and who is affected by them?

Give an example of prejudice that has affected you.

If Dr. King were alive today, what do you think he would be most concerned about? What do you think he would do about it?

**Analysis Level.** At this level, the learners are asked to describe patterns, cause-and-effect relationships, comparisons, and contrasts.

How did Rosa Parks's decision to sit in the front of the bus change King's life? How did her decision change history?

In what ways was Dr. King a minister, a politician, and a teacher?

If Dr. King had never been born, how would your life be different today?

**Synthesis Level.** At this level, the learners are asked to contribute a new and original idea on the topic.

Complete this phrase: I have a dream that one day. . .

If there were suddenly a strong new prejudice against people that look just like you, what would you do about it?

How can we, as a class, put some of Dr. King's dreams into action?

**Evaluation Level.** At this level, the learners are asked to express their own opinions or make judgments about some aspect of the topic.

What do you believe was Dr. King's greatest contribution?

Which promotes greater social change: nonviolence or violence? Give a rationale or example to defend your answer.

What social problem do you most want to change in your life?

Some teachers find that Bloom's taxonomy is a useful and comprehensive guide for planning classroom discussion questions as well as other classroom activities. Others find that the taxonomy is more complex than they desire and that it is difficult to discriminate among some of the levels, such as comprehension and analysis or application and synthesis. Other systems of classifying thinking processes are available. Doyle (1986) proposes that teachers plan classroom tasks in four categories that are readily applicable to classroom discussions: (1) memory tasks, (2) procedural or routine tasks, (3) comprehension tasks, and (4) opinion tasks.

Classroom questions and discussion starters can be created to fit these four task levels, as follows:

*Memory Questions:* Learners are asked to reproduce information they have read or heard before.

When and where was Dr. King born?

Who were the other members of his family?

*Procedural or Routine Questions:* Learners are asked to supply simple answers with only one correct response.

What jobs did King's father and mother do to earn a living?

What career did Dr. King choose?

*Comprehension Questions:* Learners are asked to consider known data and apply them to a new and unfamiliar context.

What does the term *ghetto* mean?

What does *prejudice* mean?

How did the church affect King's life?

What did Dr. King accomplish that earned him the Nobel Peace Prize?

How did Rosa Parks's decision to sit in the front of the bus change King's life? How did her decision change history?

In what ways was Dr. King a minister, a politician, a teacher?

*Opinion Questions:* Learners are asked to express their own point of view on an issue, with no correct answer expected.

Are there ghettos in this community? What are they and who is affected by them?

Give an example of prejudice that has affected you.

If Dr. King were alive today, what do you think he would be most concerned about? What do you think he would do about it?

Complete this phrase: I have a dream that one day. . .

If there were suddenly a strong new prejudice against people who look just like you, what would you do about it?

What do you believe was Dr. King's greatest contribution?

What can we, as a class, do to carry out some of Dr. King's dream?

Which promotes more social change: nonviolence or violence? Give a rationale or example to defend your answer.

What social problem do you most want to change in your life?

You will notice that the questions in Doyle's four categories are the same as the ones listed in the taxonomy's six levels. Questions at the comprehension and analysis levels are both contained in Doyle's comprehension category, and questions at the application, synthesis, and evaluation levels are contained in the opinion category. Both of these systems offer teachers a comprehensive framework for planning a range of thought-provoking questions. You may choose to write out the questions you ask ahead of time, or you may just remind yourself as you participate in a discussion that you need to include questions from the higher-level thinking categories.

## STRATEGIES FOR INTERACTIVE DISCUSSIONS

In some classrooms, what pass for discussions are really dull and repetitive question-and-answer periods. Some teachers may simply read aloud a list of questions from the teachers' manual of the textbook and call on students to recite the answers. As you probably recall from your own school experiences, when this type of "discussion" occurs, many students disengage entirely. They read ahead, doodle, or do homework surreptitiously. They seldom listen to their classmates' responses; and when it is their turn to recite, they frequently cannot find their place in the list of questions.

Reflective teachers value the process of considering alternatives and debating opinions and ideas. That is how reflective teachers approach the world themselves, and they are likely to want to stimulate the same types of behavior among their students. In the discussion centered on *The Odyssey* (Homer, translated by Butler, 1969) Michael structures the discussion to encourage the students to become actively involved, to think deeply and express their thoughts, and to compare the text to others with which they are familiar. He encourages them to relate the ancient tale to current pieces of culture with which they can personally relate. Through the process of active engagement, the students' motivation to read and understand the assignment is increased.

Authentic learning experiences depend heavily on the promotion of high-quality and actively engaged thinking. Teachers who are committed to creating authentic learning for their students do so by planning discussions that stimulate *higher-level thinking processes, problem-solving skills, critical thinking*, and *creative thinking* and acknowledge the *multiple intelligences* of their students.

These terms and concepts can be confusing and overwhelming for the beginning teacher, who may think it is necessary to establish separate programs for each of them. That is not the case, however. It is possible to discover common attributes among them and plan classroom discussions and other experiences that promote high-level thinking, problem-solving skills, and critical and creative thinking in all seven of the multiple intelligences at the same time. One question may pose a problem; another may call for a creative response; a third may be analytical; and a fourth may ask students to evaluate a situation and make a critical judgment. The best (which is to say, the most highly engaging) classroom discussions do all of these in a spontaneous, nonregimented way.

The following sections describe various thinking processes along with alternatives for planning classroom discussions to promote these processes. As you read these sections, reflect on the similarities and differences; look for patterns and sequences; and consider how you would use, modify, and adapt these systems in your classroom.

Although these processes can be applied to both academic and nonacademic areas of the curriculum, we will illustrate how classroom discussions are created and managed, using the topic of racial discrimination as a common theme. In this example, the operational goal is to promote understanding of how racial discrimination affects the lives of human beings and to generate a sense of respect for individuals who are different from oneself.

## Problem-Solving Discussions

Much has been written about the need for developing students' problem-solving and decision-making abilities. This can be done by presenting students with a complex problem and providing adequate scaffolding support for them to learn how to solve problems. Although some solutions require paper and pencil or a hands-on experimental approach, classroom discussion can solve other problems.

To create productive problem-solving discussions, the teacher must understand the processes involved in problem solving and then structure the questions to guide students through that process. A problem is said to exist when "one has a goal and has not yet identified a means for reaching that goal. The problem may be wanting to answer a question, to prove a theorem, to be accepted or to get a job" (Gagne, 1985, p. 138).

According to cognitive psychologists, the framework for solving a problem consists of identifying a goal, a starting place, and all possible solution paths from the starting place to the goal. Some individuals are efficient and productive problem solvers; others are not. An excellent classroom goal for the beginning teacher is to help students become more efficient and more productive problem solvers.

Nonproductive problem solvers are likely to have difficulty identifying or defining the problem. They may simply feel that a puzzling situation exists, but they may not be aware of the real nature of the problem. Students who are poor problem solvers need experience in facing puzzling situations and defining problems. They also need experience in identifying and selecting worthwhile goals.

When a problem has been defined and a goal established, it is still possible to be either efficient or inefficient in reaching the goal. Efficiency in problem solving can be increased when students learn how to identify the alternative strategies to reach a chosen goal and recognize which ones are likely to provide the best and quickest routes to success. This can be done by helping students visualize the probable effects of each alternative and applying criteria to help them choose the most valuable means of solving the problem they have defined.

As in the teaching of higher-level thinking processes, several useful systems are available to teachers who want to teach students to become better problem solvers. Many teachers enjoy using the technique known as *brainstorming*, which includes four basic steps:

1. Define the problem.
2. Generate, without criticism or evaluation, as many solutions as possible.
3. Decide on criteria for judging the solutions generated.
4. Use these criteria to select the best possible solution.

Brainstorming is an excellent way to generate classroom discussion about a puzzling issue. Rather than formulating a series of questions, the teacher supplies a dilemma or a puzzle, teaches the students the steps involved in brainstorming, and then leads them through the process itself.

In discussing the life of Martin Luther King, Jr., and helping students to understand the effects of racial discrimination, the teacher might use a portion of the classroom discussion to brainstorm answers to one of the most perplexing questions. For example, the teacher might choose to use brainstorming to expand discussion of the following question:

> If Dr. King were alive today, what do you think he would be most concerned about? What do you think he would do about it?

The techniques of brainstorming call for the teacher to pose the question or problem in such a way that it engages students' interest and motivates them to take it seriously. Because students may not be proficient at discussion of this sort, it is frequently necessary for the teacher to give additional cues and suggestions as a scaffold. In this instance, the teacher might need to pose the original question and then follow it up with prompts such as these:

> What do you think he'd be concerned about in our community?
>
> What has been in the news lately that might alarm him?

Who are the people in the world who are presently in need?

What about threats to our environment?

Open-ended questions such as these will generate many more responses than if they were not used. After recording all of the student responses on the chalkboard, the teacher leads the students through a process of selecting the most important items for further consideration. This may be done by a vote or general consensus. When the list has been narrowed to several important issues, the teacher must then lead the students through the process of establishing criteria for judging the items.

Because the question is related to King's values, one possible criterion is to judge whether King showed concern for the issue in his lifetime. Another criterion might be the number of people who are threatened or hurt by the problem. After judging the items by these criteria, the class makes a judgment about which items would most concern King. Then the process of brainstorming begins again, but this time the problem the class is considering is what King would be likely to do to help solve the problem. Generating responses to the first question—"If Dr. King were alive today, what would he be most concerned about?"—will help students understand the many aspects of racial discrimination that exist today. By selecting one of these as the main concern and generating responses to the question "What do you think he would do about it?" the students will reflect on their own responsibilities to other human beings and on ways to increase tolerance and build a sense of community in their neighborhoods.

To moderate a brainstorming discussion, the teacher faithfully records every response generated by the students, no matter how trivial or impossible it sounds. The teacher then leads students through the process of eliminating the least important items and finally works through a process of establishing criteria to use in evaluating the best possible solutions.

Brainstorming alone does not solve problems. It merely trains students to think productively about problems and consider many alternative solutions. In some classrooms, teachers may wish to extend the hypothetical discussion of possible solutions to an actual attempt to solve a problem or at least contribute to a solution.

## Group Investigations

Occasionally, a crisis or an unusual event will excite students' interest and concern. When the topic is appropriate, and especially if it relates to the curriculum for that grade level, teachers allow students to participate in an investigation of the puzzling event to learn as much as they can about the subject and, in the process, learn research and communication skills. Often teachers create puzzling situations or present unusual stimuli as a means of causing students to become curious and learn how to inquire and investigate to gather information that leads to accurate assessments and judgments.

Perhaps there is a change in local government or a national election that students want to know more about. Perhaps a change occurs in the way their own school is managed, or a community event that affects their lives unfolds around them. The first hint of student interest may occur in a classroom discussion. To the extent that reflective teachers are sensitive to their students' concerns, they may wish to allow students time to talk about the event.

The first discussion of the event may simply be time to air students' early opinions and express their feelings about the event. If the teacher decides that the event is a worthwhile issue, the class may be encouraged to read about it, ask questions, or interview other members of the community and bring back their findings for more expanded discussions. These, in turn, may lead students to form small investigative groups that attempt to discover as much as they can about the event and even suggest solutions to the problems or issues under discussion.

The teacher's role in this type of investigative discussion is to encourage students to find out more about the subject and to allow them opportunities to express their opinions and share their findings. The discussion may continue for a few days or a few weeks, depending upon the seriousness of the event and its impact on the students' lives. Under the guidance of a caring, reflective teacher, this type of discussion is authentic learning at its very best.

When teachers want to stimulate curiosity and discussion, they may present a social dilemma or demonstrate a strange event. For example, the teacher may drop a number of different fruits and vegetables into a large, clear bowl of water, asking students to predict and observe which will sink and which will float. Students are encouraged to ask the teacher questions and to formulate hypotheses about floating and sinking objects. As the discussion progresses, the large group discussion may be adjourned to allow small groups to make investigations of their own, reaching their own conclusions. After small group investigations are completed, class members reconvene to share their hypotheses, demonstrate their investigations, and present their conclusions.

## Discussions That Promote Critical Thinking

**PRAXIS**
Strategies for encouraging critical thinking are tested in PRAXIS™ Exam Section 2a: Instruction and Assessment.

The term *critical thinking* is not a separate and distinct concept that is different from higher-level thinking processes and problem solving. It overlaps both of them. It is presented here in a separate section because during the past few years it has become a field of study with its own research base and suggested classroom processes.

The field of study known as critical thinking grew out of the philosophical study of logic, which was designed to train people to think about a single hypothesis deductively to arrive at a rationale conclusion. Logical thinkers are prepared to deal with a single issue in depth, but sometimes they are not prepared to deal with unexpected evidence or ideas. They may be stumped when they are asked to think "outside the box," or deal with complex ideas that defy one right answer.

Critical thinking, then, is partially defined as a complex set of thinking skills and processes that are believed to lead to fair and useful judgments. Lipman (1988) points out the strong association between the words *criteria* and *critical thinking*. Through the use of problem-solving discussions, students learn the technique of brainstorming and applying criteria to select the best solution.

But critical thinking is a much more multifaceted concept than problem solving. Critical thinking involves more than simply training students to use a set of strategies or procedures. It also involves establishing some affective goals for students to support them in becoming more independent and open-minded. Richard Paul (1988), director of the Center of Critical Thinking at Sonoma State University in Rohnert Park, California, proposes that some of the affective attributes of critical thinking include independence, avoidance of egocentricity and stereotyping, and suspension of judgment until appropriate evidence has been gathered.

Paul recommends that school curricula be designed to teach students cognitive strategies such as observation, focusing on a question, distinguishing facts from opinions, distinguishing relevant from irrelevant information, judging credibility of sources, recognizing contradictions, making inferences, and drawing conclusions. Because almost every specialist in critical thinking proposes a slightly different set of thinking processes and skills that compose critical thinking, reflective teachers need to judge for themselves which of the strategies to stress in their own classrooms.

A recent addition to the knowledge base on critical thinking is the topic of critical literacy. Vasquez (2003) describes critical literacy as an approach to reading that empowers the reader to ask questions about the origin of the reading material. The reader is encouraged to ask questions about the author's point of view, the purpose of the text, and who benefits from the knowledge that is being shared. The reader is also taught to ask questions such as, "Is there another voice that should be heard in this discussion?"

## Discussions That Improve Observation Skills

Whenever possible in your curriculum, bring in photos or objects related to the subject you are studying. Invite students to read their stories, essays, or poems aloud for other students to listen and respond to. You may even be able to stage an event to elicit student observation skills. For example, as you study the concept of community, ask some students to role-play a disagreement. Then ask them to describe what they observed, using as many details as they can. Call on as many students as possible and encourage each of them to make their own response to the situation. If they seem to be making impetuous or repetitive observations, guide their thinking with questions that ask them to explain or support their observations.

Show your students that they can observe with all five senses, not just sight. As you study nutrition, for example, allow students to taste a variety of foods and describe their taste observations. During a study of sound waves, provide a variety of different sounds and ask students to identify the objects they have heard. The more students use their five senses and discuss what they observe, the more likely they are to develop accurate, detailed schemata for the subject matter they are studying.

## Discussions That Enhance Comparing Skills

In classroom discussions, compare two or more objects, stories, characters, or events by asking students first to articulate ways that the two subjects are the same. Take as many responses as possible. Then ask students to tell how the two are different. This type of discussion can occur in any subject area. You may ask them to compare fractions with percentages in math, George Washington and Abraham Lincoln in history, Somalia and the United States in geography, electric- and gasoline-powered engines in science, or the wording and effects of two different classroom rules in a classroom meeting.

## Discussions That Guide Classification Skills

Introduce a collection of words or, for young children, a set of manipulative materials appropriate to the grade level. For example, you may use a collection of buttons, small toys, macaroni shapes, or shells. When possible, conduct this type of discussion using cooperative groups. Ask each group to examine the collection, look for distinguishing attributes, and create a system for classifying the objects into groups. During follow-up discussions, a spokesperson for each group can describe the attributes the group observed and present a rationale for the classification system they used.

Older students can classify the words on their spelling lists, books or stories they have read, foods, games, clothing, famous people, or television programs. The best results occur when the teacher has no preestablished criteria or notion of right or wrong classification systems. As students discuss the characteristics of the shells or television programs they are classifying, they may discover some of the same attributes that adults have already described, or they may discover a completely original rationale on which to base their categories. The object of the discussion is not to get the most "right" answers but to participate in the open-ended process of sharing their observations and making critical judgments they can defend with evidence.

## Discussions That Identify Assumptions

Use advertisements for products your students want to buy as a means of stimulating a discussion to identify assumptions people make. Show a newspaper ad for a product and ask students to describe what they believe the product will be like based on the advertisement alone. Then discuss the actual product and compare the students' prior assumptions with the real item.

Talk about assumptions human beings make about each other. Ask students to examine the meaning of clothing fads in their lives. Whenever a subject arises that illustrates the effects of making decisions based on assumptions, take the time to discuss these events with your class. For example, ask students to discuss what assumptions are being made when they hear someone say, "He's wrong," or "She's the smartest girl in the class."

## Socratic Dialogues

One form of discussion that reveals individual assumptions to the speaker and the listeners at the same time is the technique known as *Socratic dialogue*, in which the teacher probes to stimulate more in-depth thinking among students. Teachers who use this method believe that individuals have many legitimate differences in opinion and values. They want to encourage their students to listen to each other to learn different points of view.

To conduct a Socratic dialogue, the teacher presents an interesting issue to the class and asks an individual to state an opinion on the case. With each participant, the teacher probes by asking the student to identify the assumptions and values that led to this opinion. Further questions may be posed to the same student to encourage clarification of the consequences of the student's opinion or the relative importance it has in the student's priorities.

This type of exchange between the teacher and one student may take several minutes and from 3 to 10 questions. While the teacher conducts the discussion with one student, the others are expected to listen carefully, comparing what they believe to what is being said by their classmate. Another student with a different opinion is likely to be the next subject of the Socratic dialogue. When the teacher believes that the most important issues have been raised by the dialogues, then a general class discussion can be used to express how opinions may have been changed by listening or participating in the Socratic dialogues.

## Discussions That Enhance Creative Thinking

Can individuals learn to be creative? Perhaps the more important question is, do individuals learn to be uncreative? More than a century ago, William James (1890) stated his belief that education trains students to become "old fogies" in the early grades by training them to adopt habits of convergent, conformist thinking.

Divergent thinking is the opposite of convergent thinking in that it deviates from common understanding and accepted patterns. Guilford (1967) contributed a definition of divergent thinking that is still well accepted and has become the basis for E. Paul Torrance's (1966–1984) well-known tests for creativity. Guilford describes (and Torrance's test measures) four attributes of divergent thinking: *fluency, flexibility, originality,* and *elaboration.* In other words, a divergent thinker is one who generates many ideas (fluency), is able to break with conformist or set ideas (flexibility), suggests ideas that are new in the present context (originality), and contributes details that extend or support the idea beyond a single thought (elaboration).

Classroom discussions can be designed to help students develop these four attributes of creativity. In a technique similar to brainstorming, the teacher can ask students to generate many responses to a single question as a means of helping them to become more fluent in their thinking. For example, given our topic of King's "I have a dream" speech, the teacher may begin the process with the unfinished sentence, "I have a dream that someday . . . "

Students may be asked to write their own responses for several minutes before the actual discussion begins. This allows each student to work for fluency individually. Then the ideas on paper are shared, and other new ideas are created as a result of the discussion. To promote flexibility, the teacher may ask students to imagine making their dreams come true and suggest ways that they could do this, using flexible and original strategies rather than rigid and ordinary methods. Finally, to extend the students' elaborative thought, the teacher may select one dream and ask the entire class to focus on it and create a more detailed vision and a more in-depth plan to accomplish it.

Einstein and Infeld (1938) add a further dimension to our understanding of creative thinking:

> The formulation of a problem is often more essential than its solution, which may be merely a matter of mathematical or experimental skill. To raise new questions, new possibilities, to regard old problems from a new angle, requires creative imagination and marks real advance in science. (p. 92)

Problem solving, then, is related to creative thinking. It is readily apparent that the methods described for improving problem solving involve critical thinking and that both involve the use of higher-level thinking processes. Whatever we call it, the goal of aiding students in developing better thinking skills is an integral part of any classroom discussion.

Just as we respect Einstein's ability to pose new problems, so should we respect and develop our own and our students' capacity to ask questions and suggest new ways of solving age-old problems. Certainly, the teaching profession needs people with the capability of regarding old educational problems from a new angle. Often it is the newest and youngest members of a faculty who see things from a helpful new perspective and suggest new ways of dealing with difficult school issues.

Another dimension of creativity involves the production of something useful, interesting, or otherwise valued by at least a small segment of society. In synthesis, a

**PRAXIS**
Techniques for stimulating creative thinking are tested in PRAXIS™ Exam Section 2a: Instruction and Assessment.

creative thinker is one who poses new problems, raises new questions, and then suggests solutions that are characterized by fluency, flexibility, originality, and elaboration. The solutions result in a product unique for that individual in those circumstances.

## Discussions That Encourage Imagination and Inventiveness

In the process of discussing almost any type of subject, teachers always have opportunities to ask students to consider, "What if . . . ?" Imagine living on an island with no electricity. What would your life be like? How would it be different than it is now? What could we do to make our school a better place? What would you do if you were the main character in the story? How would your actions change the ending of the book? For many reflective teachers, these questions are as important as those that test student recall of information or understanding of the main idea. While it is seldom necessary to plan a discussion with the sole intent of stimulating students' imagination, it is a worthy goal to include these types of questions in any classroom discussion.

Another technique is to assign a group of students a certain task that requires them to discuss strategies and invent a method to carry it out. For example, give students a single dollar bill and ask them to discover how high a stack of one million dollar bills would be. Give them a few pieces of cloth and some string and ask them to make an effective parachute. Have each group work together to design one map of the school property. These real-life and simulated tasks provide incentives for authentic discussions on substantive and meaningful topics.

## Prewriting Discussions

Another method teachers may use is to focus on images, analogies, and metaphors in creative discussions. These are very effective discussions before students begin writing, encouraging students to use these word pictures in their writing as well. Gordon and Poze (1975) suggest that analogies allow us to make the strange familiar and the familiar strange. In discussions, teachers can present an unfamiliar idea or object and assist students in describing it using sensory images or comparing it with another, more familiar concept. For example, when presented with a rusty old lawnmower engine, students may be led to describe it according to size, shape, imaginary sounds, or uses. They can compare it to other, more familiar objects. The teacher may ask students what the machine reminds them of. This may generate responses such as "The machine is like my old shoes." Then the teacher probes by asking the child to tell why the machine and the old shoes are alike: "Because they are both old and muddy." Another child may see the machine in a whole different context: "The machine is like a kangaroo because it has a lot of secret compartments." Discussions like this can begin to have a life of their own and can lead to fresh new ways to express one's ideas.

Do schools enhance or undermine the conditions and processes that encourage creativity? Do textbooks, curriculum guides, rules, regulations, and expectations support the development of creative thinking and the process needed to create a unique product? Caring and reflective teachers do. They work very hard to create stimulating classroom discussions that assist students in learning to become creative thinkers rather than 9-year-old fogies.

# Discussions That Address Multiple Intelligences

You have created a thematic unit plan that has an interesting topic and many opportunities for students to read, research and report on their findings. One day near the end of the unit, you will want to have a lively interactive discussion to allow your students to report on what they have learned and discovered on their own about the topic. For example, Judy Eby once planned and taught a unit called "Aviation and Mapmaking." This unit began with students making maps of their school and neighborhoods. Then, the class examined maps made by the early explorers who traveled the globe by ship and created maps of the new worlds they discovered. The students had compared the early maps with modern maps and laughed at how inaccurate the early maps appeared. As a culmination of this unit plan, Judy hired a pilot and a 10-seat airplane to take the students on short flights over their school and neighborhood. They took photos of the ground and then created new aerial maps based on their photos.

Let's imagine a discussion taking place a few days after their flights. The general topic of discussion is, "How has aviation changed mapmaking?"

To promote linguistic intelligence, questions involving vocabulary might be asked. "What is a map legend? What is the difference between latitude and longitude?" Logical-mathematical intelligence can be stimulated by asking questions about the map scales. "How accurate are the first maps you made? Does the entire map have the same scale or does it vary? How accurate are the scales of the aerial maps you are making? Why are they likely to be more consistent?"

This whole project is an excellent example of a school program that develops visual spatial intelligence. There can be many discussion questions in which students refer to their maps or show something on their photos. "Can you show us an example of how your map is more accurate now than it was before the aerial photo experience?"

Bodily-kinesthetic intelligence was involved in creating the first maps. Students can be asked to describe the process they used to walk around the school or their neighborhood and find ways to see the big picture of what they were drawing. "Did you have to climb on something high and look down at the area in order to draw it accurately? Did you pace off the distances and then convert them to inches or centimeters?"

Musical intelligence does not come easily to this unit. If it is not appropriate, there is no need to include it just for the sake of including it. Other units may have many musical applications. It would be a stretch, but you might ask students to create short songs about their experience in the air or sing a song or two from early American history that refers to maps or travels or distances.

Naturalist intelligence can be promoted by referring to the land and its uses. "In your view, is the land near our school used well or are there things that you would like to see changed? By looking at your photos and maps, what do you appreciate about the world that you did not seem to notice before?"

To promote interpersonal intelligence, the discussion could turn to how well people worked together to create their maps. If a cooperative learning model was used, the maps may have been the work of a small committee rather than an individual. "How well did your group work together on the first map you made? Did you work more effectively or less on the second maps?"

During the evaluation phase of this unit, the teacher can tap into students' intrapersonal intelligence by conducting an interactive assessment of what each student accomplished. "What are you most proud of accomplishing during this unit? What new interests have you developed during this experience? What do you want to improve?"

# THE ROLE OF THE TEACHER IN LEADING DISCUSSIONS

Discussions that promote the use of multiple intelligences and critical or creative thinking can be exciting classroom events for both students and teachers, but beginning teachers may find it difficult to elicit responses from students who are not used to taking part in such activities. What if you ask a wonderful question and the pupils do not respond? There is nothing quite so demoralizing for a teacher as a lack of response from students. "Now boys and girls, how do you think the sound got onto this tape?"

No response. Interminable silence. Finally the teacher leaps in to break the tension and gives the answer. Everybody, including the teacher, visibly relaxes. Whew! Let's not try that again.

This example of a nondiscussion is more common than is desirable. Students in your classroom may not have had opportunities to think creatively and express their own ideas. If not, they may be reluctant to do so at first. They may believe that you expect one right answer, just as most of their teachers have in the past. Because they do not know the one right answer, they may prefer to remain quiet rather than embarrass themselves by giving a wrong answer. Your response to their silence will tell them a great deal. If you jump in with your own response, they will learn that their own responses were not really wanted after all.

Scaffolding is a necessary component of teaching critical thinking and discussion strategies to students. Be explicit about what you do expect from them in a discussion. Tell them that there are no wrong answers and that all opinions are valued. If they still hesitate, provide cues and prompts without providing answers. Simplify or rephrase the question so that they are able to answer it. If the question "How do you think the sound got on this tape?" gets no response, rephrase it. "What sounds do you hear on this tape? Can you imagine how those sounds were captured on a piece of plastic like this? Do you think machinery was used? What kinds of machines are able to copy sounds?" These supporting questions provide scaffolds for thinking and talking about unknown and unfamiliar ideas.

Another consideration in leading discussions is to *value* silence rather than fear it. Silence can indicate that students are truly engaged in reflection. By allowing a few moments of silence, a teacher may find that the resulting discussions are much more creative and productive. Students need time to process the question. They need time to bring forward the necessary schema to their working memories and to consider the question in light of what they already know about the topic. Some students need more time than others to see connections between new ideas and already stored information and to generate a response of their own.

Some teachers consciously use *wait time*, requiring a short period of silence after each significant question is asked. Students are taught to listen quietly, then think quietly for several seconds and not raise their hands to respond until the wait time has passed. Rowe (1974) found that when teachers used a wait time of 3–5 seconds, more students were able to generate a response to the question. Without a planned wait time, the same group of fast-thinking students are likely to dominate all discussions. With the wait time, even slower-thinking students will have an opportunity to consider what it is they do believe before hearing the opinions of others.

Lyman (1989) recommends that teachers employ a system called *listen, think, pair, share* to improve both the quantity and the quality of discussion responses. This technique employs a structured wait time at two different points in the discussion. When a question is asked, wait time goes into effect while students jot down ideas and think about their responses. Students are then expected to discuss their ideas in pairs for a minute. Then a general discussion takes place. After each student makes a contribution, other members of the class are expected to employ a second wait time of 3–5 seconds to process what their classmate has said before they raise their hands to respond.

The quantity and quality of students' responses may be improved by introducing the questions early in the class period, followed by reading, a lecture, or another type of presentation and actual discussion of the questions themselves. This strategy follows the principle of using the question as an advance organizer. Giving students the question before presentation of new material alerts them to what to listen or read for and allows sufficient time for them to process the information they receive in terms of the question. When teachers use this technique, they rarely experience a silent response.

Another strategy that promotes highly interactive discussions involves the physical setup in the classroom. To facilitate critical and creative thinking, students must be able to hear and see one another during the discussion. Arranging the chairs in a circle, rectangle, U-shape, or semicircle will ensure that each student feels like a contributing member of a group.

Meyers (1986) notes that a hospitable classroom environment is the most important factor in engaging students' attention and interest and promoting their creative responses during discussion:

> Much of the success in teaching critical thinking rests with the tone that teachers set in their classrooms. Students must be led gently into the active roles of discussing, dialoguing, and problem-solving. They will watch very carefully to see how respectfully teachers field comments and will quickly pick up nonverbal cues that show how open teachers really are to student questions and contributions. (p. 67)

Reflective teachers are critical and creative thinkers themselves. They welcome opportunities to model their own thinking strategies for their students and plan experiences that encourage the development of their students' higher-level thinking processes. They are likely to make even the simplest discussion an exercise in problem solving, reasoning, logic, and creative and independent thinking. They examine the subjects taught in the curriculum in search of ways to allow their students to learn to think and communicate their ideas. They plan discussions involving the creation and testing of hypotheses in science. They promote thinking that avoids stereotypes and egocentricity in social studies. They teach their students to suspend judgment when they lack sufficient evidence in discussions of math problems. They promote flexible, original thinking in discussions of literature. Discussions in every part of the curriculum can be crafted in ways that teach individuals to think reflectively, critically, and creatively.

## REFLECTIVE ACTION EXPERIENCES FOR YOUR PROFESSIONAL PORTFOLIO

### Show Evidence of NBPTS Core Proposition 2: Teachers Know the Subjects They Teach and How to Teach Those Subjects to Students

**NBPTS Proposition 2 states that professional teachers generate multiple paths to knowledge and show that they are aware that there is value in both structured and inductive learning. Discussion strategies have been presented in this chapter that include both structured and inductive learning experiences.**

For this entry in your professional portfolio, plan and videotape a discussion that uses a variety of structured and inductive questioning strategies. Then, write an analysis of your discussion-leading strengths and weaknesses. Reflect on how you can improve your practice by learning from this experience.

Begin by observing a classroom and record the amount of time spent on teacher talk and on authentic student discussions. What amount of time do you want to set aside each day for students to express their ideas in discussion?

Next, plan and lead a discussion with a small group of students. Write the student outcomes you hope to achieve. Do you wish to emphasize students' critical thinking, creativity, or concept formation? Ask an experienced colleague or teacher to sit in on the discussion. What are the things that could go wrong when you lead a discussion? Think about it from the students' point of view. What will you do if they do not seem to understand the questions you ask? What will you do if some students sit quietly and seem hesitant to participate? What will you do if some students seem restless or bored? Write some special questions that you think will bring these three groups of students into your discussion.

Remember, some of the best feedback you can ask for is from the students themselves. Ask students to tell you what they enjoyed best about the discussion and what they did not understand. In a one-to-one situation, ask the quiet students to tell you why they did not feel like participating and what you could do to help them be more comfortable speaking in a group. Ask the bored or restless students what they needed or wanted to make the discussion more interesting or challenging.

Have someone videotape the discussion. Then, write a reflective critique, comparing the result to the outcomes you had hoped for and include it in your portfolio with the videotape.

## References

Bloom, B. (1981). *All our children learning.* New York: McGraw-Hill.

Bloom, B., Engelhart, M., Furst, E., Hill, W., & Krathwohl, D. (1956). *Taxonomy of educational objectives: Cognitive domain.* New York: Longman.

Butler, S. (1969). *Homer's odyssey.* New York: Washington Square Press.

Doyle, W. (1986). Classroom organization and management. In M. Wittrock (Ed.), *Handbook of research on teaching* (3rd ed.) (pp. 392–420). Upper Saddle River, NJ: Merrill/Prentice Hall.

Einstein, A., & Infeld, L. (1938). *The evolution of physics.* New York: Simon & Schuster.

Gagne, E. (1985). *The cognitive psychology of school learning.* Boston: Little, Brown.

Gordon, W., & Poze, T. (1975). *Strange and familiar.* Cambridge, MA: Porpoise.

Guilford, J. (1967). *The nature of human intelligence.* New York: McGraw-Hill.

James, W. (1890). *Principles of psychology.* New York: Holt.

Lipman, M. (1988). Critical thinking: What can it be? *Educational Leadership, 46*(1), 38–43.

Lyman, F. (1989). Rechoreographing the middle-level minuet. *Early Adolescence Magazine, 4*(1), 22–24.

Meyers, C. (1986). *Teaching students to think critically.* San Francisco: Jossey-Bass.

Paul, R. (1988). *31 Principles of critical thinking.* Rohnert Park, CA: Center for Critical Thinking and Moral Critique.

Rowe, M. (1974). Wait time and reward as instructional variables, their influence on language, logic and fate control. Part 1: Wait time. *Journal of Research on Science Teaching, 11*, 81–94.

Torrance, E. (1966–1984). *Torrance tests of creative thinking.* Bensenville, IL: Scholastic Testing Service.

Vasquez, V. (2003). Getting beyond "I like the book," Creating space for critical literacy in K–6 classrooms. Newark, DE: International Reading Association.

CHAPTER **9**

# Building a Repertoire
# of Teaching Strategies

School experiences should be enjoyable for both teachers and students. Teachers who have developed a repertoire of teaching strategies are able to provide a greater variety of learning experiences for their students. When learning experiences are varied, students are more likely to become actively engaged in the learning process and teachers are more likely to feel fresh and enthusiastic about their careers. Variety is the spice that causes students to experience an intrinsic motivation to learn. They become intrigued, involved, and active participants in the learning experience when the skill or knowledge they are learning is presented in a novel and interesting format. To promote the enjoyment of teaching and learning, many reflective teachers are continuously searching for new methods and strategies to motivate and engage their students in the learning process. Developing a repertoire of teaching strategies is also necessary because students' needs and learning styles are diverse. For this reason, teachers must be ready to modify lesson plans and present information in more than one way.

The purpose of this chapter is to introduce you to a variety of teaching strategies, and encourage you to plan engaging lessons and learning experiences for your students. As you consider each strategy, you will quickly recognize that the descriptions in this chapter are not sufficiently detailed for you to become proficient in using the new strategy. This book can provide only an overview of the descriptions, illustrations, and examples you will need to employ these methods successfully. For strategies that you wish to implement in your classroom, you will need to use the reflective action of initiating an active search for more detailed descriptions of these strategies in books and journal articles or through observations of experienced teachers.

As you read about or select a strategy to try out in a laboratory or classroom, you will find that some of them work for you while others may not. You will need to reflect about what works for you and your students and why. As you think about what works for you, it is quite acceptable for you to combine, adapt, modify, and add your own unique strategies to the ones you read about or observe. Through this process of practice and reflection, you will discover, create, and refine your own unique teaching style.

Jody Salazar employs a number of teaching strategies in her middle school classroom to help her students gain confidence in using the English language in writing and speech. Because most of her students are reading below grade level and are learning English as a second language, she has developed a strategy called vocabulary role play, because acting out new words helps her students to remember them. She uses graphic organizers frequently in order to strengthen visual learning. She often has her students work in learning teams so that they have more verbal interaction in addressing the problems she poses to them.

Jody integrates her reading/language arts lessons with social studies standards frequently because her students find the reading of the social studies texts difficult. Her eighth graders are experiencing difficulty understanding the social studies unit they are studying, so Jody designs a reading/writing/oral report project for them that helps to integrate their social studies content into her reading class.

Jody begins the study with a K-W-L (Know, Want to know, Learned) chart about Native Americans. It becomes evident in building the chart that the students know a lot about Native Americans but they have many misconceptions such as, "All Indians live in teepees" and "All Indians hunt buffalo." As they discuss what they want to know about Native Americans, Jody creates a data chart with their questions and makes individual copies for the students. See Figure 9.1 for a sample of the data chart.

| Tribe or Nation _____ | | | learning team _____ | | | |
|---|---|---|---|---|---|---|
| Tribal Name (What does it mean? | Where they lived | Dwellings | What they ate | What they wore | What tools they used | Kinds of celebrations |
| | | | | | | |
| Hunters? Gatherers? Farmers? | Form of Government | Other interesting facts | | | | |
| | | | | | | |

Books Used _____

Unique information found _____

_____

**Figure 9.1**  Data chart for Native American project.

Jody then places her students into learning teams and provides them with reading materials about Native Americans. These materials include multiple, easy-to-read books about their assigned nation or tribe, such as:

- The "Picture the Past" series (*Life in a Sioux Village, Life in a Hopi Village*, etc.)
- The "Scholastic" series (*If You Lived with the Sioux Indians, If You Lived with the Cherokee*, etc.)
- The "Watts Library" series (*The Iroquois, The Crow*, etc.)
- The "True Book" Series (*The Apache, The Shawnee*, etc.)

The students work together to read the books and answer the questions about the Native American nation their learning team has been assigned. Once the team has found answers for the questions on their data chart, they are instructed to work together to create an oral report about their nation. As a part of the report they are to create visuals and some type of demonstration.

As a class, Jody and her students create a scoring rubric for the oral reports. The students contribute standards such as:

- Talk loud enough to be heard.
- Share a visual that adds to the report.

- Provide a demonstration of something unique about the tribe or nation.
- Answer all the questions on the data chart.

Each learning team then writes a chapter on their assigned tribe or nation for the class book about Native Americans. The book is published using a word processing program, illustrated by the team members, and bound with metal rings. This class book is placed into the library in Jody's room and a second copy is contributed to the social studies teacher's class library where it can be read by other members of the social studies class.

After the completion of the Native American project, Jody teaches her students to write a poem using the "I used to think. . . but now I know. . . " format. The first line of their class poem says, "I used to think that all Indians lived in teepees, But now I know that they lived in many different types of houses depending on the natural resources in their land."

In this curriculum unit, Jody used several different teaching strategies. Her students addressed many different types of standards as well: reading for information, writing reports, preparing and giving oral reports, exploration of Native American tribes, using multiple research strategies, and comparing and contrasting Native American tribes and nations.

## EXAMPLES OF TEACHING STRATEGIES IN ACTION

### Discovery Learning

**PRAXIS**
Discovery learning is a topic tested in PRAXIS™ Exam Section 2a: Instructional Strategies.

The philosophy underlying *discovery learning* is that students will become more active and responsible for their own learning in an environment that allows them to make choices and encourages them to take initiative. To accomplish this goal, many teachers like to arrange their classrooms to provide as much space as possible for activity and learning centers. They enjoy creating curriculum units and lessons that allow students to choose from among many alternatives. The main principle of discovery learning is that students learn best by doing rather than just by hearing or reading about a concept. Teachers may still find this strategy an excellent addition to their repertoire. It can be used occasionally to provide real, rather than vicarious, experiences in a classroom.

In employing discovery learning, the teacher's role is to gather and provide equipment and materials related to a concept that the students are to learn. Sufficient materials should be available so that every student or pair of students has immediate access to them. Materials that are unfamiliar, interesting, and stimulating are especially important to a successful discovery learning experience. After providing the materials, the teacher may ask a question or offer a challenge that causes students to discover the properties of the materials. Then, as the students begin to work with the materials, the teacher's role is to monitor and observe as the students discover the properties and relationships inherent in the materials, asking occasional questions or making suggestions that will guide the students in seeing the relationships and understanding the concepts. The period of manipulation and discovery is then followed by a discussion in which students report on what they have observed and learned from the experience.

A simple example at the primary level is the use of discovery learning to teach the concept of colors and their relationships to one another. Rather than telling students that blue and yellow make green or demonstrating that they do while students watch, the strategy of discovery learning is to provide every student with a brush and two small puddles of blue and yellow paint on white paper and allow them to discover it for themselves. In this case, the opening question may simply be, "What happens when you mix blue and yellow together?" When this relationship becomes apparent and students verbalize it, the teacher can then provide additional puddles of red and white paint and challenge students to "create as many different colors as you can." Experiences can be designed to allow students to discover how and why some things float, what makes a light bulb light, how electricity travels in circuits, and the difference between solutions and mixtures.

Math relationships also can be discovered. Beans, buttons, coins, dice, straws, and toothpicks can be sorted according to size, shape, color, and other attributes. Objects can be weighed and measured and compared with one another. The concept of multiplication can be discovered when students make sets of objects in rows and columns. Many resources in the form of math curriculum projects involving discovery learning are presently being developed for schools because discovery is a part of the problem-solving process, currently a hot topic in education.

## Inquiry Training

Closely linked to the discovery method is a strategy known as *inquiry training*. Teachers who believe that their students must learn how to ask questions and carry out other types of investigations to become active learners often plan lessons that stimulate their students' curiosity and then train them in asking productive questions and using critical thinking, observation skills, and variations of the scientific method to gather information, make informed estimates or predictions, and then design investigations to test their hypotheses.

As an example, a classroom teacher wanted to train her students to think like scientists, using the skills of observation, inquiry, prediction, hypothesis testing, and experimental design to find out what they need to know. She grouped her students into pairs and distributed a clear plastic glass and five raisins to each dyad. She asked them to predict what would happen to the raisins if they were dropped into a glass of water. Most students correctly guessed that the raisins would sink to the bottom of the glass. The teacher then discussed with her students the need to keep an open mind and not jump to easy conclusions based on prior knowledge. She poured a carbonated lemon-lime beverage into the students' glasses and asked them to predict whether the raisins would sink or float. Each pair of students wrote down their prediction. The teacher generated a chart on the board showing the class predictions.

After recording the predictions, the teacher allowed the students to drop the raisins into their glasses. At first it appeared that the students who predicted that the raisins would sink were correct as the raisins fell to the bottom of the glasses, but as the students watched, several raisins began to rise to the top. In the next few minutes, the students observed a puzzling phenomenon. Raisins moved up and down in the glasses, each at their own pace.

At this stage in the lesson, the teacher encouraged the students to ask questions of her and of each other as they all tried to make sense out of what they were observing. The teacher answered their questions with "yes" and "no" answers, giving her students the responsibility of articulating the questions and gathering the information they needed to make meaning out of the situation. Soon they began to generate new investigations that they would have to undertake to discover why some raisins moved up and down more quickly and why some settled to the bottom.

To stimulate your own curiosity and encourage you to use the reflective actions of gathering information, being creative, and being persistent in solving problems, we will not disclose the reasons for the raisins' movement. Try the experiment yourself and try to think like a scientist. If you have opportunities to learn like this yourself, you will be better able to provide your students with the encouragement and support they need without rushing to provide them with answers. You will allow them to take the time they need to inquire and experiment so that they can succeed, and fully experience the "aha" moment, just as scientists do when their inquiries lead them to new understandings.

## Role Playing

When problems or issues involving human relationships are part of the curriculum, teachers may choose to use *role playing* to help students explore and understand the whole range of human feelings that surround any issue. This strategy is frequently used to resolve personal problems or dilemmas, but it can also be employed to gain understanding about the feelings and values of groups outside of the classroom.

For example, to help students understand the depth of emotions experienced by immigrants coming to a new and unfamiliar country, the teacher may ask students to role-play the interactions among family members who are separated or the dilemmas of the Cubans who set off for America in leaky boats or others who want to immigrate to the United States but are stopped by immigration quotas.

Successful and meaningful role playing has two major phases: the role playing itself and the subsequent discussion and evaluation period. In the first phase, the teacher's responsibility is to give students an overview of both phases of role playing, so that they know what to expect. The teacher then introduces and describes a problem or dilemma, identifies the roles to be taken, assigns the roles, and begins the action by setting the stage and describing the immediate problem the actors must confront. Roles must be assigned carefully. Usually teachers select students who are involved in the problem to play the role. In an academic dilemma, the roles may be assigned to students who most need to expand their experience with and understanding of the issue. Students who are not assigned roles are expected to be careful observers.

To set up the role-playing situation, the teacher can arrange some chairs to suggest the setting of the event to be played out. During the role play itself, the actors are expected to get inside the problem and "live" it spontaneously, responding realistically to one another. The role play may not flow smoothly; actors may experience uncertainty and be at a loss for words just as they would in real life. The first time a role is played, the problem may not be solved at all. The action may simply establish the problem, which in later enactments can be probed and resolved.

To increase the effect of role playing, after playing a scene out once, the actors may exchange roles and play out the same scene so that they grow to understand the other characters' points of view. Actors may be allowed to select consultants to discuss and improve the roles they are playing.

In the second phase, the observers discuss the actions and words of the initial role players. The teacher helps the observers review what they have seen and heard, discuss the main events, and predict the consequences of actions taken by the role players. Following the initial discussion, the teacher will probably decide to have new class members replay the role to show an alternative way of handling the problem. The situation can be replayed a number of times if necessary. When a role-played situation generates a useful solution or suggests an effective way of handling a problem, the situation can be adapted and subsequent role plays can focus on communication skills that will enhance or improve the situation even further.

Role playing has many applications in both the cognitive and affective goals of the curriculum. Through role playing, students can experience history by researching the life of a public figure and taking the role in a historical interaction. Each student in the class, for example, can study the life of a U.S. president and be the president for a day. Frequently, teachers ask students to play the role of characters in books that they have read as a means of reporting their own reading and stimulating others in the class to read the book. Students can enact the feelings of slaves and slave traders, the roles of scientists as they are "doing" science, or the interaction between an author and editor as they try to perfect a piece of writing.

Vocabulary role play is a simple, yet effective, tool for getting students involved in an active learning process of learning new words and applying their meanings. In this type of activity, appropriate vocabulary words are physicalized with students acting out the words in order to internalize their meanings. Primary students may participate with action words such as *jumping*, *squeezing*, and *shrugging*, words that require physical involvement and movement. Older students may use scenarios to demonstrate the meaning of more complex words and expressions such as *honesty*, *revolution*, *respect*, or *serenity*. The physicalization of these words and terms provides a different route of internalization and makes the vocabulary "come alive" for the students. This strategy has been found to be especially effective with English language learners (Herrell & Jordan, 2004).

Students can learn new behaviors and social skills that may help them win greater peer acceptance and enhance their own self-esteem. Interpersonal conflicts that arise in the classroom can be role-played as a means of helping students discover more productive and responsible ways of behaving. For example, when two students argue about taking turns with a toy in the kindergarten class, the teacher can ask the students to role-play the situation in an effort to learn new ways of speaking to one another, asserting their own desires, and creating a plan for sharing the scarce resource. In a classroom, the teacher may notice that one student is isolated and treated like a scapegoat by others in the class. The dilemma can be role-played with the role of the isolated student assigned to be played by some of the students who have been most critical and aggressive toward the student. Through this active, vicarious experience, students may learn to be more tolerant and accepting of one another.

## Simulation

Student drivers drive simulated vehicles before they learn to drive a real car on the highway. Airplane simulators provide a realistic but safe way for student pilots to practice flying in which mistakes lead to realistic consequences without threatening lives. *Simulations* usually involve some type of role playing but also include other gamelike features, such as a set of rules, time limits, tokens, or other objects that are gained or lost through the action of the simulation, and a way of recording the results of the players' decisions and actions. Simulations almost always focus on dilemmas in which the players must make choices, take actions, and then experience feedback in the form of consequences of their actions. The purpose of simulations is primarily to allow young people to experience tough, real-life problems and learn from the consequences in the safe, controlled environment of the classroom.

Many valuable academic and social simulations can be used to enrich the classroom experience and cause students to understand the relationship among their choices, actions, and the consequences. The teacher can purchase or create simulation games. A company named Interact publishes catalogs of simulations in all areas of the curriculum that can be purchased for a relatively small price. You can access its web page at *http://www.interact-simulations.com/*. Its kits include teacher manuals describing the rules, time limits, and procedures to follow, and a set of student materials that may include fact sheets, game pieces, and record-keeping devices. Titles of some of the simulations it publishes include *Goldrush, Egypt,* and *Underground Railroad.* In its web-based simulation called *Internet Cruises,* students become members of six "advance teams," each sent by a cruise line to explore a different travel destination. They use the Internet to explore geographic locations (which can be tailored to your classroom needs), conduct focused Internet research on the history, geography, nature, foods, and culture of the region, and report back to the class with travel brochures they have created.

The role of the teacher during a simulation is to explain the conditions, concepts to be covered, and expectations at the outset of the event. A practice session may be held to further familiarize participants with the rules and procedures that govern the simulation. After assigning roles or creating groups that will interact, the teacher moderates, keeps time, clarifies misconceptions, and provides feedback and consequences in response to the participants' actions. At the conclusion of the simulation, the teacher leads a discussion of what occurred and what was learned by asking students to summarize events and problems and to share their perceptions and insights with one another. At the end of the discussion, the teacher may compare the simulation to its real-life counterpart and ask students to think critically about what they would do in real life as a result of having taken part in the simulation.

An example of a simulation in economics involves the creation of small companies or stores in which students decide on a product, create the product, set up the store, price and sell the product, and keep records on the transactions. The purpose, of course, is to learn about the principles of supply and demand, as well as the practical skills of exchanging money and making change. Along with the primary goals of the simulation are secondary learning experiences. Students are also likely to increase their capacity for critical thinking and to learn about their own actions and decisions regarding competition, cooperation, commitment to a goal, and communication.

Students may simulate the writing of the U.S. Constitution by writing a classroom constitution. After studying various countries of the world, sixth-grade students may take part in a mock United Nations simulation in which students are delegates and face daily world problems presented to them by the teacher.

In language arts, students may establish a class newspaper to learn how news is gathered and printed in the real world. They may even establish a number of competitive newspapers to add another dimension of reality to the simulation. Students may simulate the writing, editing, and publishing processes as they write, print, and distribute their own original books.

Simulations may be used to introduce a unit or as the culminating activity of a unit. They may take a few minutes or the entire year. They may be continued from week to week but played for only a specified amount of time during each session. Some may take a full day or longer. Simulations are powerful learning experiences that may change the way students view themselves and the world.

## Mastery Learning

Teaching strategies known as *mastery learning* derive from the philosophy that all students can learn if they have sufficient time to master the new skill or concept. Bloom (1984) proposed that students have different *learning rates* rather than different ability levels. He created a practical system for instruction using mastery learning based on the assumption that learners can achieve the educational objectives established for them, but because they learn at different rates, they need different amounts of time to complete the required work. Bloom points to cases in which students are tutored to prove his point. In a controlled experiment, he demonstrated that "the average tutored student outperformed 98% of the students in the control class" (p. 5). He attributes this finding to the fact that a tutor is able to determine what each student knows in a given subject and is then able to plan an educational program that begins instruction at the student's level and proceeds at the student's own pace.

The basic structure of the mastery learning model, including adaptations known as *individually prescribed instruction* (IPI) and *continuous progress*, lend themselves best to the learning of basic skills in sequentially structured subjects. Very specific behavioral objectives are written for each unit of study. Pretests are used to assess students' prior knowledge, which then determines their placement or starting level. Working individually, as students master each objective in the sequence of learning, they are able to proceed to the next one. Periodically, unit tests covering several objectives are given to check on the mastery and retention of a whole range of knowledge and skills.

The teacher's role in this process is quite different from teaching skills with a whole class approach. The teacher rarely instructs the entire class at one time. Instead, as students work independently, the teacher monitors their progress by walking around the classroom and responding to requests for assistance. This frees the teacher to work with small groups of students rather than devoting all of the time responding to individual needs.

The value of mastery learning is that it allows students to actively learn new material and skills on a continuous basis. Motivation to achieve also presumably increases because students are working at their own pace and have the prerequisite skills necessary for success. Also, because testing is done individually and they have opportunities to repeat what they did not learn, students should suffer less embarrassment when they make mistakes. The effective goal of mastery learning programs is to help students become independent, self-directed learners.

## Contracts for Independent Learning

Because mastery learning is appropriate for use only in sequential subjects that require a great deal of independent practice, many teachers are searching for methods of promoting independence and self-directed learning in other subjects as well. An alternative

**PRAXIS**
Strategies for independent study are tested in PRAXIS™ Exam Section 2a: Instructional Strategies.

to direct, whole class instruction is the use of independent or group academic learning contracts. A learning contract such as the one in Figure 9.2 is usually created by the teacher at the beginning of a unit of study. The contract specifies one list of required activities, such as reading a chapter in the textbook, finding a library resource and writing a summary of the topic, completing a fact sheet, and other necessary prerequisites for developing a knowledge base on the subject.

A second list of activities is offered as choices or alternatives for students to pursue. This list includes opportunities to do additional independent research or create plays, stories, songs, and artwork on the topic. When learning contracts are offered to develop independence, individuals usually select the activities they want to accomplish. A variation on this strategy would be to combine the concepts of cooperative groups and learning contracts and allow each group to sign a joint contract specifying the tasks and products they will complete.

Science investigations, social studies research projects, and creative language arts activities can be described in learning contracts. The primary advantage of this strategy is that it allows individuals at various ability levels to work on an appropriate amount and type of work during the unit of study. Students who work quickly and accurately can select the maximum number of tasks and products, while other students can select fewer tasks. Theoretically, both types of students can actively learn and experience success during the same amount of time.

## Group Rotations Using Learning Centers

**PRAXIS**
Strategies for using Learning Centers are tested in PRAXIS™ Exam Section 2a: Instructional Strategies.

*Learning centers* or stations are areas of the classroom where students can go to do independent or group work on a given subject or topic. Learning centers vary enormously in appearance, usage, and length of time for which they are set up. Teachers who use learning centers use them for a variety of purposes and with a variety of expectations.

Some centers may be informal and unstructured in their use. For example, a classroom may have a permanent science center containing a variety of science equipment and materials. Students may go to the center to do science experiments in their free time. The same classroom may have a permanent reading center furnished with a rug, comfortable chairs, and shelves or racks of books where students can go to read quietly.

Other centers are set up for a limited amount of time and have highly structured expectations. For example, to accompany the unit on settling the western United States described in the learning contract, the teacher may have set up an area of the classroom as a research center. It would contain a computer, with the Minnesota Educational Computing Consortium (MECC) computer program called "Oregon Trail" turned on and ready for students to use. It would also contain posters and maps of the western United States and a variety of reading materials on the topic. When the unit is finished, the center will be redesigned; new learning materials will replace the ones from the finished unit, and the center will become the focus of a new unit of study.

In primary classrooms, learning centers are often an important adjunct to reading and language arts. Many teachers set up four or five learning centers or stations with different activities each week. Students in small groups travel from one station to another according to a prespecified schedule. For example, Ginny Bailey uses a weekly theme as the basis for her first-grade language arts program. Each week she sets up activities related to that theme in her five stations: art, math, writing, listening, and reading. To accompany her butterfly theme, students will find books on butterflies to read

### Westward Expansion of the United States
### Required Learning Activities

Date    Approval

_____   _____ Read Chapter 6 in the social studies textbook.

_____   _____ Write answers to the questions at the end of the unit.

_____   _____ Locate and read a book on the American West or Indians.

_____   _____ Write a 2–4 page summary of the book.

_____   _____ Play the computer game "Oregon Trail" until you successfully reach the state of Oregon alive.

### Alternative Learning Activities

_____   _____ Imagine that you are a member of a wagon train heading west. Write a series of letters back "home" describing your journey.

_____   _____ Write a play about a meeting between Indians and settlers. Find a cast for your play and present it to the class assembly.

_____   _____ Draw or paint a large picture of a scene that you imagine took place during the westward expansion.

_____   _____ Create a song or ballad about life in the west. Be prepared to play and sing it for the assembly.

_____   _____ Create a diorama or a model of a Plains Indian village.

_____   _____ Research the lives of the Plains Indians today. Be prepared to give a speech about the conditions in which they live now and how this is related to the westward expansion.

_____   _____ Create an alternative plan for a learning experience on this topic.

_____

I, _____ , agree to complete the required learning activities by the date _____ . In addition, I select two to five alternative activities to pursue on my own. I will present my creative work to my classmates at our assembly on _____ .

_____
student signature

I have reviewed this contract and understand the work my child has agreed to do. I agree to support this effort.

_____
teacher signature

_____
parent signature

**Figure 9.2** Independent learning contract.

| Group | Monday | Tuesday | Wednesday | Thursday | Friday |
|-------|--------|---------|-----------|----------|--------|
| **Blue** | Art | Math | Writing | Reading | Listening |
| **Green** | Math | Writing | Reading | Listening | Art |
| **Red** | Writing | Reading | Listening | Art | Math |
| **Yellow** | Reading | Listening | Art | Math | Writing |
| **Orange** | Listening | Art | Math | Writing | Reading |

**Figure 9.3** Learning station schedule.

Courtesy of Ginny Bailey.

at the reading station, paper and directions for a writing project at the writing center, paint and brushes to create a picture at the art station, a prerecorded tape to listen to at the listening station, and a math game involving butterflies and caterpillars at the math station.

Ginny uses five centers—one for each day—and that means each group can visit each center once a week. Figure 9.3 shows the posted schedule of groups and centers.

In Ginny's classroom, students can go to their stations only after completing their daily work assignments. In her system, the stations extend the students' learning experiences on the weekly theme but are also used as an incentive system for students to complete their required work.

Teachers who work with students who have limited English proficiency are finding that rotations from one learning center to another give the students many rich opportunities to use the English language with their peers as well as with adults. In a kindergarten classroom at Hamilton School in mid-city San Diego, Susan King recently completed her Cultural, Language, and Academic Development (CLAD) teaching credential. In her classroom, she wants to create a learning environment that enables her English language learners to take risks with English so that they develop oral fluency in their new language. In the following case study, you can read about how she changed her entire system of teaching within a few months when she became aware that her students were becoming less proficient and quieter under the conventional teacher-centered system she had been using.

## ✳ REFLECTIVE ACTION STORIES ✳

## Establishing Learning Centers

*Susan King, CLAD Kindergarten, Hamilton School, San Diego, California*

### Teacher Begins to Plan

At the beginning of my first year as a kindergarten teacher, I organized my classroom for whole group instruction in reading and language arts. I used conventional methods in which my students all worked at the same task at the same time, with a great deal of direct instruction from me.

## Teacher Considers What the Students Already Know

Then I began to perceive that the room was too quiet. Students sat quietly, waiting passively for me to tell them what to do. There were very few opportunities for oral language development using this teacher-centered approach to teaching.

## Teacher Has Expectations

One day after school, I was thinking about my classroom and I decided that I needed to take some risks and reorganize my entire classroom system to stimulate talking, problem solving, and cooperative learning.

## Teacher Does Research and Invites Feedback

Our district has designated mentor teachers who are willing to share the teaching strategies they employ with beginning teachers. I arranged to visit a mentor teacher who uses a rotation schedule for her kindergarten–first-grade classroom and I learned more in that one day than I could imagine. I was able to see the physical arrangement of her classroom and watch her students travel from one learning center to another. I took pictures of the charts and schedules she used to direct traffic in her room. I also took pictures of the students working at the various centers she had established. From this visit, I was able to envision the changes that would need to be made in my classroom.

Since many of my students are English language learners, I also decided to sign up for some courses to get my Cultural, Language, Academic Development (CLAD) credential.

## Teacher Reflects Again Using Feedback, Research, and Creativity

The new knowledge I gained from these visits and my courses caused me to become aware of the needs of the students in my class. I became aware of how important it was to include parent volunteers or peer tutors who are familiar with the primary or first language (L-1) of the English language learners in my program. In my classroom, these L-1 languages include Spanish and Laotian.

## Teacher Creates a New Action Plan

I recruited Spanish- and Laotian-speaking parents and upper-grade students to assist me in my classroom. I also decided to use the resources of my own students who are bilingual. I began to design the materials I would need to get started. In January, I plunged into the whole new system. I set up four different learning stations in my classroom: journal writing, a reading basket, a structured activity center, and the guided reading group. Peer tutors supervised the structured activity center to help children with science, math, and social studies. In all the centers I encouraged my students to talk with each other, share ideas, help each other, and solve whatever problems were at hand. I instructed them to ask everyone in their group for help and then ask the peer tutor or group captain before coming to ask me for help. With this management system, I was free to work with the guided reading group without interruptions.

### Unforeseen Problems Occur

It took about 2 weeks for the children to become accustomed to the movement from one area to the next. It took even longer for them to become independent learners. At first they would stand still, waiting for me to come give them direct teaching or instruction about every little step. When I saw this response of stillness and waiting to be spoon fed, I thought to myself. "What a disservice we are doing to children when we train them to be passive learners." I realized that the whole group teaching I had done for the first 5 months had caused this response. I had trained them to wait for my every word and not to think for themselves.

### Teacher Uses Withitness in Response to Problem

In order to be able to give my full attention to the students in the guided reading group, I had to find a way to organize the learning environment so that the other 25 students were busy and would not need to interrupt me. This felt like a real challenge to me because even though I had recruited parent volunteers, they did not come consistently. So, I went to my colleagues who teach upper grades and asked them to send me some helpers who would like to help in the kindergarten. The response was overwhelmingly positive. Just as my students needed peer tutors, the older children need this type of responsibility to enhance their own self-image.

A resource teacher who visited recently looked around to see the children working so independently. As he left, he told me, "I can't believe this is a kindergarten class. The children are so responsible—so in charge of their own learning."

---

## COOPERATIVE LEARNING STRATEGIES

**PRAXIS**
The use of Cooperative Learning is tested in PRAXIS™ Exam Section 2a: Instructional Strategies.

Cooperative groups are a welcome change of pace for many students. They enjoy the opportunity to interact with their peers for part of the school day. Teachers may be hesitant to try the strategy, however, for fear that the students will play or talk about outside interests rather than work at the task assigned. Cooperative groups can degenerate to chaotic groups if they do not meet certain conditions.

Imagine that a teacher hears some general ideas about cooperative groups at a conference or reads the first few paragraphs of an article on the strategy. Thinking that it seems to be an intriguing idea, the teacher may hurry back to the classroom, divide the class into several small groups, and tell them to study the Civil War together for a test that will be held next Friday. After a few moments of discussing what they have (or have not) read about the Civil War, the groups are likely to dissolve into chaos or, at best, evolve into groups who sit near one another and talk to one another as each person studies the text in isolation.

When the group has a poor understanding of the goals of the task, the results may be unproductive and frustrating. To prevent this, the teacher must clearly state the goals and expectations of each group task and provide a copy of them in writing so the group can refer to them from time to time. This includes assigning specific duties to each group member which, when combined, result in a smoothly functioning interaction.

*Cooperative learning* is designed to encourage students to help and support their peers in a group rather than compete against them. This purpose assumes that the perceived value of academic achievement increases when students are all working toward the same goal. Cooperative groups emphasize the notion of pride in one's "team" in much the same way that sports teams do. A teacher using cooperative learning must be constantly vigilant to ensure that one or two students are not dominating the group to the educational detriment of the other students in the group. Quite often, dominant students will disregard the contributions of other members of the group based on a perception of educational "worthiness." Students who are not strong readers, for example, are often left out of discussions, their ideas minimized or disregarded altogether. Students are sometimes the objects of negative interactions simply because of their linguistic or ethnic backgrounds. It is the responsibility of the teacher to monitor the groups' progress and intervene when necessary to make sure that all students are given the opportunity to participate in the group process (Cohen, 1994).

Another major purpose of cooperative learning is to boost the achievement of students of all ability levels. The assumption is that when high-achieving students work with low-achieving students, they both benefit. Compared to tracking systems that separate the high achievers from the low achievers, cooperative groups are composed of students at all levels so that the low-achieving students can benefit from the modeling and interaction with their more capable peers. It is also believed that high-achieving students can learn to be more tolerant and understanding of individual differences through this type of experience than if they are separated from low achievers.

Still another point is that cooperative teams are believed to be more motivating for the majority of students because they have a greater opportunity to experience the joy of winning and success. In a competitive environment, the same few high-achieving students are likely to win over and over again, but a classroom divided into cooperative teams, each with its own high- and low-achieving students, more evenly distributes the opportunity to succeed. To this end, the reward systems do not honor individuals, but depend on a group effort. As in a sports team, individual performances are encouraged because they benefit the whole team.

Teachers may believe that they are using cooperative learning when, in reality, they are simply making physical changes in the classroom desk arrangement or allowing students who work rapidly and well to tutor or mentor their slower classmates. Johnson and Johnson (1993) provide us with a valuable perspective by telling us what cooperative learning is *not*. Cooperation is *not* having students sit side by side at the same table to talk with one another as they do their individual assignments. Cooperation is *not* having students do a task with instructions that whoever finishes first is to help the slower students. Cooperation is *not* assigning a report to a group of students wherein one student does all the work and the others put their names on the product, as well.

## Learning Teams Enhance Achievement

Slavin (1995) emphasizes the team concept in cooperative learning. For example, the teacher presents information to the entire class in the form of lectures, discussion, and/or readings. As a follow-up, students are formed into four- or five-member heterogeneous teams to learn the new material or practice the new skills.

These learning teams are designed to provide a way to encourage both individual accountability and group efforts at the same time. A baseline score is computed for each team by combining the data from individual pretests. Students then work together and assist each other in learning new material. At the conclusion of the study period, individual posttests are given to determine how well each member of the group has learned the material. Students are not allowed to help one another on the tests, only during the practice sessions. The individual test scores are then combined to produce a team score; but the winning team is not necessarily the team with the highest combined score. The results that count are the *improvement scores*, computed by determining the difference between each individual's original baseline pretest score and the final posttest results and adding these individual improvement scores together to create a final group improvement score.

For example, students may be pretested on 20-word spelling lists. High-scoring students are grouped with lower-scoring students to study and practice together, with the goal of having all students in the group earn improvement points for their team. One group's scores and points might look like this example:

| Name | Pretest Score | Posttest Score | Difference = Improvement Points |
|------|---------------|----------------|---------------------------------|
| John | 13 | 15 | +2 |
| Mary | 17 | 14 | −3 |
| Jorge | 12 | 19 | +7 |
| Carla | 10 | 18 | +10 |

The teacher may use the total score of 16 (the sum of scores in the last column) or calculate an average improvement score for this group, which is 16 divided by 4, for an average group improvement score of 4. This group's score can then be compared with other groups in the class and a competition among the study groups may be used to stimulate interest and motivation in working together to improve everyone's scores. If all groups do well and achieve impressive group improvement scores, then all groups can earn awards or extra privileges. Teachers can design award certificates or plan a menu of extra privileges to encourage students to work hard individually and in cooperation with each other.

## Cooperative Learning of the Basic Skills

Cooperative learning can be used to assist students in the mastery of basic skills such as computing the basic addition, subtraction, and multiplication facts. In a traditional classroom, teachers may prepare students for this assessment by providing them with daily worksheets for practicing and memorizing the math facts. Students may win rewards or recognition for being the fastest or the most accurate on these work assignments.

Although this type of competitive environment may please and motivate the high achievers, it is not likely to encourage the remainder of the class. To modify the process of learning math facts from a competitive to a cooperative experience, teachers could adapt the student team achievement division model to fit the needs of their classrooms.

Using a learning team approach, the teacher would begin by giving a pretest of 100 math facts to the entire class. By sorting the pretests into high, medium, and low scores, the teacher can divide the class into heterogeneous groups with equivalent ability in math facts. Each group would contain one of the top scorers, one of the lowest scorers, and two in the middle range.

How the teacher sets up the conditions and expectations for this cooperative learning experience is very important. The achievement goal and the behavioral expectations must be clearly explained at the outset. For example, the teacher may state that the groups are expected to practice math facts for a given time each day. Worksheets, flash cards, and other materials will be provided, and the teams are free to choose the means they use to practice. The goal, in this instance, is to raise all scores from pretest levels as much as possible. A posttest will be given on a certain day, and each individual will have an improvement score, which is the difference between the correct responses on the posttest and the correct responses on the pretest. The group improvement score will be computed by adding up the individual improvement scores. This method of scoring encourages the group to give extra energy to raise the scores of the lowest scorers because they have the most to gain. Top scorers, in fact, may not gain many points at all, since their pretests may already be near the total. Added incentives for this group may be devised, such as a certain number of points for a perfect paper.

The incentives that will be awarded for success depend a great deal on the class itself. The teacher may choose to offer one reward for the group whose scores improve the most or reward each group, depending on their gains. For example, a single reward for the most improved group may be tangible, such as a certificate of success or temporary possession of a traveling math trophy. Less tangible incentives are also important to third graders, such as the opportunity to be first in line for a week, go to the library together during a math class, or eat lunch with the teacher. To spread the incentives to all groups, the points that each group earns may be translated into an award such as 1 minute of free time per point or the opportunity to "buy" special opportunities and materials.

Once students become accustomed to helping their classmates in one subject area, they are likely to take considerable interest in assisting and supporting their members in doing well in other subjects as well. Similar groups could operate to improve spelling, vocabulary, the mechanics of writing, or other basic skills. The membership of each group would be different because students are likely to score differently on pretests for various subjects.

## Cooperative Learning in Science

In many classrooms, the conventional approach to teaching science once centered on textbook reading, discussion, an occasional demonstration by the teacher, and written tests of understanding. More recently, science curricula have been revised to include many more hands-on experiments and investigations. The current philosophy is that students need to learn how to *do* science rather than simply learn about it.

Hands-on science is an area that has a natural fit with cooperative group strategies. By participating in cooperative science investigations, students learn how scientists themselves interact to share observations, hypotheses, and methods. Although many teachers value these current science goals, they may be reluctant to try them because they are unsure of how to manage the high level of activity in the classroom when science experiments are happening. Cooperative groups can provide the support and structure needed to manage successful science investigation in the classroom.

When a topic or unit approach is taken for teaching science, each unit offers opportunities for cooperative learning. For example, jigsaw groups may study the topic of astronomy, with each studying one planet, creating models and charts of information about their planet, and reporting their findings to others.

Investigations into the properties of simple machines, magnets, electricity, and other topics in physics can be designed by establishing a challenge or a complex goal for groups to meet by a given date. Groups may be given a set of identical materials and told to create a product that has certain characteristics and can perform a specific function. For example, given a supply of toothpicks and glue, groups are challenged to construct a bridge that can hold a pound of weight without breaking. Given a raw egg and an assortment of materials, groups work together to create ways to protect their eggs when they are dropped from a high window onto the pavement below.

Science groups can be mixed and matched frequently during the year, offering students an opportunity to work cooperatively with most other members of their class. This strategy is likely to reinforce the principles of social science as well. For example, during the astronomy unit, the emphasis could be on learning how to come together as a group quickly, quietly, and efficiently when getting started on the day's project. During the bridge-building unit, the groups could practice encouraging everyone to participate, taking time to ask for opinions and suggestions from every member of the group before making an important decision. After completing each unit, the groups should participate in evaluating how they worked together and how well they demonstrated the interpersonal skill emphasized during that unit.

## Literature Circles

Reading instruction may be conducted in a variety of formats. Primary teachers may teach small groups of students reading individual storybooks in flexible groupings that change almost weekly. These groups of students are often engaged in active learning experiences after each small book is completed. In some classrooms, more conventional methods of teaching reading, three homogeneous reading groups based on ability, may still be used at many grade levels. Each group reads stories, essays, poems, and plays collected in a basal reader geared for their reading ability. The teacher leads discussions of reading materials and assigns seatwork to be done while he or she works with other groups.

Many upper elementary teachers, however, prefer to use literary materials in their own format rather than as collections in basal readers or anthologies. They believe that students' motivation to read will improve if they are encouraged to choose and read whole books, novels, poetry collections, and plays. A variety of paperback books in sets of six to eight books apiece are needed to carry out this type of reading program.

At Our Lady of Mercy School in Chicago, sixth-grade teacher Roxanne Farwick-Owens has developed a system that allows choice, maximizes cooperative efforts, and holds individuals accountable. To maximize student motivation and enjoyment of reading, Roxanne believes students must be allowed to choose their reading materials. Each month she provides three or four reading selections, in the form of paperback books, to the class. Students are allowed to choose the book they want to read, and groups are formed according to interest rather than ability level. Roxanne may advise students about their selections and try to steer them toward appropriate selections, but in the end, she believes that they have the right to choose for themselves what they will read, especially because she has provided only books that have inherent value for sixth graders.

During initial group meetings, students decide for themselves how much to read at a time. They assign themselves due dates for each chapter. Periodically, each group meets with Roxanne to discuss what they are reading, but most discussions are held without her leadership. Usually, she holds the groups responsible for generating their own discussion on the book. To prepare for this discussion, all members are expected to prepare questions as they read. For example, each person in the group may be expected to contribute three "why" questions and two detail questions per session. Roxanne reviews the questions each day as a means of holding each individual accountable for reading the material and contributing to the group.

Another task is to plan a presentation about the books—using art, music, drama, and other media—to share with the rest of the class at the end of the month. This allows groups to introduce the books they have read to the other members of the class, who are then likely to choose them at a later date. One group made wooden puppets and a puppet stage to portray an event from Mark Twain's Tom Sawyer. After reading Judy Blume's *Superfudge*, a group created a radio commercial for the book complete with sound effects and background music. Familiar television interview shows are sometimes used as a format, as are music videos.

About once per quarter, two teams are formed to compete in a game-show–type tournament. Questions about the books are separated into categories such as characters, plot, setting, authors, and miscellaneous. Each person is responsible for writing five questions and answers on index cards to prepare for the tournament. One student acts as emcee, while another keeps track of the points. The team with the most points wins the tournament.

Roxanne finds that this cooperative group structure increases her students' social skills, especially their ability to work with others and to find effective ways to handle disagreements. But the primary reason for the program is to help her students see that reading can be enjoyable and that instead of being a solitary pursuit, reading can have a social aspect. Roxanne believes many of her students may become lifelong readers from this one-year experience.

## Peacemaking Groups

Some cooperative groups are formed for the social purpose of teaching students how to resolve conflicts, handle anger, and avoid violence in their lives. Many schools are taking an active role in training their students to incorporate conflict-management skills in their daily lives. Johnson and Johnson (1991) have created a series of learning experiences teachers can use for this purpose. Students are taught to recognize that conflict is inevitable, and that they can choose between entering into destructive or constructive conflicts. They learn how to recognize a constructive conflict through cooperative group experiences and simulations.

For example, a group of students may be told that they have just won an all-expense-paid field trip to the destination of their choice. Now comes the hard part. Where will the group choose to go? Pairs of students are formed to list their choices and create a rationale for them. Through negotiation, the group must resolve the dilemma and make a plan by consensus.

In other group sessions, students learn to identify how they personally react to conflicts and learn how to be assertive rather than aggressive or withdraw from arguments. For example, one session may be devoted to assisting students in dealing with insulting remarks and put-downs. In another they may deal with a simulated situation in which one student refuses to do her part in a cooperative group assignment. Cooperative group activities such as these are designed to encourage students to seek peaceful solutions in their school environment. Teachers who use these methods are also likely to believe they may be useful to their students as adults and may lead to future generations seeking more peaceful solutions in business, politics, or other issues in their families and communities.

## Creating Well-Balanced Cooperative Groups

Assigning students to cooperative groups can be the most difficult part of the process for teachers. The philosophy of heterogeneous grouping is excellent in theory, but is difficult to achieve in a real-life classroom. A classroom is likely to have one or two superstars whose ability cannot be matched in some subject areas. Similarly, one or two students may have very unusual learning difficulties or behavior problems. For most types of learning situations, the teacher must simply make the best judgment about the combinations that are approximately equivalent in ability.

It is advisable to put non-task-oriented students into groups with highly task-oriented teammates so that peer pressure will work to keep them on task. This theory, however, does not always work out in the classroom. Angry or highly restless students may refuse to participate or otherwise prevent their team from succeeding. When this happens, the group itself should be encouraged to deal with the problem as a means of learning how to cope with and resolve such occurrences in real life.

In arranging the room during cooperative group activities, each group should have a comfortable space, and members should be able to face one another and have eye contact with every other member of the group. Separating the groups from one another is also necessary so they can each work undisturbed by the conversations and activities taking place in other groups.

Materials intended for cooperative groups may differ from those used in conventional teaching and learning situations. It is suggested that only one set of materials explaining the task and the expectations be distributed. This causes students in the group to work together from the very beginning. In some cases, each member of the group may receive different information from other members. This promotes interdependence as each member has something important to share with the others.

Interdependence can also be encouraged by the assignment of "complementary and interconnected roles" to group members. These roles will vary with the type of learning and task, but might include discussion leader, recorder of ideas, runner for information, researcher, encourager, and observer.

Tasks that result in the creation of products, rather than participation in a test or tournament, are more likely to succeed if the group is limited to the production of one product. If more than one product is allowed, students may simply work independently on their own products. Members of the group should also be asked to sign a statement saying that they participated in the development of the group's product.

To ensure individual accountability, students must know that they will all be held responsible for learning and presenting what they learned. During the final presentations, the teacher may ask any member of the group to answer a question, describe an aspect of the group's final product, or present a rationale for a group decision.

## The Effects of Cooperative Learning

In a school setting, students learn in classes made up of their age-mates, for the most part. With conventional teaching methods, relationships among peers in a class are likely to become somewhat competitive because most students are aware of how well they are doing in relation to their classmates. Grading systems reinforce the competitive nature of school, as do standardized tests and entrance exams.

Individual competition can enhance the motivation for high-achieving students who perceive that they have a possibility of winning or being the best. However, the public nature of competitive rewards and incentives leads to embarrassment and anxiety for students who fail to succeed. When the anxiety and embarrassment are intense, students who recognize that they are unlikely to win no matter how hard they work eventually drop out of the competition in one way or another.

Even when the anxiety over competition is less intense and under control by students with average or high-average achievement, they may become preoccupied with grades to the extent that they avoid complex or challenging tasks that will risk their academic standing and grades.

Despite these negative effects of competition, it is difficult to imagine a classroom without some type of competitive spirit or reward system, and despite its obvious flaws, competition does create an energetic response from many students. Slavin's (1995) models of cooperative group structures are designed to maintain the positive value of competition by adapting it in the form of team competition so that each student is equally capable of winning.

Reflective teachers who undertake some form of cooperative learning will need to be aware of all possible effects and observe for both positive and negative interactions among teammates. When using competitive teams, teachers should take steps to ensure that every team has an equal chance to win and that attention is focused more on the learning task than on who wins and loses. When anger or conflict arise within groups, teachers must be ready to mediate and assist students as they learn the interpersonal and communication skills necessary to learn from their team losses.

Slavin (1995) and Sharan (1999) also report that cooperative groups may actually improve race relations within a classroom. When students participate in multiracial teams, studies show that they choose one another for friends more often than do students in control groups. Researchers attribute this effect to the fact that working together in a group as a part of a team causes students to promote more differentiated, dynamic, and realistic views (and therefore less stereotyped and static views) of other students (including handicapped peers and students from different ethnic groups) than do competitive and individualistic learning experiences (Johnson & Johnson, 1993).

Promoting dynamic interactions among you and your students is the likely effect if you choose to learn and master the use of cooperative learning strategies for your future classroom. All of the teaching strategies presented in this chapter have the potential of creating a stimulating, motivating, and highly interactive learning environment. They are all strategies that enhance the relational aspects of teaching. Simulations encourage interaction; role playing encourages self-awareness and understanding of others' points of view. Discovery learning and learning centers foster independence and intrinsic motivation, while cooperative groups promote interdependence. By using many of these strategies in your classroom, you will be inviting your students to learn for the sake of learning while at the same time you are providing them with opportunities for becoming reflective and relational human beings.

**PRAXIS**

This activity prepares you to write a constructed response similar to what you will be required to do on the PRAXIS™ Exam.

# REFLECTIVE ACTION EXPERIENCES FOR YOUR PROFESSIONAL PORTFOLIO

## Show Evidence of NBPTS Core Proposition 3: Teachers Orchestrate Learning in Group Settings

Proposition 3 of the NBPTS standards states that teachers need to be able to demonstrate that they know how to manage groups of students. This includes teaching students to work independently without constant supervision by a teacher. Forming cooperative groups is one significant way to manage groups and build independence at the same time. For this portfolio entry, you will analyze and reflect on the way you would use cooperative groups in your classroom.

1. Start by visiting a classroom to observe whether competition or cooperation is more highly valued. Give examples of classroom events or incentive structures to support your observation. Then reflect on whether you believe in using competition, cooperation, or some of each to motivate your students to learn. From your own experience, do you find cooperative groups enjoyable and stimulating or frustrating and discouraging? What type of role do you usually take in a cooperative group? Do you get impatient with others in your group and wish you could work on the assignment by yourself? How could the structure of the groups you participated in have been improved? Based on your own experience as a learner, are you likely to use cooperative groups in your classroom? Why or why not?

2. Visit a number of other classrooms that are using cooperative groups. This is one strategy that cannot be learned by reading alone. Observe the methods other teachers use to form the groups and to assign tasks and responsibilities. Look up the topic of cooperative learning on the web pages referred to in Chapter 1. Keep a log of the best ideas you see. Talk with the teachers to learn their best strategies for managing cooperative groups.

After your observations, has your point of view changed? Which are you now more likely to emphasize in your class—cooperation or competition?

3. Write a brief plan for using cooperative groups in the grade level you hope to teach. Organize your plan according to subject matter or thematic units. Describe three to five types of cooperative groups you will use to accomplish different purposes.

4. If possible, ask for an opportunity to field test a cooperative group in one of the classrooms you are visiting. Implement it and have someone videotape the students working on the task while you assist them. Describe the field test for your portfolio. How did you form the groups? What was the task? How did you communicate the task to the students? How did you assign roles and responsibilities? How did you interact with groups as they worked on the task? Critique the results with honesty and reflectiveness, describing what you have learned in the process.

# References

Anderson, M. K. (2000). *The Omaha.* New York: Franklin Watts.

Bloom, B. (1984). The search for methods of group instruction as effective as one-to-one tutoring. *Educational Leadership, 41*(8), 4–17.

Cohen, E. (1994). *Designing groupwork* (2nd ed.). New York: Teachers College Press.

Flanagan, A. (1998). *The Pueblos.* New York: Children's Press.

Flanagan, A. (1998). *The Shawnee.* New York: Children's Press.

Herrell, A., & Jordan, M. (2004). *50 strategies for teaching English language learners* (2nd ed.). Upper Saddle River, NJ: Merrill/Prentice Hall.

Issacs, S. S. (2000). *Life in a Hopi village.* Chicago: Heinemann Library.

Issacs, S. S. (2002). *Life in a Sioux village.* Chicago: Heinemann Library.

Johnson, D., & Johnson, R. (1991). *Teaching students to be peacemakers.* Edina, MN: Interaction Book Co.

Johnson, D., & Johnson, R. (1993). *Circles of learning.* Alexandria, VA: Association of Supervision and Curriculum Development.

Kamma, A. (1999). *If you lived with the Hopi.* New York: Scholastic.

Levine, E. (1998). *If you lived with the Iroquois.* New York: Scholastic.

McGovern, A. (1992) *If you lived with the Sioux Indians.* New York: Scholastic.

Roop, P., & Roop, C. (1998). *If you lived with the Cherokee.* New York: Scholastic.

Santella, A. (2001). *The Apache.* New York: Children's Press.

Santella, A. (2001). *The Lakota Sioux.* New York: Children's Press.

Sharan, S. (1999). *Handbook of Cooperative learning methods.* Westport, CT: Praeger.

Slavin, R. (1995). *Cooperative learning* (2nd ed.). Boston: Allyn & Bacon.

Sonneborn, L. (2002). *The Iroquois.* New York: Franklin Watts.

Sonneborn, L. (2002). *The Seminole.* New York: Franklin Watts.

Tarbescu, E. (2000). *The Crow.* New York: Franklin Watts.

Woods, G. (2002). *The Navajo.* New York: Franklin Watts.

## CHAPTER 10

# Integrating Technology into the Curriculum

Technology can empower people to create new solutions, invent new processes, and change minds and the world in which we live. As teachers, we have a new responsibility to prepare our students with all the advantages and power that technology can bring. Technology can enhance your curriculum planning and your presentation skills. With recent advances in digital and cellular technology, you can use technology in your classroom or outdoors on a field experience.

Imagine that you are a parent of a middle school student whose class has gone to a national park for several days to take part in an outdoor education experience. You might wonder what they are doing and feel somewhat disconnected from your child. However, if your child is spending the week visiting Yellowstone Park on a geology field trip with John Graves's class from Bozeman Montana, you could monitor the activities of the class online at *http://gemini.oscs.montana.edu/~graves/*.

During their autumn field experience, you might learn from the Web journal written by John's students, that they climbed and hiked for 5.2 miles. They posted pictures on their Web page of a snake and a brand-new elk calf that they observed. You could also view their pictures of travertine terraces and of travertine being deposited around the base of living trees. This outdoor education experience and the way it is being reported to the entire world online is evidence of the significant change taking place in the way that educational experiences are structured and documented. Their field trip is along ancient ground, looking at history and earth science with their own eyes. Yet, their laptop computers allow them to communicate with their parents, other classmates, and educators around the world in real time.

The importance of technology in the classroom cannot be overemphasized as we explore the cyberfrontiers of the 21st century. For many teachers, however, technology may seem to be a mixed blessing: exciting and motivating, but at the same time, bewildering and frustrating. In this chapter, we describe what we believe is a glimpse into the educational future, a peek at what may become the norm in most school districts in the next decade. For example, we predict that in the next few years, technology will make it possible for students in one school district to enroll in courses taught by other school districts throughout the United States or even the world.

## NBPTS Standards Related to Technology in the Classroom

Proposition 2 describes the repertoire of curricular strategies and resources that professional teachers are responsible for providing in their classrooms. This repertoire should include primary sources, models, reproductions, textbooks, videotapes, computer software, and musical recordings. Professional teachers are expected to keep abreast of technological developments that can add richness and depth to their teaching and learning experiences. Being able to engage students in making use of the rapidly expanding field of computer technology and how to use the computer to enhance their own teaching are both essential to the professional teacher.

As you read about or select a strategy to try out in a laboratory or classroom, you will find that some of them work for you and others do not. You will need to reflect on what works for you and your students and why. As you think about what works for you, it is quite acceptable for you to combine, adapt, modify, and add your own unique strategies to the ones you read about or observe. Through this process of practice and reflection, you will discover, create, and refine your own unique teaching style.

Technology is a valuable tool and can play a pivotal role in education, but it may never replace the types of spontaneous, invigorating class discussion that take place between students and teacher when they are actively engaged in puzzling out some dilemma or discussing the relative merits of an abstract idea such as liberty. The most effective teaching is still a human experience, and great teachers thrive and take advantage of these teacher–student interactions. In today's classroom, that interaction may be initiated and conducted through technological formats such as online discussion boards and chat rooms. Teachers and their students may e-mail one another after school hours or parents may be monitoring what is happening in their children's classes by logging on to the class's Web page.

## Other National Standards for Technology Use

The International Society for Technology in Education (ISTE) has established and published national technology standards for teachers (ISTE 2002). The standards and suggestions for meeting them in the classroom can be viewed online at *www.iste.org*. Broadly stated, these standards state that all teachers should be prepared to meet the following standards:

**PRAXIS**
This approach addresses content tested in PRAXIS™ Exam Section 2b: Planning Instruction.

1. Teachers demonstrate a sound understanding of technology operations and concepts.
2. Teachers plan and design effective learning environments and experiences supported by technology.
3. Teachers implement curriculum plans that include methods and strategies for applying technology to maximize student learning.
4. Teachers apply technology to facilitate a variety of effective assessment and evaluation strategies.
5. Teachers use technology to enhance their productivity and professional practice.
6. Teachers understand the social, ethical, legal, and human issues surrounding the use of technology in K–12 schools and apply that understanding in practice.*

## Reasons to Incorporate Technology into Your Curriculum

Although it is true that excellent teaching can take place with little assistance from current technology, most teachers are enjoying the new doors and windows that computers have opened for extending students' learning experiences beyond the classroom walls. We view technology as an essential ingredient in a well-run classroom, for the following reasons:

1. *Technology adds variety to classroom experiences.* During any class, using a variety of teaching methodologies with students is very important. Integrating the appropriate technology into your classroom will provide more options. Students can, for example,

---

use word processing to create final drafts of written materials, use video cameras to capture class projects, create PowerPoint© presentations covering a broad span of topics, search the Internet for material related to assigned investigations, engage e-pals in electronic conversations, electronically scan work into e-portfolios, take virtual tours to other classrooms and locations to broaden their views of our global community, and perform a host of additional activities. Students become more engaged in the curriculum when it offers them new and novel ways to explore and learn. Bringing the world to their doorstep through electronic means offers them more excitement and brings their learning into the real world of application and understanding.

2. *Technology mirrors the world beyond the classroom.* The classroom environment should reflect what is happening beyond the classroom. Our students are going to be continually challenged by technological innovations when they leave school. We must make certain that they are computer literate and confident in their interactions with a technological world.

3. *Technology is an effective teaching tool.* To enhance learning, technological devices can add to teachers' presentations and make subject matter more meaningful in new and unusual ways. Students can see changes to variables and subsequent ramifications at the click of a mouse. The "what ifs" can be explored in seconds. Students can generate their own patterns and make judgments when large blocks of data are gathered from many sources and displayed on computer screens.

4. *Learning to master technology prepares students to cope with change.* In every historical era, there have been skeptics who believe that because technology changes so rapidly, school curricula are perpetually out of date and will never keep up. Nonetheless, we believe that by using the most up-to-date technological methods available, teachers are helping their students envision the future and prepare themselves for living in a world in which change is occurring more rapidly than ever before. Teachers who keep current themselves and use the most up-to-date technological equipment possible in their classrooms are modeling for students that there is immense value in technology. Students who become accustomed to using technology will be motivated to adapt to the times and keep current with future technological advances.

## MANAGING YOUR CLASSROOM WITH (AND FOR) TECHNOLOGY

Technology can assist teachers in classroom management, but at the same time, technology creates new classroom management issues. As a means of making teachers' professional lives more manageable, the market provides excellent software packages that can be adapted or are designed for seating charts, grades, attendance, lesson plans, room inventories, rubrics, test masters, word processing, spreadsheets, and other classroom needs. Keeping a computer file of these important daily functions saves office space and paper.

Many teachers have developed classroom management systems that include having students do their homework on computers. They may "turn in" their papers by e-mailing their homework to the teacher. Independent or group projects can be done by students working on their home or school computers. Some schools now provide laptop computers for each student.

When there is a computer laboratory in the school, the classroom teacher and the computer specialist may frequently confer about what the students need to accomplish when they come into the laboratory. Occasionally, the computer specialist will initiate and manage a series of experiences for each grade level.

Having computer activities in a centralized laboratory has certain advantages. The teacher in the lab is likely to be more familiar with various programs and can efficiently select and instruct students in their use. Computer programs can be stored in the lab and distributed easily when students need them. On the negative side, when the entire school must be scheduled for time in the lab, each class may get only an hour or two per week to spend working with the computers.

Media center computers are managed by media center personnel. They may designate one or more computers to be used for CD-ROM research stations. Students use these computers whenever they want to search for information on the CD-ROM encyclopedia, atlas, or other database. Other computers in the media center may be available for a variety of uses, including word processing, tutoring programs, and literature-based software packages. When the media center has a collection of software programs available, students may be allowed to check them out and use them on a computer in the room, getting assistance from media center personnel when needed.

Just appearing above the technological horizon is a new technology that may revolutionize the way we think about teaching and learning. The Smart Spaces Laboratory provides a potential for people to be able to interact with one another in a life-size and real-time setting. Through the Internet, a teacher and students may be separated by thousands of miles, but they will be able to interact as if they were in the same room. For example, a social studies teacher attending a conference in San Francisco could deliver a lecture to her students in New York City. During the teaching session, the teacher in San Francisco will see her class projected onto a wall in a room at the conference center and students will see her projected on a wall in the classroom. The teacher will appear to her students as if she is really there. A teacher can lecture, perform demonstrations, and view her virtual wall to see student responses. The teacher can respond to questions as they are asked, and students' body language and other important feedback cues will be clearly visible in a real-time life-like setting.

Does one have to be a technological super-geek to deliver these presentations? No. Through implicit computing, small nested computers around your neck and on your clothes will activate all commands through voice recognition. Universities are researching this technology today. Although the Smart Spaces Laboratory does not appear to be available any time soon, we should be aware of its possibilities and respect its potential.

Similar technologies are, however, currently available in the form of course management and delivery systems such as Blackboard.com *<http://www.blackboard.com>*. These systems allow for much of the same types of interaction between students and instructors as are mentioned in the previous example. Assignments may be easily passed back and forth between student and instructor. Chat rooms and discussion boards allow for high levels of interaction between and among students and instructors. Assignments may be posted on the site for students to access and review 24 hours a day, 7 days a week. Virtual classrooms allow instructors to be located away from the physical classroom, yet conduct the class session in real time by having all the students signed onto the site at the same time. Individual lessons may also be posted to the Web site so that students who, for whatever reason, are unable to attend the face-to-face lessons may access them at a later time as if they were actually (or virtually, in this case) attending the class.

When teachers have more than one computer in a classroom for use by the students and the teacher, they may designate one or more computers for a specific use. In the primary grades, rotating schedules are often created that allow each child to use a computer to accomplish a specified task for the week. For example, while studying addition, students may rotate through four to six stations that allow them to practice addition. In a primary classroom, one of the stations may be a computer with a program such as Number Muncher (MECC), an addition learning activity.

In the upper grades, schedules are often created so that students can sign up to use a computer. Cliff Gilkey, for example, has four computers in his classroom. He has collected a variety of software programs over the years. For some projects, he uses a rotation system that allows one cooperative group to use the computers at a time. He tries to keep the computers busy as much as possible during the day, so he rotates students to the computers for one task or another. During free time, students can choose to use the computer to play educational games.

A video camera can also be used to record lessons for students who are absent. Also, for teacher absences, a video camera can be used to record a lesson and then allow a substitute teacher to show the material at a later time. Important concepts that are difficult to perform in class can be taped and played over several times for student comprehension. Intricate events that are videotaped as they unfold over time can be replayed one frame at a time. Videotaping student laboratory work and pertinent class presentation discussions and then showing vignettes can be an incontestable review session at the end of a unit. However, make sure parents agree to the taping of their children and that signed permission slips are kept on file.

The information recorded by a digital camera can be downloaded into a computer and then either printed or projected on a television screen. These pictures can be displayed in the classroom at a nominal cost. The pictures from a digital camera can also be used to document accomplishments for teacher or student portfolios. Digital photographs can also be printed on transparencies using inexpensive inkjet printers and can then be projected using a simple overhead projector, thus enhancing the image and providing visual input to aid in understanding and comprehension. Students also enjoy seeing themselves in videos and projected "larger than life" on the overhead screen. They can use these relatively simple technologies to create projects and enhance oral reports presented in class.

If your school district has a photocopy network, you can add to your classroom management system by preparing and binding handouts for each unit of study. At the middle school or high school, teachers can plan for a packet of handouts needed for each semester. The typical bound handout may include a calendar of events, unit objectives, homework assignments with due dates, lab experiments, review sheets, supplementary reading materials, and pictures of key transparencies, with each page perforated for easy removal. With a bound packet, students are less likely to lose a big packet of material compared to individual sheets, which might end up in the wrong folder or be lost. Using colored divider sheets between the units of study lets students easily locate material and allows students to see upcoming work at a glance. Classroom packets are extremely helpful for teachers when students are absent and want to be able to keep up with class assignments.

# ENHANCING YOUR INSTRUCTIONAL STRATEGIES WITH TECHNOLOGY

## Word Processing Programs

Word processing programs are among the most versatile software available for classrooms. Early experiences, especially in the primary grades, may be devoted to very simple writing assignments with a dual purpose: composing and learning keyboarding. Many programs are available to teach students how to type and use the special function keys on the keyboard. As students learn to identify letters and numbers, they can often begin to type them before they can hold a pencil and write them on paper.

Learning to operate a keyboard also provides new opportunities for older students with special needs related to small motor functioning. Students with visual and motor difficulties that prevent them from writing neatly or cause them to erase and redo their work can now create neat papers. The delete key may save students from embarrassment and frustration, just as it does for teachers.

When students master keyboarding skills, they are free to compose many types of verbal products, including letters, stories, poems, essays, reports, and plays. Studies have shown that students write longer pieces on a word processor than they do by hand. The other major benefit is that the word processor greatly simplifies the editing and revision processes. Students can learn to use spelling checkers, grammar checkers, and thesaurus programs. Their motivation to write is increased in part because of the attraction of working on a computer, but also because the final products that are printed out are neat and relatively error-free. Rather than experiencing writing as drudgery, students are likely to feel pride and success related to the writing process when they are allowed to compose and edit using a word processing program.

Students with limited English proficiency benefit from writing and composing with a word processor. By pairing a proficient English speaker with a less proficient student, the two can work together at the computer to compose and illustrate stories and poems. In the process, they are communicating orally as well as in writing, giving the less proficient English speaker an opportunity to use the new language in a meaningful context.

Using word processing programs or more specialized desktop publishing programs, students can create newspapers, magazines, posters, invitations to events, and other materials that have the appeal of a professionally published product. Many teachers employ these media to help students create gifts for families, such as published books of poetry or calendars illustrated by the class.

## Educational Software

Computer programs are available for classroom use that can diagnose students' skill levels in math, reading, vocabulary, and other basic skills and prescribe lessons at the appropriate level. In "teaching" the lessons, computers make excellent tutors because they are endlessly patient in waiting for a student response and give the appropriate feedback without emotional side effects. Like manipulatives in mathematics, many computer games provide students with realistic or simulated experiences that allow them to experiment, observe relationships, test hypotheses, and use data to reach conclusions supported by evidence.

From the thousands of software packages available today, how do you select the best program for your students? You will find many resources for evaluating software at the Web site called Superkids (*http://www.superkids.com*). This Web site provides reviews and ratings of software programs in terms of educational value and ease of use.

Some gamelike programs are useful in expanding students' experiences beyond the classroom walls into simulated journeys, laboratories, foreign countries, earlier periods of history, and the future. Many of these programs increase students' decision-making and problem-solving abilities by offering them opportunities to make choices and get immediate feedback on the consequences of their decisions.

## EXTENDING CLASSROOM EXPERIENCES BEYOND THE CLASSROOM WALLS

Yen-Ling Shen is a sixth-grade teacher in Barrington, Rhode Island. She likes to introduce her students to her ancestral land of China and does so through a study of ancient China and its geography by showing a PowerPoint presentation of photos taken while she was there visiting relatives. She then has the students explore maps of the ancient land and trade routes.

Yen-Ling uses technology in preparing and teaching her unit in several ways:

- She researches Internet sites for information.
- She prepares overhead slides using the computer.
- She shows photos using pictures she has integrated into PowerPoint presentations using the computer and a projector.
- She shows KidPix paintings using a computer and projector.
- She prepares handouts for the students on the computer.
- She uses the scanner to create color transparencies from relevant illustrations and travel folders.

During the unit of study, her students use technology in the following ways:

- They research information using Internet sites Yen-Ling predesignates.
- They create slides using KidPix paint.
- They write summaries using a word processor.
- They print out their summaries on the computer.

Yen-Ling's learning goals for this unit include the students' discovery of China's geography and how it impacted early settlements and an understanding and respect for those whose way of life is different from their own.

Through a series of explorations and the use of technology, Yen-Ling is able to address history and social science standards related to the structures of early Chinese civilizations (geographic, economic, religious, and social). She also addresses visual arts standards by having the students use various observational drawing skills to depict a variety of subject matter as well as creating a drawing using various tints, shades, and intensives.

Yen-Ling addresses English and language arts standards by exploring the organizational features of electronic text (e.g., bulletin boards, databases, keyword searches, e-mail addresses). The students also gain experience in composing documents with appropriate formatting by using word-processing skills and principles of design (e.g., margins, tabs, spacing, columns, and page orientation). The students also research their topics using a variety of resources and compose and organize informational text. Yen-Ling addresses technology standards by giving the students experience in using a variety of technologies including word-processing, Internet research, and multimedia presentations. Yen-Ling concludes her unit of study by inviting the parents to an evening where the students share maps and reports they have created using technology with PowerPoint visuals.

## Slide Show Presentations

Jim Hicks uses slide shows to outline the day's activities and inform students of the objectives for class each day. These slides can be stored on a computer and retrieved for any purpose. Students also display what they have learned in a class project by creating their own slide shows using a word-processing document displayed on a television screen, or making a PowerPoint demonstration complete with digital pictures, graphs, charts, and lesson plans all on a series of screen snapshots. These slides can be stored for review sessions in class or at a computer resource center. A summary can be written for each day's presentation, which is especially helpful for students who have been absent.

Slide shows are particularly helpful for parent-night presentations when course content and expectations need to be outlined quickly. Many teachers post these documents on a bulletin board, but with this setup you have a living document that can be easily updated, deleted, expanded, and stored for future use. Documents can be shared effortlessly with team members. In fact, team meetings can be used to establish the format and content of these slides, thereby making sure every one is on the same page—excuse me, the same slide.

Another powerful tool with slide shows is concept mapping, which allows students to see the total picture and to make connections between key ideas. This educational technique can be used to help students write more coherently in language arts classes as well as assist science students in understanding major conceptual schemes and social studies students in seeing the cause-and-effect relationships of historical events.

## Digital High School in Action

High school students may even travel back in time via the Internet. Tom Berger teachers high school English at Rancho Buena Vista High School in Vista, California. He publishes his courses online to make them available to his students, their parents, and the school administration. To view them, log on to *http://rbvhs.vusd.k12.ca.us/~tberger/index.htm*. You will enter the world of a high school sophomore or senior enrolled in one of Tom's classes. Let's say, for example, that you are a senior taking Tom's English class. First, go to the Web page containing the course outline to see the topics that are covered this year. After the course begins, you will log on to the Web page for daily assignments to see what Tom will be covering in class this week and learn your homework assignment.

Here are the assignments for the first part of September 2004:

| ENGLISH 12 |
| --- |
| **DAILY ASSIGNMENTS** |

| | |
| --- | --- |
| 9/7, 8/04 | *Beowulf.* Vocabulary Lesson 2. |
| 9/9/04 | Reflective Writing: The personal statement, the prompt, and examples. |
| 9/10/04 | Counseling Presentation in the PAC. Report to class first. |
| 9/13/04 | Finish Vocabulary Lesson 2. Bring Theban plays to class! |

The term "Internet Field Trip" is highlighted on the Web page. When students click on it, they are linked to another page on the high school Web site that has questions about the history and politics of England. Then they click on a link to a Web site about King Arthur where they can find the answers to their questions. Of course, this is just the beginning of the search, and students may branch off in many directions depending on their interest in the topic.

Tom plans to create an Internet field trip for each unit of study in both the classes he teaches this year. He structures these Internet activities to link with preselected sites because he wants them to encounter quality information from sites that have integrity. In previous years, Tom would take students to a computer lab and they would search for information on the topic he assigned. Search engines would come up with nonrelated sites that would pull students' attention off track.

Tom posts a Web page called Class Standards in order to ensure that all students are aware of what is expected of them. This page includes his grading, make-up work, and computer policy. Here is an excerpt from that page.

*Grades and Points*

Students should put their best effort into all their assignments. Some class and homework will be checked off for credit, while essays, quizzes, and tests will be evaluated for a grade. Students' grades are compiled in the following categories:

40% Essays, Tests, & Quizzes

20% Class & Homework

20% Final Exam/Project

20% Participation & Materials

Students receive 10 points every day. Students lose points for absences, tardies, leaving the room, and forgetting materials. To make up points (for excused absences only) students must call my voice mail to hear the homework message *and* leave me a message. This way the student will be able to keep up with the class and will be accountable for reading assignments.

Tom's rules for using the computer are also clearly defined on the Class Standards Web page:

*Computer Rules*

No food or drinks in the room.
Do your assignment, don't play.
Do not aimlessly "surf the net."

We will be using the computers for researching the novels and the histories of our subjects, for publishing our writing, and for creating presentations. It is more important to put your effort into your content rather than creating flashy presentations. The writing portion of your grade will always outweigh the appearance portion. This is an English class, not a computer class.

Tom has put a lot of effort into creating and maintaining these Web pages for his courses. But, he says it is the most satisfying year of his teaching career. Students use computers at least three times per week, but the work they are doing is similar to what they would do in a noncomputerized English class. In the past, he found that English was often disliked by students because of its emphasis on reading and writing. Most students are not excited at the prospect of studying grammar and vocabulary. By bringing in technology, we provide students with a hands-on learning experience. Instead of using pen and paper, students can create PowerPoint presentations or Web pages of their essays, chapter summaries, poem explications, research projects, and oral presentations in class. The Internet provides a means for students to publish their work. They can create interactive essays incorporating graphics and reader-selected materials. Tom elaborates:

> *In my classroom I have 18 computers that are connected to the Internet and a school-wide network. The school applied for a California Digital High School Grant, which enables us to infuse technology into the existing curriculum. Every student has his or her own network I.D. and folder, which enables them to access their work from any computer on campus.*

Tom still lectures, students still read and write, but the difference is that they write on a computer and save their essays to Tom's network folder.

One benefit of Tom's Web-page assignment is that it opens communications with parents and increases their accountability. At a recent back-to-school night, parents were overjoyed to learn that they could log on to the English 10 Daily Assignment Web page and know exactly what is expected of their students. One parent provided Tom with additional links to add to the Web page on Arthurian Legends.

# EXAMPLES OF K–12 TECHNOLOGY PROGRAMS

## The Onalaska Experience

The Onalaska School System in western Wisconsin has a 5-year technology plan supported by both the community and staff. We present it here as an example of a well-planned infrastructure that makes technology available to every member of the school community.

Kevin Capwell, the coordinator of the program, likens the district's technology plan to an inverted pyramid. "At the bottom of the pyramid are the classrooms with appropriate hardware and software. As the pyramid broadens, each classroom is connected to the school, each school is connected to the district's grid, and finally, the district to the world. Connecting this entire superstructure between schools and district headquarters is fiber optic cable."

The school district was the recipient of a fortuitous technological partnership when it contracted with the local cable company to use the newly installed fiber optic cable system between school buildings for its technological grid. Consequently, every computer in each school is not only linked to appropriate support systems within a building, but to every computer and support system throughout the district. Onalaska Library, which is located adjacent to the high school, is also connected to the school system's grid. This permits students and staff to reference any book in both the school district and public libraries. Every classroom has a mounted television set with a VCR. Information can be channeled into each television from a central audio visual department. However, teachers have the flexibility of using their VCRs for in-class videos. The computer-to-student ratio throughout the district is between 1:3 and 1:2. In addition, teachers each have their own computers plus access to laptop computers that can be checked out day or night.

Because the community–school relationship and communication is an important component in the daily operations of the school district, the district maintains an extensive Web site. E-mail addresses for every staff member—teachers and cooks—along with department phone numbers are available from a directory on that site. Community members can also access this Web site from computers at the public library free of charge.

Onalaska High School has a long-distance learning program that serves students, staff, and community members. The distance learning lab (DLL) was funded with state and federal grant monies. Many high schools in the area, along with the University of Wisconsin, LaCrosse, belong to the DLL consortium, which is interconnected by fiber optic cable running at DS3 speed.

The DLL lab itself consists of a regular-size classroom with six to eight student computer stations. Each station has a computer and keyboard under a glass-counter desk. A microphone sits on top. Two banks of four televisions each are at opposite ends of the room. One set of four televisions, located in the front of the room, is for student viewing while the second set of four televisions, located in the back of the room, is for instructor use, if needed.

This DLL lab allows a student at Onalaska to enroll in a course offered by another school within the consortium. For example, if an Onalaska High School student wants to enroll in an agriculture business class not offered by the district, he can take the course long distance from Holmen High School, a member-school in the consortium. Also, students or community members can take courses offered by the University of Wisconsin at LaCrosse, via the DLL if the class is scheduled at an appropriate time for both LDL consortium schools.

The interaction between students and teacher is live and in real time because of three cameras that are installed in the DLL schools. Camera 1 is mounted next to the front bank of four televisions and automatically shows an entire class of Onalaska students to a Holmen High School teacher, who views them from a second set of TVs in the back of the room. Camera 2, located at the base of the second bank of four TVs at Holmen High School, shows the instructor teaching the course. There is also a corresponding Camera 2 at Onalaska. If a student at Onalaska has a question at any time during the presentation, he or she presses a bar on the microphone and Camera 1 automatically zooms in on his or her face during the questioning. Camera 2 at Holmen automatically zooms in on the instructor during the explanation phase. A third camera can be used at any time to show documents on the front table at Holmen with uncanny clarity. Camera 3 at Onalaska is not functional when the instruction is at Holmen, and vice versa. While Camera 2 and Camera 3 are operating at Holmen, these two views can be seen in a picture-within-a-picture format on the TVs provided for student viewing at Onalaska. At Holmen, the teacher also has a picture-within-a-picture format so the instructor will be able to see both views simultaneously.

A teacher at one school can teach students from four other schools, with each school shown on a separate TV for instructor viewing. The school's name appears at the bottom of each screen. All together, five classes can use the DLL format: four schools using DLL instruction and one class at the instructor's school. All five classes concurrently receive instruction.

Eagle Bluff Elementary, also in the Onalaska system, is a two-story building arranged in wings or "pods," with a state-of-the-art media room in the center. One of the many activities planned for this room are staged television productions that can be transmitted to locations within the district or community via cable.

Computer stations are located in the corridors. There are six computers at each station arranged on a huge circular table. Each computer along with keyboard and earphones is arranged every 60 degrees allowing ample room for two students, if necessary, to operate one computer. Because the computers are arranged in a circle, all connecting cables are funneled to the back of each computer through the center of the table to connecting links in the floor. From a distance, the area looks wire-free.

All classrooms next to shared corridors contain a computer, VCR, and approximately 20 students. For each classroom, huge interior windows allow teachers to view any location in the shared corridor. Consequently, teachers can instruct students inside classrooms or in the shared corridor, simultaneously. "Since all of the technology is hooked together, a student finishing a project anywhere within the pod can record it directly to VHS tape and take it home with him," Kevin adds enthusiastically.

Onalaska High School has computer laboratories for business, language arts, mathematics-science, applied arts (CAD), and foreign language. There are two computer labs for business, one with Macintosh computers and another containing Windows-based machines. The two computer labs, which have at least 30 student stations, are arranged like bookends with a classroom and a teacher business office nested between them. Students can easily attend class discussions, and then adjourn to either lab to perform computer tasks. The entire yearbook and school newspaper are composed on these computers.

The mathematics computer lab is adjacent to the mathematics rooms. It is not uncommon for students to attend class discussion, and then during the same class period adjourn to the computer lab to complete tasks with carefully chosen mathematical software, including ones for remediation and graphical analyses.

The language arts lab is used the most throughout the school. Students can access this room as early as 6:30 A.M. and can stay as late as 9 P.M. These late-night episodes usually take place at the end of a grading period. The room is located near an entrance to the school and can be easily accessed by students after school hours.

A school–community alliance forms the heart of this computer lab. Paraprofessionals supervise this lab during the day, community volunteers at night. Each supervisor is well versed in computer technology so students can easily get help when working on projects.

The computer aided drafting (CAD) lab, consisting of at least 30 computers, is adjacent to the applied arts classrooms so that students have the ability to attend class discussions, and then within just a few feet, work on computer-assisted drawings. Many times students from nearby English classrooms can be found working on writing projects in this computer lab. Digital editing also takes place in the CAD lab. This allows students to produce *Topper TV*, a biweekly show dedicated to news and events about Onalaska High School. The news anchors, camera operators, and digital video editors are all students.

Onalaska is a district that has infused technology into every aspect of its curriculum and community relations. We hope you will be able to teach in a district that has such a pioneering spirit.

## COMPUTER LITERACY PROGRAM AT BEARDSLEY MIDDLE SCHOOL

Another district that has encouraged and supported teachers to infuse technology into the curriculum is Crystal Lake District 47, Crystal Lake, Illinois. Diane Jensen brings a great deal of expertise to her computer technology instructor position at Hannah Beardsley Middle School (grades 6–8) in Crystal Lake. Teaching is a second career for Diane, who was a managing editor of 13 community newspapers when she retired at age 40. The lack of excitement she experienced while in the workplace encouraged her to go back to college and pursue a career in teaching. She has never looked back and immensely enjoys her teaching assignment.

Diane's main responsibility is to teach computer technology skills to students in seventh and eighth grades. Because different levels of keyboarding skills of her students can present a problem, one focus of the sixth-grade program is to ensure that there is a minimum level of keyboarding competency for all students.

The first topic in her 9-week course for seventh graders is file management, which is very important for data storage and retrieval. Then, a PowerPoint assignment called "About Me," helps Diane learn more about the students while students become familiar with this presentation program. Included in this assignment is information about their family plus their activities, hobbies, and dreams for the future. Once finished, students take this project one more step by making their presentations to their classmates.

The major project for seventh graders is a report and presentation on an endangered species, which is a collaborative effort with seventh-grade science teachers Fran Hicks and Ann Min. The science teachers evaluate the content of the project; Diane evaluates its technical side. "I like to say I grade the style and pizzazz whereas the science teachers grade the substance," she says.

Before students get started, they are given two rubrics for grading the project: one from their science teacher and one from Diane. That way everyone knows what is expected.

Working with seventh- and eighth-grade language arts teachers, Diane uses Inspiration—a webbing and graphic organizing software program—to teach her students how to create a book report. Using circles, rectangles, clouds, and a host of other graphics and symbols available in Inspiration, students craft a concept flowchart using arrows that are drawn between main and complementary ideas. With the click of a mouse, Inspiration transforms this right-brain activity into a traditional outline complete with Roman numerals and subcategories.

Diane believes computers can enhance the education of all students, including students with special needs. Some students in special education do very well on computer tasks. Diane doesn't let those labels interfere with how she treats her students. "Several years ago one of my best students was in special education for support and I didn't even know it," she says. "Because some students have a hard time getting ideas on paper, which could result from having trouble with their handwriting, the computer somewhat standardizes each writing assignment. When writing second or third drafts, students readily appreciate, like all of us, that we do not have to rewrite what is correct. By copying and pasting, only the mistakes have to be corrected. Also, there is a creative side to using computers, especially in PowerPoint presentations and Web-page designs. The computer is seen as less frustrating for many students. I always like to think I teach children, not the curriculum."

One teaching technique Diane uses to improve efficiency and independence involves placing a cup on top of the computer. For example, when working on computer tasks, Diane encourages students to be self-directed with her as the guide on the side. If students do have questions, then, instead of raising their hands or shouting out distress signals, they place a plastic cup on top of their computer and continue to troubleshoot. "I use this approach so students can keep working even though they need my help in one area. I don't know very many people who can keyboard efficiently with one hand up in the air and the other one on the keys," she quips. "Sometimes students can remedy their own problems in seconds after the cup alert. Also, neighbors seeing the cup can assist, thereby encouraging students to see themselves as drivers rather than passengers."

The eighth-grade curriculum emphasizes telecommunications. The major project involves students creating their own Web pages featuring a social studies topic. Geography is the focus for some of the students; a Civil War battle is the focus for others. Like with the PowerPoint science project, this is a collaborative effort and students earn a grade for both classes.

The eighth-grade telecommunications curriculum includes history of the Internet, e-mail usage, the substance of a URL address and its purpose, vocabulary pertinent to telecommunications, search engines, and netiquette. Students often surf chat rooms outside of the classroom so Diane makes them aware of the dangers associated with this type of activity. That is one reason why she and the school's police liaison officer, Terri Nowak, co-teach a lesson on Internet safety and computer crimes. "Young people in this age group think they're invincible and nothing will happen to them. We try to break down that myth. They also think there's nothing wrong with loading someone else's program onto their computer. Hopefully they'll understand that it is tantamount to stealing," says Diane.

Beyond the classroom, Diane works with middle school students who apply what they have learned in the classroom to a real-world experience: the school newspaper. Four to five times a year, *The Beardsley Roar* newspaper provides faculty, parents, and students with a first-class student publication—complete with photos, coupons, advertisements, news and features, editorials, sports, and a Dear Hannah column. The tabloid format of the newspaper is published on actual newsprint at a nearby printing plant. Readers pay 25 cents a copy or $1 for a year's subscription. This is an after-school club activity with students being responsible for all content, including advertisements. The activity is entirely self-supporting. The school newspaper provides a sense of community for the school, with the latest issue 20 pages long. The Dear Hannah advice column reveals an openness and sensitivity that rivals national publications. One entry reads:

> Dear Hannah,
>
> I'm having trouble with my parents. You see, they are going through a divorce and I don't know what to do. I'm so upset about it that I barely talk to them anymore. I know they are starting to worry, but I just can't talk to them because I am so mad. How can I fix my problem?
> Divorce

> Dear Divorce,
>
> Your voice will come back, but for now use your writing skills. Instead of talking to your parents, write to them about how you feel. You might learn writing is a powerful thing. It is often easier to write out your feelings than to say them.
> Hannah

In addition to mentoring the computer skills of her students, Diane assists other faculty members at Beardsley as they develop programs and curricula that make use of technology. Fran Hicks is a science teacher at Beardsley who expects, and usually gets, quality work from her students. She has been recognized by her district for her creative curriculum designs, and has the enthusiasm of a first-year teacher but the knowledge of a sage veteran. In the following Reflective Action Story, Fran, recalls how one of her favorite curriculum units has changed and developed over the years. New technology and the support of her fellow teachers has permitted her to keep growing as a teacher as she interacts with her colleagues to develop courses of study that not only engage her students in a creative and active search for knowledge but also hold them accountable for basic skills.

## ✳ REFLECTIVE ACTION STORIES ✳

# Planning a Technology-Based Endangered Species Unit

*Fran Hicks, Life Science Teacher, Hannah Beardsley Middle School, Crystal Lake, Illinois*

## Teacher Begins to Plan

We talk a lot about interdisciplinary studies these days. But, what does this term really mean? For me, the answer to this question got a little bit clearer when I began to notice how much it bothered me to see students' science reports filled with misspelled words and grammar errors. I believe that the more emphasis there is on interdisciplinary studies in each classroom, the better the education we are offering. Whether students are in science or in English classes, when answering questions they should be able to spell correctly and use complete sentences with proper grammar.

## Teacher Considers What the Students Already Know

Using a computer-TV interface. I decided to display the most frequently misspelled science words for the week. With a click of a mouse, I can compare this week's list with the previous top 10 to give students feedback on their spelling growth.

## Teacher Has Expectations

As the culmination to an ecology unit. I wanted to give students a project that would encourage them to use good spelling and grammar in communicating good science. I wanted to evaluate the unit using something other than a paper and pencil format, so I decided to have them design a poster publicizing various endangered species. I also believed that they would be motivated to do their best if they knew that their posters would be hung up around the school. The posters would also have the effect of making other students be aware of the plight of the endangered animals and plants.

## Teacher Does Research and Invites Feedback

I spent a considerable amount of time in the school and community libraries researching current material available to make sure the students would have ample resources. I also talked to my colleagues. Ann Min. another science teacher, and Diane Jensen, the computer instructor, to get their perspectives on this topic. Ann and Diane suggested that since the school had a new Windows computer lab it might be possible to create PowerPoint presentations. I also asked for, and received, assistance on this project from the language arts teachers and Marilyn Harfst, the media director, making this even more of an interdisciplinary unit.

## Afterward, Teacher Reflects on the Event

With all this input. I began to see that making posters was just the beginning of what my students could do to generate interest in saving endangered species. We could turn this project into a schoolwide curriculum plan that encourages students to think like scientists and communicate their ideas effectively using the latest technology.

## Teacher Reflects Again, Using Feedback, Research, and Creativity

We wanted our students to understand from the outset what was expected of them and how they can succeed. Each of the teachers in the project created a separate evaluation rubric. Diane's rubric is used to grade the technical skills, the language arts rubric is used to cheek for spelling errors, and my rubric evaluates the science content. We give these rubrics to students at the beginning of the unit, so that they know upfront what we expect of them.

## Teacher Creates a New Action Plan

The new plan that developed from this collegial planning is that each student will take the role of a fund raiser for the World Wildlife Federation. Their goal is to get money for a project that will protect an endangered species of their choice. Each student must create and present an informative and persuasive presentation using PowerPoint. To do this they must go beyond just researching the background of their endangered animals or plants. They also have to focus on the problems that are threatening the animal's or plant's existence and then come up with a plan that will effectively save it from extinction. Then they must use technology and good English skills to produce their PowerPoint presentation.

## Tracking the Return of Spring on the Internet

When one enters Ann Min's seventh- and eighth-grade physical and life science room, the place oozes with science. It's easy to understand why she is one of the first middle school science teachers in Illinois to attain the coveted National Board Certified Teacher designation. Ann challenges her students each day to hypothesize, evaluate, and reach a consensus when finalizing answers. The Internet plays a pivotal role in her seventh-grade life science curriculum called "Cycles." Beginning on Groundhog Day, she coordinates her curriculum unit called "The Return of Spring" with the Annenburg Foundation's online program, "Journey North" at *http://www.learner.org/jnorth/current.html*.

On campus, students are assigned to teams that monitor the return of springlike conditions around Hannah Beardsley Middle School. Teams monitor tulips, monarch butterflies, earthworms, and robins. By recording soil temperature as a function of days, number of hours of sunlight each day, arrival dates of certain birds, and emergent dates for assigned plants, correlations are noticed between measured variables.

The student teams fill out a template of information and then log on to the Internet. The Annenburg Foundation's Web page processes the information and shares it with the world. Each group identifies its position by latitude and longitude. After downloading information weekly from the Internet, the seventh graders tape little robin stickers onto a huge map of the United States at locations where robins were sighted. Because this map is located in the hallway, all students in the school are virtually able to see a wave of springlike happenings starting in the south and traveling north.

To heighten interest in scientific observation skills, the Annenburg Foundation picks 10 mystery schools. Students are asked to locate these mystery schools by observing weekly data from their positions.

The monarch butterfly study also has an international component. Each fall, Ann has her students mail paper butterflies to middle school students in Mexico. "The fall mailing, of course, symbolizes monarch butterflies heading south for the winter," Ann explains. When the monarchs arrive south of the border in the spring, the middle school students in Mexico mail the butterflies back to her students. But Ann adds a twist to this. "Our students have to write in Spanish to the students in Mexico, and the students in Mexico write in English to the students at our school." This project, then, is truly international as well as interdisciplinary.

## Technology Support for Teachers of English Language Learners

The Internet holds a wealth of resources for teachers of English and foreign languages. For example, leveled lesson pans, articles and resource guides are available at *http://esl.about.com/cs/teachingresources*. Projects and programs in ESL and foreign language instruction are evaluated and discussed at *http://www.esl.net*. The Intercultural Development Research Association offers a number of teaching resources and professional development opportunities at *http://www.idra.org*. A list of Web sites full of teacher resources and free downloads is available at *http://www.esl-group.com/tres.html*.

One of the most valuable Web sites for teachers is found at Matt Stanton's CyberEFL at *http://members.tripod.com/matt_stanton*. Mr. Stanton provides step-by-step instructions for teachers of ESL and foreign languages in how to create interactive Web sites, download free software, and create learning games and quizzes. He also provides ways for teachers to share ideas, network, and submit success stories. The Telus Learning Connection Web site also provides a format for teachers to network and share ideas and concerns (*http://www.2learn.ca*).

The Internet serves as a resource in finding translations for use in planning lessons, also. Many times a teacher needs a word in the student's native language in order to build on prior knowledge and make lessons more comprehensible. Two good sites for translations are: *http://www.babylon.com* and *http://www.babelfish.altavista.com*.

# THE ADVANTAGES OF TEACHER-TO-TEACHER NETWORKING

A major premise of the reflective action model presented in this text is that teachers learn a great deal by interacting with respected colleagues. We encourage beginning teachers to ask for feedback when they have questions or problems. One of the best methods teachers use today to interact and exchange ideas is through networking. While networking still occurs on the telephone or in meetings, the Internet has created many more exciting opportunities for "meeting" people and interchanging ideas.

Today, teachers and their students can belong to a community of learners who are willing to share ideas, explain complex issues, or suggest alternative solutions. And while other forms of networking may invoke travel expenses or long-distance phone charges, most of the information from Internet networks is free. For example, at *http://www.teachers.net*, you are greeted with this welcome message: "Take part in a nationwide Mentor Support Center, bringing together hundreds of thousands of educators in an environment specially designed to foster peer support and development. Take advantage of this incredible panel of experts and friends—you won't find teacher support like this anywhere else on Earth!" At this site, you can choose chat boards or chat rooms on the following topics:

**PRAXIS**
Teacher networking is a strategy addressed in PRAXIS™ Exam Section 4a: Profession & Community.

**General Interest Forum**

**English Center**

**Tech Center**

**Teacher Chatboard**

**Administrators Chatboard**

Preschool (EC)
Kindergarten
Primary Elementary
Upper Elementary
Middle School
High School
College Profs
Multiage Classroom

Beginning Teachers
Student Teachers
Substitute Teachers
Golden Apples
Retired Teachers
Gifted/Talented Ed
Special Education
Adult Education
Private School
Montessori
Prof Readings
Classroom Discipline
Classroom Mgmt
Counseling

**Curriculum Chatboards**

Math Teacher
Science Teacher
Social Studies/Geog
Music Teacher

Fine Arts & Art Education
PE/Coaching
Health
Brain-Compatible Learning

**English Center**

Reading & Writing
HS English
Books & Literature
Remedial Reading
Accelerated Reading
4 Blocks Literacy
Building Blocks (K)
6 Traits Writing
Library/Media Specialists

**Language Center**

ESL/EFL
French Teacher
Spanish Teacher
Travel/Study Abroad

**Project Center**

Project Switchboard
Learning Centers
Grant Writing

**Career Support Center**

JobTalk Support Board
Teacher Job Listings

At *http://www.teachnet.org*, you can search for lesson plans, grant information, online courses for teachers, and other resources to support teachers in the search for successful teaching practices.

New teachers are sure to receive many responses from fellow teachers willing to share their valuable resources and expertise. Perhaps not all the responses will be useful or match all teachers' teaching styles. It is the responsibility of the teacher who requests the information to reflect on all the responses and make use of the material that is most appropriate and useable. This is true of all Internet exchanges today. There is always more information than we can possibly use and we must be willing to consider each source to determine its value.

We encourage teachers at all levels and subject matter to join network groups to help support and promote excellent teaching techniques. It is only when we work together and pool our resources that the students of this nation will have the best education possible.

After reading this book, you can continue to interact with the authors at *http://www.reflectiveaction.com*. At this site, you can learn about how to plan and lead a professional book club at a teacher inservice program for your school. You can learn how to mentor and support other teachers who want to become more reflective and proactive in their careers. You can contact us and tell us your stories of being a reflective teacher. We may add your stories to the next edition of this book. You can also plan a professional book club for your faculty. We are providing materials at our site for you to take a self-assessment of your present capacity for withitness. We also provide materials you can use to lead a discussion of your peers on the many aspects of reflective teaching. We hope to see you there.

## REFLECTIVE ACTION EXPERIENCES FOR YOUR PROFESSIONAL PORTFOLIO

### Show Evidence of NBPTS Core Proposition 2: Teachers Command Specialized Knowledge of How to Convey a Subject to Students

**Proposition 2 states that professional teachers keep abreast of technological developments that can be used in their classrooms for many purposes. Teachers will be able to demonstrate that they know how to engage students in the rapidly expanding field of computer technology, as well as how to use the computer to enhance their own teaching.**

To prepare yourself to demonstrate your mastery of educational technology, visit a classroom where technology is used. Keep a log of how the teacher uses technological equipment. Take notes about the way the classroom is set up so that students can get access to the computer. Observe the students to see how they respond to using technology. Are they active and motivated by this type of learning?

Consider what you would do in the classroom you have observed. How would you rearrange furniture and equipment to improve students' access to the equipment? What would you add in the way of technology?

Think about a curriculum unit you are planning for this course. What type of learning experiences do you have planned that feature the use of technology? How will you use the equipment to make your presentations for the unit? How will students use the technology to create their final products? What do you want your students to be able to do with all of this information? How can your curriculum unit help them achieve your goal for them?

Rewrite your curriculum unit to include more options for technology both in your presentations and in the way your students research and gain information. Add several new technological options for students to make presentations on what they've learned.

Refer to Fran Hick's Reflective Action Story in this chapter. Note how she and her colleagues provided rubrics for evaluation at the beginning of her unit on endangered species. Create one or more rubrics for your curriculum unit that can be used to evaluate the use of technology as well as the content or subject matter.

## Reference

International Society for Technology in Education (2002). *National educational technology standards for teachers*. Eugene, OR: ISTE.

## CHAPTER 11

# Assessing and Reporting Student Accomplishments

**PRAXIS**

This chapter prepares you for PRAXIS™ Exam Section 2c: Assessment Strategies.

What is good work? As a teacher, you may find evaluating students' accomplishments among the most difficult judgments you have to make. You have worked hard to create authentic learning experiences. Now, how can you create an assessment system that allows students to demonstrate what they learned? How can you create an assessment system that allows students a range of possibilities to demonstrate their own particular strengths and talents? How can you create an assessment system that is fair and that your students can understand?

Educators committed to providing authentic learning for their students are also searching for meaningful and useful assessment systems that provide the kinds of information that allow students to move ahead and develop their skills and knowledge base.

## NBPTS Standards on Student Assessment

The NBPTS Proposition 3 subsection "Teachers Regularly Assess Student Progress" discusses the fact that teachers use assessment devices in their classrooms for two very different purposes. On the one hand, teachers give students tests that will be used to assess the progress of the class as a whole. Teachers want information on how their students are doing on average as a guide to making judgments about what to teach and how to teach it most effectively. Teachers use test data for the purpose of planning for the group as a whole.

The second purpose of assessment is to inform teachers of individual student progress, and the NBPTS states that professional teachers are astute observers of students—tracking their movements, their words, and their minds. Teachers use a variety of assessment devices to collect information on individual student progress and they recognize that each assessment tool has its own strengths and weaknesses. These assessments may be *formative* in nature, given during a sequence of instructions to help determine what learning is taking place and whether more instruction might be needed to assist the students in mastering needed material before further progress can be made in the study. *Summative* assessments are typically given at the end of a unit of study or sequence of lessons in order to determine how well individual students have mastered the material presented.

Professional teachers create their own assessment tools, including, but not limited to, portfolios, videotapes, demonstrations, and exhibitions. In addition, they use more traditional methods of assessment such as quizzes and exams. Teachers use questions and group discussions to determine how well students are responding to the lesson. They also talk with individuals in conference to learn more about each student's needs and accomplishments.

## HOW TEACHERS SELECT AND USE ASSESSMENT PROCEDURES

One piece of the authentic learning puzzle is to be sure to link your grading and reporting criteria with the criteria used in the learning process. When students know what the criteria for success are and see how they are linked to the learning experiences in the classroom, the learning environment seems fair to them (Guskey & Bailey, 2000). Varying evaluation procedures is also seen as beneficial. No one evaluation strategy works well for all subjects, grade levels, or student learning styles. For that reason, students should have a variety of ways to demonstrate their understandings and earn their grades.

Imagine you are a teacher planning a unit on astronomy for your classroom. You have gathered some interesting learning materials, including filmstrips on the solar system, National Aeronautics and Space Administration (NASA) material on the space shuttles and telescopes, and many exciting books with vivid illustrations. You have planned a field trip to an observatory and invited an astronomer to visit the classroom. You have worked out a time line for several weeks' worth of individual and group investigations and projects.

Now it is time for you to think about evaluation and to clarify your values regarding complex evaluation issues. How will you know what students have learned at the end of this unit? What do you expect them to learn? What techniques will you use to find out whether they have learned what you expect? What about the possibility that they may learn something different from what you expect or even that some students who become actively engaged in the study may learn more than you expect? How will you know what they learned? How will you assign students science grades at the end of this unit? How will you communicate to the students' parents what each has gained from it?

The following sections describe a variety of assessment devices. Each one has a variety of uses and applications. Each one provides answers to different questions teachers have about evaluation. Reflective teachers will consider each alternative and decide whether and how to use such measures in their own classrooms. Recognizing that this introductory text can only provide minimal information about each assessment method, the reflective teacher will want to search actively for more information about certain methods in order to fully understand their value and use before incorporating them into a program that affects students' lives.

## Informal Observations

Teachers use informal observation intuitively from the first moment the students enter the classroom at the beginning of the term. They watch groups to see how students relate to one another; they watch individuals to spot patterns of behavior that are either unusually disruptive or extremely productive. To manage a classroom effectively, withit teachers are alert to the overt and covert actions of their students at all times.

Informal observations also have academic implications. Teachers who observe their students while teaching a lesson are able to evaluate their understanding. Spotting a blank look, a nervous pencil tapping, or a grimace of discomfort on a student's face, the teacher can stop the lesson, check for understanding, and reteach the material to meet the needs of the students who did not understand.

As students read aloud, primary teachers observe and listen for patterns of errors in decoding words. They may also listen to the expression in the student's voice to determine whether the student is comprehending the material or simply saying words aloud. They listen for signs that indicate whether the student is interested in or bored with the material. An additional tool in informal observation is asking the student pertinent questions to check for understanding and determine the student's thought processes. This one-to-one interaction provides data and information not measured in any paper-and-pencil test.

By observing the student read, asking a few questions, and comparing the results with other students of the same grade or age, the teacher is able to assess many things, including (1) the extent to which the student is able to use phonics and context clues to decode reading material, (2) the student's approximate reading level in terms of sight vocabulary, and (3) the student's comprehension level. In addition, the reflective teacher uses the informal observation to gather information about the student's affective qualities, including confidence level, interest in the subject or in reading itself, amount of effort the student is willing to give to the task, and expectations the student has about success or failure in the subject.

By observing as students write or by reading what they have written, teachers can gather similar data about students' writing abilities, interests, and expectations. As students work out unfamiliar math problems, teachers are careful to observe who works quickly and who is struggling. Then they can gather the struggling students together for an extra tutoring session.

In order to form groups for appropriate instruction, teachers record their observations in the form of anecdotal records, checklists, or scoring rubrics. They can then use these records to plan subsequent instruction or grouping.

In the astronomy unit, the teacher may observe as students take part in discussions to determine the extent to which various students understand the concepts. When students are visiting the observatory, the teacher will watch them to learn about their interests in various aspects of the topic. When an astronomer visits the classroom, the teacher will listen to the students' questions to assess the depth of understanding they have achieved.

Informal observations are one of the most powerful assessment devices the teacher can use to gather new information about students' learning patterns and needs. Teachers may gather data about a student from academic and psychological tests, but in the end, it is the informal observation that most teachers rely on to understand the test data and make a final evaluation about appropriate placement or a grade value for a student's work.

## Performance Tasks to Show Mastery of Objectives

In contrast to informal evaluations, which provide useful subjective information, behavioral objectives are relatively formal and provide useful objective data about what students have learned. Do not assume that teachers choose one or the other of these two devices. Many reflective teachers know that it is valuable to gather both objective and anecdotal data. They may choose behavioral objectives as a means of gathering hard data about what students have achieved during classroom learning experiences and compare those data with the anecdotal information they have gathered during their informal observations.

To plan an assessment system based on students showing mastery of certain specified outcomes or objectives, the teacher must begin before teaching the lesson. By preplanning a unit with specific outcomes or a lesson with very concrete behavioral objectives, the teacher specifies the skills that students should be able to demonstrate at the conclusion of the lesson and the criterion for success. Teachers then plan learning experiences that are linked with the outcomes. After each objective has been taught and students have had an opportunity to practice the new skill, a quiz, worksheet, or other assessment product asks students to demonstrate that they have mastered the new skill and can perform it with few errors.

When each lesson is introduced, the teacher describes the prespecified criterion for success to the students. The criterion for success may be specified as a percentage or as a minimum number of correct responses. For example, the following behavioral objective specifies 80% (or 16 of the 20 possible items) as the acceptable demonstration of mastery of this objective:

*Spelling Objective:* When the teacher reads the list of 20 spelling words aloud, students will write 80% of the words, using correct spelling and legible handwriting.

A criterion-referenced test such as the weekly spelling test common in many classrooms demonstrates whether the students have mastered the new skill. To record student achievement, teachers may write the percentage of correct responses that each student attained in a grade book.

For more complex objectives, teachers design performance tasks that require students to demonstrate what they have learned. Marzano (2000) describes a system that allows teachers to design performance tasks that measure growth in communication skills, information processing, and other such complex acts. For example, students may present oral reports on a NASA satellite launch, and the teacher may evaluate students' knowledge and communication skills by using a scoring rubric. A scoring rubric consists of a fixed scale and a list of the characteristics for describing performance for each of the score points on the scale. Since rubrics describe levels of performance, they provide important information to teachers, parents, and others interested in what students know and are able to do. Perhaps most importantly, rubrics provide a clear statement to students, teachers, and parents on what is considered important and worth learning, even before the learning has occurred. Often teachers involve students in determining the criteria for the various scores on the rubric. By asking students to help write the criteria for success, the teacher ensures that students understand the criteria for success. A sample rubric is shown as follows.

### Rubric for communication skills and oral presentations

4. Clearly and effectively communicates the main idea or theme and provides support that contains rich, vivid, and powerful detail.

3. Clearly communicates the main idea or theme and provides suitable support and detail.

2. Communicates important information but without a clear theme or overall structure.

1. Communicates information in isolated pieces in a random fashion.

## Criterion-Referenced Quizzes and Tests

Quizzes are frequently used with behavioral objectives to determine whether students are successfully gaining each new skill or bit of knowledge in a unit of study. Quizzes are generally short, consisting of only a few questions or items, and are thought of as formative assessments, providing teachers with a way to know whether the students are learning the material day by day.

Tests, however, may consist of many items and are generally thought of as summative assessments. Tests are often given at the end of a unit and contain a variety of items that measure students' achievement of content and skills that have been taught during a period.

In both cases, the term *criterion-referenced* refers directly to the criterion established for each behavioral objective. Each item on a criterion-referenced test should match a preestablished criterion. Criterion referencing provides objective data about material that all students in the class have had an equal opportunity to learn.

Objective tests may take a variety of forms. The most common are matching, true-false, multiple choice, and short answer or completion forms.

*Matching* items are those that provide both the question and response. Students have only to recognize the correct response for each item and draw a line to connect the two. Items appear in a column on one side of the paper and the responses in a different order on the other side. In terms of Bloom's taxonomy, matching items are an excellent way of measuring knowledge-level objectives that require students to recognize correct responses. An example of a matching quiz related to the astronomy unit might look like this:

| | |
|---|---|
| Jupiter | Planet with rings and many moons |
| Earth | Planet closest to the sun |
| Mercury | Planet that is 3/5 water |
| Saturn | Largest planet |

To construct fair matching items, each right-column response must be clearly identified with only one item on the left. In our astronomy test, for example, descriptions of the planets need to contain unambiguous elements so that only one matches each planet. If several responses are vaguely correct, the reliability and therefore the objectivity of the test decline.

*True-false* items are also knowledge-level items, consisting of a statement that students must recognize as either true or false. These items are difficult to write, as they must be factual and objective if they are to provide useful data. If items contain unsupported opinions or generalizations, the students must guess what the teacher intended.

For our astronomy unit, we might construct a quiz with statements such as these:

| | | |
|---|---|---|
| True | False | The sun orbits the Earth. |
| True | False | Venus is smaller than Jupiter. |
| True | False | Mars is closer to the sun than Neptune. |

These items are reliable in that the correct responses are not likely to change in our lifetime. They are also valid because every item is an element directly related to our objective of teaching students about the physical characteristics of the solar system.

As examples of less reliable and less valid items, consider these:

| | | |
|---|---|---|
| True | False | Venus is a more interesting planet than Uranus. |
| True | False | The sun will never stop shining on the Earth. |

*Multiple-choice* items also measure knowledge-level objectives because they call for the student to recognize a fact or idea. A multiple-choice item contains a question, problem, or unfinished statement followed by several responses. The directions tell the student to mark the one correct answer. While college admission tests may contain several near-right responses and students are expected to use reasoning to determine which one is best, classroom tests should probably be constructed with only one correct response. As in other objective measures, reliability and validity of each item must be considered.

To fit the astronomy unit, two valid and reliable items are these:

1. Which planet is known as the red planet?
   A. Venus
   B. Orion
   C. Mars
   D. Jupiter

2. It would take longest to travel from Earth to:
   A. Neptune
   B. Mercury
   C. Venus
   D. Saturn

*Short answer* or *completion* items supply a question or an unfinished statement, and students are expected to supply a word, phrase, number, or symbol. These items are used primarily to test students' knowledge of specific facts and terminology. In our astronomy unit, two examples are these:

1. The planet Saturn has _____ rings around it.
2. Which planet has the most moons?

The advantage of the four types of objective items that comprise most criterion-referenced tests is that they objectively measure students' knowledge of the basic content of a subject. They can be written to match directly the criteria of the teacher's objectives for the lessons. They are also relatively easy to correct, and the scores are easily recorded and can be averaged together to provide the basis for report card grades.

The disadvantage of such items is that they only measure students' understanding of basic knowledge-level content and skills. They do not provide information about what students comprehend, how they would apply the knowledge they have gained, what they would create, or how they analyze and evaluate the ideas they have learned.

## Mastery Learning Assessment

Some teachers prefer to use a teaching strategy known as *mastery learning* to motivate students to learn a sequence of skills. In mastery learning, individual students work through a series of learning experiences at their own pace and demonstrate mastery as they complete each objective. The teacher uses the information gained on the tests to provide helpful feedback for reteaching rather than as a record of achievement. Summative evaluations occur only at the end of a unit of study, when students are expected to demonstrate mastery of a whole sequence or unit of learning. Grades of unit tests are recorded and become the basis for determining students' grades.

In the astronomy unit, the teacher may have written a number of outcome statements, such as these:

**Outcome 1:** After viewing the filmstrip on the solar system, the students will be able to match pictures of each planet with its name, with no more than one error.

**Outcome 2:** Students will be able to draw and label an illustration of the solar system with the sun and nine planets in their respective orbits, with 100% accuracy.

Together these two outcomes will inform the teacher whether students have learned the names, distinctive visual elements, and locations of the planets in the solar system. To measure whether students have mastered this content, the teacher simply carries out the tasks described in the objectives after students have had sufficient opportunity to learn the material. The teacher prepares a matching quiz with a column of nine names and another column of nine pictures of the planets. For those who do not achieve the criterion of eight correct answers, the teacher can provide a reteaching experience or require students to do additional reading on their own. They can be retested until they achieve the criterion.

On another occasion, the teacher distributes blank paper and asks students to draw and label the solar system. From these two objectives and others like them, the teacher can begin to answer the question, "How will I know what they have learned?" Also, the data gathered from this assessment system are more readily translated into letter grades than are the data from informal observations.

## Essays Evaluated with Rubric Guidelines

**PRAXIS**
Scoring methods are assessed in PRAXIS™ Exam Section 2c: Assessment Strategies.

Essays have the exact opposite advantages and disadvantages of criterion-referenced tests. They are subjective rather than objective. Unless they are given specific criteria upon which to base their ratings, two or more teachers rarely evaluate an essay the same way. Essays are also time consuming to read and mark.

However, essays provide teachers with an excellent means of knowing what students comprehend, how they would apply their new learning, and how they analyze and evaluate the ideas and concepts. Essays also provide students with opportunities to be creative by asking them to synthesize a number of previously unrelated notions into an original expression of their own. Essays can answer the question, "How much more have they learned than what I taught in this unit?"

To improve the way teachers rate essays, many school systems employ a rubric guide that specifies what an essay must contain and how it must appear on the page to earn a specific mark or grade. Teachers who use a rubric to guide their assessment of essays usually limit the topic of the essay with specific parameters and may even specify what must be included in the response. For example, in the astronomy unit, the teacher may want to assess whether students can describe the concept of outer space in their own words. This will provide information about how much students truly comprehend about the subject rather than what they simply remember. For example, a teacher may present students with the following guidelines for writing their essay on the solar system:

Write a two-paragraph essay in your own words comparing the Earth's atmosphere with space. Tell why humans cannot live in outer space without life support. Use examples and provide evidence to support your ideas.

These guidelines are fairly explicit in terms of both length and content. For these reasons, this form of essay is relatively objective. To make it even more likely that two or more teachers would look for similar elements when correcting the papers, school systems may provide teachers with *rubric evaluation* samples of student work, along with specific descriptions for measuring success on a particular essay topic.

---

**Grade characteristics of essay**

**A**   Paragraphs are well organized and contain at least six sentences. Facts are accurate and evidence is clearly given to support the student's viewpoints.

**B**   Paragraphs contain at least four sentences. Most facts are accurate. Examples are given to support ideas.

**C**   Paragraphs contain at least three sentences. Some facts are accurate, although one or more errors are present. One example is given.

**D**   Paper contains only one paragraph. Some facts are accurate, though no evidence or examples are given to support them.

**F**   Unconnected sentences contain few accurate facts. Many errors are stated. No examples given.

---

This format for essay evaluation is especially useful for assessing students' levels of comprehension on a topic. It also provides an opportunity for students to demonstrate their ability to analyze the topic, but limits the use of synthesis and evaluation. If students are provided with the rubric system before they begin writing, they are more likely to know what the teacher expects of them and thus be able to deliver it.

For other purposes, the *extended response essay* gives students more freedom to express ideas and opinions and to use synthesis-level thinking skills to transform knowledge into a creative new idea. In the astronomy unit the teacher may hope that students will gain a sense of responsibility for the Earth after studying its place in the universe. This affective goal for the unit may also be expressed as a series of problem-solving or expressive objectives. For example:

> At the end of the unit, students will write an essay entitled "The Big Blue Marble," in which they express their own hopes and fears for the future of the Earth. The essays will be edited, rewritten, illustrated, and displayed for parents to view on parent's night.

This extended response essay calls on students to integrate all that they have learned in this unit and combine it with previous learning from geography and social studies units. Their individual experiences and outside readings are likely to affect their responses as well. Objectivity in marking this essay is very low. It is quite likely that teachers will view the responses differently from one another. Nevertheless, within a single classroom, a teacher can say or state a set of criteria or expectations that can lead students to write a successful essay. In this instance, as stated in the objective, students will have an opportunity to receive critical feedback and make corrections on their essays before the final products are displayed.

Despite the lack of objectivity of extended response essays, there is good reason to include them in an educational program. They provide invaluable information about the creativity, values, philosophy, and maturity of students. Moreover, they encourage students to become more creative and give them practice in making difficult judgments. One of the most effective ways to provide students with the information they need to succeed is to provide them with the rubric descriptions prior to the time they write their essays. When students can see the criteria upon which their work will be evaluated, they are able to meet the expectations with much greater degrees of success than when they try to guess what the teacher expects or wants from them.

## Oral Reports and Examinations

Like essays, *oral reports* can be restricted or unrestricted depending on the type of assessment the teacher wants to generate. To increase objectivity and communicate expectations to students, teachers can create rubric systems describing the length and format of the oral report as well as what must be included. Examples of *restricted* oral reports include book reports in which students are expected to describe the main characters, the setting, the plot, and their favorite part of the story. In a restricted oral examination, teachers may ask questions that students must answer within specified parameters. In the astronomy unit, an oral examination may be scheduled for a certain day. Students are told to prepare for it by reading material supplied by NASA on the U.S. space program. In the examination, teachers ask questions taken from the reading material, and students are expected to respond in their own words. For example:

> Tell how the astronauts prepared for weightlessness.
> Describe the food astronauts eat in space.

As teachers listen to the students' responses, it is possible to make a judgment about whether their answers are right or wrong. It is also possible to assess whether the students have a poor, average, or unusually good understanding of the ideas they speak about. The teacher's evaluation of the students' responses can be recorded in some form, to be shared with the student later.

*Unrestricted* oral reports allow students more opportunities to speak about matters of great interest and importance to them. They encourage students to use their imagination to generate synthesis-level responses or to be persuasive about a matter of opinion or judgment. For example:

> Describe the space journey you'd like to take.
> Tell what you think should be NASA's next big undertaking.

*Debate* is a form of oral examination in that it provides students with an opportunity to prepare to speak about a subject by learning a great deal of content and evidence for opinions prior to the event. During the debate, teachers can assess the students' energy and effort used in gathering information, as well as their understanding of the topic.

In evaluating oral presentations, teachers may write comments as they listen, or they may videotape the presentations so that they can evaluate them more comprehensively later. Students may be involved in self-evaluation of their own efforts as well. They can view the videotapes and discuss with the teacher what they did well and what they need to improve.

# DESIGNING AUTHENTIC ASSESSMENT TASKS

It is possible to construct assessment tasks that measure student performance in terms of using higher-level thinking skills of analysis and evaluation, as well as critical thinking skills of observation and inference and problem-solving strategies such as the creation and testing of hypotheses. These tests can be constructed as paper-and-pencil exams, presenting a situation or dilemma and asking students to respond to it in various ways. Such a test may consist of a passage to be read that describes a problem or dilemma. Maps, charts, graphs, or other forms of data might also be available on the test. The test items then consist of questions that allow the student to observe, infer, formulate a hypothesis, design methods of testing the hypothesis, and speculate about the possible outcome.

Another common method of assessing student's authentic learning is to encourage them to do independent research on one aspect of a unit theme and to create a product that shows what they have learned. This method allows students to demonstrate their knowledge, comprehension, and all four of the higher-level thinking skills on a topic. This assessment technique is appropriate for every area of the curriculum. Students can do independent research or make an independent investigation in math, science, social studies, literature, music, or art. This method lends itself especially well to interdisciplinary units.

The strategy is for the teacher to introduce a unit or theme and provide some teacher-centered instruction on it at the outset. Readings may be assigned, and quizzes and worksheets may be used to assess the extent to which the student is developing a knowledge base about the topic. Essays or oral presentations may be assigned to assess whether students comprehend the main ideas and concepts of the topic. Finally, each student selects one aspect of the main topic on the basis of individual preference or interest and begins to research that subtopic independently. Each student decides on a final product that will demonstrate what has been learned and achieved during the independent study.

The kinds of products that students might create as a result of this type of investigation are limitless. Many teachers prefer to plan their evaluations of student accomplishment to correspond with Bloom's taxonomy. Specific student products are appropriate for learning objectives at all six levels. A sample of them can be found in Figure 11.1.

Teachers may evaluate these student products using a rubric checklist or rating scale. Specific rubric systems may be prespecified so that students know exactly what their product must demonstrate to earn a high mark or positive evaluation from the teacher. Reflective teachers who wish to encourage critical thinking and reflectiveness among their students are also likely to involve the students in self-evaluation of their own products. When students evaluate their work critically, they are learning how to become more independent and responsible for revising and improving their work without an outside evaluator.

## Rubrics, Checklists, and Rating Scales

When teachers wish to assess students' products or presentations, they can tell the students their reactions in a conference or write comments on a piece of paper and give these comments to the students. These methods suffice for informing the students, in

| Characteristics of Each Level | Products Associated with Each Level |
|---|---|
| **Knowledge Level** | **Knowledge Level** |
| Can recognize and recall specific terms, facts, and symbols. | Worksheet; label a given diagram; memorize poem or song; list; quiz; recognition of math symbols; spelling bee; response to flashcard. |
| **Comprehension Level** | **Comprehension Level** |
| Can understand the main idea of material heard, viewed, or read. Is able to interpret or summarize the ideas in own words. | Written paragraph or summary of main idea; oral retelling of story; use of math symbols and numbers in simple calculations; report. |
| **Application Level** | **Application Level** |
| Is able to apply an abstract idea in a concrete situation, to solve a problem, or relate it to prior experiences. | Diagram; map; model; illustration; analogy; mental problem solving; action plan; teaches others; diorama; costume; diary; journal. |
| **Analysis Level** | **Analysis Level** |
| Can break down a concept or idea into its constituent parts. Is able to identify relationships among elements, cause and effect, similarities and differences. | Graph; survey; chart; diagram; report showing cause and effect, differences and similarities, comparisons and contrasts. |
| **Synthesis Level** | **Synthesis Level** |
| Is able to put together elements in new and original ways. Creates patterns or structures that were not there before. | Artwork; story; play; skit; poetry; invention; song; composition; game; collection; hypothesis; essay; speech; videotape; film; computer program. |
| **Evaluation Level** | **Evaluation Level** |
| Makes informed judgments about the value of ideas or materials. Uses standards and criteria to support opinions and views. | Debate; discussion; recommendation; letter to editor; court trial; panel; chart showing hierarchies, rank order, or priorities. |

**Figure 11.1** Student products related to Bloom's taxonomy.

Created by Judy Eby from *Taxonomy of Educational Objectives: Handbook I: Cognitive Domain* by B. S. Bloom et al. Copyright 1956, 1984 by Longman Publishing Group.

a general way, whether they have met the teacher's expectations in the product, and they may be adequate for evaluating an unrestricted product or presentation.

When the teacher has prespecified the criteria for a product or presentation and several important elements must be included, the teacher may choose to create a *rubric* or *checklist* to use for notation when listening, for example, to the speech. This is frequently done when the objective is for students to use effective speaking skills in a presentation.

In preparing the students for the speech, the teacher will likely specify several important elements that the students should incorporate, such as maintaining eye contact with the audience, using appropriate volume to be heard by everyone in the room, and speaking rather than reading during the presentation. By preparing a simple checklist with these items on it, the teacher can quickly and accurately record whether each student used these skills in their presentations. To make the whole system even more valuable, when the teacher shares the rubrics with the students ahead of time, students are able to make much better judgments about what to study, what to include, or how to present the information they have learned.

Rubrics and checklists can record mastery of many basic skills in the primary grades. Each item on the checklist can correspond directly to a behavioral objective. Together the items on a checklist provide an overview of a sequence of objectives. Kindergarten teachers frequently employ checklists to record the letter recognition of each pupil, letter by letter. Primary teachers use checklists to record mastery of basic math operations. Intermediate and middle school teachers may use checklists to record whether students have demonstrated fundamental research skills. In our astronomy unit, for example, the teacher may combine a goal of developing research and study skills with the goal of content mastery. To record the accomplishment of these skills the teacher may use a checklist such as the one in Figure 11.2.

*Checklists* provide useful and efficient means of recording information about the accomplishments of individual students. They are also valuable during a student-teacher conference. Both teacher and student can quickly see what has been achieved and what still lies ahead. Checklists are also valuable when teachers confer with parents about the student's progress along a set of learning objectives.

*Rating scales* are used in circumstances similar to those of checklists. They provide additional information, however, in the form of a rating of how well the student achieved each element or skill on the list. Rating scales are useful in providing students

---

**Name** _____ **Grade** _____

This is a record of research and study skills demonstrated by this student. The teacher's initials and date indicate when the skill was successfully demonstrated.

| Date | Initials | Skill Area |
|------|----------|------------|
| _____ | _____ | A. Located a book on astronomy in the card catalog |
| _____ | _____ | B. Located a book on astronomy on the library shelves |
| _____ | _____ | C. Used the table of contents to find a topic |
| _____ | _____ | D. Used the index to find a subtopic |
| _____ | _____ | E. Orally interpreted a graph or chart |
| _____ | _____ | F. Took notes on a chapter in a book on astronomy |
| _____ | _____ | G. Summarized the chapter from notes |
| _____ | _____ | H. Wrote a bibliographic entry for the book |

**Figure 11.2** Astronomy unit checklist of research and study skills.

Name _____ Grade _____

To the student: Please evaluate your own product, using the following scale:

   O = OUTSTANDING; one of my best efforts
   S = SATISFACTORY; I accomplished what I set out to do
   N = NEEDS IMPROVEMENT; I need to revise and improve this element

| Student's Rating | Skill Area | Teacher's Rating |
|---|---|---|
| _____ | Did adequate research and information gathering | _____ |
| _____ | Elements of the model are accurate in shape | _____ |
| _____ | Elements of the model are accurate in scale (except for orbits of planets) | _____ |
| _____ | Labeling is accurate and legible | _____ |
| _____ | Legend is accurate and legible | _____ |
| _____ | Model is visually interesting and pleasing | _____ |

**Figure 11.3** Astronomy unit rating scale of the solar system model.

with feedback that rates their performance on an objective. In the astronomy unit, for example, students' products may be turned in and evaluated by the teacher, using a rating scale of important elements. In many classrooms, teachers involve the student in their own evaluation of the product and the efforts expended in creating them. In Figure 11.3, a rating scale is structured so that both the student and the teacher rate the finished product.

A rubric system is similar to a checklist, but also employs detailed descriptions of the specific levels of mastery the teacher hopes students will attain. Student products are then compared to the levels of mastery described in the rubric system. Figure 11.4 shows a rubric system that allows the teacher to compare student products related to the astronomy research project against a set of specific criteria. As has been suggested before, if students are given this rubric system prior to beginning the unit, they are empowered to make better choices about how to use their time, what to study, and how to present the material they have learned.

Many times you will see rubrics with four levels of quality as shown in Figure 11.4. What do the levels 4 through 1 mean? Are they the same as the grades A, B, C, and D? Andrade (2000) observes that "satisfactory labels are hard to come by, although it is obvious at a glance that a 4 is what everyone should try to achieve and a 1 is something to avoid. Some teachers indicate a cutoff point on the rubric, for instance, by drawing a box around the level that is considered acceptable.

How do you, as a classroom teacher, learn how to create fair and useful rubrics for your classroom assignments? Andrade (2000) suggests that you look at other models of rubrics, but then involve your own students in the process. She envisions the teacher and students discussing the criteria together, listing the most important criteria, and then writing descriptions of the various levels of quality.

*To the student: Read these criteria before you begin your research so that you will know how to earn the level you want to attain.*

**Turn in a 5–10 page booklet on the solar system.** The booklet may contain a combination of words, pictures, graphs, and any other types of illustrations that show an understanding of the physical elements of the planets, moons, and sun that make up our solar system. The booklets will be evaluated according to the following criteria.

**Level 4:** The student clearly and completely identifies the important planets and moons of the solar system and shows how they are related to the sun and each other in size and space. There is a combination of verbal descriptions and visual illustrations that make the distinguishing features of each planet very evident. The writing is well organized and references are given for sources of information. At least four references are provided.

**Level 3:** The student clearly identifies the planets and some of the most important moons of the solar system. Relationships of size and space are given, though they may be distorted in some cases. Verbal information is fairly well organized and illustrations are useful in distinguishing among the planets. At least two references are given as sources of information.

**Level 2:** The student correctly names the nine planets and shows that they travel around the sun. Relationships among planets are not accurate. The booklet uses more pictures than words. Only one source of information is provided.

**Level 1:** The student incorrectly labels planets and shows little understanding of their relationship to the sun and to each other. Verbal information is given as captions for illustrations only. No source of information is given.

**Figure 11.4** Rubric grading evaluation system for astronomy research project.

One method Andrade suggests for creating rubrics uses these four sentence stems: *Yes; Yes, but; No, but;* and *No.*

For example, if the criterion is "Briefly summarize the plot of the story," the four levels might be the following:

Level 4—"**Yes,** I briefly summarized the plot."

Level 3—"**Yes,** I summarized the plot, **but** I also included some unnecessary details or left out key information."

Level 2—"**No,** I didn't summarize the plot, **but** I did include some details from the story."

Level 1—"**No,** I didn't summarize the plot." (Andrade, 2000, p. 14)

## Learning Contracts

A learning contract is a device that can be thought of both as a teaching strategy and a means of assessment. The learning contract described in Chapter 10 lists several required activities and a number of options for the unit on settling the western United States. Teachers using this strategy meet with individual students to agree on a suitable number and type of optional activities. The activities on the contract then provide the structure for daily learning experiences. When the unit is complete, the contract is used as the basis for assessing what each student has accomplished. Just as in adult life, students are held accountable for meeting the terms of their contracts. If they succeed, they can expect a positive evaluation. If they have not met the terms of their contract, they can expect to have to explain why and describe what they will do to honor their contract.

Learning contracts can take several forms and can even be structured so that the student makes a contract to receive a certain grade for a specified amount of work. A point system can be employed to allow students to select from among options and earn the grade they desire. For example, in the astronomy unit, a learning contract with a built-in point system for earning a grade is shown in Figure 11.5.

Learning contracts also serve as the basis for recording accomplishments. In the sample learning contract for the astronomy unit, the parent is also required to sign the contract, agreeing to support the student's efforts. This strategy is an efficient way to communicate with parents about the goals and expectations of the class. Later, during parent–teacher conferences, the parent can see the work that was accomplished. If a student did not complete the contract, the parent can see what was left undone.

## Portfolios of Student Products

Portfolios are collections of work samples designed to illustrate a person's accomplishments in a talent area. Photographers collect portfolios of their best photos; artists collect their artwork; composers collect their compositions. Assessment portfolios are used to document what a student has achieved in school. To use this technique, teachers collect samples of each student's work and put them in a file folder with that student's name on it. Some teachers collect many types of work in a single portfolio; others have writing portfolios that contain only writing samples, math portfolios filled with worksheets and tests, and other portfolios for other subject areas.

It is important to understand that a collection of student work in a folder is not a portfolio assessment. As an assessment tool, a portfolio contains a selection of work samples, anecdotal records, tests, and other materials that document the students' progress. The student's progress must then be analyzed and summarized by the teacher and the student. There should be a statement of goals written jointly by the student and teacher. Students can select samples of work to be included in the portfolio and write brief explanations of the reason the item was selected and the progress it shows. Often there are summary sheets that serve to document the students' growth.

Portfolio assessment allows students to demonstrate their content knowledge without being dependent on English fluency or reading ability. Portfolios allow the teacher and student to approach the anxiety-laden process of evaluation more comfortably because it celebrates progress rather than weaknesses.

Portfolios may be kept for a long or short time. Many teachers collect writing samples in the first week of school, then periodically throughout the school year. In some cases the teacher may assign a writing topic during the first week and then assign the very same topic during the last week of school. When the two samples on the same topic are compared, the growth and development of the students' writing abilities are plain for everyone to see.

A short-term portfolio may be collected for the duration of a learning unit. For example, in the astronomy unit, all of the student's work, including quizzes, essays,

**Astronomy Unit Learning Contract**

I, _____ , a student in the fifth grade at
_____ School, do hereby contract to complete the following tasks during my
investigation of the solar system.

Furthermore, I agree to complete these tasks by _____ .

I understand that I am agreeing to earn _____ points, which will earn a
grade of _____ if my work is evaluated to be acceptable. I understand that the point values listed below are the maximum number that can be
earned for each task and that fewer points may be awarded.

---

**Points Needed to Earn Specific Grades**

> 90 = A        > 80 = B          > 70 = C          > 60 = D          < 60 = F

---

_____   10 pts   Read chapter 7 in the science text. Do exercises, pp. 145–146.

_____   10 pts   Matching quiz

_____   10 pts   True-false quiz

_____   10 pts   Multiple-choice quiz

_____   10 pts   Short-answer quiz

_____   15 pts   Drawing of the solar system, labeled correctly

_____   20 pts   Model of the solar system, labeled and scaled to size

_____   10 pts   Essay on Earth's atmosphere and outer space

_____   10 pts   Essay on "The Big Blue Marble"

_____   05 pts   Per answer on NASA oral exam

_____   10 pts   Oral report on "A Space Journey I'd Like to Take"

_____   10 pts   Finished Checklist on Research Skills

Signed this day _____ , 20 _____ at _____ School.

_____                    _____
     student signature                              teacher signature

_____                    _____
     parent signature                               witness signature

**Figure 11.5** Sample learning contract.

pictures, and photos of the model solar system can be collected in a portfolio to document that student's accomplishment during the unit. If a contract was used during the unit, the contract will be included in the portfolio along with the work samples. In the following Reflective Action Story, Diane Leonard, a first-grade teacher, shares her experience on developing portfolios.

## ❋ REFLECTIVE ACTION STORIES ❋

## Teacher's Reflection on Portfolio Assessment

*Diane Leonard, First-Grade Teacher, Balderas Elementary School, Fresno, California*

### Teacher Begins to Plan

I teach in an inner-city school, where the vast majority of the students are from lower socioeconomic settings and are second-language English learners. I notice that my students respond best when I can give them concrete examples and model what I want them to do.

### Teacher Considers What Students Already Know

Because my students are all second-language learners, I feel it's important to document and celebrate their growth. For first graders, their work changes rapidly and I've found collecting samples of their work showing the growth they've made to be a good way to communicate with their parents, many of whom speak very little English. It also helps me to focus on exactly what they need to be taught based on where they are in relation to the achievement of standards.

### Teacher Has Expectations

I needed a system to accomplish several things at once. I need to be able to relate the students progress to their achievement of the standards. I need to be able to clearly summarize the growth they make on their report cards. I need to be able to show their parents the progress that they are making and I need to be able to give 6-year-olds concrete examples of things they can be working on to improve their own learning. I had heard about portfolios, but no one at my school was actually using them. I wanted to find out more about them and so I went on a search for resources.

### Teacher Does Research and Invites Feedback

Because I was in a master's program at my university, I decided that researching and implementing portfolios in my classroom might be a good project. I did a literature review on portfolio assessment and decided that I could implement this approach and create my master's project at the same time. Because my undergraduate major had been video production, I decided to document each step of my implementation on video. I hoped that the implementation would be successful and then I could share the process and the product with my colleagues.

## Reflective Teachers Use Withitness

I started with a small piece of portfolio assessment by setting up storage boxes in my classroom. Each child had an individual portfolio labeled with his/her name. I collected baseline examples of their writing, drawing, cutting, and reading (a running record). I made video clips of each step of the process and shared the video with three of my colleagues. Their input into the ongoing process helped to clarify the elements in the video and make adjustments and include explanations of the process.

## Afterward, Teacher Reflects on the Event

As I continued my refinement of the portfolios and sharing with my colleagues, it became obvious that documenting progress was more than just a classroom problem, it was a schoolwide challenge. Because I had included my colleagues in the process, several of them asked if they could implement portfolio assessment in their classrooms, based on my model. By the end of the school year, all of the first-grade teachers were using portfolio assessment. This gave us the opportunity to sit together and help each other evaluate the products in the portfolios in relation to the first-grade content standards. It also gave us an opportunity to share ideas for lessons that would help our students move toward meeting the standards.

---

Portfolios may be used at all grade levels and for any subject or course a student takes. When portfolios are meant to be used to document student accomplishment, they must be organized so that they reveal the development of a skill or the growing understanding of a set of ideas. To demonstrate growth and change, Wolf (1989) suggests collecting "biographies of works, a range of works and reflections" (p. 37).

The biography of a work consists of several drafts of a work, showing the student's initial conception of the project, the first attempts, and the final product. By collecting these items, the teacher can document the growth and development of the student. Wolf (1989) further recommends that after completing this collection, the teacher may ask the student to reexamine all the stages of the work and reflect on the process and the products from beginning to end. The student's reflection may be done in writing or captured on audiotape (and later transcribed onto paper) and should then be included in the portfolio itself. This self-evaluation process is valuable in helping the student develop metacognitive abilities that can be applied to future self-assessments in academic or real-life settings.

Wolf (1989) also suggests that teachers deliberately collect a range of works, meaning a diverse collection, consisting of journals, essays, poems, drawings, charts, graphs, letters, tests, and samples of daily work. When using the portfolios as a basis for a parent–teacher conference, this range allows the teacher to discuss and document many different aspects of the student's school accomplishments.

Primary teachers must take responsibility for setting up a system for assisting the children in collecting and filing items in their portfolios. Colored portfolios in storage boxes or bins can be used so that the younger students don't have to search the whole box to locate their own folios. The teacher should take care to put similar names in different colored folders to assist the students in locating their personal work. Each item entered into the portfolio should be date stamped and even young students can be taught to put their work in chronological order by date in the folder. This adds another dimension to the portfolio in that it adds authentic learning tasks (alphabetizing and filing in chronological order) to the process of maintaining the portfolios. The portfolios should contain periodic representative examples of the child's sequential improvement and advancement through the learning process. At the upper grades, however, students may be asked to assume more responsibility for choosing representative examples that document their growth and learning. The teacher may suggest items to be included, and the student may decide on others. At the end of a people and nature unit, for example, each student may have a portfolio containing the tests, lab reports, essays, creative writing, and charts created for the unit. Portfolios are especially powerful in documenting the growth of English learners through representative samples of class work when the teacher encourages students to document their understandings in less traditional ways. Diagrams, illustrations, recordings, and multimedia presentations can be included to document content knowledge growth without being bound by the student's English writing ability. Their growth in English language development, both oral and written, is also documented in the portfolio.

Portfolios of student work are an excellent way to communicate with parents about a student's accomplishments. When the parent and teacher look at the representative writing samples together, they can both reflect on the student's growth and better understand what the student's strengths and weaknesses are at a glance. When a parent sees the signed contract and the completed work, both parent and teacher see the same evidence to support the resulting grades.

Some teachers, and even entire schools, schedule portfolio days at the end of the school year. Each student selects his/her best work for the year and prepares a short presentation to talk about the work, and what it represents in the way of effort and accomplishment. Parents and community members are invited to the school to hear the students talk about their work and to ask questions of the students. In schools where portfolio days are a regular part of the school schedule, teachers help the students to plan by being made aware of these presentation days in advance so that they have an opportunity to carefully select the work they will present and to write and practice their presentations. Teachers may also choose to assess the students' oral presentation skills as a part of the portfolio day.

## Videotape Records

When the purpose of evaluation is to record the accomplishment of a student and allow later analysis and more comprehensive evaluation, a videotape is an excellent way to capture and store a variety of learning events. Speeches can be videotaped easily. So can dramas, skits, presentations, and displays of students' products.

Videos are also excellent ways to communicate to parents the accomplishments of a student or the entire class. They allow all interested parties to view the final products or performances of a unit of study. Teachers can store on tape a whole year's worth of accomplishments.

Video recordings also provide teachers with data they need to evaluate their own plans. By reviewing a video of a classroom learning event, reflective teachers are able to gain new understandings about what students need from their learning environment to be successful.

## Grading Cooperative Group Projects and Products

Many of the assessment methods described in this chapter can be adapted for cooperative groups. Evaluation of cooperative group efforts should include an assessment of both a task that requires a group effort to complete and an assessment of individual efforts to ensure that each member of the group takes responsibility for doing personal reading and preparation.

As an illustration of how to adapt ordinary lessons and units into cooperative lessons and units, consider the astronomy unit. To adapt this unit for use by cooperative groups, each group can function as a study team with directions to assist one another in reading and preparing for the quizzes. Group scores can be computed and recorded for each quiz at the same time that individual scores are recorded.

The contract system works well with cooperative groups. When used in this way, there is one contract per group instead of per individual. Each group negotiates what they will accomplish together. Evaluations can include peer assessments, with members of the group providing critical feedback for one another.

# REPORTING STUDENT ACCOMPLISHMENTS

Assessment of student accomplishments is a complex and multifaceted undertaking. There is no one best way to assess what students have learned or accomplished in school. Some methods work better than others at various grade levels. Some work better than others with different individuals. This chapter has provided you with a number of assessment methods so you can develop a repertoire of assessment devices to use as the basis for making judgments about the accomplishments of your students.

## Computation of Grades

At the end of the astronomy unit described earlier, the grades for all of the reports, tests, and projects may be recorded in the teachers' grade books as shown in Figure 11.6.

Computation of the final grades for this curriculum unit involves a straightforward computation of an average grade by awarding numerical equivalents to each letter grade, adding the seven items, and dividing the total score by seven. The average scores can then be assigned a letter grade. After they are computed, the grades are recorded in the student's cumulative folder and on the report cards that are sent home to parents. Intermediate report cards are likely to use letter grades to sum up the student's achievement in each academic subject. Some report cards may also provide checklists of subskills beneath the letter grade as a means of explaining to parents how the letter grade was determined.

## Writing Anecdotal Records

In most school districts, teachers are responsible for writing three or four report cards per year. These contain descriptions of each student's current level of accomplishment

| Name of Student | Graded Objectives | | | | | Average Score | Report Card Grade |
|---|---|---|---|---|---|---|---|
| | 1 | 2 | 3 | 4 | 5 | | |
| Lisa | A | B | B | A | C | | |
| | 4 + | 3 + | 3 + | 4 + | 2 | = 16/5 = 3.2 | B |
| Peter | B | C | A | C | D | | |
| | 3 + | 2 + | 4 + | 2 + | 1 | = 12/5 = 2.4 | C+ |
| Alejandro | B | A | A | B | A | | |
| | 3 + | 4 + | 4 + | 3 + | 4 | = 18/5 = 3.6 | A– |

A = 4 points
B = 3
C = 2
D = 1
F = 0

**Figure 11.6** Teacher's grade book.

in each of the major areas of the curriculum, plus a summary of the student's work habits and social adjustment to school and peers. At the primary grades, report cards usually consist of either anecdotal records or checklists of skills rather than letter grades. Some school districts may use both. The advantage to this double format is that it allows teachers to describe and report their direct observations of a student's actual behaviors and accomplishments with sufficient detail so that parents understand the student's strengths and deficiencies. This is especially useful for such skill areas as listening, speaking, writing, study habits, social skills, and interests (Linn & Gronlund, 2000).

When a concern about a student arises, the teacher's daily observations of the student's work habits or social interactions can be important sources of data to help parents or other school personnel understand the student's particular needs and strengths. These observations may be augmented by the use of written anecdotal records of what the teacher observes. For example, if a student comes to school late, appears tired, and has difficulty sitting still in her desk, the teacher may want to document these observations by keeping a short anecdotal record for a week, recording how late the student is every morning and describing episodes of falling asleep or inattentiveness. When this written record is shown to the parents, it is more likely to enlist their cooperation with the teacher in seeking answers to the problem than if the teacher simply reports orally that the student is "always late and too tired to work."

To be used to their best advantage, anecdotal records should be limited to observations of specific skills, social problems, or behavioral concerns. If a teacher sets out to record every behavior and event in a student's school day, the process will become too tiring and difficult to be feasible. Instead, when a student is exhibiting a particular behavior or deficiency in a skill area, the teacher can focus on daily descriptions of that one area and be successful in producing a useful document.

The major limitation or disadvantage of the anecdotal record is teachers' tendency to project their own value judgments into the description of a student's behavior or accomplishment. This is due, in part, to the tendency to observe what fits one's preconceived notions. For example, nonreflective teachers may tend to notice more desirable qualities in those pupils they like best and more undesirable qualities in those they like least. The recommended way to avoid this tendency is to keep descriptions of observed incidents separate from your interpretation. First, state exactly what happened in nonjudgmental words. Then, if you wish to add your interpretation of the event, do so in a separate paragraph and label it as such (Linn & Gronlund, 2000).

In general, a single observation is seldom as meaningful as a series of events in understanding a student's behavior. Therefore, anecdotal records should contain brief descriptions of related incidents over time to provide a reliable picture of a student's behavior.

## Involving Students in Evaluation Procedures

For reflective teachers, the natural extension of the teaching process is the interactive evaluation process that encourages students to become active evaluators of their own efforts and products. The current writing programs organized around periodic student–teacher conferences and the grouping of students who edit one another's work are excellent examples of this type of evaluation. In classrooms that feature such writing programs, the teacher's role in evaluation is to confer with the students about their current writing projects and to ask questions that engage them in analyzing what they have written.

Teachers may use open-ended questions designed to gather information on what the student has intended to do in a piece of writing. When the teacher has a sufficient understanding of the student's goal, the teacher and student may begin to zero in on ways to improve the quality of the writing so that it more nearly matches the student's purpose. This may mean correcting the mechanics of the writing so that it can be understood by others, or guiding the student to rethink the way a passage is written and to consider new ways of stating the ideas.

The editing groups used in such writing programs encourage students to learn how to listen to and respect the work their peers are creating. Typically, in a group, students each read aloud from a current piece of writing and then answer questions about the content from the other students in the group. Through this type of interactive evaluation, students may be learning how to work cooperatively, accept critical feedback, and write better at the same time.

This interactive evaluation system can be used in other parts of the curriculum as well. "What did you learn?" should form the core of the classroom evaluation. The more often this question is asked, the easier it is for students to identify and receive the help they need. It is a question students can learn to ask themselves (Oakes & Lipton, 1990, p. 132).

Providing students with self-evaluation checklists or rating scales assists them in learning more specific types of questions about their own progress and achievement. Checklists and rating scales that ask the student to evaluate specific outcomes may be developed for any learning activity, especially a unit of study that takes place over several weeks. Teacher evaluations may be entered on the same form to allow students and their parents to compare the student's self-evaluation with the teacher's assessment of the student's accomplishments. For example, in Figure 11.7, students are allowed to assess themselves after completing a research unit on leadership.

Interactive evaluation procedures are designed to breed success and enhance students' metacognitive capacities. They are as much a part of the *learning process* as they are a part of the assessment process. In fact, the long-term goals of most caring, reflective teachers are likely to emphasize the development of independence, self-responsibility,

---

**Leadership Unit**

**Student/Teacher Evaluation**

Name of student _____ Grade _____ Date _____

Leader selected for research _____

The student completes the left side of this evaluation and then the teacher will complete the right side. Afterward, student and teacher discuss the accomplishments made by the student, decide on areas that need to be improved, and plan goals for future learning experiences.

O = Outstanding     S = Satisfactory     N = Needs Improvement

**Student Evaluation:**                                                                                       **Teacher Evaluation:**

_____  I completed the readings and assignments for this unit on time.                       _____

_____  I showed responsibility by bringing appropriate materials to class.                    _____

_____  I showed growth in my planning, decision-making, and organizational skills.      _____

_____  I have gained skills in doing research and taking notes to gather information.     _____

_____  I used a variety of relevant and challenging resources to learn about my subject.  _____

_____  I improved my ability to speak in public.                                                        _____

_____  I gained confidence in my ability to speak in public.                                         _____

_____  I gained independence in working on my own to achieve a goal.                        _____

_____  I am able to evaluate my own accomplishments and identify what                     _____

_____  I need to improve with accuracy and honesty.                                                  _____

The most important thing I learned in this unit was:

Regarding my work in this unit, I am most proud of:

**Figure 11.7** Interactive student/teacher evaluation for a leadership unit.

self-discipline, and self-evaluation as important affective goals of education. These goals are achieved through the development of metacognitive processes as students learn to understand how to succeed in any learning environment.

## Report Cards

Report cards. These two words are likely to elicit memories filled with anxiety and a variety of other conflicting emotions for most people.

In your many years of schooling, you have probably received more than 50 report cards. You probably viewed many with relief and happiness and proudly displayed them to your parents; others may have caused torment and disbelief. On occasion, you may have questioned the teacher's fairness or integrity; you may have questioned whether the teacher really got to know you or understood the effort you put into your work. Perhaps you have even approached a teacher and challenged the grade you received, showing evidence of why the assigned grade was unjustified.

Eight or 9 weeks into your first school year, you will face the task of deciding on and recording report card grades for your students. Many first-year teachers consider the responsibility one of their most difficult challenges. Experienced teachers often report that the task does not seem to get easier as the years pass. In fact, many reflective teachers find that the more they know about grades and children, the more difficult it is to sum up the work and efforts of a student in a single letter grade.

Reflective teachers struggle with many conflicting ideas, thoughts, and concerns when they confront existing evaluation systems. Systems using letter grades are likely to be based on the assumption that students vary in ability and acquire learning by passively receiving knowledge from the teacher. From this assumption, it is logical to conclude that students should be evaluated by determining what they have learned and how this compares to other students of the same age. Categorizing and rank ordering of students is the next step and is done by assigning letter grades to label their respective categories of ability. Teachers with this perspective can be overheard saying, "John is an A student, and Sally is a C student."

Reflective, caring teachers are often very uncomfortable with such statements. They recognize the complex mix of environmental, nutritional, genetic, and experiential factors that contribute to each student's success or lack of success in school. Moreover, according to their view of teaching and learning, it is the teachers' responsibility to diagnose their students' needs and then plan a series of learning experiences and the scaffolding each student needs to experience success. The competitive nature of letter grades contrasts sharply with this philosophy.

Due to the time-consuming nature of the task of correcting students' work and the complexities of the evaluation processes described previously, it is easy to see why school personnel have resorted to a form of shorthand to record and report student progress. Most teachers have too many students and too little time to hold discussions with each student's parents or to write extensive narratives of each student's learning on a regular basis. Schools use standardized shorthand methods known as *grades* and *test scores* to communicate with parents, future teachers, college admissions personnel, and future employers (Oakes & Lipton, 1990).

The practice of awarding letter grades as measures of individual achievement has been part of the U.S. educational scene for many decades. In the 1960s and 1970s, personnel in some school districts attempted to replace conventional report cards with detailed anecdotal records, describing what each student had accomplished in each subject area during the course or term. But these attempts to change the prevailing evaluation system met with opposition from parents, who insisted on a return to the letter grade system with which they had grown up. Parents were not satisfied with a description of their own child's achievements. They wanted to know how their child compared with other students. They expressed concern that these records would not be accepted at the most prestigious colleges.

In response to these debates, school boards and administrators in most school districts arrived at a compromise. While they reestablished the letter grade report cards for the intermediate and upper elementary grades, they retained the use of anecdotal report cards for the primary grades. As more and more states have adopted standards-based education, reporting systems are being developed to reflect the student's progress toward meeting the standard in each content area. That means that if you are planning to teach at the primary grades (kindergarten through the second or third grades), you may be expected to write anecdotal report cards describing and documenting the progress each student in your classroom has made toward meeting the content standards for that grade. If you are planning to teach at the intermediate grades (second or third through sixth grade), you may still be expected to compute letter grades for the students' report cards. However, the letter grade computation may include reference to the student's progress toward achievement of standards, in a standards-based system.

## Standards-Based Reporting Systems

Greenberg Elementary School opened in Fresno, California, in August 2000 as a demonstration school where state standards and students' needs are the two driving forces behind curriculum development and teaching practices. They needed to create a means of monitoring students' achievement of the standards. Because each standard consists of a number of elements, tracking each student was much more complex than the traditional grading system. The management of tracking student progress threatened to become an impediment to the real objective, which was to use this information to inform instruction and also improve the match between student instructional needs and teacher planning and instruction.

Darrell Blanks, a fifth-grade teacher and the school's math coach, developed a database file using Microsoft® Access with the help of supporting teachers at his school in documenting their students' achievement of standards.

The teachers at Greenberg are linked on their computers to Darrell's system where they can enter each child's progress in the meeting of grade level content standards, element by element. Once the teachers enter the data they can access class reports that show exactly which of their students have met each element of each standard. This allows them to form small groups for instruction. The program also links the standards to suggested assessments and teaching strategies for each standard.

Once the data have been entered the teachers can print standards-based report cards, which indicate to the parents the child's progress in meeting standards and what percentage of the elements are met for each standard. Although Greenberg does not assign letter grades to these percentages, it would be an easy task to do, by assigning a letter grade to a certain percentage of elements met. The administration and teachers at Greenberg have decided that, in their students' case, the reporting of progress in relation to the standards is more appropriate than letter grades.

Carolyn Calmes, principal of Greenberg, says, "This system allows me to generate tracking sheets that tell me what percentage of the students are meeting standards at any given time. I can print tracking sheets for individual students, classes, grade levels, or tracks." (Greenberg has four attendance tracks as a year-round school.) The data that is entered by the teachers can also be used to document the students' academic progress toward meeting the requirements for promotion to the next grade level.

When it comes time to report progress to the students' parents, the teacher enters the data in English, but the Access program offers choices of printing the report cards in English or in other languages such as Spanish or Hmong. This system permits teachers to communicate effectively with all parents about the important matter of student achievement and promotion requirements.

Darrell, Carolyn, and the teachers are continually upgrading the system. Darrell is responsive to teacher and administration input and is always refining the system to make it more teacher-friendly. The Greenberg team wants the standards to drive instruction. They also want to be able to compare students' progress in meeting the standards to their individual reading levels and test scores. The comparison of these more traditional progress monitors with the progress in meeting standards can be done using Darrell's program and serve as checks and balances, alerting teachers when there appears to be a mismatch. This also gives the administration the ability to survey progress and schedule staff development without waiting for centralized services to process information from standardized test scores or burden teachers with data collection activities.

## School Report Cards That Compare Schools

Standardized tests are now being required and widely used for "grading" schools in most states. These tests scores along with other factors such as percentage of improvement in scores from year to year, parental involvement, and socioeconomic data such as number of students on free or reduced lunch are being used to judge the effectiveness of schools. These scores are published in local newspapers, and schools that don't raise their scores in a timely and consistent manner are placed in programs designed to increase the effectiveness of the instruction. Some states publish these scores in the form of numerical scores and set a goal for each school to meet in the form of increased scores. Other states grade each school with letter grades (A, B, C, D, F). Again, these states set goals for the schools, with the ultimate goal being schools that all score an A or B.

Federal legislation known as the No Child Left Behind Act of 2001 requires that states publish annual report cards on the performance of individual school districts. Districts must also provide similar report cards showing school-by-school data. Schools must be able to demonstrate that their students are achieving a "proficient" level on tests that are aligned with state academic standards. Individual schools must meet state "adequate yearly progress" targets toward this goal based on a formula spelled out in the law. If a school receiving federal Title I funding fails to meet the target 2 years in a row, its students must be offered a choice of other public schools to attend.

# REFLECTIVE ACTION EXPERIENCES FOR YOUR PROFESSIONAL PORTFOLIO

## Respond to NBPTS Proposition 3: Teachers Regularly Assess Student Progress by Designing an Interactive Portfolio Assessment System

**Proposition 3 states that professional teachers are knowledgeable about tracking student progress with a variety of evaluation methods, including portfolios, videotapes, demonstrations, and exhibitions.**

**PRAXIS**
This exercise prepares you to write a constructed response similar to those required on the PRAXIS™ Exam.

To begin designing your own interactive portfolio assessment system, find a teacher who is using one and schedule an observation. What system does this teacher use for assessing student progress? Are there elements of this system that seem useful to you? Do the students appear to understand the teacher's grading policies and expectations? What would you do to improve their understanding?

Read more about portfolio assessment. Do research on the topic on the World Wide Web. Visit classrooms to observe the systems other teachers use to collect student work in portfolios.

For the unit plan you are working on, plan an interactive student–teacher evaluation system that encourages students to use metacognitive processes to assess their own performance. Create a contract, checklist, or rating scale that students and teachers can use to look at the students' positive achievements as well as provide realistic and useful information about what students need to improve.

Share your assessment plan with other prospective teachers. Get feedback from them on how clear and understandable your system is likely to be with students. Try using the system with one student. Ask the student to tell you what is needed to make the plan clear and fair.

Reflect on your own relationship with grades and evaluation. Did you get good grades in school? Do you believe that the grades you received were an accurate reflection of your effort and achievement? How would a portfolio assessment system have changed the way you viewed your own progress in school?

# References

Andrade, H. (2000). What do we mean by results? Using rubrics to promote thinking and learning. *Educational Leadership, 57*(5), 11–14.

Guskey, T., & Bailey, J. (2000). *Developing grading and reporting systems for student learning.* Berkeley, CA: Corwin Press.

Linn, R., & Gronlund, N. (2000). *Measurement and assessment in teaching* (8th ed.). Upper Saddle River, NJ: Merrill/Prentice-Hall.

Marzano, R. (2000). *Transforming classroom grading.* Alexandria, VA: Association for Supervision and Curriculum Development.

Oakes, J., & Lipton, M. (1990). *Making the best of schools.* New Haven, CT: Yale University Press.

Wolf, D. (1989). Portfolio assessment: Sampling student work. *Educational Leadership, 46* (7), 35–39.

## CHAPTER 12

# Reflective Teachers in the School Community

The teacher's role in the school community becomes more complex each day. Most school districts are undergoing some form of reform or systemic change that calls upon teachers to take more responsibility for decision making beyond their own classrooms. School reform can be compared to piloting an airplane and conducting a major overhaul while in flight. While attempting to maintain a stable environment for students and faculty, many schools are overhauling their curriculum, schedules, student evaluation systems, and administrative relationships.

The motivation for many of these changes appears to be a shift in what people see as the basic purpose of schools. When reforms appear to be succeeding, teachers share in the glory. When reforms appear to be failing to meet their objectives, principals, teachers, and other staff must respond by working harder and longer hours to accomplish the many complex tasks needed to turn things around. They must also be able to reduce a natural tendency to become defensive upon hearing criticism. Instead, teachers must be able to examine what it is the community wants them to accomplish and communicate to the community what they themselves view as important. This process is likely to generate conflict. It is probably unavoidable, and may perhaps be necessary to induce change. Reflective teachers, however, are not afraid of conflict. They recognize that conflict is part of any important change, and they are willing to use their reflective action skills to perceive the needs of all members of the school community.

## NBPTS Standards Related to Parent/Teacher Relationships

**PRAXIS**
This chapter prepares you for PRAXIS™ Exam Section 4b: The Larger Community.

NBPTS Proposition 5 states that *teachers are members of learning communities.* There are two major ways that teachers can demonstrate their commitment to being active members of their school community. One way is to take an active role in collaborating with other professional educators. The second way is to look for ways to collaborate with parents.

The ability to work collaboratively with other professionals may be demonstrated by sharing responsibilities for developing curriculum or planning other aspects of the instructional program of the school. Teachers may work in grade level or subject matter teams to establish goals and coordinate learning experiences that will achieve these goals. Teachers serve on committees to select new textbooks, design new forms of report cards, and even to select new faculty. Teachers may work together to strengthen their teaching proficiency. They may observe one another and engage in discussions about teaching and learning strategies. They may collaborate in trying out new instructional strategies. All of these opportunities for collaboration are viewed as important by the NBPTS. It believes that the reality of teachers working as solo performers is both narrow and outdated. The new image of the professional teacher is a team player who seeks opportunities to share knowledge and ideas with colleagues.

Reflective, caring teachers also recognize that they share with parents the responsibility for educating students. They communicate frequently with parents and guardians, listening as often as they speak in order to learn parents' perspectives and enlist their support in fostering good learning habits. Professional teachers recognize that there are circumstances that complicate parent–teacher relationships, such as cultural and language differences or the variation among parents in the amount and type of support they are willing to provide for their children. Nevertheless, reflective teachers demonstrate that they value and welcome parental input into their children's educational needs and experiences.

## No Child Left Behind

In 2002, the federal government passed the legislation No Child Left Behind, which is intended to motivate every public school in the nation to make improvements that will result in higher achievement for its students. One of the federal mandates in this legislation forces each state to identify schools that are not showing positive results as described in Chapter 11. But the large numbers of schools identified as needing improvement under the No Child Left Behind Act have alarmed many state education officials.

When you are hired as a teacher, the school you select may be struggling to meet federal mandates or raise test scores. You will be on the front line of meeting the expectations in these and other guidelines. As a teacher, you will have both the opportunity and the responsibility to create the curriculum and the classroom conditions that will motivate your students to achieve success on the standardized tests and other measures that determine how your school is evaluated.

## TWO-WAY COMMUNICATION WITH PARENTS

Parents do have a right to know how their children's school is evaluated as well as how the curriculum meets the needs of the students. For beginning teachers, the thought of interacting effectively with parents is not always a high priority, however. They are struggling to cope with all the planning and preparation for teaching the many subjects in the K–12 curriculum and for establishing a welcoming classroom environment for their students.

At the beginning of Chapter 4, Diane Leonard described the many thoughts, feelings, and decisions she had to make on her first day of teaching. In the week prior to that first day, Diane spent a lot of time in her classroom setting up bulletin boards and learning centers. As she worked that week, many of her new students and their parents who had come to the school for registration stopped by her classroom to see the "new teacher." Some stood outside her door looking in quietly until she approached them and introduced herself. Others came into the room and looked around, exclaiming over the brightly decorated walls. The students were all interested in trying to discern whether the new teacher was "nice" and whether they thought they would be happy in her class.

Their visits, before the first day of school had even arrived, alerted Diane to the fact that she had more than just the needs of 20 or more students to consider. She realized that she had to use withitness and concern for their parents' needs as well.

Some parents of primary students may be especially reluctant to see the beginning of school because, for them, it marks an end to an important phase in their lives. For 5 years, they have had complete jurisdiction over the lives of their sons and daughters. Now they recognize that the teacher may have almost as much influence over their children as they have. I have observed the parent of a first grader, for example, standing outside the school after dropping off the child, saying tearfully, "But we've had lunch together every day of his life."

For the majority of parents, many of whom work outside of the home and whose children have gone to day-care centers and preschools, this leave-taking may not be so abrupt, but it is still a significant event in their own lives, as well as those of their children. Many parents feel a strong interest in, and responsibility for, determining whether this particular classroom is a healthy and welcoming environment for their children. For this reason, parents of primary students are likely to come to school on one pretext or another in the first days of school, just to see for themselves that their children are in good hands.

Beginning teachers may feel somewhat overwhelmed by these visits. All of their available energy has gone into planning the curriculum, moving furniture, decorating the classroom, and meeting and becoming acquainted with other teachers in the school. When a parent suddenly shows up unannounced, it can be unsettling, especially if the parent wants to ask questions when the students are present. When this occurs, it is necessary for the teacher to suggest politely but assertively, another time for this impromptu conference: "I'm sorry, Mrs. Jones, but all of my attention is needed in the class right now. Would you prefer to talk about this after school or tomorrow morning at 8:15?"

On many occasions throughout the school year, the teacher is expected to communicate with parents either singly or in large groups. In addition, many classroom teachers invite parents to become involved in the life of the classroom. Some students come from single-parent families, blended families in which divorced parents have remarried and have children with previous and current spouses, foster parents, and guardians. Teachers meet students who do not have the same last names as their parents. Teachers must recognize that the home lives they may have experienced may be different from those of their students. When the term *parents* is mentioned in this chapter, it is meant to refer to the people who are being contacted or are meeting with the teacher on behalf of a particular child.

## Fall Open House

When parents come to visit the classroom early in the year, one method of deflecting their concerns is to suggest that they will be able to have many of their questions answered within a few weeks at the annual fall open house (sometimes called Back to School Night). This event is planned especially for that purpose in many school districts.

The fall open house is usually held on an evening in late September. To prepare for the event, teachers are asked to be ready to describe their goals for the year and give an overall picture of the school's curriculum at that grade level. The event usually begins in the school auditorium or other large meeting room, where the principal welcomes everyone to the school and describes the important events that the entire school has planned for the coming year. The teachers, counselors, other administrators, and sometimes the president of the parent–teacher organization are introduced. Special attention is given to introducing any new teachers on the faculty. At the conclusion of this general meeting, the teachers are released to go to their classrooms and make themselves ready for the open house. After a few minutes, the visitors are dismissed from the general meeting to find their children's classrooms. Some schools may ring a bell periodically so that parents who have more that one child in a school have an opportunity to move from classroom to classroom in order to meet all of their children's teachers.

When the parents assemble in the classroom, the teacher makes a short presentation to the entire group, describing what is planned for the year. A time for questions and answers of interest to the entire group is also likely to occur. Because most school districts intend the fall open house to be a time for general discussions of goals and curriculum, there is no planned opportunity for individual parents to ask teachers for specific information about their child's achievement or behavior. If parents approach the teacher and begin to discuss personal concerns, it is expected that the teacher will suggest an alternate time and place for an individual conference.

# Parent–Teacher Conferences

Conferences between individual parents and teachers vary greatly in purpose. Some are primarily used for diagnosing a problem or concern, and others are set up to report to the parents about a child's progress in school. Diagnostic conferences were described in Chapter 3, but are discussed briefly in this context as well because they are such valuable means of evaluation.

If either the teacher or the parent has a serious concern about a child, one or the other may arrange a conference in the first weeks of school. When teachers, for example, observe unusually aggressive, passive, depressed, or antisocial behavior in a child, they are wise to call home immediately and set up a conference right away to gain information about the nature of the child's problems. This is especially true when a child's behavior disrupts other students in the class.

Setting up a conference sends an important signal to a student who is exhibiting unusual or unacceptable behavior. It tells the student that the teacher has withitness and is going to take action to correct the problem rather than let it go. It allows the teacher to seek information about the underlying reasons for the observed behavior. In a conference of this type, it is recommended that the student attend with the parents to gain a better understanding of the adults' views of the behavior.

When the conference takes place, the teacher should describe the behavior and, if possible, supplement the oral description with written anecdotal reports of examples of the behavior. The teacher should express concern about the behavior and then ask both the student and the parents to explain why it is occurring.

Good and Brophy (2002) point out that students usually cannot explain fully why they act as they do, and teachers should not expect them to be able to do this. If the students had such insight, they probably would not be behaving badly in the first place. Instead, the hope is that clues or helpful information will emerge from the discussion.

When the parents discuss their own views of the child's problem, the teacher may gain significant insight by learning about the home environment. For example, the parents may agree that they have observed the same behavior at home and that it seems to be related to a crisis the family is dealing with, such as a death, divorce, drugs, lost job, or move. When the teacher, the child, and the parents confront this matter together, they can begin to devise a workable plan to help support the student during this difficult period and, at the same time, help the child gain awareness about the effects of the behavior on others.

Conferences do not always result in such harmonious cooperation. Parents may not present much useful information. On occasion, they may become very defensive or resentful of the suggestion that their child's behavior is unacceptable. In their family, this behavior may be okay. For example, a fifth-grade teacher was alarmed to see a boy walk into her class on the first day of school wearing a T-shirt that read, "Born to Raise Hell!" True to the message on the shirt, the child fought with other students at least once a day. When the parents were called in for a conference and the teacher described this behavior to them, the father replied, "So what? I tell my kids not to let anyone get the best of them." From the words and the father's tone of voice, the teacher learned that fighting was an acceptable behavior in that family. No happy resolution was discovered in this conference, but it did give the teacher some additional insight into the source and the depth of the boy's difficulties in social interactions with his peers.

At times, a teacher may need to involve others in the conference. Counselors may need to be present to suggest alternative ways of dealing with problems. If the teacher, parents, and counselor cannot effectively address a problem with the student, additional professional help may need to be offered to the parents. At times, parents admit that they cannot even handle their child at home. Interpreters may also be needed for parents who are not proficient English speakers. If you are using an interpreter, it is important to remember to maintain eye contact with the parent, and not conduct the conference focusing on the interpreter. The use of older students as interpreters, while convenient and sometimes the only choice available, is not recommended. Not only is there the chance that it is demeaning to the parent, but that it may also result in some purposeful miscommunication by the child, depending on the content and repercussions of the conversation.

Conferences designed for reporting on student progress rather than for diagnostic purposes usually take place in the late fall to coincide with the end of the first marking period and the first report card. In many districts, the parents are asked to come to the school for a conference with the teacher shortly after report cards are sent home. This gives the parents an opportunity to look at the report card and think about the questions and concerns they may want to raise at the conference. Some school districts require parents to come to the school to pick up the child's report card and have a conference with the teacher. In this case, the teacher explains the grades and observations to the parent as the parent views the report card for the first time. This second strategy is used primarily to make sure that parents do attend the conference.

Report card conferences are generally 15 to 30 minutes in length. They may be offered during the day and at night so that parents who work during the day may choose a night conference. Usually one or two school days are used for the fall conferences. In some school districts, the entire process is repeated in the spring. In the K–12 school, a schedule of 30 conferences over a period of one or two days is a tiring experience for most teachers, who may find that conference days are more exhausting than regular teaching days. This is due primarily to the tension caused by the teachers' recognition that they are responsible for the smooth flow of conversation and information. When this feeling of responsibility is multiplied by a factor of 30 or more in a few short days, it is easy to see how draining it can be.

To minimize the tension, it is important that teachers plan each conference carefully. Prior to the event, reflective teachers often write a page of notes about each student, highlighting the accomplishments and the matters of concern that the teacher wants to discuss with the parents. It is important for the teacher to be able to identify the child correctly in the conference. Teachers have mentioned embarrassing moments when parents have a puzzled look on their faces only to discover that the teacher was talking about another student and not their child.

In addition to planning what you want to say about each child, it is a good idea to make a general plan for how you will conduct your conferences. The primary purpose of report card conferences is for you to inform the parents about the child's progress in your class. Teachers like Diane Leonard, who use portfolio assessment, find that sharing the student's progress by talking about specific assignments and progress tend to make the conferences more meaningful. But the conference is also designed to elicit information from the parents that may help you to help the child. The parents may also have concerns that they wish to discuss. To accomplish all of these things in 20 minutes can be difficult. To do so, you must act as the timekeeper and allot a reasonable amount of time to each purpose. The parent will not be concerned about going overtime, but you will because you will be aware that the next set of parents is waiting outside the door for their appointment with you.

Linn and Gronlund (2000) suggest considering the following elements when you plan your conferences:

1. Make plans for each conference. For each child, make a list of the points you want to cover and the questions you want to ask. Prepare a folder with work samples that represent the quality of the work the student does.

2. Begin the conference in a positive manner. Making a positive statement about the child, such as "Betty really enjoys helping others" or "Derek is an expert on dinosaurs" is likely to create a cooperative and friendly atmosphere.

3. Present the student's strong points before describing areas needing improvement. Present samples of work and focus on what the child can do and what he or she still has to learn. Put these work samples into perspective for the parent by sharing the grade-level standards that the student will be expected to meet by the end of the school year and comparing them with the work samples.

4. Encourage parents to participate and share information. You must be willing to listen as well as talk. They may have questions and concerns about the school and about their child's behavior that need to be brought out into the open before constructive, cooperative action can take place.

5. Plan a course of action cooperatively. Guide the discussion toward a series of steps that can be taken by the teacher and the parents to assist the child. At the end of the conference, review these steps with the parents. If possible, provide the parent with a brief written record of the conference to take home. Much of this form can be written before the conference as part of the teacher's preparation. See Figure 12.1 for an example of a conference record form.

**Parent Conference Record**

**Student name** _____     **Date of conference** _____

**Present at conference:** _____

Student's strengths:




Areas of concern:




Actions to be taken:

By teacher:                                        By parents:

**Figure 12.1**  Parent conference record form.

6. End the conference with a positive comment. Thank the parents for coming and say something positive about the student such as, "Erik has a good sense of humor and I enjoy having him in my class."

The regularly scheduled report card conferences may be the only time you will meet with the parents of most of your students. For others, those whose behavior or learning problems are quite serious, you will need to continue to contact the parents by telephone or in follow-up conferences to monitor whether the cooperative plan of action is being implemented and what effects it is having.

## Talking to Parents About Underachievement

Effective two-way communication with parents is essential for assisting students with severe problems. In working with students whose behavior interferes with their learning in school, an excellent resource for both teachers and parents is Rimm's (1995) *Why Bright Children Get Poor Grades.* This book describes many of the most feared behavior problems that teachers must face: hyperactivity, passiveness, perfectionism, rebellion, bullying, and manipulative behaviors. Rimm believes these behaviors cause students to achieve much less than they are capable of in school. In her studies of underachievement, Rimm has discovered that students learned most of these behaviors in response to some elements of their home environment. Changing the behavior takes a concerted effort by the parents to isolate the causes and create new procedures to help students learn healthier, more productive behavior patterns that can lead to success.

Often it is the teacher who spots the self-defeating behavior. Parents have been living with the child for so long that they may not see that the child's behavior is unusual, and they may not be able to recognize how it affects the child's school achievement. Some examples of home situations that may lead to underachievment include the following:

*The overwelcome child.* Although it has long been recognized that an unwelcome or rejected child is likely to have problems in life, it is also likely that excessive attention can cause achievement and emotional problems. When parents overprotect and overindulge, the child may develop a pattern of not taking initiative and of waiting for others to do his or her bidding.

*Child with early health problem.* When children are born with allergies, birth defects, or other disabilities and parents respond by investing themselves almost totally in the child's well-being, a set of behaviors similar to those of the overwelcome child can develop.

*Particular sibling combinations.* Birth order and sibling rivalry affect all students, but some combinations may be particularly damaging to a child's achievement. A student who is the sibling of a child with severe health problems or is considered to be extremely gifted may feel left out or inadequate in comparison to the sibling. This can lead to the development of attention-getting behavior patterns, such as clowning or mischief-making, that may prevent the child from achieving fully.

*Specific marital problems.* A single parent may develop a very close relationship with the child as a result of seeing the child as the only purpose for living. The parent may treat the child more like a spouse or a partner than a child, thus giving the child too much power. The child may learn to expect power and may not be willing to give it up to conform to the requirements of school. (Rimm, 1995)

These are only four of many possible situations that can cause students to develop behaviors that may prevent them from achieving well in school. When a teacher spots a child who is exhibiting overly dependent or overly aggressive behaviors, it is important to confer with the child's parents, to report the problem, and to learn how the behavior first developed and how the parents are responding to it. The first step toward a positive behavior change is for the teacher to describe and give examples of the behavior and its effects on the child's achievement. The parents may deny that the behavior exists or that it is serious, but if the teacher can establish a cooperative two-way dialogue with the parents, it may lead to new insights for all of them.

If parents do acknowledge the behavior, the next step is for you to describe the changes you are going to make at school to support the development of new, more positive behavior patterns and to suggest modifications that the parents may make at home. Together with the parents, set some reasonable goals for the child in terms of both behaviors and grades. Discuss methods of helping the child reach these goals, and agree on a plan that fits the child and the situation.

Rimm cautions that students will not change their behavior just because the adults in their lives want them to do so. The child must want to break the underachieving patterns and substitute them for behaviors that lead to success. Both the teacher and the parents must also confer with the child, describing the behaviors and their effects in words the child can understand and accept. When the teacher, parent, and child all have the same goal and are working together on a plan of action tailored to fit the needs of the child, it is quite possible that the child will succeed.

Independent contracts are also useful support systems for helping students change behavior. A contract can specify work the child is to accomplish with deadlines and expectations for success. It can also be used to specify behavioral expectations. When the teacher negotiates the contract with the child ahead of time, the child has an intrinsic incentive to complete it—after all, the child helped to create it and decide what would be required. A sense of ownership is likely to increase the likelihood of the contract being fulfilled (see Figure 12.2).

The teacher may employ additional extrinsic incentives if these seem useful in a given circumstance. It is most often recommended that students receive a reward that supports academics. For example, a student could earn points toward additional time at a learning activity or game. The major point is that the reward is something a student really would like to receive. Some things a teacher thinks would be rewarding are not rewarding to students. The types of rewards would vary by grade level.

This type of plan may be created as a result of a successful parent–teacher conference, a visit by the teacher to the student's home, or a telephone conversation, followed by written documents specifying what the teacher expects, what the parents agree to take responsibility for, and what the student agrees to do to earn the agreed-upon incentive.

For example, if the teacher observes that a student is not turning in homework, the teacher may call the students' parents and ask for a conference at school or suggest that the teacher come to visit the home to discuss the matter. Alerting the parents to this concern is likely to result in a discussion of probable causes. The parents may or may

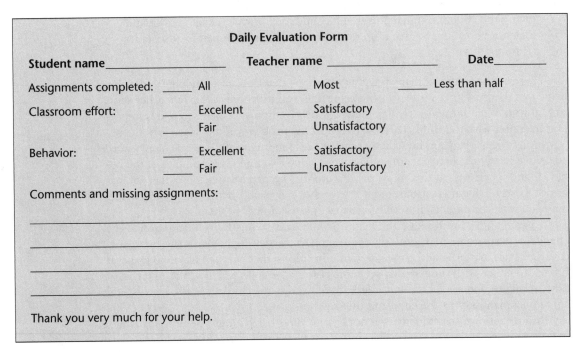

**Figure 12.2** Daily evaluation form.

not accept the teacher's perceptions of the problem and its negative consequences for their child's achievement. After a frank discussion of conditions at home that may support or interfere with the student doing homework, the parents may come to recognize that the major cause might be the fact that the child and the family watch a great deal of television, beginning right after school and continuing up to bedtime. If the parents express a willingness to do their part to help change the child's behavior, then together they can draft an agreement or contract, specifying when the student will do homework and when he or she can watch television. It is a good idea for the teacher to follow up on this type of agreement by sending the parents daily reports specifying whether the homework is actually being turned in. These daily reports are likely to help everyone remember the commitment they have made. Later, when the student appears to have learned the new pattern of behavior and is more consistent about turning in homework, the reports can be sent home weekly instead of daily (see Figure 12.3).

When the student is beginning to show more responsibility and independence, the teacher may choose to involve the student in writing a study plan contract such as the one in Figure 12.4. This contract describes what the goal is and how the student plans to accomplish the goal. It may specify a reward or positive consequence that the student wants to earn when the goal is reached.

One final caution about conducting parent–teacher conferences: Occasionally, participants in the conference may reveal a family problem that is unusual and extremely serious. The students or parents may describe extreme poverty, desertion, or physical or sexual abuse to a teacher as a desperate attempt to get help. The classroom teacher is well advised not to try to deal with such problems alone. If this happens to you, ask the parent to allow you to discuss this matter with the school's social services personnel

**Weekly Evaluation Form**

Name _____ Grade_____ Date_____

Week of _____

| Subject | Behavior | Effort | Grade this week (optional) | Grade to date (optional) | Teacher initials |
|---|---|---|---|---|---|
| 1. | | | | | |
| 2. | | | | | |
| 3. | | | | | |
| 4. | | | | | |
| 5. | | | | | |
| 6. | | | | | |
| 7. | | | | | |
| 8. | | | | | |
| 9. | | | | | |

Comments and missing assignments:

_____

_____

_____

_____

**Rating Key**

Please use the same rating for effort, behavior, and achievement:

A–Excellent     B–Above average     C–Average     D–Below average     F–Failing

**Figure 12.3** Weekly evaluation form.

and immediately contact the principal, school psychologist, social worker, and other members of the crisis team to assist in the matter.

## Through the Eyes of Parents

When parents send their students to school, they have many hopes and fears for their children's future. They want to be able to trust the school to create a safe, stable, nurturing environment for their students. They want their students' developing sense of self to be enhanced and their individual talents to be appreciated. But many parents feel

**Sample Study Plan Contract**

Richard, his mom, his dad, and Mrs. Norbert agree that Richard will spend at least one hour each day, five days a week, studying and doing his homework independently at his desk in his room. He will do this before he watches TV and there will be no radio, stereo, or TV on in his room during study time. After his work is complete, his dad will review his materials. At the end of the week, if all work is complete in class and homework has been handed in on time, Richard will receive ten points, which may be saved toward a bicycle. Each point is worth one dollar toward the price of the bike. Richard may also receive extra credit points for doing special projects. Richard's mom and dad will not remind him to study, and he will take the initiative independently. If Richard has not completed his homework, he will bring all his books home on Friday and Richard will not be allowed any weekend activities until he completes all missing work.

Richard

Dad

Mom

Mrs. Norbert

**Figure 12.4** Sample study plan contract.

left out of the decision-making process within their children's schools. If teachers describe their goals or programs using educational jargon unfamiliar to the parents, they may be reluctant to attend conferences or meetings at the school.

When parents are involved in establishing the school's vision statement, or invited to participate on advisory groups, they may contribute many valuable ideas. In Jefferson County, Colorado, a school created a parent–teacher focus group to provide teachers with feedback on how to increase student self-esteem. At first, teachers were reluctant to have the parent observers visit their classrooms, but team members worked collaboratively to design a set of guidelines for the observations and agreed to provide teachers with copies of their observation notes after each visit. A parent–teacher retreat was held to build trust and clarify roles and expectations. After observing classrooms and playgrounds, the parent observers worked with faculty to develop a statement of their beliefs about how the schools could enhance students' self-esteem. Their statement of beliefs includes the following:

Provide experiences that allow for individual differences.

Provide opportunities to express creativity.

View mistakes as learning opportunities.

Provide a safe and clean learning environment. (Meadows, 1993, p. 32)

Although these recommendations were not new to the faculty, they were helpful in clarifying what the community wanted and expected from their school. From the team effort, both teachers and parents had a better understanding of the complexity of education.

In some communities, parents take a very active role in governance. Parents serve as members of school boards or advisory groups that work closely with the school administrators to make the important decisions about school funding and hiring and firing of personnel. On occasion, some parents have strong views about a single issue and may try to influence school boards or administrators to provide a certain program or modify an existing program to coincide with the parents' values or philosophy. When this occurs, opinions can become strongly stated and conflict is likely to arise among parent factions and faculty. For the beginning teacher, it is important to try to learn as much as possible about the values of a school community prior to submitting an application for employment or accepting a teaching contract. If your own values and philosophy differ greatly from that of the majority of the school governance teams, then you are unlikely to feel at home teaching in that school district.

## Teaching and Learning in a Multicultural Community

When the language, culture, and values of the parents match those of the teachers in the child's school, communication is likely to be relatively clear and agreements relatively simple to achieve. When the culture of the child's home differs significantly from the culture of the teacher, the teacher must be especially willing to listen as well as talk during parent–teacher conferences.

Before the *Brown v. Board of Education* Supreme Court decision in 1954, students who were racially different from the "white majority" were often segregated in separate (and inferior) schools. Since that time, federal mandates have required school systems to integrate both the student bodies and the faculties of their schools. But federal laws have not been able to mitigate the subtler forms of racism that still exist in some educational settings.

Although the United States is known as a nation of immigrants and a melting pot of cultures, the traditionally accepted cultural norm has mirrored the philosophy of the white Anglo-Saxon majority. Other cultures have been known as minority cultures. The prevailing belief is that students from minority cultures must be taught the language and habits of the majority. Florio-Ruane (2001) found that when the home culture's practices and values are not acknowledged or incorporated by the school, parents may not feel capable of supporting students in their academic pursuits. This may explain why some parents seem to withdraw from the educational process. It may be that they don't feel welcome or comfortable in the school. It may also be a cultural assumption on the part of the parents. In some cultures coming to school to talk to the teacher is considered to be an insult, implying that the teacher is not doing a good job. Using cultural liaison personnel in highly diverse neighborhoods has helped to inform parents so that they begin to realize that they are expected to be a part of the educational team in this country.

Reflective teachers are aware that their own values and expectations may vary considerably from those of the families in their school community. Rather than assume that the students and their parents should be taught to mimic the language, behavior, and norms of the teacher's own culture, however, reflective teachers strive to gain a better understanding of the various cultures that comprise the school community and to celebrate these differences by incorporating them into the curriculum.

In parent–teacher conferences, the reflective teacher is likely to ask with great interest about the home environment and the parents' cultural values as a means of

**PRAXIS**

Strategies for encouraging home/school partnerships are addressed in PRAXIS™ Exam Section 4b: Profession and Community.

better understanding the various cultures and conveying respect to the parents. When parents sense this respect from the teacher, they are more likely to return it and to believe that the teacher shares their own concerns for their child. The teacher may need to be especially encouraging to parents of other cultures, urging them to share their own concerns and ask questions. People from many cultures were not raised to ask questions of teachers and may be reluctant to do so. If the teacher encourages them to ask questions or make suggestions for the child's benefit, they may feel comfortable enough to do so. This two-way communication and mutual understanding can lead to a more productive arrangement to work together in supporting the child's achievement at home and at school.

Hodgkinson (2003) points out that people from various cultures see the world differently and have different perspectives, needs, and values. While some teachers may expect students to speak up and show their individuality, students from many other nations have great difficulty doing so. This type of behavior, known as "putting yourself forward" in Asian cultures, is considered to be a negative character trait. Some students are raised not to meet other people eye to eye, especially someone with as much authority as a teacher. Teachers must be aware that their own way of doing things and the expectations they were raised to emulate may not be shared by their students.

The classroom teacher must demonstrate a willingness to assist culturally different students and their parents as they make the difficult transition from one land to another. One of the best ways to accomplish this is to show sensitivity and respect for the various cultures of all the students in the class. Each year, the teacher may plan a special unit of study on the contribution of the cultures represented by the class members. Parents can be invited to participate in the learning experience by visiting the classroom and sharing with students the crafts and food of their countries. They can teach the students the songs and games of their homelands. When teachers involve the parents in their children's education, they send a powerful message that the school cares about them.

However, a teacher should not feel offended if the parent does not want to be involved. This could be viewed as parental disinterest, even though in some cultures parents have been taught that the school is responsible for their youngster's education and they should not be involved in the process on the school campus.

## Visits to Students' Homes

When teachers care sufficiently about understanding the particular home and cultural environments that surround their students, one way to seek information is to visit the students and their families in their homes. Teachers may do this by sending home a newsletter early in the year, announcing that the teacher would enjoy meeting the parents and seeing the students in their homes, and that invitations to do so will be gladly received. This allows the parents to invite the teacher when it is a good time for them.

The visit will probably take place after school or during the evening meal. No agendas need to be established for such a visit; in fact, doing so would be counterproductive. The visit is not a structured parent–teacher conference. It is simply an opportunity for the teacher to understand more fully the conditions in which the child lives. As the teacher shares the family's meal, looks at their photographs, and hears some of their family stories, it greatly enhances the feelings of the child and the parents that they are respected members of the school community.

On occasion, it may become necessary for school personnel to make a more structured visit with an agenda. This may occur if a child is having extreme problems and is referred for special services and a psychological evaluation. In that case, the school social worker or psychologist may visit the home to determine what factors in the home environment may be causing the child's problems.

## Newsletters and Notes

Many K–12 teachers communicate with parents by sending home handwritten notes describing a particular behavior or accomplishment of their child. In some classrooms, a note from the teacher signifies only bad news that is sent home when the teacher wants to describe an incident or pattern of misbehavior, a poor test result, or excessive tardiness. More recently, many reflective teachers have considered how to use the note home to encourage good behavior and reward achievement. Many teachers now send home notes describing a special accomplishment, an improvement in classwork, or an act of friendliness or generosity shown by the child.

To ensure that all students benefit from this system, the teacher may send a note of good news home to a certain number of students per week until every child has had one. Others prefer not to use a schedule, but send a note whenever they observe a child doing something especially well. Without a schedule, however, it is important that teachers be careful not to favor some students over others.

In some classrooms, teachers prepare and send home classroom newsletters describing the important events planned for that week or month. The newsletter may contain items describing completed projects and new ones just getting underway. In the newsletter, the teacher can request parent volunteers for various projects and write notes of appreciation to parents who have recently helped out in some way.

In primary classrooms, the teacher generally takes full responsibility for creating the newsletter. But in intermediate and upper elementary classrooms, many teachers allow students to help write the items. They may use a computer program designed for creating newspaper-like formats. In this case, the production of the newsletter becomes more than just a method of communicating with parents. It becomes an enriching learning experience as well.

## Telephone Calls

The telephone provides an important link between school and home. Teachers often call students' homes for the same reasons as they write notes. Some use a telephone call to report a child's misbehavior and poor achievement and to enlist the support and assistance of parents in correcting the problems. Other teachers try to call home to report both positive and negative news. It is often of great value to make the first call to a parent a positive interaction. Tell them how excited you are to have their child in your class. Be prepared to mention one or two specific things that have occurred since the beginning of school that reflect the positive impression that their child has made on you. Lastly, remind them that you are seeking their assistance in making this a successful year for their son or daughter in your classroom. If the first call to a parent is made to report a problem or concern, we recommend that you follow up several days later with a second telephone call to (hopefully!) report that the student is making progress in solving the problem.

**PRAXIS**

Effective communication strategies are assessed in PRAXIS™ Exam Section 3a: Communication Techniques.

Teachers are often on the receiving end of telephone calls from students' parents as well. Parents may call to clarify something about an assignment or an announcement that they cannot understand from their child's description. If parents hear confusing stories about something that happened during the school day, they may call the teacher to find out what really occurred. Responding to these promptly and in an open and informative manner promotes a positive pattern of communication between home and school.

Occasionally parents call in anger or frustration. They may disagree with the contents of the curriculum, the way a test was graded, or the way a classroom incident was handled. The teacher receiving one of these calls may easily become defensive and angry as well. Dealing effectively with these calls takes mature, well-developed communication skills. It is difficult, but very important, to listen empathetically to what the parent says. Even when the instinctive reaction of most teachers is to break into the parent's statements and present their own side of the situation, it is more productive if the teacher's initial responses encourage the parent to describe the problem in more detail and express personal feelings.

After the parent has had an opportunity to fully describe the reason for the telephone call, the teacher's side of the story can be presented in a quiet, nonthreatening, and nondefensive voice. In a situation such as this, the teacher has the responsibility for attempting to resolve the conflict and creating a mutually acceptable solution.

For example, suppose a fight occurs in the classroom during the day and Dean punches John in the face and bloodies his lip. The first thing the teacher may decide to do is send John to the nurse. Then, the teacher may talk to Dean to find out what prompted the fight. Suppose that Dean claims he was provoked by John's name-calling, and many students in the class support that claim. When John returns from the nurse, the teacher tells him that both he and Dean will have to stay in during recess for fighting. John seethes with anger for the rest of the day.

After school, the teacher is called to the telephone to find John's very angry parent on the other end. "Why did you keep my son in for recess when he got hit by that bully? And why did you not call me immediately when he got hit? Did you know he was bleeding? I'm going to come in right now and talk to your principal about this matter, and you will be sorry you treated my son this way!"

The instinctive reaction for most teachers is to jump in and explain after the first few words are spoken. If the parent continues to question the teacher's judgment, the teacher may soon feel as angry as the parent does. But reflective teachers recognize that there will be days like this in the classroom with 30 students and one adult. They will try to keep their feelings in control and say something to soothe the parent's hurt pride and upset feelings.

"I'm glad you called, Mrs. Jones. I can understand how you feel. Tell me how John's lip is now." This type of comment will help the teacher gather information and gain time to formulate a good response. Not all such problems can be readily resolved. Perhaps the teacher and the parent will continue to have different points of view no matter how much they discuss it. If this is the case, it is necessary to acknowledge it and end the conversation with a comment such as, "I recognize how you feel about this situation. I'm sorry John got hurt today, and I'll do my best to see that he is not involved in any more fights this year."

The key point of this section is expressed in the phrase "reflective teachers recognize that there will be days like this." Every school year has days like these. Values clash and feelings are hurt. The beginning teacher may be shocked the first time this happens and overreact by feeling angry, guilty, or defensive. If possible, when incidents such as these occur in your classroom, remember that every teacher experiences conflict. Conflict is unavoidable in this career, and the first step in learning how to handle it is learning to expect and accept it as part of the job.

## Spring Open House and Other Special Events

In the fall, the purpose of most conferences and open house events is to allow parents and teachers to get to know each other, communicate their goals for their students, and make plans for accomplishing these goals. As the year goes by, the focus of most meetings between parents and teachers is for the teacher to demonstrate to the parents how these goals are being met.

Many classroom teachers invite parents frequently, perhaps as often as once a month, to attend exhibits, plays, assemblies, or other occasions for students to display what they are learning and what they have accomplished. Some of these events may be schoolwide assemblies, such as Thanksgiving plays, concerts, and feasts, winter pageants, midwinter cultural fairs, and spring open houses in which collections of student work are displayed throughout the school.

Individual teachers may also invite their students' parents to school to view the performances or an exhibit of products resulting from a unit of study. These events are usually highly prized by students and parents, and are an excellent way for the teacher to interact and communicate continually with the parents.

Consider, though, how some parents might feel if they attend a spring open house and find that their own child's work is not displayed. In some competitive classrooms, teachers tend to display only the papers with "100%" written across the top. For those students who rarely get perfect papers, this can be a discouraging experience; for their parents, it is likely to be equally discouraging. If classroom displays include examples of students' work, it is important to display the best works of every student in approximately equal numbers.

To avoid creating a competitive environment, you may want to display students' work inside their portfolios on their desks so that each parent can view the work done by his or her own child alone. General classroom displays can consist of group projects and murals so that every child and parent can take equal pride in the classroom.

# COMMUNITY INVOLVEMENT IN CLASSROOM ACTIVITIES

## Parents as Volunteers

Parents volunteer to do many things in schools to benefit their own children and the larger community. Many parents enjoy being members of an all-school organization known as the Parent Teacher Association (PTA) or Parent Teacher Organization (PTO). These organizations have regularly scheduled meetings and yearly fundraising events to serve the needs of the school. In most cases, parents do the greatest part of the work on the committees, although teachers are usually represented as well.

Many schools encourage parents to volunteer their time during the school day to assist teachers in educational or extracurricular programs. Parents can serve as coaches, assistant coaches, or referees for some sports events such as all-school field day events. They often serve as helpers on class field trips, accompanying the class on the bus ride and throughout the day. Usually, teachers ask each adult to be responsible for a small group of students during the trip, reducing the adult to child ratio from 28:1 down to 4:1 or 5:1.

In the classroom, many primary teachers invite parent volunteers to serve as assistants in the reading and language arts program. A parent can work with one small group while the teacher works with another, or with the rest of the class. In this way, parents can serve many important functions. They can read aloud to a group of students or listen to an individual or a small group of students read aloud to them. Parents can write the words as a child dictates a story or can edit a piece of writing done by a child. Parents can listen to book reports and keep records of the number and type of books each child has read.

With the advent of computers in the classroom, many teachers appreciate having parents who are knowledgeable about computers volunteer to work with groups of students as they learn to operate a computer or to monitor students' progress as they work with tutorial or problem-solving computer programs.

During individualized mathematics or spelling programs, or those structured on a mastery learning model, parents can serve as assistants who correct formative tests and provide feedback to students. They can also help to organize the large amounts of paperwork, filing, and record keeping that often accompany individualized instructional programs.

Having parents volunteer to work in your classroom has many benefits, and often you will find knowledgeable and experienced parents who enjoy this type of work. Many parents have interrupted their own careers to raise children and look forward to having a regular volunteer job.

Not all teachers, however, enjoy having parent volunteers in their classrooms. Some teachers are reluctant to have parents view the ups and downs that occur in any school day. Other teachers are not comfortable with parent volunteers because the teacher must be ready with activities and materials when the parent arrives. For some teachers, this is a burden that outweighs the benefit of having the extra help. It is true that working with parent volunteers means greater responsibility for the teacher, who must manage the other adults as well as the students in the class.

Whether you wish to use parents as volunteers in your classroom is one of those issues that you will need to reflect on, considering the benefits against the costs. One of the best ways to gather information about the efficacy of this practice in your classroom is to try it out with one subject area and a knowledgeable, experienced parent volunteer to see if it is a system you want to employ.

To increase the likelihood that the practice will work in your room, you and the parent volunteer should discuss in advance what you expect the parent to do and agree on the times the parent will visit. Usually parents do only routine tasks or monitor students as they work on a program planned by you and your colleagues. When these matters are clarified, you will probably find the volunteer effort to be very productive, allowing you to reduce the amount of time you spend on routine tasks.

# Community Resources

Parents with special interests, abilities, careers, and accomplishments can also enrich your program by visiting to speak to the class about their specialties. A unit on community helpers can certainly benefit from visits by parents who are nurses, police officers, fire fighters, and others who perform community services. Parents who are manufacturers or waste haulers can provide their input during a unit on ecology. When the class is studying economics, parents who work as merchants can describe the theory of supply and demand to the class.

During the first parent–teacher conference in the fall, you may be able to discover what talents your students' parents possess and create a community resource file to draw on throughout the year. In some schools, these files are kept for schoolwide use and parents listed in the file are happy to come to any classroom in the school to share their knowledge and experience with the students. The file may also contain names of adults in the community who are not parents of children attending the school but who are willing to visit as a service to the community.

Some schools seek financial contributions from the community to fund music, art, or other enrichment programs that have been eliminated from their school budgets. Booster clubs are often formed by parents, and other community members raise money to finance sports teams, the arts, or technological programs that require expensive equipment.

Some districts have established an educational foundation that is run by an administrator. People in the community donate money to the foundation, and teachers apply for grants to be used within their department or classroom. If your school does not have such a foundation it might be worthwhile to encourage one.

Getting a foundation started can be an arduous task. A wall of donors prominently displayed at a conspicuous place within the school with plaques indicating the range of support for donating families is an effective procedure for encouraging funding. Auctions and other enjoyable pastimes may be occasions for bringing together families from the school community for a fun evening as well as fund raising.

Occasionally, parents may approach a teacher and offer to pay for something or contribute something of value to the class. A parent who works in a scientific or technological field may approach a high school science teacher, for example, and say, "I would like to donate a used cathode ray oscilloscope or a used computer to the department. Can you use one?" It is very hard to turn down this type of request when you may need the equipment and there are no funds available from other sources. It is important that you check with your administration before accepting an offer of this type or before making an appeal for funding at an open house or parent conference.

There could be confusion about whether money or gifts have been exchanged for grades. To reduce this fear for yourself and for the administration, send a letter to each parent stating that in the past some parents have approached you to donate certain items or money, and therefore, you would like to inform all parents about the procedures to be followed for classroom donations. Items of value or donations of money should be sent to the school office with a letter stating which department should receive the money. The teacher is not to be informed who donated the money or equipment. A ledger should be kept with all receipts so at any time during the year appropriate personnel can check how much money was collected and what was purchased. An administrator should be asked to oversee the fund. This procedure standardizes all gift-giving practices for your class or department so that everyone is protected.

## Character and Moral Education Programs

The interaction between home and school becomes more complex and controversial when the school's objective changes from supporting the child's academic development to supporting the child's moral development. Nevertheless, schools in the 21st century are likely to be at the center of a growing concern about the need for greater emphasis on moral education. This concern grows out of an awareness that schools must take more responsibility for countering the influence of drugs, violence on television and other media, the fragmentation of the family, and the publicity about questionable ethical practices in business and industry.

When teachers and parents discuss the schools' role in teaching values, there is general agreement that, due to the enormous temptations and distractions facing students today, schools must take an active role in teaching students about the nature of right and wrong. The ever-increasing social, religious, and ethnic diversity of the schools also makes it difficult to agree on one set of values.

Gardner (1999) explored the concept of a moral intelligence but chose not to include it as one of the multiple intelligences he describes because of the difficulty of defining it. He is able to state that, "central to a moral domain is a concern with those rules, behaviors, and attitudes that govern the sanctity of life."

Lickona (1992) recommends that school–parent support groups think locally rather than globally in order to achieve a meaningful set of moral values. Within the school community, we hope that you as teachers will take an active role in trying to: (1) arrive at a consensus of the moral values most important to your community and (2) write a moral education curriculum that will be taught at school and in the home at the same time.

Saterlie (1992) illustrates how such a school–parent partnership can be formed and what it can produce. As a school administrator, she describes the Baltimore public schools' experience, in which school administrators created a community task force to participate in an open dialogue on community values. They purposely invited people with different religious and political beliefs to serve on the task force. After extensive reading and debate, the task force was able to agree upon a "common core" of values appropriate for a democratic and pluralistic society. They are compassion, courtesy, critical inquiry, due process, equality of opportunity, freedom of thought and action, honesty, human worth and dignity, integrity, justice, knowledge, loyalty, objectivity, order, patriotism, rational consent, reasoned argument, respect for others' rights, responsible citizenship, rule of law, self-respect, tolerance, and truth.

After identifying these community-acknowledged values, the task force wrote outcome statements for development of these moral values. The board of education discussed and ratified their report. The PTA developed a brochure on the values education program and distributed it to all parents in the system.

The method used to implement this program allowed each of the 148 schools in the district to appoint its own values committee, which was encouraged to select certain task-force–identified values to emphasize in its own school projects. This encouraged a creative response from most schools. Some addressed additional values such as computer ethics or academic honesty, as well as those identified by the task force. The Baltimore model linked parents, schools, and the community in a unified examination of moral and ethical issues to strengthen the character of students, which in turn will contribute to strengthening a free society (Saterlie, 1992).

As a beginning teacher, you may find that your school district is taking similar measures, and you may wish to become an active part of the task force that identifies the moral values of your community and creates school programs to educate students in these values. If you find that your school district has not yet considered such a challenge, perhaps you can be the one who initiates the idea. Reflective individuals who are committed to upholding the moral values of the community can serve as important role models for the students they teach.

# TEACHERS MENTORING AND COACHING ONE ANOTHER

In recent history, the school principal was responsible for observing and evaluating teachers' classroom performance. The top-down hierarchy implied that only administrators could and should supervise teachers and make recommendations about improving their performance.

There is a growing consensus that teachers' growth and development is enhanced when they think of themselves as members of professional communities whose members take responsibility for teaching each other, learning together, and focusing on the successes and challenges of educating their students (Shaps, Watson, & Lewis, 1996). The idea of belonging to a community changes the way teachers think about their own learning. It tends to break the pattern of isolation that individual teachers used to experience when they went into their classrooms and closed their doors to the outside world. In supportive communities, teachers support one other, share teaching strategies, try out new ways of teaching, and ask for and receive feedback, which leads them to be able to redesign their curriculum and methods of instruction. Teachers in professional communities learn how to reflect on their abilities and gain confidence for changing their practice to better meet students' needs (Lieberman, 1995).

One promising approach being implemented in a number of schools is the formation of professional book clubs. Groups of teachers purchase copies of professional books and read assigned chapters and meet to discuss the possibilities of using the ideas contained in the book in their classrooms. We believe that this book could be used very effectively in that context. By discussing the issues raised in these chapters, teachers can provide the feedback and support for one another that reflective teachers seek in order to improve their practice.

Being part of a teaching community encourages the type of reflective action in teaching that we have recommended throughout this book. When teachers seek out other, more experienced teachers to discuss their classroom dilemmas and ask for feedback, they are demonstrating their willingness to reflect on their own practice in an effort to improve it.

In many school systems today teachers are sharing their own perspectives with each other as part of the evaluation process. Experienced classroom teachers, sometimes called *coaches* or *mentor teachers*, observe less-experienced teachers as they work with students in their classrooms. Afterward, the two teachers discuss the observed classroom events. This practice allows the mentor teacher to provide critical feedback and to share personal knowledge with colleagues. It also encourages the beginning teachers to reflect on what they do, the effects of their actions, and decisions and ways to improve their teaching.

In Watsonville, California, teachers in two schools created a program called Professional Partnerships to decrease isolation and build collegial support systems. In this program, two teachers selected each other on a voluntary basis to become teaching partners. They observed one another's classrooms each month for a minimum of 30 minutes each visit. The partners meet prior to each observation to define the focus of the lesson and then discuss the visit afterwards. Quarterly, the partners meet with the principal and two additional teachers in the school, who serve as facilitators. Here are how two of the teacher partners described the project:

> My partner is coming to visit so I do not let things slide. My area of interest is improving the quality of student interactions. But I've also improved management, groupings, and materials because everything surrounding the lesson affected what I wanted to have happen.

> The postconferences give me a chance to talk about the details of the lesson that I could not pay attention to while I was teaching. My partner always gives me new ideas. I feel very supported, and I'm making changes. (Stobbe, 1993, p. 41)

Teachers are also actively involved in selecting the type of staff development they need to accomplish the goals they have established for themselves. When teachers get interested in a new curriculum such as the whole language approach, or mathematics programs that emphasize problem solving, they are likely to propose conferences they would like to attend and arrange to bring in consultants knowledgeable about the new methods.

Another powerful new result of being part of a professional community is teachers' role as researchers. Asking questions of one another and generating ideas often leads teachers to investigate areas of concern. Informally, and quite naturally, they often begin doing active research to improve their own instructional practices. When they learn something valuable about their own efforts, they are increasingly taking the role of collaborating with other educators to communicate what they have found. To share the results of their investigations, many teachers are writing about their experiences and describing the investigations they have made. They submit their papers to journals and take part as presenters in local and regional conferences.

## Interacting with Colleagues in Creating Professional Portfolios

Beginning teachers are frequently interested in creating professional portfolios as a means of demonstrating their knowledge, awareness of issues, ability to communicate, and reflectiveness on the important issues of K–12 education. Many school systems engage experienced teachers as mentor coaches and ask beginning teachers to create professional portfolios that document their accomplishments and strengths. Judy Eby has worked with beginning teachers as a mentor coach and finds that the most valuable aspect of creating the professional portfolio is not the product itself, but the growth that occurs during the process of selecting what to include, reflecting on each document and work sample, and talking with other collegues and the mentor coach about the experiences that resulted in each document or page of the portfolio.

In this text, we have encouraged the creation of a professional portfolio and have offered specific suggestions of what might be included. We also highly recommend that you view your portfolio as a work in progress, changing it weekly or monthly as new ideas or accomplishments occur. We also heartily recommend that you share your portfolio with other trusted colleagues and look at theirs. The ideas you will gain from one another will enable you to make your portfolio more interesting and useful as a means of communicating your strengths.

We hope that you have a mentor coach when you begin teaching, and that your mentor will assist you in collecting artifacts and documents for your portfolio. A mentor can be asked to photograph your classroom while you are teaching, so that you can include the photos in your portfolio. You may also ask your mentor to videotape you while you present your first unit or teach with manipulatives or lead a lively discussion. These videos are wonderful additions to your portfolio.

Many states are now mandating beginning teacher programs in all districts, whereby new teachers are involved in an "induction" process. Through this process the beginning teachers are assigned support personnel to assist them in areas that they (the teachers themselves) identify as needing more training or attention. New teachers are encouraged to write a professional development plan outlining the steps, courses, and professional development workshops and seminars they will participate in over the first 2 to 3 years of their teaching. These programs have met with high approval from new teachers and are responsible for a dramatic increase in the number of teachers remaining in the profession after their initial 3 years of teaching.

If there are no mentor coaches in your district during your first year of teaching, you can find one for yourself. In the first few weeks of teaching, listen and watch for the teachers who have the most in common with your philosophy or curriculum orientation. Approach one and ask the teacher to serve as your informal mentor. The teacher is likely to be delighted with this invitation, as it offers both of you the opportunity to grow and learn. You will learn from the experience of your chosen coach, and the mentor will learn what's new from you. We hope that you will share this book with your coach and work on the professional portfolio pages together.

## The Powerful Influence a Teacher Can Make

At the center of all of this change is the teacher, and the growing power, responsibility, and respect the teacher has earned. Good and Brophy (2002) report that since the early 1970s there has been a surge of activity in research on teaching. Much of it has been predicated on a deceptively simple thesis: Effective school learning requires good teaching, and good teachers are those who exercise good judgment in constructing the education of their students. In our view, as we expressed in Chapter 1, we believe that good teachers may have their own hopes and expectations when they enter the profession, but they choose to use withitness and reflective action to put the needs of their students above their own. Not satisfied with their own self-perceptions, they consciously seek out respected colleagues to ask for feedback on their actions and plans.

We hope that we have made our case in this text that there is a strong, undeniable link between *reflective* and *effective* teachers.

As we discussed in Chapter 2, research shows that the most effective teachers are good classroom managers. This management skill grows directly out of reflective, relational, and democratic leadership from the first day of school. As shown in Chapter 3, the role of the teacher includes the responsibility for making accurate assessments of students' needs. Students from all cultures, ethnic groups, and economic conditions can thrive in the classroom of a caring and relational teacher, who uses formal and informal sources of information as a means of ensuring that all students in the class can achieve success.

Throughout the research on effective teaching and effective schools the attribute of *teacher clarity* continues to surface. Effective teachers are clear about what they intend to accomplish through their instruction, and they keep these goals in mind both in designing instruction and in communicating its purposes to the students (Good & Brophy, 2002). Clarity in articulating the goals and outcomes expected of students is described in Chapter 4, while clarity in presentation skills requires the strategies described in Chapter 7.

It is also becoming apparent that it is very effective to combine or integrate subjects into multidisciplinary units of study, as described in Chapters 5 and 6. Rather than being textbook technicians, reflective teachers prefer to create their own learning experiences either individually or with teammates. They frequently focus on interesting themes or topics in which students use and develop their reading, writing, and research skills as they gain new knowledge about a variety of subjects.

Another common element identified throughout the literature on effective teaching is that effective teachers create learning experiences in which students are not simply passive recipients of fact-based knowledge; instead, they teach their students how to use many *cognitive processes*, how to organize information in new ways, and how to solve problems for themselves. It takes a reflective, relational teacher to recognize and select the appropriate teaching strategies that will engage students in active learning, as described in Chapters 7, 8, 9, and 10.

Reflective teachers are eager to use a variety of assessment techniques, such as those described in Chapter 11, rather than rely on one objective method. This is an especially effective practice because it allows students with a variety of learning styles to demonstrate their accomplishments and succeed. Effective practitioners are also talented at providing students with useful, timely, and detailed *critical feedback* so that students know what is expected and what they must do to succeed. We also now know that simply being a good evaluator is not enough; the most effective teachers are those who cause their students to take an active role in the evaluation of their own learning by teaching them how to apply *metacognitive strategies* to become independent and self-reliant, able to monitor and regulate their own learning.

In addition to their responsibilities to their students, effective teachers are able to communicate well with the parents and other members of the school community in order to support the moral development of students, as we have described in this chapter and in Chapter 2.

The teacher's role in the educational community is changing. Teaching shows considerable promise of becoming a highly respected profession in the United States during the 21st century. This is largely due to the efforts of reflective teachers who are asking the important questions about how they can improve classroom events and children's lives. Alone or in collaboration, relational teachers are seeking out new alternatives and selecting the ones they believe might improve their teaching. They are taking responsibility for evaluating their classroom practices by gathering data from their own observations and from the current research and knowledge base on teaching and learning. They are disseminating what works for them in faculty meetings, workshops, conferences, and articles in professional journals. The result is a new emphasis on inquiry, reflection, and building a knowledge base about the most successful and effective practices that create a stimulating and healthy learning community.

A single teacher can exert a powerful influence on the community and has the potential to literally change the lives of students in perceptible ways. Chaos theory in physics tells us that only slight changes to the initial conditions of two identical dynamical systems will result in two completely different outcomes as time proceeds. The classic example is a pinball machine where each pinball is as identical to the others as we can possibly make them. No matter how precisely we try to produce the same initial conditions for each release and operate each flipper the same way as our ball cascades down our slight incline, minute variations along the way result in different scores and different paths for each ball. No two games are identical.

Our teaching influences others just like the pinball machine, as we "touch" each student's life. A teacher's acts of kindness or courage take on huge proportions months or even years down the road. What each individual does today to improve the lives of the next generation is the most lasting contribution any of us can make. The athlete Michael Jordan's greatest contribution to society will not be his feats on the basketball court, but how he raises his children, how he treats his wife, and how he interacts with other people. A teacher has the opportunity to make an impact on the lives of many more young people than basketball stars or business executives do. Although we may not experience the notoriety of a film star or receive the signing bonuses of a professional athlete, teaching is one of the most important professions in society.

Just imagine the life your students will live 10 years from now if you do your best to instill in each one the following goals:

1. To be a lifelong learner
2. To erase the fear of failure, learn from mistakes, and know that sometimes we have to fail to succeed
3. To explore meaningful and productive paths in life

Just as we have seen in the movie starring Jimmy Stewart, the profession of teaching can lead us to conclude that yes, it is a wonderful life. Occasionally, when a student comes back to visit you after 5 or 10 years, you may have the opportunity to understand the impact your life has had on others, that your influence was significant, and that the caring, reflective actions you worked so hard to achieve in your classroom are, indeed, very much appreciated.

## REFLECTIVE ACTION EXPERIENCES FOR YOUR PROFESSIONAL PORTFOLIO

## Demonstrate Your Commitment to Collaborative Teaching

Arrange to visit a faculty meeting or another decision-making body at a school you are visiting. How are decisions made? Do teachers work as colleagues to propose programs or solve problems? Does the administrator respect the ideas of the faculty? Visualize yourself as a member of this faculty. What responsibilities would you be willing to assume?

Are you a person who is comfortable or uncomfortable with decision-making power? If you work in a school district that encourages teachers to take responsibility for many important decisions, will you welcome this as an opportunity or look on it as a burden? Would you prefer to make decisions about your own classroom independently, or would you rather share the power and the responsibility with your teammates?

Ask several experienced teachers to tell you stories of their interactions with other faculty members at their schools. If there are mentor teachers at the schools you visit, talk with them about the way teachers coach one another in that setting. What are the advantages of having teachers visit one another's classrooms to offer support and suggestions? What are the possible disadvantages or fears related to these visits? In your view, how can these fears or disadvantages be minimized?

You may have learned from your discussions with colleagues that it is difficult or impossible for teachers to please every student, every colleague, or every administrator. When a controversial issue arises in a school community, your point of view will be welcomed by some but not all of your colleagues on the faculty. If you accept that condition, how can you present your opinions to others on your faculty who may have different opinions from yours?

Choose an educational issue or dilemma that you are observing in schools you visit. Create an action plan to approach this problem that you would propose to your colleagues if you were a full-time faculty member at the school. Include a method to gather information from a variety of people who make up the school community.

Show your action plan to an experienced teacher. Get feedback on how to improve your plan or make it more realistic. What will you do if other teachers are reluctant to discuss your plan? What will you do if they think your issue is of little interest or value? What will you do if they disagree with you? Revise your plan and include it in your portfolio along with your reflective analysis of the collaborative process you used to achieve your goals.

# References

Florio-Ruane, S. (2001). *Teacher education and cultural imagination: Autobiography, conversation, and narrative.* Mahwah, NJ: Lawrence Erlbaum.

Gardner, H. (1999). *Intelligence reframed: Multiple intelligences for the 21st century.* New York: Perseus Books.

Good, T., & Brophy, J. (2002). *Looking in classrooms* (9th ed.). Boston: Allyn & Bacon.

Hodgkinson, H. (2003). Educational demographics: What teachers should know, in A. Ornstein et al. (Eds.), *Contemporary issues in curriculum.* Boston: Pearson.

Lickona, T. (1992). *Educating for character: How our schools can teach respect and responsibility.* New York: Bantam.

Lieberman, A. (1995). Practices that support teacher development: Transforming conceptions of professional learning. *Phi Delta Kappan, 76,* 591–596.

Linn, R., & Gronlund, N. (2000). *Measurement and assessment in teaching* (8th ed.). Upper Saddle River, NJ: Merrill/Prentice Hall.

Meadows, B. (1993). Through the eyes of parents. *Educational Leadership, 51*(2), 31–34.

Rimm, S. (1995). *Why bright children get poor grades.* New York: Crown.

Saterlie, M. (1992). Schools, parents, and communities working together, in T. Lickona (Ed.), *Educating for character: How our schools can teach respect and responsibility.* New York: Bantam.

Shaps, E., Watson, M., & Lewis, C. (1996). A sense of community is key to effectiveness in fostering character education. *Journal of Staff Development, 17*(2), 42–47.

Stobbe, C. (1993). Professional partnerships. *Educational Leadership, 51*(2), 40–41.

# NAME INDEX

# SUBJECT INDEX